Lecture Notes in Computer Science 9392

Commenced Publication in 1973
Founding and Former Series Editors:
Gerhard Goos, Juris Hartmanis, and Jan van Leeuwen

Mehdi Dastani · Marjan Sirjani (Eds.)

Fundamentals
of Software Engineering

6th International Conference, FSEN 2015
Tehran, Iran, April 22–24, 2015
Revised Selected Papers

 Springer

Editors
Mehdi Dastani
Intelligent Systems
Utrecht University
Utrecht
The Netherlands

Marjan Sirjani
School of Computer Science
Reykjavik University
Reykjavik
Iceland

ISSN 0302-9743   ISSN 1611-3349   (electronic)
Lecture Notes in Computer Science
ISBN 978-3-319-24643-7   ISBN 978-3-319-24644-4   (eBook)
DOI 10.1007/978-3-319-24644-4

Library of Congress Control Number: 2015949443

LNCS Sublibrary: SL2 – Programming and Software Engineering

Springer Cham Heidelberg New York Dordrecht London

Printed on acid-free paper

Springer International Publishing AG Switzerland is part of Springer Science+Business Media
(www.springer.com)

Preface

The present volume contains the proceedings of the sixth IPM International Conference on Fundamentals of Software Engineering (FSEN), held in Tehran, Iran, April 22–24, 2015. This event, FSEN 2015, was organized by the School of Computer Science at the Institute for Research in Fundamental Sciences (IPM) in Iran, in cooperation with ACM SIGSOFT and IFIP WG 2.2.

The topics of interest span all aspects of formal methods, especially those related to advancing the application of formal methods in the software industry and promoting their integration with practical engineering techniques. The Program Committee of FSEN 2015 consisted of 46 top researchers from 38 different academic institutes in 17 countries. We received a total of 62 submissions from 22 countries out of which we have accepted 14 regular papers, 5 short papers and 6 posters. Each submission was reviewed by at least 3 independent referees, for its quality, originality, contribution, clarity of presentation, and its relevance to the conference topics. These proceedings include the regular and short papers, as well as two papers by the invited speakers.

Three distinguished keynote speakers delivered their lectures at FSEN 2015. Paola Inverardi gave a talk on "Automated Integration of Service-Oriented Software Systems", Holger Giese presented his work on "Towards Smart Systems of Systems", and John Hughes gave a presentation on "Experiences with Property-Based Testing: Testing the Hard Stuff and Staying Sane."

We thank the Institute for Research in Fundamental Sciences (IPM), Tehran, Iran for their financial support and local organization of FSEN 2015. We also thank the members of the Program Committee for their time, effort, and excellent contributions to making FSEN a quality conference. We thank Hossein Hojjat for his help in preparing this volume. Last but not least, our thanks go to the authors and conference participants, without whom FSEN 2015 would not have been possible.

July 2015

Mehdi Dastani
Marjan Sirjani

Organization

Program Committee

Mohammad Abdollahi Azgomi	Iran University of Science and Technology, Iran
Gul Agha	University of Illinois at Urbana-Champaign, USA
Christel Baier	Technical University of Dresden, Germany
Ezio Bartocci	Vienna University of Technology, Austria
Borzoo Bonakdarpour	McMaster University, Canada
Marcello Bonsangue	Leiden University, Netherlands
Mario Bravetti	University of Bologna, Italy
Michael Butler	University of Southampton, UK
Fabiano Dalpiaz	Utrecht University, Netherlands
Mehdi Dastani	Utrecht University, Netherlands
Frank De Boer	CWI, Netherlands
Erik De Vink	Technische Universiteit Eindhoven, Netherlands
Klaus Dräger	Oxford University, UK
Wan Fokkink	Vrije Universiteit Amsterdam, Netherlands
Masahiro Fujita	University of Tokyo, Japan
Maurizio Gabbrielli	University of Bologna, Italy
Fatemeh Ghassemi	University of Tehran, Iran
Jan Friso Groote	Eindhoven University of Technology, Netherlands
Kim Guldstrand Larsen	Aalborg University, Denmark
Hassan Haghighi	Shahid Beheshti University, Iran
Holger Hermanns	Saarland University, Germany
Hossein Hojjat	Cornell University, USA
Mohammad Izadi	Sharif University of Technology, Iran
Mohammad Mahdi Jaghoori	CWI, Netherlands
Einar Broch Johnsen	University of Oslo, Norway
Joost-Pieter Katoen	RWTH Aachen University, Germany
Narges Khakpour	KTH Royal Institute of Technology, Sweden
Ramtin Khosravi	University of Tehran, Iran
Zhiming Liu	Birmingham City University, UK
Jose Meseguer	University of Illinois at Urbana-Champaign, USA
Hassan Mirian-Hosseinabadi	Sharif University of Technology, Iran
Ugo Montanari	Università di Pisa, Italy

Peter Mosses	Swansea University, UK
Mohammadreza Mousavi	Halmstad University, Sweden
Ali Movaghar	Sharif University of Technology, Iran
Peter Olveczky	University of Oslo, Norway
Jose Proenca	Katholieke Universiteit Leuven, Belgium
Niloofar Razavi	University of Toronto, Canada
Wolfgang Reisig	Humboldt-Universität zu Berlin, Germany
Philipp Ruemmer	Uppsala University, Sweden
Gwen Salaün	INRIA Grenoble, France
Cesar Sanchez	IMDEA Software Institute, Spain
Wendelin Serwe	INRIA Grenoble, France
Marjan Sirjani	Reykjavik University, Iceland
Meng Sun	Peking University, China
Carolyn Talcott	SRI International, USA
Samira Tasharofi	University of Illinois at Urbana-Champaign, USA
Tayssir Touili	CNRS, LIPN, France
Danny Weyns	Linnaeus University, Sweden

Additional Reviewers

Aflaki, Saba	Li, Xiaoshan
Amini, Morteza	Mafi, Zohreh
Azadbakht, Keyvan	Mashayekhi, Hoda
Bartocci, Ezio	Mauro, Jacopo
Beohar, Harsh	Melgratti, Hernan
Boudjadar, Jalil	Moelle, Andre
Bruni, Roberto	Motallebi, Hassan
Bucchiarone, Antonio	Nooraee, Maryam
Dalvandi, Mohammadsadegh	Nyman, Ulrik
Dan, Li	Petre, Luigia
Devismes, Stéphane	Sammartino, Matteo
Din, Crystal Chang	Savicks, Vitaly
Entezari Maleki, Reza	Schlatte, Rudolf
Evans, Cain	Serbanescu, Vlad Nicolae
Fernandez Anta, Antonio	Sürmeli, Jan
Giallorenzo, Saverio	Talebi, Mahmoud
Helvensteijn, Michiel	Tapia Tarifa, Silvia Lizeth
Heydarnoori, Abbas	Varshosaz, Mahsa
Jensen, Peter Gjøl	Vignudelli, Valeria
Keramati, Hossein	Völlinger, Kim
Keshishzadeh, Sarmen	Ye, Lina
Klein, Joachim	Zeljić, Aleksandar
Klueppelholz, Sascha	

Contents

X   Contents

Towards Smart Systems of Systems[*]

Holger Giese, Thomas Vogel, and Sebastian Wätzoldt

Hasso Plattner Institute at the University of Potsdam
Prof.-Dr.-Helmert-Str. 2-3, D-14482 Potsdam, Germany
{Holger.Giese,Thomas.Vogel,Sebastian.Waetzoldt}@hpi.de

Abstract. Systems of Systems (SoS) have started to emerge as a consequence of the general trend toward the integration of beforehand isolated systems. To unleash the full potential, the contained systems must be able to operate as elements in open, dynamic, and deviating SoS architectures and to adapt to open and dynamic contexts while being developed, operated, evolved, and governed independently. We name the resulting advanced SoS to be *smart* as they must be self-adaptive at the level of the individual systems and self-organizing at the SoS level to cope with the emergent behavior at that level. In this paper we analyze the open challenges for the envisioned smart SoS. In addition, we discuss our ideas for tackling this vision with our SMARTSOS approach that employs open and adaptive collaborations and models at runtime. In particular, we focus on preliminary ideas for the construction and assurance of smart SoS.

1 Introduction

Systems of Systems (SoS) [1, 2] nowadays become a highly relevant challenge as the general trend can be observed that beforehand isolated systems are integrated into larger federations of systems. To unleash the full potential of such federations, SoS must be *smart* such that the contained systems are able to operate as elements in open, dynamic, and deviating SoS architectures and to adapt to open and dynamic contexts while being developed, operated, evolved, and governed independently.[1] Therefore, the resulting smart SoS must be self-adaptive at the level of the individual systems and self-organizing at the SoS level to cope with the emergent behavior at that level.

For a smart SoS holds that each of its systems has to be *independent* in the sense that it is developed, operated, evolved, and governed independently from

---

[*] This work was partially developed in the course of the project "Quantitative analysis of service-oriented real-time systems with structure dynamics" (Quantum) at the Hasso Plattner Institute at the University of Potsdam, published on its behalf, and funded by the Deutsche Forschungsgemeinschaft. See http://www.hpi.de/en/giese/projects/quantum.html

[1] Similar needs are observed for specific cases of SoS, such as *ultra-large-scale systems* [3] focusing on issues arising from the complexity of SoS or *cyber-physcial systems* [4] emphasizing the integration of the physical and cyber world.

© IFIP International Federation for Information Processing 2015
M. Dastani and M.Sirjani (Eds.): FSEN 2015, LNCS 9392, pp. 1–29, 2015.
DOI: 10.1007/978-3-319-24644-4_1

the other systems in the SoS. Furthermore, these systems interact with each other in an open and dynamic world (cf. [5]), which causes individual systems to dynamically join or leave the SoS over time, the SoS architecture to deviate, and emergent behavior at the *SoS level*. Moreover, each independent system must adapt its behavior autonomously according to its own needs and peer systems in the SoS (*self-adaptation* [6, 7]) while considering the interplay between its own behavior, the other systems' behavior, and the required SoS-level behavior (*self-organization* [8]). The envisioned interaction between the systems involves independently developed systems and requires means for exchanging knowledge between these systems at runtime. This knowledge covers aspects of a running system itself and the context or the requirements of a running system. While the outlined rich interaction is key, the development of the systems has to scale and thus only can take into account the publically available knowledge about possible collaborations with the other systems. Finally, the systems as part of a smart SoS will evolve in order to adjust to new needs or changing regulations (cf. *software evolution* [9]). Since it seems today improbable or even impossible that all the required evolution steps can be covered automatically by a system itself (e.g., by self-adaptation or self-organization), it must still be possible that required evolution steps for each individually governed system are performed during the operation of the SoS. These challenges for engineering smart SoS are currently hardly covered by the available approaches.

The current state of the art suggests constructing SoS using an architecture perspective and services (cf. [10]) employing, for example, the *Service oriented architecture Modeling Language* (*SoaML*) [11] and the *Unified Modeling Language* (*UML*) [12] to specify the cooperation of systems by means of service contracts and collaborations. In these collaborations, roles with dedicated interfaces describe the behavior of the systems while the SoS-level behavior emerges from the interactions of these roles.

The use of collaborations for the modeling of services [13, 14], the use of class diagrams for the structure and graph transformations for the behavior modeling [15, 16], and a formal model of ensembles [17] have been proposed. However, none of these approaches supports the construction of dynamic collaborations as required for smart SoS where systems dynamically join or leave the federation. And even though well-established formal approaches such as π-calculus [18] or bigrahs [19] tackle such structural dynamics, to the best of our knowledge no work exists that especially covers the problem of providing assurances for dynamic collaborations of arbitrary size. Either the approaches require an initial system configuration and only support finite state systems (or systems for which an abstract finite state model of moderate size exist) [15, 20–24] or they lack the expressive power to describe typical problems concerning the structural dynamics [25, 26].

In our own MECHATRONIC UML approach (mUML) [27] for the model-driven development of self-optimizing embedded real-time systems, we already support collaborations of self-optimizing autonomous systems in a rigorous manner by means of role protocols. For mUML and its collaboration concepts an overall assurance scheme has been presented in [28]: it combines a modular verification approach [29] for the component hierarchies of the autonomous systems, the compositional verification [30] of ad hoc real-time collaborations between the autonomous systems, and a fully automatic checker for inductive invariants of graph transformation system rules [31] describing the possible changes of the dynamic architecture at the SoS level. Additional work on assurances for MUML employs a multi-agent system view on an SoS to study how commitments between the collaborating systems can be modeled and analyzed [32]. Therefore, with MUML an approach exists that provides assurances for systems that combine self-adaptive autonomous systems similar to an SoS. However, in contrast to the challenges of smart SoS, which are discussed in the next section, MUML provides no solution for collaborations with structural dynamics of the roles, is restricted to homogeneous systems (i.e., systems that evolve jointly and similarly and that have complete knowledge about each other), and does not support the runtime exchange of complex knowledge. Moreover, the self-adaptation is limited to pre-planned reconfigurations in hierarchical architectures.

Our EXECUTABLE RUNTIME MEGAMODELS approach (EUREMA) [33] for the model-driven engineering of self-adaptive systems supports – in contrast to MUML – the flexible specification of self-adaptation by allowing us to employ abstract runtime models (cf. [34]) of the context and the system itself such that the self-adaptation behavior can be specified by rules operating on such abstractions. However, EUREMA is so far limited to centralized and non-distributed systems and does not address collaborations or the self-organizing SoS level.

In this paper, we will first analyze open challenges for engineering smart SoS. We will then discuss our *Software with Models at Runtime for Systems of Systems* (SMARTSOS) vision that employs collaborations and generic models at runtime for trustworthy self-organization and evolution of the systems at the SoS level and self-adaptation within the systems while taking the independent development, operation, management, and evolution of these systems into account. We will particularly outline the formal foundations underlying SMARTSOS based on graph transformation systems [35,36] which cover in principle the identified challenges for the construction and assurance of smart SoS.

The rest of the paper is structured as follows: In Section 2, we discuss open challenges for smart SoS. Afterwards, our SMARTSOS vision is outlined in Section 3. Then, the concepts for constructing smart SoS with collaborations, components, and runtime models are outlined in Section 4. Afterwards, the results that enable the assurance for the smart SoS are presented in Section 5. The paper closes with a discussion of these results in Section 6 and provides in Section 7 some concluding remarks and an outlook on future work.

2 Challenges

SoS as a composition of systems that are operationally and managerially independent from each other [1] is characterized by uncoordinated evolution steps and geographic distribution of these systems (cf. [37]). Additionally, dynamic

Table 1. Summary of the Identified Challenges.

Construction/Assurance of Self-Adaptation (C1/A1)
Construction/Assurance of SoS-Level Interactions for Self-Organization (C2/A2)
Construction/Assurance of SoS-Level Structural Dynamics (C3/A3)
Construction/Assurance of SoS-Level Runtime Knowledge Exchange (C4/A4)
Construction/Assurance of Evolution of Smart SoS (C5/A5)
Scalable Construction/Assurance of Smart SoS (C6/A6)
Construction/Assurance of Smart SoS with Restricted Knowledge (C7/A7)

configuration capabilities, resilience, the ability to dynamically adapt and absorb deviations in the SoS structure, and the ability to deal with emergent behavior in context of self-organization that goes beyond developing contractual descriptions are crucial [2] for smart SoS. These issues are challenging since each system as part of a smart SoS is *independent* in the sense that it is developed, operated, evolved, and governed independently from the other systems in the same SoS. Furthermore, the systems interact with each other in an open and dynamic world (cf. [5]), which causes individual systems to dynamically join or leave the smart SoS over time, the SoS architecture to deviate, and emergent behavior at the *SoS level*. Consequently, the SoS-level architecture and behavior are not controlled by a single, centralized authority.

As example in this paper we consider a large-scale transport system where different organizations operate fleets of autonomously driving shuttles that share a track system. This constitutes an SoS since the shuttles are operated, managed, and evolved by different authorities, they dynamically interact with each other (e.g., to build convoys), and they adapt to their own and the other shuttle's states and behavior (e.g., to decrease the speed when the shuttle's own battery level is low or when the speed of the shuttle running ahead decreases).[2]

Engineering such smart SoS imposes several challenges that we outline in Table 1. All of them aim for means for the construction and assurance of smart SoS and its individual systems, which must take the operational and managerial independence of the individual systems and the emergent behavior at the SoS level into account.

The first challenge considers the *Construction/Assurance of Self-Adaptation (C1/A1)* of the individual systems as each system within a smart SoS must adapt its behavior according to its own needs and the behavior of other systems as well as the emergent SoS-level behavior (cf. [38,39]). For instance, a shuttle adapts its speed to its battery level, to the speed of the shuttle running ahead, or to an agreement established by all shuttles in a convoy. Such changes of the behavior must be systematically constructed and assured to enable trustworthy operation and in particular self-adaptation [6,7].

Due to the operational and managerial independence of the systems, the *Construction/Assurance of SoS-Level Interactions for Self-Organization (C2/A2)* challenge captures that the interactions among these systems must be self-organizing (cf. [8]) to achieve the SoS-level goals. For example, shuttles from different organization must interact to avoid collisions or they may even

---

[2] See http://www.railcab.de for an example with the outlined characteristics.

cooperate to build convoys in order to save energy. Such interplays of autonomous shuttles must be systematically constructed and assured to provide confidence for satisfying SoS-level goals (e.g., reliable and safe rail traffic).

Furthermore, since the operational context changes or the systems dynamically join or leave the SoS such that the SoS-level architecture dynamically changes, the challenge of the *Construction/Assurance of SoS-Level Structural Dynamics (C3/A3)* must be supported. For instance, autonomous shuttles may join or leave a convoy and the other shuttles already part of the convoy must account for it. Such dynamics must be constructed and assured to guarantee certain SoS-level behavior resulting from the interactions.

Additionally to the structural dynamics, the *Construction/Assurance of SoS-Level Runtime Knowledge Exchange (C4/A4)* is required since no system in the SoS typically has *all* the knowledge needed to achieve the SoS-level goals at runtime. This calls for exchanging knowledge between interacting systems. This knowledge refers to the current state, context, and requirements of individual systems. For instance, shuttles establishing a convoy may exchange their driving modes to agree on a common mode for the whole convoy. Such a knowledge exchange must be constructed and assured when engineering interactions to gain confidence that the SoS-level goals can be achieved.

In parallel to the self-adaptive and self-organizing behavior of systems in the SoS, the systems evolve in an uncoordinated way as they are managed independently from each other by different organizations. Evolution is caused by the permanent need to change the software in response to changing requirements of the stakeholders, no longer valid assumptions, or changing regulations the software has to adhere to (cf. *software evolution* [9]). With evolution, we refer to introducing new or removing existing types of systems or interactions (and therefore, also behavior) from the SoS. For example, new shuttle versions that support new cooperation mechanisms are integrated into the SoS and they must not interfere with the already existing versions. To handle such radical changes in a trustworthy manner and to support the long-term existence of the SoS, the *Construction/Assurance of Evolution of Smart SoS (C5/A5)* is a main challenge.

In general, engineering smart SoS is challenging due to the ultra-large scale and complexity of such systems and due to the different authorities managing such systems. Therefore, the *Scalable Construction/Assurance of Smart SoS (C6/A6)* and the *Construction/Assurance of Smart SoS with Restricted Knowledge (C7/A7)* are also important aspects for the engineering. The first aspect is motivated by the fact that it is not feasible to construct the whole SoS upfront before its deployment, or to analyze *all* possible SoS configurations or architectures that grow exponentially with the number of participating systems. For instance, any number of shuttles of arbitrary types may run on the track system or may cooperate in a convoy. Thus, the construction and assurances for SoS must scale with the size of the SoS. The second aspect refers to the construction and assurances for smart SoS, which must work despite the restricted knowledge that participants of the SoS have. An organization responsible for an individual system in the SoS or the system itself might have no global view of the SoS and no concrete information about the other participants and possible interactions among participants. Nevertheless, assurances for each system and the SoS must be provided to enable trustworthy operations. For example, when constructing and assuring new shuttle versions supporting a certain interaction, details about other organizations' shuttle versions that are potential cooperators for the interaction might not be available. However, the construction and assurance must cope with the limited knowledge available.

These open challenges, each with a construction and assurance dimension as summarized in Table 1, reveal the difficulty of engineering and ruling smart SoS due to the complexity, dynamics, emergence, and decentralized management and governance.

3   SMARTSOS

In our vision SMARTSOS, we suggest combining the benefits of MUML and EUREMA to tackle the challenges for smart SoS. However, we do not suggest simply integrating the ideas of both approaches. Instead we developed a radically different and more abstract perspective on the SoS-level interactions to overcome the limitations of the state-of-the-art and former approaches and to master the complexity of smart SoS. This novel perspective is based on the combination of runtime models and collaborations.

3.1   Runtime Models

To realize the challenge of the Construction/Assurance of SoS-Level Runtime Knowledge Exchange (C4/A4), SMARTSOS employs *models at runtime* [34] that suggest following model-driven engineering principles to engineer abstract runtime representations of running systems or their contexts and requirements. Such models are said to be *causally connected* to the running system, which means that changes in the system are reflected in the model and vice versa. Thus, "change agents (e.g., software maintainers, software-based agents) use [abstract] runtime models to modify executing software in a controlled manner" [40, p. 39] rather than directly adapting the running software at the code level.

With EUREMA we have extended this perspective by providing runtime models at different levels of abstraction [41] and by specifying the adaptation itself, that is, software-based agents, using runtime models [33]. The latter aspect leverages the flexibility of runtime models for managing the change agents at runtime in addition to the running systems. In SMARTSOS, we go another step further and suggest using *generic* in contrast to highly specific and optimized runtime models, which eases interoperability and evolution of systems in an SoS, as it excludes individual optimization and specific solution for the runtime models.

For an individual system in a smart SoS, such generic runtime models may capture the system's state, context, requirements, and adaptation logic. These models may be used locally for self-adaptation and assurances that each system

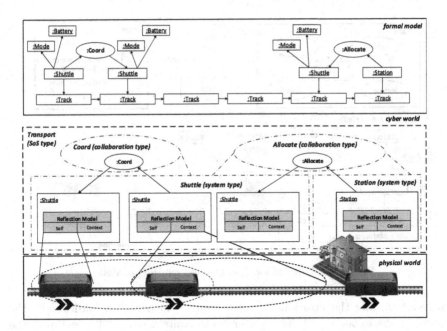

Fig. 1. Local and shared runtime models of a complex SoS architecture.

fulfills its requirements. As discussed in the following, they may also be used for collaborations among systems leading to the self-organization of the SoS, which requires the exchange of runtime knowledge.

The basic idea to integrate runtime models and collaborations for the construction of smart SoS is depicted in Fig. 1. At first, each running system living in the cyber world may have a view on its physical context and its own state in the cyber and physical world by means of runtime models of the *context* and the *self*. In general, we consider runtime descriptions reflecting the running system and its context as *Reflection Models*. Particularly, *System Models* (Self in Fig. 1) reflect about architectural and behavioral key aspects of the system and they are causally connected to the system. *Context Models* (Context in Fig. 1) describe the environmental situation of a system (cf. [42, 43]). In our example, models of the Context and Self are depicted in the individual Shuttle systems in Fig. 1. This supports designing the self-adaptation of the shuttles as MAPE-K feedback loops (**M**onitor/**A**nalyze/**P**lan/**E**xecute-**K**nowledge) [44] while the knowledge part is implemented by the runtime models. Such feedback loops are realized by analyze and plan activities that operate on the basis of the runtime models while linking the runtime models to the system and context is realized by the monitor and execute activities. The Self and Context runtime models can refer to the local state of a shuttle (e.g., the Mode and Battery status) as well as the available information about the context (e.g., whether there is another shuttle driving on the tracks ahead of the shuttle). This context does not only consist of the physical context such as the shuttle's position, the topology of the

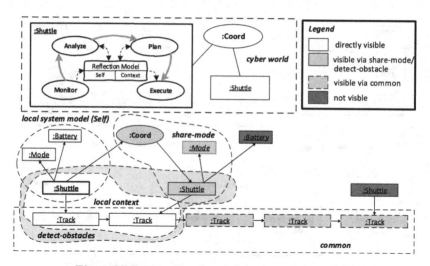

Fig. 2. Visibility of local and shared runtime models.

track system, and the positions of other shuttles nearby, but additionally the context in the cyber world. This cyber-world context covers, for instance, the established collaboration instances and context shared with other roles of these collaboration instances.

As depicted in Fig. 1, these runtime models of the context and self constitute an overall local runtime model, that is, the Reflection Model, for each :Shuttle system. As described in Fig. 2 in more detail, each system does not only operate on information about its own local context and itself, but can also get access to the information stored in runtime models of other systems concerning their context or themselves.[3] In our example, the left most Shuttle system has also access to information in form of runtime models in quite different ways. The directly visible elements are the information available local to the shuttle by means of runtime models (white with solid frame). Additional information like the position of the shuttle in front of it, which is encoded by the on edge between that shuttle and its current track, is accessible for shuttles that knows the Coord collaboration type (gray with dashed frame). Finally, information about the mode of the shuttle system in front of it is accessible for a shuttle, if it is connected to this via a Coord collaboration instance (gray with solid frame).

Likewise to EUREMA, the behavior of the systems in reaction to particular situations can now be directly described based on such overall local runtime models. This is illustrated at the top of the left-hand side of Fig. 2 showing the feedback loop (i.e., the monitor, analyze, plan, and execute activities) of a shuttle realizing the self-adaptation and therefore, addressing the Construction

---

[3] In the case of heterogeneous local runtime models, efficient incremental model synchronization techniques such as triple graph grammars [45] can be employed. Such techniques realize required translation steps between runtime models that are specified in different modeling languages but that capture similar content. We already applied them to create and maintain multiple runtime models of a system in [41].

of Self-Adaptation (C1) challenge. In the following, we will elaborate the use of such generic runtime models in the context of collaborations. In general, such models as employed by SMARTSOS provide an idealization of the systems and contexts, which is discussed in Section 4.3.

3.2 Collaborations

To approach the challenges of the Construction/Assurance of SoS-Level Interactions for Self-Organization (C2/A2) and the Construction/Assurance of SoS-Level Structural Dynamics (C3/A3) while taking aspects of the Scalable Construction/Assurance of Smart SoS (C6/A6) and the Construction/Assurance of Smart SoS with Restricted Knowledge (C7/A7) into account, *SoaML* and *UML* provide basic concepts of modeling collaborations. They support specifying abstract collaboration types and corresponding roles. The interaction of roles is defined by sequence or activity diagrams and *UML* interface descriptions (in form of class diagrams). Role behavior may be also covered by protocol state machines. The MUML approach goes beyond the ideas of *SoaML* and *UML* by describing the possible interaction always via real-time variant of state machines for each role and the communication medium. Due to the well-defined semantics for all employed formalism such as the real-time variant of state machines, MUML enables the basic verification of the interactions through model checking.

SMARTSOS supports a more flexible concept for collaborations compared to MUML and *SoaML/UML*. In SMARTSOS a richer language to specify the collaborations is provided, which also covers the exchange of complex information as well as specifying structural dynamics covering, for example, how systems can join the collaboration, leave the collaboration, or how the structure of the collaboration may change at runtime. In order to ensure interoperability and achieve trustworthy behavior at the SoS level, we furthermore need also more sophisticated analysis capabilities, for example, to investigate the impact from one system part to another through collaborations.

The basic idea of separating the required interactions into separated collaborations is depicted in Fig. 1. The autonomous systems of the SoS can connect with each other as specified by the collaboration types and can establish collaboration instances to cooperate as needed. For example, the two left most Shuttle instances in Fig. 1 are linked by a Coord collaboration instance to build a temporary convoy and the right most Shuttle instance is linked to a Station instance by an Allocate collaboration instance.

It has to be noted that different collaboration types and their involved views on the physical or cyber world may not be disjoint. In such a case, the construction and assurance for the collaboration types that share some of their elements of the physical or cyber world have to take such overlapping into account. The required concepts for abstract shared collaborations types that includes runtime models with overlapping entities are discussed in Section 4.3.

The elements of the Coord collaboration type are defined in the class diagram depicted on the left hand side of Fig. 3. The Coord collaboration element as well as the Shuttle role with its Mode and Battery status are introduced using the

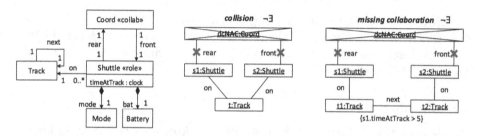

Fig. 3. Class diagram of the collaboration type Coord (left); properties of the collaboration type Coord as forbidden SPs (middle and right).

stereotypes ≪collab≫ for collaborations and ≪role≫ for roles. The class diagram also defines the track topology, that is, multiple Track elements connected with each other by the next relationship, as well as the positioning of the Shuttles on the tracks by the on relationship.

The class diagram of a collaboration type implicitly specifies in form of all valid object configurations for the class diagram the possible states the collaboration may be in. Later on, we define rules that refer to such object configurations to capture the system behavior. We formally define these object configurations as attributed graphs in Section 4.

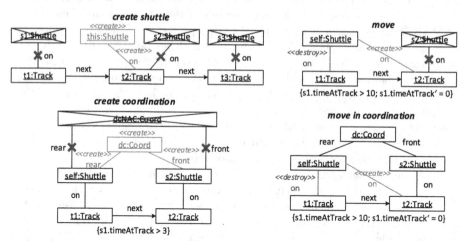

Fig. 4. Behavior rules for the Shuttle role of the Coord collaboration as SPs.

To capture the laws that should hold for the different collaboration types, we specify *behavior rules* with Story Patterns (SPs) [45] that define the permitted and mandatory behavior of each role, *read rules* with SPs having no side effects that define the visibility of shared runtime models, and the *properties* the collaboration has to ensure. These properties are described by SPs without side effects in the case of simple state properties and with Timed Story Sequence Diagrams (TSSDs) [46] in the case of sequence properties. A major duty for the SoS-level assurance is to ensure that the properties are the guaranteed outcome of the roles' behavior.

Fig. 4 depicts the *behavior rules*, that is, the SPs defining the permitted and mandatory behavior of each role of the Coord collaboration (we refer to [47] for the complete set of behavior rules). The SP called move in coordination on the lower right-hand side of Fig. 4, for example, describes that after the building of a platoon encoded by the existence of the Coord instance, the rear shuttle instance can move with a reduced distance behind the front shuttle instance and therefore, both shuttle instances may even be positioned on the same Track instance. The instance name self used in a rule determines the role of the collaboration, for which this rule is intended, in this example, for the shuttle role (cf. self:Shuttle element). Furthermore, the create coordination SP defines that shuttles must create a collaboration if they are on neighboring tracks and do not yet collaborate (i.e., there is no Coord instance yet).

A simple SP denotes two graphs at once. The first one is the left-hand-side graph L that you try to find in the current instance situation encoded in the graph G and that consists of all unmarked elements and those marked with ≪destroy≫. The second one is right-hand-side graph R that consists of all un-marked elements and those marked with ≪create≫. If L can be matched in G, the SP rule can be applied. A rule application on G results in the replacement of the match of L in G by R. In the case of complex SPs that have a negative application condition (NAC) that defines a graph L' resulting from extending L by all the crossed-out elements. Then, besides finding the left-hand-side graph L in G there must exist *no* match for the NAC L' in G that extends that match for L. Otherwise, the rule cannot be applied.

On the upper right-hand side of Fig. 4, the move SP specifies using such a NAC that shuttles can move forward along the track over time if there is no other shuttle on the next track. Additionally, the SP defines a temporal condition that a shuttle must stay on a track at least ten time units before it can move to the next track. This temporal condition ensures that the move SP can only be applied with respect to realistic physical movement conditions of the shuttles. If the shuttle moves, the on reference is created on the t2 Track and the clock attribute timeAtTrack of the shuttle is reseted to zero. As a consequence, the shuttle has to stay on the next track again at least for ten time units before the move SP can be applied again.

Fig. 5 shows an example of an application of a graph transformation rule. If we consider the instance situation (start graph) on the left-hand side and apply the move SP rule from Figure 4, first a match for the move SP has to be found.

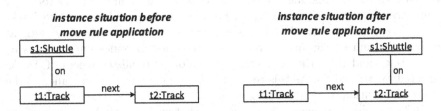

Fig. 5. Application of the move SP from Figure 4 on an exemplary instance situation.

Thereby, we can find a match, where the shuttle instance *self* from Figure 4 is matched to the *s1* shuttle instance on the left side in Figure 5. Because there is no other shuttle on the next track t2, the move SP can be applied for the found match with the consequence that the on link from shuttle s1 to track t1 is deleted and a new on link from shuttle s1 to track t2 is created. Thus, we obtain the instance situation (result graph) as depicted on the right-hand side on Figure 5.

The *properties* the collaboration type Coord should guarantee are depicted in Fig. 3. We have the forbidden situations collision and missing collaboration that must not happen. Hence, these properties are marked with $\neg\exists$. For example, the collision SP in the middle of Fig. 3 shows the situation where two shuttles that are not collaborating with each other are on the same track, that is, these two shuttles may collide. Furthermore, the missing collaboration SP on the right-hand side of Fig. 3 reflects the faulty situation where two shuttles are on neighboring tracks but they do not collaborate with each other. Both situations have to be excluded to ensure a proper operation of the collaboration. For both instance situations in Figure 5 must hold that all specified properties are fulfilled (that the forbidden collision and missing collaboration SP cannot be matched).

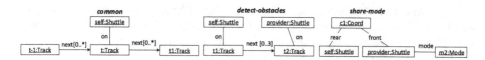

Fig. 6. Read rules for the Shuttle role of the Coord collaboration type as SPs.

The *read rules* for the collaboration type Coord are depicted in Fig. 6 using SPs and so called *path expressions* that allow us to describe the fraction of the runtime models that can be accessed in a more compact form than standard SPs without such path expressions. In general, read rules on the one hand describe what the roles can access (read) but also imply on the other hand that the other roles somehow have to provide the related information. In any case, the self instance name in a read rule that must always be present determines for which role this rule specifies access to other runtime models. The optional provider instance name if present in a rule indicates whether a related role is in charge of providing that information.

The first read rule, called common, describes that it is assumed that a shuttle (marked with the self instance name) has access to the complete track topology because the path expression next[0..*] denotes any finite path between two Tracks with arbitrary many omitted and thus not visible nodes in between. Looking at the class diagram in Fig. 3, it reveals that the omitted nodes must always be of type Track and thus, the path expression represents all sequences of Tracks connected by next edges. As this read rule does not require any instance of the Coord collaboration, it denotes that each shuttle knows the track topology on its own (a possible implementation would be that each shuttle has a map of the track topology).

The read rule detect-obstacle for the Shuttle role (cf. self instance name) employs the path expression next[0..3] to denote a path between two Tracks with 0 to 3 not visible Tracks in between. The provider instance name for the other Shuttle role indicates that this role must provide this fragments of its runtime model. As this read rule does not require any instance of the Coord collaboration, it defines that the shuttles are able to see other shuttles nearby even though no collaboration has been established yet (a possible implementation can be based on GPS and a related protocol to broadcast position data to the shuttle's vicinity [48]). The read rule share-mode for the Shuttle role (cf. self instance name) is different as it always requires an instance of the Coord collaboration. Otherwise, it does not allow a shuttle to retrieve (read) the mode of the other Shuttle role. The provider instance name for that Shuttle role indicates that this role must provide this data.

4   Construction

To cover in particular the challenges of the Construction of SoS-Level Interactions for Self-Organization (C2), Construction of SoS-Level Structural Dynamics (C3), Construction of SoS-Level Runtime Knowledge Exchange (C4), Construction of Evolution of Smart SoS (C5), and Scalable Construction of Smart SoS (C6), SMARTSOS supports collaborations with a dynamic number of roles, runtime models, the independent evolution of the autonomous systems and their collaborations, and the specification of individual autonomous systems without having complete knowledge about the overall SoS. These aspects require at first a solid foundation for the concepts used for the construction and assurance of smart SoS. Based on this foundation we then can formally introduce types and instances of collaborations, systems, and SoS as well as the notions of runtime models and overlapping collaborations. Finally, we cover the evolution of smart SoS, that is, the set of types and instances of the SoS evolve (e.g., new types and instances are introduced).

4.1   Foundation

The formal foundation of SMARTSOS can be based on our former results in the context of MUML and experience in formal models for self-adaptive systems [49] and model transformations [50] based on graph transformation systems. In this context, graphs serve as a *formal model* to represent object configurations capturing the SoS-level architecture and runtime models (see the formal model depicted in Fig. 1) while the graph transformation rules such as SPs denote the behavior of the collaboration roles and graph conditions the required properties. To address various software aspects, we have developed extended attributed graph transformations systems covering real-time [51], probabilistic [52], and hybrid [47,53,54] behavior. These extensions can be used in the formal foundation of SMARTSOS.

In this paper, we will only introduce the basic ideas of the underlying formal model and refer to [54] for more details. The formal model we use can be described as follows:

Typed attributed graphs G with attributes describe the states of our model elements (system of systems, systems, and collaborations). They relate to the possible object configurations that a class diagram CD defines (cf. Figure 3 for the Coord collaboration). We use $\mathcal{G}_\emptyset(CD)$ to denote all those possible typed attributed graphs that fit to a class diagram CD and do not contain any role objects. We will further refer to the empty graph as $G_\emptyset$. An example of an object configuration is depicted in Figure 2, where two shuttles are linked by a Coord collaboration. The corresponding elements can also be found in the formal model depicted on top of Fig. 1.

Sets of graph transformation rules $\mathcal{R}$ define the behavior. They related to the SPs we employed earlier (cf. Figure 4 for the Coord collaboration). Rules $r \in \mathcal{R}$ can match a certain fragment of a graph representing the state and in addition describe how the graph changes when the rule is applied. Given a start graph and a number of rule applications we get a path π.

Furthermore, a suitable logic for state and sequence properties is assumed and we can describe whether a sequence property ϕ holds for a path π ($\pi \models \phi$) or for all paths generated by a start graph G and a set of rules $\mathcal{R}$ applied on G ($G, \mathcal{R} \models \phi$). Simple state conditions are specified by SPs without side effects (cf. Fig. 3), while TSSDs [46] can be employed to describe sequence properties.

Additionally, we use a refinement notion for graph transformation rule sets $\mathcal{R}' \sqsubseteq \mathcal{R}$ that guarantees preservation of safety properties while allowing us to extend the rules unless guaranteed behavior will be blocked.

We further exploit the fact that the different elements in our formal model are by construction separated either by their types or so-called pseudo types[4] For two rules separated by their types or pseudo types holds that the behavior cannot interfere in unexpected ways.

4.2   Collaborations, Systems, and System of Systems

Collaborations. Similar to *SoaML* and MUML, collaborations are the main elements to address the interactions among individual systems in SMARTSOS. However, we need an extended formalization as presented in more detail in [54] to cover also the structural dynamics such as joining a collaboration, leaving a collaboration, or changing the structure of a collaboration.[5] At first and in addition to the simplified view depicted in Fig. 1, we have to add extra nodes in the graphs for the role instances of a collaboration:

Definition 1 (see [54]). *A role type ro^i equals a node type ro_i.*

---

[4] Their types separate two rules if they have no node and edge type in common. Their pseudo types separate them, if for all nodes of shared type holds that always a single link to a special node with not shared type at the instance level are demanded.

[5] The terminology used in [54] has been adjusted and extended in this paper to better fit the concepts of SoS.

In our application example, the Shuttle element of the Coord collaboration is such a role type.

In addition to the basic notion of collaborations used in *SoaML/UML* and the extended one provided by μUML, we have to cover more information for a collaboration type as depicted in Fig. 1, 2, 3, and 4.

Definition 2 (see [54]). *A collaboration type* $\mathsf{Col}_i = (\mathsf{col}_i, (ro_i^1, \ldots, ro_i^{n_i}), CD_i, R_i, \Phi_i)$ *consists of a collaboration type node* col_i, *a number of role types* ro_i^j, *an UML class diagram* CD_i, *a function* $R_i : \{\mathsf{col}_i, ro_i^1, \ldots, ro_i^{n_i}\} \mapsto 2^{\mathcal{R}}$ *assigning rules to role types, and a guaranteed property* Φ_i.

A collaboration instance of collaboration type Col_i is represented by a node of type col_i. In our example we have the Coord and Allocate collaboration types (see related dashed oval shapes in Fig. 1) as well as single :Coord and :Allocate collaboration instances (see related solid oval shapes in Fig. 1).

For two different role types ro_i^k and ro_i^l the set of assigned rules has to be disjoint $R_i(ro_i^k) \cap R_i(ro_i^l) = \emptyset$. The creation of collaboration instances of collaboration type Col_i is only possible through the collaboration type's roles ro_i^k and their assigned behavior $R_i(ro_i^k)$. E.g., see the create shuttle SP in Fig. 4.

The relation among the collaboration Col_i's role types $ro_i^1, \ldots, ro_i^{n_i}$ and any additional data types that are used within the collaboration are specified by the class diagram CD_i. The class diagrams of different collaborations have to be separated by different name spaces.

In our example, we have a role type Shuttle and its behavior rules are given by the set { create shuttle, move, create coordination, move in coordination } of SPs as depicted in Fig. 4. The corresponding class diagram CD_i defining the roles and all the other elements in the rules is depicted on the left-hand side of Fig. 3. The guaranteed property Φ_i is in our example the and-combination of two forbidden properties collision and missing collaboration depicted in the middle and right-hand side of Fig. 3. The read rules that are depicted in Fig. 6 are not explicitly covered in the formal model but the behavioral rules of the systems that realize the roles have to take them into account. This issue will be discussed in more detail in Section 4.3.

Within a collaboration many styles of interactions, particularly, synchronous or asynchronous ones can be used. For asynchronous message passing, the following scheme can be employed: an instance of the Shuttle role creates a new message (i.e., a node in the graph) and links it to another instance of the Shuttle role that should be the receiver of the message. The latter shuttle instance can afterwards process the message that has been linked to this instance. For synchronous interactions, an instance of a role may directly modify links and data of another instance. For example, an instance of the Shuttle role may if permitted directly change the mode of another instance of the Shuttle role (cf. Fig. 1).

Systems. Similar to *UML* and *SoaML*, we employ components to represent systems that interact through collaborations by realizing the related roles. Our specification of a system further comprises safety properties that have to be fulfilled by the system's implementation.

Definition 3 (see [54]). *A system type* $\mathsf{Sys}_i = (\mathsf{sys}_i, (ro_i^1, \ldots, ro_i^{m_i}), CD_i, R_i, I_i, \Psi_i)$ *consists of a system type node* sys_i, *a number of role types* ro_i^j, *a class diagram* CD_i, *a function* $R_i : \{\mathsf{sys}_i, ro_i^1, \ldots, ro_i^{m_i}\} \mapsto 2^{\mathcal{R}}$ *assigning rules to role types, a set of initial rules* $I_i \subseteq R_i(\mathsf{sys}_i)$, *and a safety property* Ψ_i.

A system as an instance of system type Sys_i is represented by a node of type sys_i, which also fulfills the pseudo-typing requirements and thus separates elements from each other that belong to different systems. In our example we have the Shuttle and Station system types (see related dashed boxes in Fig. 1) as well as several :Shuttle and one :Station system of the corresponding types (see related solid boxes in Fig. 1).

All rules of Sys_i preserve a pseudo-typing linking of all nodes to sys_i. The function R_i is defined as for collaboration types (see Definition 2). The only way a system/instance of type Sys_i can be created is through the execution of any of the creation rules in I_i. The system type's class diagram CD_i contains all class diagrams of the collaboration types that are used by the system type.[6] Additionally, the system itself represented by a class sys_i (node type) and all data types required by the system are contained in CD_i. We further write $R_i(ro_i^k) \subseteq R_i(\mathsf{sys}_i)$ to refer to the set of all rules that belong to the system Sys_i's implementation of role ro_i^k.

System of Systems. To cover SoS, we employ system of system types and instances. System of systems combine collaboration and system types to a conceptual unit (depicted by the outer dashed box in Fig. 1).

Definition 4 (see [54]). *A system of system type* $\mathsf{SoS} = ((\mathsf{Col}_1, \ldots, \mathsf{Col}_n), (\mathsf{Sys}_1, \ldots, \mathsf{Sys}_m))$ *consists of a number of collaborations types* Col_i *and a number of system types* Sys_j.

Definition 5 (see [54]). *A system of system instance is a pair* $\mathsf{sys} = (\mathsf{SoS}, G_{\mathsf{sys}})$ *with system of system type* $\mathsf{SoS} = ((\mathsf{Col}_1, \ldots, \mathsf{Col}_n), (\mathsf{Sys}_1, \ldots, \mathsf{Sys}_m))$ *and an initial configuration* G_{sys} *that is type conform to* SoS.

As this paper does not include the details of a system type and system of system type for our example, we refer to [47,54] to obtain these details and an example that cover abstract system specifications and a system of system type.

4.3   Runtime Models

As depicted in Fig. 1, in our formal model an idealized view of the context is directly visible and accessible by the shuttle systems. This idealization reflects

---

[6] A system type uses a collaboration type if it implements a role that has been defined for this collaboration type.

that the systems handle the related information about the physical and cyber world by means of runtime models and their exchange. The idea of the read rules depicted in Fig. 6 generalizes the concept of [32] to capture the capabilities of sensors and actuators for the physical world. Consequently, the formal model describes what can be read directly by local sensors or indirectly by the exchange of runtime models reflecting the context or the other systems' internal states.

The read rules are not formalized but the behavior rules of the systems have to adhere to them, that is, the rules must not access information that should not be visible to them through local runtime models or the exchange/sharing of runtime models. In the example of Fig. 1, this visible information of the local and shared runtime models relates to the local context as well as the mode and battery status of the shuttle itself, the topology as given by the common read rule, the position of the shuttles nearby as given by the detect-obstacle read rule, and the mode of the other shuttles that are connected by a Coord collaboration instance as given by the share-mode read rule (cf. Fig. 6).

It has to be noted that the outlined formal model is an *idealization*. It assumes that the systems operate on consistent and not delayed observations and ignore the risk of partial failures. However, it many cases the outlined idealization is quite reasonable. At first, any solution that would not work for the idealization will also likely not work under more realistic assumptions. Secondly, a more detailed design would in particular acknowledge that the effects due to partial failures and delayed and inconsistent observations are limited to the extent which can be tolerated for the considered problem addressed by the collaboration type (e.g., see the protocol developed in [48] that covers the loss of connection while preserving a basis for a safe behavior).

Another issue that has to be taken into account is that even though different collaborations can be employed to talk about different required interactions, as soon as they refer to the same phenomena of the physical or cyber world, the observations in the different collaborations must be consistent. Therefore, we require that in these cases an initial collaboration has to cover the interrelated phenomena of the domain that should be considered in a consistent manner and share these phenomena with the other collaborations.

If other and more specific collaboration types take a subset of the phenomena of the physical or cyber world covered by such an initial collaboration type into account, they have to extend the initial collaboration type. Then, these more specific collaboration types cannot be specified completely separated from each other and the shared one.

Definition 6. *An* overlapping collaboration type $\mathsf{Col}_i = (\mathsf{col}_i, (ro_i^1, \ldots, ro_i^{n_i}),$ $CD_i, R_i, \Phi_i)$ *extending a shared collaboration type* $\mathsf{Col}_j = (\mathsf{col}_j, (ro_j^1, \ldots, ro_j^{n_j}),$ $CD_j, R_j, \Phi_j)$ *consists of a collaboration type node* col_i, *a number of roles* ro_i^j *with* $n_i \geq n_j$ *and for all* $1 \leq l \leq n_j$ $ro_i^l = ro_j^l$, *an UML class diagram* CD_i *extending* CD_j, *a function* $R_i : \{\mathsf{col}_i, ro_i^1, \ldots, ro_i^{n_i}\} \mapsto 2^{\mathcal{R}}$ *extending* R_j *assigning rules to roles, and a guaranteed property* Φ_i.

In our example depicted in Fig. 1, the Allocate collaboration type refines the Coord collaboration type and therefore is aware that the shuttles may move.

4.4   Evolution

One aspect of our motivation for this work is that individual systems in a smart SoS are subject to independent changes (evolution), which has to be handled by construction and assurance. In the following, we will explicitly consider the modeling of evolution, which is not addressed by *SoaML* or MUML.

Definition 7 (see [54]). *An* extended evolution sequence *is a sequence of system of systems* $(\mathsf{SoS}_1, G_S^1), \ldots, (\mathsf{SoS}_n, G_S^n)$ *such that (1)* SoS_{i+1} *only extends* SoS_i *by additional collaboration and system types, (2)* G_S^{i+1} *is also type conform to* SoS_i, *and (2)* G_S^{i+1} *can be reached from* G_S^i *in the system of system* (SoS_i, G_S^i).

An evolution sequence *is a sequence of system of system types* $\mathsf{SoS}_1, \ldots, \mathsf{SoS}_n$ *such that at least one related extended evolution sequence* $(\mathsf{SoS}_1, G_S^1), \ldots, (\mathsf{SoS}_n, G_S^n)$ *exists.*

As presented in [54], type conformance for the introduced evolution concepts can be defined that ensure a proper typing of collaborations, systems, and system of systems.

5   Assurance

Existing instance-based formal approaches do not scale and are often not applicable to the specific settings of SoS such as openness, dynamic structures, and independent evolution. Thus, the challenges of establishing Assurance of SoS-Level Interactions for Self-Organization (A2), Assurance of SoS-Level Structural Dynamics (A3), and Assurance of Evolution of Smart SoS (A5) and in particular the Scalable Assurance of Smart SoS (A6) and the Assurance of Smart SoS with Restricted Knowledge (A7) for the assurance for smart SoS are not covered.

Therefore and similar to the MUML approach, we propose establishing the required guarantees for the assurance by referring only to the collaboration and system types rather than to the instance level. For the verification at the type level we show that the correctness proven for the collaboration and system types and only type conformance for the system of systems type will by construction imply that the related correctness also holds at the instance level for any possible configurations of the related system of systems. The scalability of our approach comes from the fact that the size of the type level is independent of the size of the instance level. However, we have to show as a general property of our approach that the results we yield for the type level are also valid for the instance level.

To tackle assurance for the envisioned SMARTSOS approach, we will first address the correctness at the type level looking into collaboration and system types. Then, we will look at the instances of collaboration and system types and show that the correctness established for the types can be transfered to the instances. Afterwards, we outline how the special case of collaborations with overlapping runtime models can be handled. Finally, we cover evolution where the set of types and instances of a SoS may evolve.

5.1 Collaboration and System Types

We start our considerations with defining what we mean by correct types for collaborations and systems (see dashed inner elements in Fig. 1).

Definition 8 (see [54]). *A collaboration type* $\mathsf{Col}_i = (\mathsf{col}_i, (ro_i^1, \ldots, ro_i^{n_i}), CD_i,$ $R_i, \Phi_i)$ *is correct if for all initial configurations* $G_I \in \mathcal{G}_\emptyset(CD_i)$ *holds that for* $R_i(\mathsf{Col}_i) = R_i(ro_i^1) \cup \cdots \cup R_i(ro_i^n) \cup R_i(\mathsf{col}_i))$ *the overall behavior of the collaboration the reachable collaboration configurations are correct:* $G_I, R_i(\mathsf{Col}_i) \models \Phi_i$.

Please note that looking only at the behavior of all roles and to consider only the initial object configurations G_I without any roles is sufficient to cover all possible behavior, as we have a closed model where only the behavior of the roles is allowed to create or delete roles or any other considered elements.

For our example and the behavior rules of the Coord collaboration type as depicted in Fig. 4, it can be formally verified that the collaboration type is correct employing an automated checker (cf. [47, 51]). These checks only work for state properties and operate at the level of the types. Therefore, they do not have to consider the instance situation that would require checking infinite many and arbitrary large object configurations over arbitrary long sequences of steps. Another option that would allow us to cover sequence properties might be to use incomplete techniques such as simulation/testing or bounded or statistical model checking to establish a certain confidence for the correctness of a specific collaboration type.

A correct system type requires that the resulting behavior ensures the guarantees and that the system's implementation refines the combined role behavior.

Definition 9 (see [54]). *A system type* $\mathsf{Sys}_i = (\mathsf{sys}_i, (ro_i^1, \ldots, ro_i^{m_i}), CD_i, I_i, \Psi_i)$ *is correct if for all initial configurations* $G_I \in \mathcal{G}_\emptyset(CD_i)$ *holds that (1) the reachable configurations are correct* $G_I, R_i(\mathsf{sys}_i) \cup COMP(\mathsf{Sys}_i) \cup I_i \models \Psi_i$ *and that (2) the system behavior* $R_i(\mathsf{sys}_i)$ *refines the orthogonally combined role behavior and creation behavior* $R_i(\mathsf{sys}_i) \sqsubseteq R_i(ro_i^1) \cup \cdots \cup R_i(ro_i^{m_i}) \cup I_i$. *To add the collaboration behavior to the system behavior for each role without the role itself, we employ here* $COMP(\mathsf{Sys}_i) = \bigcup_{1 \le l \le m_i} COMP(\mathsf{Sys}_i, ro_i^l)$ *with* $COMP(\mathsf{Sys}_i, ro_i^l) = R_j(\mathsf{Col}_j)$ *which is covered by* $R_i(\mathsf{sys}_i)$ *to derive a related closed behavior.*

Due to lack of space, we do not discuss an example for a correct system type and refer to [47,54] for such an example and its formal verification. Again, another option might be to employ incomplete techniques such as simulation/testing or bounded or statistical model checking to establish a certain confidence for the correctness of a specific system type.

5.2   Collaborations and System Instances

After defining our notion of correctness for the types, we have to define the related notion of correctness at the instance level (cf. the solid elements in Fig. 1).

Definition 10 (see [54]). *A concrete system of system* sos $= (\mathsf{SoS}, G_S)$ *with system of system type* SoS $= ((\mathsf{Col}_1, \ldots, \mathsf{Col}_n), (\mathsf{Sys}_1, \ldots, \mathsf{Sys}_m))$ *is* correct *if it holds:*

$$G_S, R(\mathsf{sys}_1) \cup \cdots \cup R(\mathsf{sys}_m) \cup R(\mathsf{col}_1) \cup \cdots \cup R(\mathsf{col}_n) \models \Phi_1 \wedge \cdots \wedge \Phi_n \wedge \Psi_1 \wedge \cdots \wedge \Psi_m.$$

Then, we can show in the following Theorem 1 that the type conformance of the system of system type and the correctness of collaboration types and system types ensures correctness at the instance level for the system of system.

Theorem 1 ([54]). *A system of systems* sos $= (\mathsf{SoS}, G_\emptyset)$ *with system of system type* SoS $= ((\mathsf{Col}_1, \ldots, \mathsf{Col}_n), (\mathsf{Sys}_1, \ldots, \mathsf{Sys}_m))$ *is* correct *if (1) the system of system type* SoS *is type conform, (2) all collaboration types* $\mathsf{Col}_1, \ldots, \mathsf{Col}_n$ *are* correct, *and (3) all system types* $\mathsf{Sys}_1, \ldots, \mathsf{Sys}_m$ *are* correct.

Theorem 1 provides sufficient but not necessary conditions to ensure the correctness. It permits us to straightforward establish the required correctness of the types by checking refinement and the guarantees for the properties using the rule sets as employed in condition (2) and (3).[7]

Due to lack of space, we do not present an example for a correct system of system type here and refer to [47,54] for such an example. In general, at the system of systems level, we only have to collect the evidence for correctness that is provided for the collaboration and system types being part of this system of systems.

5.3   Runtime Models

The sharing of runtime models by a single collaboration type as depicted in Fig. 1 for the Coord collaboration can be covered with the introduced basic concepts for collaborations. Thus, the results of Theorem 1 also apply in such cases and permit us to provide the required assurance. However, this does not hold for overlapping collaborations.

For collaboration types that refine a shared collaboration type we can exploit the following Definition 12 and Lemma 1 that outline under which circumstances the correctness of the composition of all overlapping collaboration types can be derived only on the basis of the correctness of all the overlapping collaboration types, the correctness of the refined shared collaboration type, and the compatibility of their roles.

---

[7] As outlined in [54] in detail, based on the refinement of the rule sets for the involved roles the result of Theorem 1 can also be extended to abstract system and collaboration types.

Definition 11. *An overlapping collaboration type* $\mathsf{Col}_i = (\mathrm{col}_i, (ro_i^1, \ldots, ro_i^{n_i}),$ $CD_i, R_i, \Phi_i)$ *extending the shared collaboration type* $\mathsf{Col}_j = (\mathrm{col}_j, (ro_j^1, \ldots, ro_j^{n_j}),$ $CD_j, R_j, \Phi_j)$ *is correct if for all initial configurations* $G_I \in \mathcal{G}_{\emptyset}(CD_i)$ *holds that the reachable collaboration configurations are correct* $G_I, R_i(\mathsf{Col}_i) \models \Phi_j \wedge \Phi_i$ *for* $R_i(\mathsf{Col}_i) = R_i(ro_i^1) \cup \cdots \cup R_i(ro_i^n) \cup R_i(\mathrm{col}_i))$ *the overall behavior of the collaboration and that all added roles refine roles of the refined shared collaboration type:* $\forall l \in [n_j + 1, n_i] \exists k \in [1, n_j] R_i(ro_i^l) \sqsubseteq R_i(ro_j^k)$.

We can combine a set of overlapping collaboration types of the same shared refined collaboration type to obtain the related resulting collaboration type.

Definition 12. *For a set of overlapping collaboration types* $\mathsf{Col}_{i_1}, \ldots, \mathsf{Col}_{i_m}$ *extending a shared collaboration type* $\mathsf{Col}_0 = (\mathrm{col}_0, (ro_0^1, \ldots, ro_0^{n_0}), CD_0, R_0, \Phi_0)$ *the resulting collaboration type is defined as* $\mathsf{Col}_i = (\mathrm{col}_i, (ro_i^1, \ldots, ro_i^{n_i}), CD_i, R_i, \Phi_i)$ *with a collaboration type node* col_i, *a set of roles that unites the roles sets of* $\mathsf{Col}_0, \mathsf{Col}_{i_1}, \ldots, \mathsf{Col}_{i_m}$, *an UML class diagram* $CD_i = CD_0 \cup \bigcup_{1 \leq k \leq m} CD_{i_k}$, *a function* $R_i : \{\mathrm{col}_i, ro_i^1, \ldots, ro_i^{n_i}\} \mapsto 2^{\mathcal{R}}$ *extending* R_0 *and all* R_{i_k} *for* $1 \leq k \leq m$ *assigning rules to roles, and a guaranteed property* $\Phi_i = \Phi_0 \wedge (\wedge_{1 \leq k \leq m} \Phi_{i_k})$.

In a next step we can show with the following Lemma that the resulting collaboration type is correct, if all overlapping collaboration types of the related shared collaboration types are correct.

Lemma 1. *If all overlapping collaboration types* $\mathsf{Col}_{i_1}, \ldots, \mathsf{Col}_{i_m}$ *and the shared refined collaboration type* $\mathsf{Col}_0 = (\mathrm{col}_0, (ro_0^1, \ldots, ro_0^{n_j}), CD_0, R_0, \Phi_0)$ *are correct, then the resulting collaboration type* $\mathsf{Col}_i = (\mathrm{col}_i, (ro_i^1, \ldots, ro_i^{n_i}), CD_i, R_i, \Phi_i)$ *is also correct.*

Proof. *For any correct overlapping collaboration type* $\mathsf{Col}_{i_k} = (\mathrm{col}_{i_k}, (ro_{i_k}^1, \ldots,$ $ro_{i_k}^{n_{i_k}}), CD_{i_k}, R_{i_k}, \Phi_{i_k})$ *of the shared refined collaboration type* $\mathsf{Col}_0 = (\mathrm{col}_0, (ro_0^1,$ $\ldots, ro_0^{n_j}), CD_0, R_0, \Phi_0)$ *holds that* $G_I, R_{i_k}(\mathsf{Col}_{i_k}) \models \Phi_0 \wedge \Phi_{i_k}$. *As the extension of each overlapping collaboration type are disjoint and the shared behavior is refining the roles of the shared collaboration, we can conclude that also* $G_I, R_i(\mathsf{Col}_i) \models \Phi_{i_k}$ *will hold. As* $\Phi_i = \Phi_0 \wedge (\wedge_{1 \leq k \leq m} \Phi_{i_k})$ *we only have to combine this finding for all* $1 \leq k \leq m$ *and get* $G_I, R_i(\mathsf{Col}_i) \models \wedge_{1 \leq k \leq m} \Phi_{i_k}$ *and thus* $G_I, R_i(\mathsf{Col}_i) \models \Phi_i$ *such that* Col_i *is correct.* $\square$

Due to Lemma 1 we can now employ Theorem 1 to cover overlapping collaborations.

5.4 Evolution

So far the presented results for assurance do not cover the evolution of SoS. Therefore, we will extend the former results to cover typical evolution scenarios such as adding new collaboration or system types. If we look at our former results in more detail, we can notice that the assumption has been made that all types are known at verification time. This assumption is not true for a steadily evolving system where new type definitions are added over time. Furthermore, the different organizations involved in an SoS will only have a partial view and thus do not know all currently existing types in the SoS. For a given *extended evolution sequence* (cf. Definition 7) we can define correctness as follows:

Definition 13 (see [54]). *An extended evolution sequence* $(\mathsf{SoS}_1, G_S^1), \ldots,$ (SoS_n, G_S^n) *with* $\mathsf{SoS}_n = ((\mathsf{Col}_1, \ldots, \mathsf{Col}_p), (\mathsf{Sys}_1, \ldots, \mathsf{Sys}_q))$ *is* correct *if for any combined path* $\pi_1 \circ \cdots \circ \pi_n$ *such that* π_i *is a path in* SoS_i *leading from* G_S^i *to* G_S^{i+1} *for* $i < n$ *and that* π_n *is a path in* SoS_n *starting from* G_S^n *holds:* $\pi_1 \circ \cdots \circ \pi_n \models$ $\Phi_1 \wedge \cdots \wedge \Phi_p \wedge \Psi_1 \wedge \cdots \wedge \Psi_q$. *An evolution sequence* $\mathsf{SoS}_1, \ldots, \mathsf{SoS}_n$ *is* correct *if all possible related extended evolution sequence* $(\mathsf{SoS}_1, G_S^1), \ldots, (\mathsf{SoS}_n, G_S^n)$ *are* correct.

A first observation is that SoS_n contains all types defined in any SoS_i. However, for a combined path $\pi_1 \circ \cdots \circ \pi_n$ such that π_i is a path in SoS_i leading from G_S^i to G_S^{i+1} for $i < n$ does not hold in general that an equal path π in SoS_n exists that goes through all G_S^i, as the rules added by later added types may influence the possible outcomes if added at the start.[8] Another observation is that the properties guaranteed for newly introduced collaboration or system types have to be true as long as the types have not yet been introduced as otherwise the evolution cannot be correct. We can exploit these observations and construct related collaboration types $E(\mathsf{Col}_i)$ and system types $E(\mathsf{Sys}_j)$ encoding that the types come into existence later. Based on this we can then define $E(\mathsf{SoS}_1, \mathsf{SoS}_n)$ as that system of system type where the types of SoS_n not present in SoS_1 can come into existence later. $E(\mathsf{SoS}_1, \mathsf{SoS}_n)$ therefore includes all possible combined paths of any possible extended evolution sequences for a given evolution sequence $\mathsf{SoS}_1, \ldots, \mathsf{SoS}_n$.

We can then use the fact that the related dynamically evolving system of system type includes all possible extended evolution sequences to check also the correctness for all possible evolution sequences.

Theorem 2 (see [54]). *An evolution sequence of systems* $\mathsf{SoS}_1, \ldots, \mathsf{SoS}_n$ *is* correct *if the related dynamic evolving system of system type* $E(\mathsf{SoS}_1, \mathsf{SoS}_n)$ *is* correct.

Lemma 2 (see [54]). *For a correct collaboration type Col holds also that its dynamic extension* $E(Col)$ *is correct. For a correct system type* Sys *holds also that its dynamic extension* $E(\mathsf{Sys})$ *is correct.*

Due to Lemma 2, it is sufficient to simply check the collaboration and system types and this already guarantees that any extended evolution sequence will also show correct behavior.

Moreover, due to Theorem 2 and Lemma 2, an organization that wants to extend the system of system type accordingly does not require any knowledge about all the other types besides those which are refined or where an overlap

---

[8] For example, in a refined model there may be urgent rules that have to be executed if enabled and thus may preempt other rules when added during the evolution.

exists. Furthermore, if two independent extensions are done which do not refer to each other, the concrete order of these extensions does not matter as the checks remain the same. Therefore, each organization can simply check its own extension by means of added collaboration and system types without considering when the other extensions are enacted.

Due to lack of space, we do not present an example for a correct system of system type with evolution here and refer to [47,54] for such an example.

6 Discussion

In SMARTSOS, we combine ideas from MUML and EUREMA to tackle the challenges for smart SoS that are discussed in Section 2. A radically different and more abstract perspective on the SoS-level interactions based on runtime models and collaborations is employed to overcome the limitations of the state-of-the-art and our former approaches and to master the complexity of smart SoS. In the following, we will discuss which challenges are addressed by the proposed ideas, particularly, by the concepts of collaborations and runtime models, the novelty of these ideas, and the additional benefits of these ideas.

6.1 Runtime Models

As discussed for the envisioned SMARTSOS approach in Section 3 and its formal model in Sections 4 and 5, SMARTSOS employs *generic runtime models*.

On the one hand, this supports the engineering of the self-adaptation for individual systems in the smart SoS as required by the challenge of Construction/Assurance of Self-Adaptation (C1/A1) (cf. Section 2). Similar to EUREMA, the self-adaptation for each system is implemented in SMARTSOS by a feedback loop with monitor, analyze, plan, and execute activities that operate on the generic runtime models. For instance, the self-adaptive behavior of each shuttle in the large-scale transport system is specified by such feedback loops operating on partially shared runtime models that reflect the shuttle itself and the shuttle's context (cf. top of the left-hand side of Fig. 2).

On the other hand, SMARTSOS uses the generic runtime models to exchange information between individual collaborating systems, which addresses the challenge of Construction/Assurance of SoS-Level Runtime Knowledge Exchange (C4/A4). This aspect distinguishes SMARTSOS from the state of the art in engineering SoS that employ specific and optimized runtime models without exchanging them among individual systems.

Therefore, SMARTSOS goes beyond the MUML approach and the state of the art by supporting *generic runtime models* of the contexts and the systems in the SoS. SMARTSOS also goes beyond EUREMA and the state of the art by supporting the runtime exchange of these models between the individual collaborating systems in an SoS. In the context of collaborations, such runtime models can also reflect agreements between the collaborating systems which is a prerequisite for jointly achieving the SoS-level goals. Thereby, such collaborations may be established in a self-organizing manner while each system still evolves and self-adapts independently from the other systems in the SoS.

While the *generic* nature of the runtime models used in SMARTSOS clearly leads to a higher complexity of the models compared to the state of the art, it also leverages a number of benefits: (B1) As a "success in regulation implies that a sufficiently similar model must have been built," [55], it is consequently unavoidable that the software captures all the relevant variety of the controlled system itself, the requirements, and the context to be able to control their variability effectively. (B2) Herbert A. Simon observed for the example of an ant that "[t]he apparent complexity of its behavior over time is largely a reflection of the complexity of the environment in which it finds itself" [56, p. 52]. Thus, it can be expected that including the physical and cyber environment by runtime models will in fact help to reduce the complexity of the remaining software solution that operates on the basis of these runtime models. Finally, (B3) while specialized solutions that only capture a minimal amount of information about the environments lead to simpler software in the short run, it can be expected that the envisioned generic runtime models without such optimizations result in a *direct-mapping* [57] between the original (e.g., the system or context) and the model. Such a mapping is usually more stable in the long run and considerably eases interoperability. The latter aspect is a critical issue to achieve open and dynamic collaborations in smart SoS.

6.2   Collaborations

Based on the generic runtime models, SMARTSOS employs *open and dynamic collaborations* (cf. Section 3) to achieve self-organizing interactions between individual systems of the smart SoS. The collaboration concept of SMARTSOS is also covered in the formal model for the construction and assurance of smart SoS (cf. Sections 4 and 5). In contrast to state of the art approaches, this perspective on the SoS-level interactions addresses the challenges of Construction/Assurance of SoS-Level Interactions for Self-Organization (C2/A2) and Construction/Assurance of SoS-Level Structural Dynamics (C3/A3) (cf. Section 2). Moreover, it is key to address the challenges of Construction/Assurance of Evolution of Smart SoS (C5/A5), Scalable Construction/Assurance of Smart SoS (C6/A6), and Construction/Assurance of Smart SoS with Restricted Knowledge (C7/A7).

In this context, SMARTSOS extends EUREMA that does not consider collaborations at all since EUREMA focuses on centralized and non-distributed systems. In contrast to MUML, SMARTSOS employs *open and more dynamic collaborations* that are governed by laws supporting self-organization at the SoS level and that support the structural dynamics of smart SoS where, for example, systems may dynamically join or leave the SoS. The collaboration concept of SMARTSOS supports abstracting details of individual systems in the SoS by means of roles, runtime models, and behavioral contracts while distinguishing the type and instance levels (cf. Section 3). This collaboration concept leverages the independent development, operation, management, and evolution of these systems (cf. Sections 4 and 5). Thus, the evolution of smart SoS and its contained systems with respect to construction (cf. Section 4.4) and assurance (cf. Section 5.4) aspects is supported. By abstraction and explicitly distinguishing the type and instance levels of smart SoS, the construction and assurance are scalable as they mainly work at the type level – hence abstracting from the sheer scale and number of all possible instance situations of a smart SoS. In the same line of reasoning, the construction and assurance of smart SoS works despite not considering the complete instance situation and thus all details of the SoS. Therefore, SMARTSOS can handle the restricted knowledge of SoS caused by multiple authorities governing the SoS.

In general, the collaboration concept of SMARTSOS is motivated by the beneficial observations that (B4) in our society we have established legal domains, which we consider independent of each other. We can expect that the individuals behave according to the laws of each of these legal domains independent of the other domains. This approach allows us to cooperate even though the systems and legal domains evolve and adapt in principle independently from each other (cf. law-governed interaction [58]). In the traffic domain, for example, rules for driving vehicles and related regulations and laws impose what individual drivers are allowed to do while within these bounds the individuals are free to act. In our example, the Coord collaboration in Fig. 1 establishes such a solution with respect to the driving behavior of the shuttles. As another example, individuals in the traffic domain may establish contracts with each other to allocate parking slots. In our example, a Shuttle may establish such a contract to have the privilege to stop at a specific platform of a Station by means of an Allocate collaboration instance as depicted in Fig. 1.

7 Conclusion and Future Work

In this paper we analyzed the open challenges for the envisioned smart SoS looking in particular into construction and assurance of such SoS. In this context, we presented our ideas how to tackle this vision with our SMARTSOS approach, specifically, by employing open and adaptive collaborations and generic models at runtime. We discussed that by supporting generic runtime models at the SoS level, the challenge of Construction/Assurance of SoS-Level Runtime Knowledge Exchange (C4/A4) can be covered by SMARTSOS. Furthermore, based on such runtime models, the SMARTSOS collaboration concept directly covers the challenges of Construction/Assurance of SoS-Level Interactions for Self-Organization (C2/A2) and Construction/Assurance of SoS-Level Structural Dynamics (C3/A3). Moreover, it provides the required foundation to tackle the challenges of Construction/Assurance of Evolution of Smart SoS (C5/A5), Scalable Construction/Assurance of Smart SoS (C6/A6), and Construction/Assurance of Smart SoS with Restricted Knowledge (C7/A7). While SMARTSOS addresses the challenges related to the SoS level, the challenge of Construction/Assurance of Self-Adaptation (C1/A1) of individual systems in the SoS is mainly addressed by our former work on MUML and EUREMA.

Our plans for future work are to further elaborate SMARTSOS by extending the model-driven EUREMA approach [33] with open and adaptive collaborations and means for the distributed management of runtime models. Additionally, we plan to further strengthen the links between runtime and development-time models [59] and model-driven techniques in runtime scenarios [45].

Acknowledgment. We thank Basil Becker for his contribution to the presented results and his comments on draft versions of this paper.

References

1. Maier, M.W.: Architecting principles for systems-of-systems. Systems Engineering 1(4), 267–284 (1998)
2. Valerdi, R., Axelband, E., Baehren, T., Boehm, B., Dorenbos, D., Jackson, S., Madni, A., Nadler, G., Robitaille, P., Settles, S.: A research agenda for systems of systems architecting. Intl. Journal of System of Systems Engineering 1(1-2), 171–188 (2008)
3. Northrop, L., Feiler, P.H., Gabriel, R.P., Linger, R., Longstaff, T., Kazman, R., Klein, M., Schmidt, D.: Ultra-Large-Scale Systems: The Software Challenge of the Future. Software Engineering Institute, Carnegie Mellon University, Pittsburgh, PA (2006)
4. Broy, M., Cengarle, M.V., Geisberger, E.: Cyber-Physical Systems: Imminent Challenges. In: Calinescu, R., Garlan, D. (eds.) Monterey Workshop 2012. LNCS, vol. 7539, pp. 1–28. Springer, Heidelberg (2012)
5. Baresi, L., Di Nitto, E., Ghezzi, C.: Toward Open-World Software: Issue and Challenges. Computer 39(10), 36–43 (2006)
6. Cheng, B.H.C., et al.: Software Engineering for Self-Adaptive Systems: A Research Roadmap. In: Cheng, B.H.C., de Lemos, R., Giese, H., Inverardi, P., Magee, J. (eds.) Software Engineering for Self-Adaptive Systems. LNCS, vol. 5525, pp. 1–26. Springer, Heidelberg (2009)
7. de Lemos, R., et al.: Software Engineering for Self-Adaptive Systems: A Second Research Roadmap. In: de Lemos, R., Giese, H., Müller, H.A., Shaw, M. (eds.) Software Engineering for Self-Adaptive Systems. LNCS, vol. 7475, pp. 1–32. Springer, Heidelberg (2013)
8. Di Marzo Serugendo, G., Gleizes, M.P., Karageorgos, A. (eds.): Self-organising Software. Natural Computing Series. Springer (2011)
9. Mens, T., Demeyer, S.: Software Evolution. Springer (2008)
10. Mittal, S., Risco Martin, J.: Model-driven systems engineering for netcentric system of systems with DEVS unified process. In: Simulation Conference (WSC), pp. 1140–1151 (Winter 2013)
11. Object Management Group (OMG): Service oriented architecture Modeling Language (SoaML) Specification, Version 1.0.1. (2012)
12. UML 2.4 Superstructure Specification, Version 2.4, ptc/2010-11-14 (2010)
13. Sanders, R.T., Castejón, H.N., Kraemer, F., Bræk, R.: Using UML 2.0 Collaborations for Compositional Service Specification. In: Briand, L.C., Williams, C. (eds.) MoDELS 2005. LNCS, vol. 3713, pp. 460–475. Springer, Heidelberg (2005)
14. Broy, M., Krüger, I., Meisinger, M.: A formal model of services. ACM Trans. Softw. Eng. Methodol. 16 (2007)

15. Baresi, L., Heckel, R., Thöne, S., Varró, D.: Modeling and Validation of Service-Oriented Architectures: Application vs. Style. In: Proceedings of the 9th European Software Engineering Conference Held Jointly with 11th ACM SIGSOFT International Symposium on Foundations of Software Engineering, ESEC/FSE-11, pp. 68–77. ACM, New York (2003)
16. Baresi, L., Heckel, R., Thöne, S., Varró, D.: Style-based modeling and refinement of service-oriented architectures. Software and Systems Modeling 5(2), 187–207 (2006)
17. Hölzl, M., Wirsing, M.: Towards a System Model for Ensembles. In: Agha, G., Danvy, O., Meseguer, J. (eds.) Formal Modeling: Actors, Open Systems, Biological Systems. LNCS, vol. 7000, pp. 241–261. Springer, Heidelberg (2011)
18. Milner, R.: Communicating and mobile systems: the π-calculus. Cambridge University Press, New York (1999)
19. Milner, R.: The Space and Motion of Communicating Agents. Cambridge University Press (2009)
20. Varró, D.: Automated formal verification of visual modeling languages by model checking. Software and System Modeling 3(2), 85–113 (2004)
21. Rensink, A.: Towards model checking graph grammars. In: Proc. of the 3rd Workshop on Automated Verification of Critical Systems, AVoCS, University of Southampton, pp. 150–160 (2003)
22. Frias, M.F., Galeotti, J.P., López Pombo, C.G., Aguirre, N.M.: DynAlloy: Upgrading Alloy with actions. In: Proceedings of the 27th International Conference on Software Engineering. ICSE 2005, pp. 442–451. ACM (2005)
23. Ölveczky, P.C., Meseguer, J.: Specification and Analysis of Real-Time Systems Using Real-Time Maude. In: Wermelinger, M., Margaria-Steffen, T. (eds.) FASE 2004. LNCS, vol. 2984, pp. 354–358. Springer, Heidelberg (2004)
24. Zhang, J., Goldsby, H.J., Cheng, B.H.: Modular verification of dynamically adaptive systems. In: Proceedings of the 8th ACM International Conference on Aspect-oriented Software Development, AOSD 2009, pp. 161–172. ACM, New York (2009)
25. Baldan, P., Corradini, A., König, B.: A Static Analysis Technique for Graph Transformation Systems. In: Larsen, K.G., Nielsen, M. (eds.) CONCUR 2001. LNCS, vol. 2154, pp. 381–395. Springer, Heidelberg (2001)
26. Bauer, J., Wilhelm, R.: Static Analysis of Dynamic Communication Systems by Partner Abstraction. In: Riis Nielson, H., Filé, G. (eds.) SAS 2007. LNCS, vol. 4634, pp. 249–264. Springer, Heidelberg (2007)
27. Burmester, S., Giese, H., Münch, E., Oberschelp, O., Klein, F., Scheideler, P.: Tool Support for the Design of Self-Optimizing Mechatronic Multi-Agent Systems. International Journal on Software Tools for Technology Transfer (STTT) 10(3), 207–222 (2008)
28. Giese, H., Schäfer, W.: Model-Driven Development of Safe Self-Optimizing Mechatronic Systems with MechatronicUML. In: Cámara, J., de Lemos, R., Ghezzi, C., Lopes, A. (eds.) Assurances for Self-Adaptive Systems. LNCS, vol. 7740, pp. 152–186. Springer, Heidelberg (2013)
29. Giese, H., Burmester, S., Schäfer, W., Oberschelp, O.: Modular Design and Verification of Component-Based Mechatronic Systems with Online-Reconfiguration. In: Proceedings of the 12th ACM SIGSOFT Twelfth International Symposium on Foundations of Software Engineering, SIGSOFT 2004/FSE-12, pp. 179–188. ACM (2004)

30. Giese, H., Tichy, M., Burmester, S., Schäfer, W., Flake, S.: Towards the compositional verification of real-time uml designs. In: Proceedings of the 9th European Software Engineering Conference Held Jointly with 11th ACM SIGSOFT International Symposium on Foundations of Software Engineering, ESEC/FSE-11, pp. 38–47. ACM, New York (2003)
31. Becker, B., Beyer, D., Giese, H., Klein, F., Schilling, D.: Symbolic Invariant Verification for Systems with Dynamic Structural Adaptation. In: Proceedings of the 28th International Conference on Software Engineering, ICSE 2006, pp. 72–81. ACM (2006)
32. Giese, H., Klein, F.: Systematic verification of multi-agent systems based on rigorous executable specifications. Int. J. Agent-Oriented Softw. Eng. 1(1), 28–62 (2007)
33. Vogel, T., Giese, H.: Model-Driven Engineering of Self-Adaptive Software with EUREMA. ACM Trans. Auton. Adapt. Syst. 8(4), 18:1–18:33 (2014)
34. Blair, G., Bencomo, N., France, R.B.: Models@run.time. Computer 42(10), 22–27 (2009)
35. Rozenberg, G. (ed.): Handbook of Graph Grammars and Computing by Graph Transformation: Foundations, vol. 1. World Scientific Pub. Co. (1997)
36. Rozenberg, G., Ehrig, H., Engels, G., Kreowski, H. (eds.): Handbook of graph grammars and computing by graph transformation. applications, languages, and tools, vol. 2. World Scientific (1999)
37. The Open Group Architectural Framework (TOGAF), version 9.1. Open Group Standard (2011)
38. Vassev, E., Hinchey, M.: The Challenge of Developing Autonomic Systems. Computer 43(12), 93–96 (2010)
39. Marconi, A., Bucchiarone, A., Bratanis, K., Brogi, A., Camara, J., Dranidis, D., Giese, H., Kazhamiakink, R., de Lemos, R., Marquezan, C., Metzger, A.: Research challenges on multi-layer and mixed-initiative monitoring and adaptation for service-based systems. In: 2012 Workshop on European Software Services and Systems Research - Results and Challenges (S-Cube), pp. 40–46. IEEE (2012)
40. France, R., Rumpe, B.: Model-driven development of complex software: A research roadmap. In: 2007 Future of Software Engineering, FOSE 2007, pp. 37–54. IEEE Computer Society, Washington, DC (2007)
41. Vogel, T., Giese, H.: Adaptation and Abstract Runtime Models. In: Proceedings of the 2010 ICSE Workshop on Software Engineering for Adaptive and Self-Managing Systems, SEAMS 2010, pp. 39–48. ACM (2010)
42. Vogel, T., Seibel, A., Giese, H.: The Role of Models and Megamodels at Runtime. In: Dingel, J., Solberg, A. (eds.) MODELS 2010. LNCS, vol. 6627, pp. 224–238. Springer, Heidelberg (2011)
43. Wätzoldt, S., Giese, H.: Classifying Distributed Self-* Systems Based on Runtime Models and Their Coupling. In: Proceedings of the 9th International Workshop on Models@run.time. CEUR Workshop Proceedings, vol. 1270, pp. 11–20. CEUR-WS.org (2014)
44. Kephart, J.O., Chess, D.: The Vision of Autonomic Computing. Computer 36(1), 41–50 (2003)
45. Giese, H., Lambers, L., Becker, B., Hildebrandt, S., Neumann, S., Vogel, T., Wätzoldt, S.: Graph Transformations for MDE, Adaptation, and Models at Runtime. In: Bernardo, M., Cortellessa, V., Pierantonio, A. (eds.) SFM 2012. LNCS, vol. 7320, pp. 137–191. Springer, Heidelberg (2012)
46. Klein, F., Giese, H.: Joint Structural and Temporal Property Specification using Timed Story Sequence Diagrams. In: Dwyer, M.B., Lopes, A. (eds.) FASE 2007. LNCS, vol. 4422, pp. 185–199. Springer, Heidelberg (2007)

47. Becker, B.: Architectural modelling and verification of open service-oriented systems of systems. PhD thesis, Hasso-Plattner-Institut für Softwaresystemtechnik, Universität Potsdam (2014)
48. Giese, H., Burmester, S., Klein, F., Schilling, D., Tichy, M.: Multi-Agent System Design for Safety-Critical Self-Optimizing Mechatronic Systems with UML. In: Henderson-Sellers, B., Debenham, J. (eds.) OOPSLA 2003 - Second International Workshop on Agent-Oriented Methodologies, Anaheim, CA, USA, pp. 21–32. Center for Object Technology Applications and Research (COTAR), University of Technology, Sydney, Australia (2003)
49. Becker, B., Giese, H.: Modeling of Correct Self-Adaptive Systems: A Graph Transformation System Based Approach. In: Proceedings of the 5th International Conference on Soft Computing As Transdisciplinary Science and Technology, CSTST 2008, pp. 508–516. ACM (2008)
50. Giese, H., Hildebrandt, S., Lambers, L.: Bridging the gap between formal semantics and implementation of triple graph grammars. Software and Systems Modeling 13(1), 273–299 (2014)
51. Becker, B., Giese, H.: On Safe Service-Oriented Real-Time Coordination for Autonomous Vehicles. In: Proc. of the 11th IEEE International Symposium on Object Oriented Real-Time Distributed Computing (ISORC), pp. 203–210. IEEE Computer Society Press (2008)
52. Krause, C., Giese, H.: Probabilistic Graph Transformation Systems. In: Ehrig, H., Engels, G., Kreowski, H.-J., Rozenberg, G. (eds.) ICGT 2012. LNCS, vol. 7562, pp. 311–325. Springer, Heidelberg (2012)
53. Becker, B., Giese, H.: Cyber-Physical Systems with Dynamic Structure: Towards Modeling and Verification of Inductive Invariants. Technical Report 64, Hasso Plattner Institute at the University of Potsdam, Germany (2012)
54. Giese, H., Becker, B.: Modeling and Verifying Dynamic Evolving Service-Oriented Architectures. Technical Report 75, Hasso Plattner Institute at the University of Potsdam, Germany (2013)
55. Conant, R.C., Ashby, W.R.: Every good regulator of a system must be a model of that system. Intl. J. Systems Science 1(2), 89–97 (1970)
56. Simon, H.A.: The Sciences of the Artificial, 3rd edn. The MIT Press (1996)
57. Meyer, B.: 30. In: Concurrency, Distribution, Client-Server and the Internet, 2nd edn., pp. 951–1036. Prentice Hall (1997)
58. Minsky, N.H., Ungureanu, V.: Law-governed interaction: a coordination and control mechanism for heterogeneous distributed systems. ACM Transactions on Software Engineering and Methodology (TOSEM) 9(3), 273–305 (2000)
59. Vogel, T., Giese, H.: On Unifying Development Models and Runtime Models. In: Proceedings of the 9th International Workshop on Models@run.time. CEUR Workshop Proceedings, vol. 1270, pp. 5–10. CEUR-WS.org (2014)

Automated Integration of Service-Oriented Software Systems

Marco Autili, Paola Inverardi, and Massimo Tivoli

Università dell'Aquila, Dipartimento di Ingegneria e Scienze dell'Informazione e
Matematica, L'Aquila, Italy
{marco.autili,paola.inverardi,massimo.tivoli}@univaq.it

Abstract. In the near future we will be surrounded by a virtually infinite number of software applications that provide services in the digital
space. This situation radically changes the way software will be produced
and used: (i) software is increasingly produced according to specific goals
and by integrating existing software; (ii) the focus of software production
will be shifted towards reuse of third-parties software, typically black-
box, that is often provided without a machine readable documentation.
The evidence underlying this scenario is that the price to pay for this
software availability is a lack of knowledge on the software itself, notably
on its interaction behaviour. A producer will operate with software artefacts that are not completely known in terms of their functional and
non-functional characteristics. The general problem is therefore directed
to the ability of interacting with the artefacts to the extent the goal is
reached. This is not a trivial problem given the virtually infinite interaction protocols that can be defined at application level. Different software
artefacts with heterogeneous interaction protocols may need to interop-
erate in order to reach the goal. In this paper we focus on techniques and
tools for integration code synthesis, which are able to deal with partial
knowledge and automatically produce correct-by-construction service-
oriented systems with respect to functional goals. The research approach
we propose builds around two phases: elicit and integrate. The first concerns observation theories and techniques to elicit functional behavioural
models of the interaction protocol of black-box services. The second deals
with compositional theories and techniques to automatically synthesize
appropriate integration means to compose the services together in order
to realize a service choreography that satisfies the goal.

1 Introduction

In the near future we will be increasingly surrounded by a virtually infinite
number of software services that can be composed to build new added value
applications in the Digital Space. According to John Musser, founder of Pro-
grammableWeb[1], the production of Application Programming Interfaces (APIs)
grows exponentially and some companies are accounting for billions of dollars

---

[1] http://www.programmableweb.com.

© IFIP International Federation for Information Processing 2015
M. Dastani and M.Sirjani (Eds.): FSEN 2015, LNCS 9392, pp. 30–45, 2015.
DOI: 10.1007/978-3-319-24644-4_2

in revenue per year via API links to their services. Moreover, the evolution of today Internet is expected to lead to an ultra large number of available services, hence increasing their number to billions of services in the near future. This situation radically changes the way software will be produced and used: (i) software is increasingly produced according to specific goals and by integrating existing software; (ii) the focus of software production is on integration of third party and typically black-box software, that is only provided with an interface that exposes the available functionalities but does not provide the assumed interaction protocol. The first characteristic implies a **goal oriented, opportunistic use** of the software being integrated, i.e., the producer will only use a subset of the available functionalities, some of which may not even be (completely) known. The second one implies the need to (a) **extract suitable interaction models** from discoverable and accessible pieces of software, which are made available as services in the digital space, and (b) devise appropriate **integration** means (e.g., architectures, connectors, mediators, integration patterns) that ease the composition of existing services so to achieve the goal.

The aim of the proposed research is to **provide automatic support** to the production of software systems by **integrating** existing software services **according to a specified goal**.

Our proposal builds on the model-based software production paradigm while accounting for the inherent incompleteness of information about existing software. This evidence suggests the use of an experimental approach, as opposed to a creationistic one, to the production of software. Software development has been so far biased towards a creationist view: a producer is the owner of the artefact and, if needed, she can declaratively supply any needed piece of information (interfaces, behaviours, contracts, etc.). The digital space promotes a different experimental view: the knowledge of a software artefact is limited to what can be observed of it. The more powerful and extensive the observations are, the deeper the knowledge will be; the knowledge will always remain partial, though. Indeed, there is a theoretical barrier that limits, in general, the power and the extent of observations.

Beyond automation, a further big challenge underlying this scenario is therefore to live up with the fact that this immense software resources availability corresponds to a lack of knowledge about the software, notably on its behaviour. A software producer will know less and less the precise behaviour of a third-party software service, nevertheless she will try to use it to build her own application. This very same problem recognized in the software engineering domain [16] is faced in many other computer science domains, e.g., exploratory search [39] and search computing [12].

In order to face this problem and provide a producer with a supporting framework to realize software applications via **automated integration**, we envision a process that implements a radically new perspective. First results can be found in [22]. This process builds around **elicit** and **integrate** phases.

From now on, when referring to models of services we always mean models of the interaction protocols of the services, that is models of the sequences of actions/messages exchange that need to be performed in order to consume the service, e.g., "login" and "get authorized", before "access bank account".

The elicit phase automatically produces an interaction protocol model for each service that has been discovered as a candidate to provide a desired functionality with respect to a specified system goal. This model is complete enough to allow the service to be integrated with others in order to satisfy the goal.

The integrate phase assists the producer in creating the appropriate integration means to compose the observed services together in order to produce a system that satisfies the goal.

In this paper we present a specific instance of the above reuse-based elicit-integrate development process, which is suitable for service-oriented systems.

The paper is organized as follows. Section 2 describes an instance of the elicit phase, which is suitable for the automatic elicitation of the interaction protocol of a Web Service. Section 3 discusses in detail an instance of the integrate phase, which allows the producer to automatically enforce the realization of a specific form of service composition, namely a choreography. Thus, this instance is suitable for the automatic production of choreography-based service-oriented systems. Section 4 discusses related work in the domains of behavioral model elicitation techniques and of service choreography development. Section 5 discusses final remarks and future research directions.

2   The Elicit Phase

Given a software service S that has been discovered as a candidate to provide a desired functionality with respect to a system goal G, elicitation techniques must be defined to produce interaction protocol models that are complete enough to allow the service to be integrated with others in order to satisfy G. This means that we admit partial models of the service interaction protocols. For the integration phases to be automated, a goal G specification is a machine-readable model achieved by the producer by operationalizing the needs and preferences of the user [36].

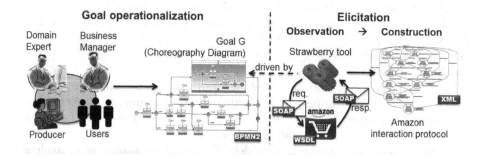

Fig. 1. Elicit phase

Referring to Figure 1, a concrete example of a goal specification can be found in [7], where domain expert and user goals are operationalized into a BPMN2[2] choreography specification, after being transformed into a CTT (ConcurTask-Trees) intermediate model [32]. The elicit phase is composed of two steps, namely *observation* and *construction* [22]. For each service to be integrated, the observation step is driven by G and collects a set of observation data. We focus on observations devoted to the identification of a set of functional behaviours, e.g., the SOAP response to a Web-Service (WS) operation invocation. Construction takes as input the set of observation data and produces a (partial) model of the observed service. This model represents the observed behaviours enriched with inferred information that is relevant for achieving G. For instance, as done in [11], the collection of the SOAP responses to WS operation invocations, enriched with the inferred partial order of the invocations, can be represented as an automaton that models the interaction protocol of the observed WS. Note that, as it is shown in Section 3, having a partial model of the interaction protocol, for each observed WS to be integrated, is sufficient to automatically synthesize the code of proxies that allow for integrating the WSs so to realize the specified BPMN2 choreography. An important aspect is that the elicit phase produces models that, although partial, are still good enough to achieve G. Goal driven elicitation can be very effective, e.g., as observed on the Amazon E-commerce WS (AEWS) where we apply the approach in [11] to elicit the AEWS interaction protocol. The experiment considered a goal-independent elicitation versus a goal-driven one [5]. Starting from the AEWS WSDL consisting of 85 XML schema type definitions and 23 WSDL operation definitions, the goal independent elicitation resulted in an interaction protocol made of 24 states and 288 transitions by using 10^6 test cases, each executed in 10^{-2} secs, e.g., few hours of testing. By considering a goal specification that the user wished to "develop a client for cart management only", the interaction protocol computed was made of 6 state and 21 transitions only. The goal driven elicitation required the generation and execution of 10^5 test cases, e.g., few seconds of testing.

As it is shown in Section 3, having a partial model of the interaction protocol, for each observed WS to be integrated, is sufficient to automatically synthesize the code of additional software entities that, proxyfing the WSs, allow for integrating them so to realize the specified BPMN2 choreography. An important aspect is that the elicit phase produces models that, although partial, are still good enough to achieve G.

Goal driven elicitation can be very effective, e.g., as observed on the Amazon E-commerce WS (AEWS) where we apply the approach in [11] to elicit the AEWS interaction protocol. The experiment considered a goal independent elicitation versus a goal driven one [5]. Starting from the AEWS WSDL consisting of 85 XML schema type definitions and 23 WSDL operation definitions, the goal independent elicitation resulted in an interaction protocol made of 24 states and 288 transitions by using 10^6 test cases, each executed in 10^{-2} secs, e.g., few hours of testing. By considering a goal specification that the user wished to

---

[2] http://www.omg.org/spec/BPMN/2.0.

"develop a client for cart management only", the interaction protocol computed was made of 6 state and 21 transitions only. The goal driven elicitation required the generation and execution of 10^5 test cases, e.g., few seconds of testing.

The following section summarizes the elicit technique that we describe in detail in [11]. It represents a specific realization of the elicit phase, which is suitable for producing the interaction protocol of a WS.

2.1   StrawBerry: Automated Synthesis of WS Interaction Protocols

By taking as input a syntactical description of the WS signature, expressed by means of the WSDL notation, StrawBerry [11] derives in an automated way a partial ordering relation among the invocations of the different WSDL operations. This partial ordering relation is represented as an automaton that we call *Behavior Protocol automaton*. It models the interaction protocol that a client has to follow in order to correctly interact with the WS. This automaton also explicitly models the information that has to be passed to the WS operations. StrawBerry is a black-box and extra-procedural method. It is black-box since it takes into account only the WSDL of the WS. It is extra-procedural since it focuses on synthesizing a model of the behavior that is assumed when interacting with the WS from outside, as opposed to intra-procedural methods that synthesize a model of the implementation logic of the single WS operations [29, 38].

Figure 2 graphically represents StrawBerry as a process that is split in five main activities that realize its **observation** and **construction** phases.
Observation: the observation phase is in turn organized in two sub-phases. The first sub-phase exploits the WSDL of the WS, and performs data type analysis.

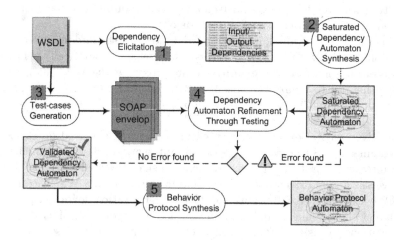

Fig. 2. Overview of the StrawBerry technique

The *Dependencies Elicitation* activity elicits data dependencies between the I/O parameters of the operations defined in the WSDL. A dependency is recorded whenever the type of the output of an operation (called *source*) matches with the type of the input of another operation (called *sink*). The match is syntactic. The elicited set of I/O dependencies (*Input/Output Dependencies* in Figure 2) may be optimized under some heuristics [11]. It is used for constructing a data-flow model (*Saturated Dependencies Automaton Synthesis* activity and *Saturated Dependencies Automaton* artifact) where each node stores data dependencies that concern the output parameters of a specific operation and directed arcs are used to model syntactic matches between output parameters of an operation and input parameters of another operation. This model is completed by applying a saturation rule. This rule adds new dependencies that model the possibility for a client to invoke a WS operation by directly providing its input parameters.

The second sub-phase validates the dependencies automaton through testing against the WS to verify conformance (*Dependencies Automaton Refinement Through Testing* activity). The testing phase takes as input the SOAP messages produced by the *Test-cases Generation* activity. The latter, driven by coverage criteria, automatically derives a suite of test cases (i.e., SOAP envelop messages) for the operations to be tested, according to the WSDL of the WS. Tests are generated from the WSDL and aim at validating whether the synthesized automaton is a correct abstraction of the service implementation. Testing is used to refine the syntactic dependencies by discovering those that are semantically wrong. By construction, the inferred set of dependencies is syntactically correct. However, it might not be correct semantically since it may contain false positives. The testing activity is organized into three steps. `StrawBerry` runs positive tests in the first step and negative tests in the second step. Positive test cases reproduce the elicited data dependencies and are used to reject fake dependencies: if a positive test invocation returns an error answer, `StrawBerry` concludes that the tested dependency does not exist. Negative test cases are instead used to confirm uncertain dependencies: `StrawBerry` provides in input to the sink operation a random test case of the expected type. If this test invocation returns an error answer, then `StrawBerry` concludes that the WS was indeed expecting as input the output produced by the source operation, and it confirms the hypothesized dependency as certain. If uncertain dependencies remain after the two steps, `StrawBerry` resolves the uncertainty by assuming that the hypothesized dependencies do not exist.

Construction: the construction phase consists in a synthesis stage which aims at transforming the validated dependency automaton (a data-flow model) into an automaton defining the behavior protocol (a control-flow model), see the *Behavior Protocol Synthesis* activity in Figure 2. This automaton explicitly models also the data that has to be passed to the WS operations. More precisely, the states of the behavior protocol automaton are WS execution states and the transitions, labeled with operation names plus I/O data, model possible operation invocations from the client of the WS.

3   The Integrate Phase

The integrate phase assists the producer in creating the appropriate *integration means* to compose the observed services together in order to produce a system that satisfies G. Multiple models may exist for each service (e.g., behavioural, interfaces, stochastic or Bayesian), each of them representing a view of the interaction protocol. Model transformation techniques ensure coherence and consistency among the different views, hence providing a systematic support to model interoperability [14, 19]. *Model and code synthesis techniques* produce an Integration Architecture (IA), including the the corresponding code for the actual integration, out of the elicited models by suitably instantiating architectural styles [34] and integration patterns [15]. If needed, extra integration logic can be synthesized as connectors, coordinators, mediators and adapters [7, 23, 24, 30] to guarantee correctness of the IA with respect to G.

Continuing the example introduced above, Figure 3 shows a possible concrete instance of the Integrate phase [7, 8]. Here, the elicit phase has produced the interaction protocol of each participant service in the choreography specified by G (AEWS included). Starting from G and the elicited models, the Integrate phase synthesizes a set of software coordinators. The synthesis exploits model transformations implemented by means of the Atlas Transformation Language (ATL[3]). The developed ATL transformations consist of a number of rules each devoted to the management of specific BPMN2 Choreography Diagram modelling constructs. Coordinators are implemented in Java and their deployment descriptors are codified in XML. By instantiating a fully distributed architectural style, coordinators are interposed among the participant services that need to be coordinated. By exploiting a request/response delegation pattern, coordinators proxify the services and coordinate their interaction in a way that the resulting collaboration realizes G.

Next section briefly describes the integration synthesis techniques we have implemented in the CHOReOSynt tool. More details can be found in [7, 8].

3.1   CHOReOSynt: Automated Synthesis of Service Choreographies

From the BPMN2 specification of a choreography (i.e., the goal G), CHOReOSynt allows for deriving the coordinators, hereafter called Coordination Delegates (CD). CHOReOSynt offers bespoke functionalities to:

- start the synthesis process giving as input a BPMN 2.0 Choreography Diagram;
- transform the BPMN2 Choreography Diagram into an intermediate automata-based model, which is amenable to automated reasoning;
- derive a set of Coordination Models containing information that serve to coordinate the services involved in the choreography in a distributed way;

---

[3] ATL is a domain specific language for realizing model-to-model transformations - www.eclipse.org/atl

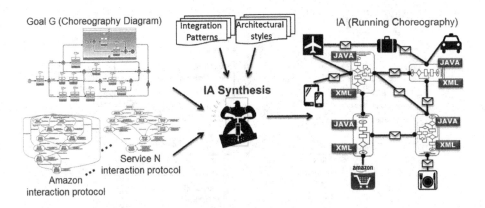

Fig. 3. Integrate phase

- extract the participants of the choreography and project the choreography on their behavioral role;
- simulate the behavioral role of the participants in the choreography against the interaction protocol of the services discovered by the service discovery;
- generate the Coordination Delegate artefacts and the so called "ChorSpec" specification to be used by the Enactment Engine component for deploying and enacting the choreography;

We have implemented these functionalities in a set of REST (Representational State Transfer) services, which are called by CHOReOSynt as shown in Figure 4 and described below.

M2M Transformator – The Model-to-Model (M2M) Transformator offers a set of model transformations. Specifically, it offers an operation bpmn2clts() that takes as input the BPMN2 specification of the choreography and transforms it into a model called CLTS. The latter is an extended Labeled Transition System (LTS) that allows for automatically handling complex constructs of BPMN2 Choreography Diagrams, such as gateways, loops, forks and joins.

Then, starting from the CLTS, CHOReOSynt extracts the list of the participants and, applying a further M2M transformation, automatically derives, for each participant, the CLTS model of the expected behavior with respect to the specified choreography. To this end another operation named extractParticipants() is offered. The CLTS model of expected behavior is achieved by projecting (projection()) the choreography onto the participant, hence filtering out those transitions, and related states, that do not belong to the participant. Basically, for each participant, this CLTS specifies the interaction protocol that a candidate service (to be discovered) has to support to play the role of the participant in the choreography.

Synthesis Discovery Manager – The Synthesis process and the Discovery process interact each other to retrieve, from the service registry, those candidate

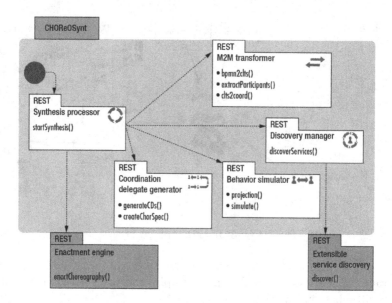

Fig. 4. CHOReOSynt REST architecture

services that are suitable for playing the participant roles, and hence, those services whose (offered and required) operations and protocol are compatible with the CLTS models of the expected behavior. In particular, for each participant, the call to the `discoverServices()` operation is performed. It takes the participant (abstract) CLTS as input. Then, a query is issued to the eXtensible Service Discovery (XSD) component (not in the focus of this paper). Note that, although for each choreography participant a suitable third-party service may have been discovered (and hence, its interaction protocol fits the behavior of the participant in isolation), the uncontrolled (or wrongly coordinated) composite behavior of all the discovered services may show *undesired interactions* that prevent the choreography realization. For a detailed and formal description of the notion of undesired interaction, refer to [4, 6, 9].

Behavior Simulator – Once a set of concrete candidate services has been discovered, the synthesis process has to select them by checking, for each participant, if its expected behavior can be simulated by some candidate service. Note that, for a given participant, behavioral simulation is required since, although the discovered candidate services for it are able to offer and require (at least) the operations needed to play the role of the participant, one cannot be sure that the candidate services are able to support the operations flow as expected by the choreography. Thus, in order to simulate the expected behavior of a participant with the behavior of a service, the Behavior Simulator offers an operation named `simulate()` that takes as input the projected (abstract) CLTS of the participant and the extended (concrete) LTS of the service as retrieved by the URI returned by the discovery service. It might be interesting to mention that the simulation method implemented a notion of strong simulation suitably extended to treat the CLTSs and extended the LTSs we use in CHOReOS. After simulation, if all the participant roles have been "covered" by (some of) the discovered services, the abstract CLTS is concretized with the actual names of the selected services and the actual names of the offered and requested operations. Then, the automated synthesis process distributes the coordination logic specified by the obtained CLTS into a set of Coordination Models by means of the functionality clts2coord().

Coordination Delegate Generator – Once the services have been selected for all the choreography participants, and hence the CLTS has been concretized, the synthesis processor can generate the Coordination Delegates through the operation generateCDs() offered by the Coordination Delegate Generator component.

Next Step in the Process – Once the Coordination Delegates have been generated, the Coordination Delegate Generator component can further generate a specification of the choreography (called ChorSpec) to be passed to the choreography Enactment Engine (not in the focus of this paper). To this end, the operation createChorSpec() is offered. It takes as input the selected services and the coordination delegates generated for them. The ChorSpec is an XML-based declarative description of the choreography that specifies the locations of the selected services and of the generated Coordination Delegate artifacts that can be deployed. Indeed, before passing the ChorSpec to the Enactment Engine, the Choreography Offline Testing process activity is performed to assess the quality of the choreography specification, its well formedness, etc.

4   Related Work

In this section we discuss related work in the domains of behavioral model elicitation techniques and of service choreography development.

Elicitation Techniques. We focus on black-box/grey-box techniques able to elicit behavioural models of the software. The reader interested on white-box techniques can refer to [3, 37, 38] and references therein.

LearnLib [21] is a framework to automatically construct a finite automaton through automata learning and experimentation. Active automata learning tries to automatically construct a finite automaton that matches the behavior of a given target automaton on the basis of active interrogation of target systems and observation of the produced behavior.

The work described in [27] presents a comprehensive approach for building parametrized behaviour models of existing black-box components for performance prediction. Those parameters represent three performance-influencing factor, i.e., usage, assembly, and deployment context; this makes the models sensitive to changing load situations, connected components, and the underlying hardware. The approach makes use of static and dynamic analysis and search-based approaches, namely genetic programming. These techniques take as input monitoring data, runtime bytecode counts, and static bytecode analysis.

SPY [17] is an approach to infer a formal specification of stateful black-box components that behave as data abstractions (Java classes that behave as data containers) by observing their run-time behavior. SPY proceeds in two main stages: first, SPY infers a partial model of the considered Java class; second, through graph transformation, this partial model is generalized to deal with data values beyond the ones specified by the given instance pools. The inferred model is partial since it models the intentional behavior of the class with respect to only a set of instance pools provided as input, which are used to get values for method parameters, and an upper bound on the number of states of the model.

GK-Tail [29] is a technique to automatically generate behavioral models from (object-oriented) system execution traces. GK-Tail assumes that execution traces are obtained by monitoring the system through message logging frameworks. For each system method, an Extended Finite State Machine (EFSM) is generated. It models the interaction between the components forming the system in terms of sequences of method invocations and data constraints on these invocations. The correctness of these data constraints depends on the completeness of the set of monitored traces with respect to all the possible system executions that might be infinite.

The work described in [10] presents an approach for inferring state machines with an infinite state space. By observing the output that the system produces when stimulated with selected inputs, they extend existing algorithms for regular inference (which infer finite state machines) to deal with infinite-state systems. This approach makes the problem of dealing with an infinite state space tractable, but may suffer a higher degree of model approximation.

The work described in [31] presents a learning-based black-box testing approach in which the problem of testing functional correctness is reduced to a constraint solving problem. Functional correctness is modeled by pre- and post-conditions that are first-order predicate formulas. A successful black-box test is an execution of the program on a set of input values satisfying the pre-condition, which terminates by retrieving a set of output values violating the post-condition. Black-box functional testing is the search for successful tests with respect to the program pre- and post-conditions. As coverage criterion the authors formulate a convergence criterion on function approximation.

The work in [13] presents an approach that, through a combination of systematic test case generation (by means of the TAUTOKO tool) and typestate mining, infers models of program behavior in the form of finite state automata describing transitions between object states. The generation of test cases permits to cover previously unobserved behavior, and systematically extends the execution space, and enriches the inferred behavior model. In this sense, it can be said this approach goes in an opposite direction with respect to StrawBerry.

The work in [2] concerns an application of active learning whose aim is to establish the correctness of protocol implementations relative to a given reference implementation. The work in [1] shows how to fully-automatically construct the typical abstractions needed to perform automata learning.

Choreography Realization Techniques. CHOReOSynt is related to several approaches developed for automated choreography enforcement.

The approach described in [18] enforces a choreography's realizability by automatically generating monitors. Each monitor acts as a local controller for its peer. Monitors are built by iterating equivalence-checking steps between two centralized models of the whole system. A monitor is similar to our coordination delegate (CD). However, our approach synthesizes CDs without producing a centralized model of the whole system, hence preventing state explosion.

The method described in [26] checks the conformance between the choreography specification and the composition of participant implementations. Their framework can model and analyze compositions in which the interactions can also be asynchronous and the messages can be stored in unbounded queues and reordered if needed. Following this line of research, the authors of [26] provided a hierarchy of realizability notions that forms the basis for a more flexible analysis regarding classic realizability checks [25, 26]. These two approaches are novel in that they characterize relevant properties to check a certain degree of realizability. However, they statically check realizability and do not enforce it.

The ASTRO toolset [35] supports automated composition of Web services and the monitoring of their execution. It aims to compose a service starting from a business requirement and the description of the protocols defining available external services. Unlike our approach, ASTRO deals with centralized orchestration-based business processes rather than fully decentralized choreography-based ones.

The CIGAR (Concurrent and Interleaving Goal and Activity Recognition) framework aims for multigoal recognition [20]. CIGAR decomposes an observed sequence of multigoal activities into a set of action sequences, one for each goal, specifying whether a goal is active in a specific action. Although such goal decomposition somewhat recalls CHOReOSynt's choreography decentralization, goal recognition represents a fundamentally different problem regarding realizability enforcement.

Given a set of candidate services offering the desired functionalities, the TCP-Compose* algorithm [33] identifies the set of composite services that best fit the user-specified qualitative preferences over non-functional attributes. CHOReOSynt could exploit this research to extend the discovery process to enable more flexible selection of services from the registry.

The research we described in this paper is an advance over our previous research [4, 6]. Although the synthesis process described in our previous research treated most BPMN2 constructs, it considered a simplified version of their actual semantics. For instance, as in [18], the selection of conditional branches was simply abstracted as a non-deterministic choice, regardless of the runtime evaluation of their enabling conditions. Analogously, the synthesis process enforced parallel flows by non-deterministically choosing one of their linearizations obtained through interleaving, thus losing the actual degree of parallelism. To overcome these limitations, CHOReOSynt relies on a choreography model that, being more expressive than the choreography model in CIGAR and

TCP-Compose*, preserves the BPMN2 constructs' actual semantics. Relying on a more expressive model led us to define a novel, more effective distributed coordination algorithm [9].

5   Final Remarks and Future Perspectives

Our past experience in behavioural models elicitation and integration code synthesis gives a first evidence, yet concrete, that the proposed approach is viable once referring to specific application domains, e.g., choreography-based systems.

Our experiments with strawberry have shown that it is practical and realistic in that it only assumes: (i) the availability of the WSDL; and (ii) the possibility to derive a partial oracle that can distinguish between regular and error answers. Furthermore, we observed that strawberry nicely converges to a realistic automaton. In future work, we intend to investigate if and how assumption (ii) could be relaxed.

Our experiments with CHOReOSynt demonstrated that considering domain-specific interaction patterns mitigates the complexity of coordination enforceability when recurrent business protocols must be enforced. Generally, choreography synthesis is difficult in that not all possible collaborations can be automatically realized. This suggests we could improve CHOReOSynt with a combination of domain-specific choreography patterns, as well as protocol interaction patterns that correspond to service collaborations that are tractable through exogenous coordination. Currently, CHOReOSynt supports pure coordination. It doesn't deal with protocol adaptation because it doesn't account for mismatches at the level of service operations and related I/O parameter types. To support data-based coordination through the elicitation and application of complex data mappings, CHOReOSynt should be enhanced to automatically infer mappings to match the data types of messages sent or received by mismatching participant services. This means effectively coping with heterogeneous service interfaces and dealing with as many Enterprise Integration Patterns [15] and protocol mediation patterns [28] as possible, in a fully automatic way. Toward that end, we achieved promising results in automated synthesis of modular mediators [24].

We want to enable the market acceptance and further enhancement of CHOReOSynt by third-party developers, especially small and medium enterprises, including development of applications for commercialization. So, we released CHOReOSynt under the umbrella of the Future Internet Software and Services Initiative (FISSi[4]). Using a market-oriented approach, FISSi aims to develop awareness of OW2 Future Internet software in both FISSi members and non-members and both open source vendors and proprietary vendors. Our primary objective, to be achieved in the near future, is to establish a community of developers and third-party market stakeholders (for example, users, application vendors, and policy makers) around CHOReOSynt.

Last but not least, an interesting future direction is the investigation of non-functional properties at the level of the elicited interaction protocols and of the

---

[4] http://www.ow2.org/view/Future_Internet/CHOReOS

synthesized choreography. For instance, this requires considering operation invocation response time, extending the choreography specification with performance or reliability attributes, and accounting for them in the CDs synthesis process.

Acknowledgments. The research work so far has been supported by the Italian MIUR, prot. 2012E47TM2 (project IDEAS - Integrated Design and Evolution of Adaptive Systems), and by the EC FP7 under grant agreement n. 257178 (project CHOReOS - Large Scale Choreographies for the Future Internet - www.choreos.eu). Future research efforts will be supported by the EC H2020 under grant agreement n. 644178 (project CHOReVOLUTION - Automated Synthesis of Dynamic and Secured Choreographies for the Future Internet).

References

1. Aarts, F., Heidarian, F., Kuppens, H., Olsen, P., Vaandrager, F.: Automata learning through counterexample guided abstraction refinement. In: Giannakopoulou, D., Méry, D. (eds.) FM 2012. LNCS, vol. 7436, pp. 10–27. Springer, Heidelberg (2012)
2. Aarts, F., Kuppens, H., Tretmans, J., Vaandrager, F., Verwer, S.: Improving active mealy machine learning for protocol conformance testing. Machine Learning 96(1-2), 189–224 (2014)
3. Alur, R., Černý, P., Madhusudan, P., Nam, W.: Synthesis of interface specifications for java classes. SIGPLAN Not. 40(1) (2005)
4. Autili, M., Di Ruscio, D., Di Salle, A., Inverardi, P., Tivoli, M.: A model-based synthesis process for choreography realizability enforcement. In: Cortellessa, V., Varró, D. (eds.) FASE 2013 (ETAPS 2013). LNCS, vol. 7793, pp. 37–52. Springer, Heidelberg (2013)
5. Autili, M., Di Ruscio, D., Inverardi, P., Pelliccione, P., Tivoli, M.: Modelland: Where do models come from? In: Bencomo, N., France, R., Cheng, B.H.C., Aßmann, U. (eds.) Models@run.time. LNCS, vol. 8378, pp. 162–187. Springer, Heidelberg (2014)
6. Autili, M., Di Salle, A., Tivoli, M.: Synthesis of resilient choreographies. In: Gorbenko, A., Romanovsky, A., Kharchenko, V. (eds.) SERENE 2013. LNCS, vol. 8166, pp. 94–108. Springer, Heidelberg (2013)
7. Autili, M., Inverardi, P., Tivoli, M.: Automated synthesis of service choreographies. IEEE Software (99) (2015)
8. Autili, M., Ruscio, D.D., Salle, A.D., Perucci, A.: Choreosynt: enforcing choreography realizability in the future internet. In: Proc. of FSE 2014 (2014)
9. Autili, M., Tivoli, M.: Distributed enforcement of service choreographies. In: Proc. of FOCLASA 2014 (2014)
10. Berg, T., Jonsson, B., Raffelt, H.: Regular inference for state machines using domains with equality tests. In: Fiadeiro, J.L., Inverardi, P. (eds.) FASE 2008. LNCS, vol. 4961, pp. 317–331. Springer, Heidelberg (2008)
11. Bertolino, A., Inverardi, P., Pelliccione, P., Tivoli, M.: Automatic synthesis of behavior protocols for composable web-services. In: Proc. of ESEC/FSE (2009)
12. Ceri, S., Braga, D., Corcoglioniti, F., Grossniklaus, M., Vadacca, S.: Search computing challenges and directions. In: Dearle, A., Zicari, R.V. (eds.) ICOODB 2010. LNCS, vol. 6348, pp. 1–5. Springer, Heidelberg (2010)

13. Dallmeier, V., Knopp, N., Mallon, C., Fraser, G., Hack, S., Zeller, A.: Automatically generating test cases for specification mining. IEEE Transactions on Software Engineering 38(2), 243–257 (2012)
14. Di Ruscio, D., Malavolta, I., Muccini, H., Pelliccione, P., Pierantonio, A.: Model-driven techniques to enhance architectural languages interoperability. In: de Lara, J., Zisman, A. (eds.) Fundamental Approaches to Software Engineering. LNCS, vol. 7212, pp. 26–42. Springer, Heidelberg (2012)
15. Hohpe, B.W.G.: Enterprise Integration Patterns: Designing, Building, and Deploying Messaging Solutions, pp. 1–480. Addison-Wesley (2004)
16. Garlan, D.: Software engineering in an uncertain world. In: Proc. of FoSER 2010, pp. 125–128 (2010)
17. Ghezzi, C., Mocci, A., Monga, M.: Synthesizing intensional behavior models by graph transformation. In: Proc. of ICSE 2009, pp. 430–440 (2009)
18. Güdemann, M., Salaün, G., Ouederni, M.: Counterexample guided synthesis of monitors for realizability enforcement. In: Chakraborty, S., Mukund, M. (eds.) ATVA 2012. LNCS, vol. 7561, pp. 238–253. Springer, Heidelberg (2012)
19. Hilliard, R., Malavolta, I., Muccini, H., Pelliccione, P.: On the composition and reuse of viewpoints across architecture frameworks. In: Proc. of WICSA-ECSA 2012, pp. 131–140. IEEE Computer Society (2012)
20. Hu, D.H., Yang, Q.: CIGAR: Concurrent and Interleaving Goal and Activity Recognition. In: Proc. of AAAI 2008, pp. 1363–1368 (2008)
21. Hungar, H., Margaria, T., Steffen, B.: Test-based model generation for legacy systems. In: Proc. of ITC 2003, vol. 2, pp. 150–159 (2003)
22. Inverardi, P., Autili, M., Di Ruscio, D., Pelliccione, P., Tivoli, M.: Producing software by integration: Challenges and research directions (keynote). In: Proc. of ESEC/FSE 2013, pp. 2–12 (2013)
23. Inverardi, P., Spalazzese, R., Tivoli, M.: Application-layer connector synthesis. In: SFM (2011)
24. Inverardi, P., Tivoli, M.: Automatic synthesis of modular connectors via composition of protocol mediation patterns. In: Proceedings of ICSE 2013 (2013)
25. Kazhamiakin, R., Pistore, M.: Analysis of realizability conditions for web service choreographies. In: Najm, E., Pradat-Peyre, J.-F., Donzeau-Gouge, V.V. (eds.) FORTE 2006. LNCS, vol. 4229, pp. 61–76. Springer, Heidelberg (2006)
26. Kazhamiakin, R., Pistore, M.: Choreography conformance analysis: Asynchronous communications and information alignment. In: Bravetti, M., Núñez, M., Zavattaro, G. (eds.) WS-FM 2006. LNCS, vol. 4184, pp. 227–241. Springer, Heidelberg (2006)
27. Krogmann, K., Kuperberg, M., Reussner, R.: Using genetic search for reverse engineering of parametric behavior models for performance prediction. IEEE Transactions on Software Engineering 36(6), 865–877 (2010)
28. Li, X., Fan, Y., Wang, J., Wang, L., Jiang, F.: A pattern-based approach to development of service mediators for protocol mediation. In: Proceedings of WICSA 2008, pp. 137–146. IEEE Computer Society (2008)
29. Lorenzoli, D., Mariani, L., Pezzè, M.: Automatic generation of software behavioral models. In: Proc. of ICSE 2008 (2008)
30. Mateescu, R., Poizat, P., Salaün, G.: Adaptation of service protocols using process algebra and on-the-fly reduction techniques. IEEE Transactions on Software Engineering 38(4), 755–777 (2012)
31. Meinke, K.: Automated black-box testing of functional correctness using function approximation. In: Proc. of ISSTA 2004, pp. 143–153 (2004)

32. Paternó, F., Santoro, C.: Preventing user errors by systematic analysis of deviations from the system task model. International Journal of Human-Computer Studies 56(2), 225–245 (2002)

33. Santhanam, G.R., Basu, S., Honavar, V.G.: TCP − compose* – A TCP-net based algorithm for efficient composition of web services using qualitative preferences. In: Bouguettaya, A., Krueger, I., Margaria, T. (eds.) ICSOC 2008. LNCS, vol. 5364, pp. 453–467. Springer, Heidelberg (2008)

34. Taylor, R.N., Medvidović, N., Dashofy, E.M.: Software Architecture: Foundations, Theory, and Practice, pp. 1–736. Wiley and Sons (2009)

35. Trainotti, M., Pistore, M., Calabrese, G., Zacco, G., Lucchese, G., Barbon, F., Bertoli, P., Traverso, P.: Astro: Supporting composition and execution of web services. In: Benatallah, B., Casati, F., Traverso, P. (eds.) ICSOC 2005. LNCS, vol. 3826, pp. 495–501. Springer, Heidelberg (2005)

36. van Lamsweerde, A.: Requirements Engineering - From System Goals to UML Models to Software Specifications. Wiley (2009)

37. Wasylkowski, A., Zeller, A.: Mining temporal specifications from object usage. In: Proc. of ASE 2009, pp. 295–306 (2009)

38. Wasylkowski, A., Zeller, A., Lindig, C.: Detecting object usage anomalies. In: Proc. of ESEC-FSE 2007, pp. 35–44 (2007)

39. White, R.W., Roth, R.A.: Exploratory Search: Beyond the Query-Response Paradigm. Synthesis Lectures on Information Concepts, Retrieval, and Services (2009)

Software Architecture Modeling and Evaluation Based on Stochastic Activity Networks

Ali Sedaghatbaf and Mohammad Abdolahi Azgomi

School of Computer Engneering, University of Science and Technology, Tehran, Iran
ali_sedaghat@comp.iust.ac.ir,
azgomi@iust.ac.ir

Abstract. Quantitative and integrated evaluation of software quality attributes at the architectural design stage provides a sound basis for making objective decisions for design trade-offs and developing a high quality software. In this paper we introduce a formal method for modeling software architectures and evaluationg their quality attributes quantitatively and in a unified manner. This method is based on stochastic activity networks (SANs) and the quality attributes considered include security, dependability and performance.

Keywords: Software architecture, quality attributes, quantitative evaluation, stochastic activity networks (SANs), reward structures.

1 Introduction

Dealing with quality attributes is one of the most difficult tasks in software engineering. To know whether a quality attribute is achieved, it has to be quantified by analysis or measured. However, not only quantification of each attribute has its own difficulties, but also they have complex dependencies.

In software systems, quality attributes are principally determined by the system's architecture. Evaluating quality attributes at the architectural design stage not only helps in assuring that stakeholders expectations are met, but also aids in discovering flaws in a shorter time and with lower cost than latter stages.

According to an investigation on different types of quality attributes and their application domains [1], security, dependability and performance are among the top quality attributes important for software systems. The necessity of the integrated evaluation of security and performance has gained much attention in research communities. However, a few have contributed to the quantitative evaluation of security. Dependability is a quality attribute closely related to both security and performance [2]. The necessity of the integrated evaluation of dependability and performance led to the derivation of a new quality attribute called perfomability. On the other hand, many of the methods proposed for quantitative security evaluation are inspired from dependability evaluation techniques. Therefore, despite the significant differences between security and performance, their integrated and quantitative evaluation can be performed regarding their close relation to dependability.

M. Dastani and M.Sirjani (Eds.): FSEN 2015, LNCS 9392, pp. 46–53, 2015.
DOI: 10.1007/978-3-319-24644-4_3

The purpose of this paper is to take a small step in the direction of developing a unified approach for reasoning about multiple quality attributes. The attributes considered include security, dependability and performance (called the SDP attributes in this paper). In this approach hierarchical colored stochastic activity networks (HCSANs) [5,6] are used for architecture modeling and activity-marking oriented reward structures [5] are used for evaluation.

Stochastic activity networks (SANs) [6] are stochastic extensions of Petri Nets, which are more powerful and more flexible than other stochastic extensions such as GSPNs and have been effectively used for performance, dependability, performability and security evaluations. HCSANs are extensions of SANs, whose hierarchical nature facilitates top-down and bottom-up model construction and their support for colored tokens facilitates complex data manipulations.

The remainder of this paper is organized as follows: in section 2 the related work is discussed. An introduction to HCSANs and activity-marking oriented reward struc-tures is provided in section 3. Section 4 presents the proposed approach and finally section 5 provides the concluding remarks and outlines the future work.

2   Related Work

Discrete-time Markov chains (DTMCs) are used in [7] to model software architectures and evaluate their security, performance and reliability. In this approach each component is modeled as a simple state and the arcs between states model the control flow between components. Quality attributes are evaluated by assigning reward functions to the states of the model.

In [8] a framework is proposed for analyzing the performance degradation induced by different security solutions. In this approach UML is used for modeling both the architecture and different security solutions. These models are then composed and converted to GSPN models for performance evaluation.

A methodology is proposed in [9] for combined performance and security risk analysis for border management systems. These systems are good examples of the systems in which both security and performance are critical. On one hand travelers should not linger because of security checks and on the other hand impostors should be distinguished from genuine travelers. In this approach the UML models of systems architecture are annotated with performance requirements. From these models LQN models are extracted for performance analysis. Also, cost curves are used to estimate the risk of misclassifying travelers with different classifiers.

In comparison to the above methods, the approach presented in this paper has the following distinguishing features:

- all the three SDP attributes can be evaluated quantitatively,
- the internal behavior of components can be modeled and analyzed,
- error propagation between components can be modeled,
- in contrast to many evaluation methods, any distribution function can be used for estimating the time spent by each software activity and

- the generality of the activity-marking oriented reward structures makes this approach extensible to other quality attributes.

3   HCSAN-Based Reward Models

In addition to the five primitives of ordinary SANs (i.e. place, input gate, output gate, instantaneous activity and timed activity), Colored stochastic activity networks (CSANs) [3,4] have the following two primitives: (1) token type: a non-integer data type specifying the type of each token stored in a colored place and (2) colored place: a place maintaining a list of tokens with a specific token type. A selection policy (e.g. FIFO, LIFO, Priority) may be associated to each colored place specifying the order in which tokens are removed from that place.

HCSANs as an extension of CSANs, have one additional primitive, i.e. macro activity. A macro activity is a sub-model of an HCSAN model with a predefined interface. This interface includes a set of fusion places, which are virtual (colored) places that must be bound to concrete (colored) places in the encompassing model.

As a modification of the SAN-based reward structures, the reward structure of an HCSAN model can be defined formally as follows:

Definition 1. *An activity-marking reward structure of an HCSAN model with places $P = SP \cup CP$ and activities $A = IA \cup TA \cup MA$ is a pair of functions:*

- *$C : A \to \Re$ where for $a \in A$, $C(a)$ is the reward obtained due to the completion of activity a, and*
- *$R : \wp(P, M) \to \Re$ where for $v \in \wp(P, M)$, $R(v)$ is the rate of reward obtained when for each $(p, m) \in v$ the marking of place p is m,*

where $\Re$ is the set of real numbers, and $\wp(P, M)$ is the set of all partial functions between P and M.

In order to quantify the total reward associated with an HCSAN model at an instant of time t, variable V_t can be used, which is defined as follows:

$$V_t = \sum_{v \in \wp(P,M)} R(v).I_t^v + \sum_{a \in A} C(a).I_t^a \tag{1}$$

where I_t^v is a random variable indicating that for each $(p, m) \in v$, the marking of place p is m at time instant t, and the random variable I_t^a indicates that activity a is the most recently completed activity with respect to time instant t. If I_t^v and I_t^a converge in distribution for all v and a with non-zero rewards as t approaches ∞, then steady-state reward evaluation is also possible:

$$V_{t \to \infty} = \sum_{v \in \wp(P,M)} R(v).I_{t \to \infty}^v + \sum_{a \in A} C(a).I_{t \to \infty}^a \tag{2}$$

In order to evaluate the total reward accumulated in an interval $[t, t + \tau]$ variable $Y_{[t,t+\tau]}$ can be used, which can be expressed as:

$$Y_{[t,t+\tau]} = \sum_{v \in \wp(P,M)} R(v).J_{[t,t+\tau]}^v + \sum_{a \in A} C(a).N_{[t,t+\tau]}^a \tag{3}$$

where J_t^v is a random variable indicating the total time the model is in a marking such that for each $(p, m) \in v$, the marking of place p is m during $[t, t + \tau]$, and the random variable N_t^a indicates the number of completions of activity a during $[t, t + \tau]$. Variable $W_{[t,t+\tau]} = \frac{Y_{[t,t+\tau]}}{\tau}$ can be used to evaluate time-averaged measures.

4   The Proposed Approach

In this section we explain how to model software architectures and evaluate their SDP attributes with HCSAN-based reward models. We call this approach SAN-based architecture modeling (SANAM). In SANAM, HCSANs are used to define the behavior models of components and connectors and HCSAN-based reward structures are used to define and evaluate quality attributes.

A SANAM-based architecture model can be formally defined as a 4-tuple $SANAM = (CM, CN, HD, RS)$, where:

- $CM = \{cm_1, cm_2, \ldots, m_n\}$ is a set of component models such that each component model $cm = (IBM, PS, RS)$ consists of: an internal behavior model IBM specified with HCSANs, a set PS of provided services such that each provided service is modeled by a concrete macro activity and a set RS of required services, each modeled by a virtual macro activity which should be bound to a concrete macro activity providing the service.
- $CN = \{cn_1, cn_2, \ldots, cn_n\}$ is a set of connector models. Connectors are building blocks for modeling interactions among components.
- $HD = \{hd_1, hd_2, \ldots, hd_n\}$ is a set of hardware device models. Each software component or connector may be bound with a set of hardware devices such as processors, disks, links, etc. Speed, capacity, and failure behavior of these devices have significant impacts on the SDP attributes of software and
- RS is a set of HCSAN-based reward structures which can be used for specifying and evaluating the quality measures of interest.

As an illustrative example, consider a Group Communication System (GCS) used to store a set of documents and give users access to them. Several use cases can be defined for a GCS (e.g. subscribe, unsubscribe, submit a document, retrieve a docu-ment and update a document). In this paper we focus on document retrieval. The SANAM model of this system is depicted in Fig. 1. This model includes two software components (i.e. $CApp$ and $Serv$) representing the client application and the communication server respectively. $Serv$ provides one service (i.e. $rDoc$) which facilitates retrieving a document. This component is bound with two hardware resources i.e. the processor $SPrc$ and the disk $SDsk$, and its communication with $Serv$ is handled by the connector $CSPr$, which represents a client-server protocol. The behavior model of $CApp$ is depicted in Fig 2. This component iteratively generates requests, sends them to $Serv$ and displays the responses. In this model the timed activities $genReq$ and $display$ are bound with the processor $CPrc$. The activity $genReq$ ($display$) is enabled whenever a token is put in the place $resp$ (doc) and it has acquired an idle processor i.e.

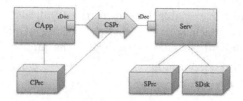

Fig. 1. SANAM model of a GCS system

the ID of this activity is put in the place *acID* by *CPrc*. After completion, this activity releases the acquired processor. If *display* fails, an error message will be displayed. Otherwise, the response of the server will be displayed which may be either a valid document or a server-side error message. The virtual macro activity *rDoc* corresponds to the required service of *CApp*. The behavior model

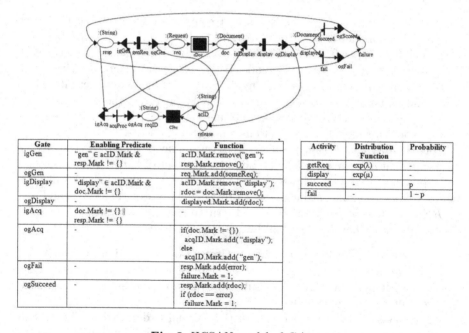

Gate	Enabling Predicate	Function
igGen	"gen" ∈ acID.Mark & resp.Mark != {}	acID.Mark.remove("gen"); resp.Mark.remove();
ogGen	-	req.Mark.add(someReq);
igDisplay	"display" ∈ acID.Mark & doc.Mark != {}	acID.Mark.remove("display"); rdoc = doc.Mark.remove();
ogDisplay	-	displayed.Mark.add(rdoc);
igAcq	doc.Mark != {} || resp.Mark != {}	-
ogAcq	-	if(doc.Mark != {}) acqID.Mark.add("display"); else acqID.Mark.add("gen");
ogFail	-	resp.Mark.add(error); failure.Mark = 1;
ogSucceed	-	resp.Mark.add(rdoc); if (rdoc == error) failure.Mark = 1;

Activity	Distribution Function	Probability
getReq	exp(λ)	-
display	exp(μ)	-
succeed	-	p
fail	-	1 - p

Fig. 2. HCSAN model of *CApp*

of the service *Serv.rDoc* is presented in Fig. 3. This activity first requests access to the local disk and processor. If it acquires these resources, it will seek for the requested document. In case of success, the content of the found document is put in the place *doc*, and a token representing an error message otherwise.

The behavior model of *CSPr* includes two timed activities for transferring requests and documents between *Serv* and *CApp* (see Fig. 4). The activity *send* is enabled whenever a request is received from *CApp* and an idle processor is

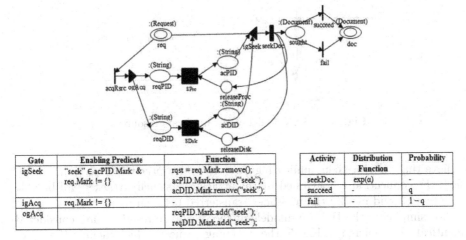

Gate	Enabling Predicate	Function
igSeek	"seek" ∈ acPID.Mark & req.Mark != {}	rqst = req.Mark.remove(); acPID.Mark.remove("seek"); acDID.Mark.remove("seek");
igAcq	req.Mark != {}	-
ogAcq		reqPID.Mark.add("seek"); reqDID.Mark.add("seek");

Activity	Distribution Function	Probability
seekDoc	exp(α)	-
succeed	-	q
fail	-	1−q

Fig. 3. HCSAN model of *Serv.rDoc*

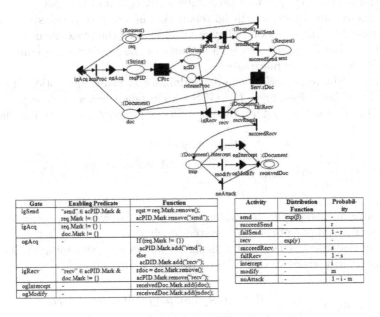

Gate	Enabling Predicate	Function
igSend	"send" ∈ acPID.Mark & req.Mark != {}	rqst = req.Mark.remove(); acPID.Mark.remove("send");
igAcq	req.Mark != {} | doc.Mark != {}	-
ogAcq	-	If (req.Mark != {}) acPID.Mark.add("send"); else acDID.Mark.add("recv");
igRecv	"recv" ∈ acPID.Mark & doc.Mark != {}	rdoc = doc.Mark.remove(); acPID.Mark.remove("recv");
ogIntercept	-	receivedDoc.Mark.add(idoc);
ogModify	-	receivedDoc.Mark.add(mdoc);

Activity	Distribution Function	Probability
send	exp(β)	-
succeedSend	-	r
failSend	-	1−r
recv	exp(γ)	-
succeedRecv	-	s
failRecv	-	1−s
intercept	-	i
modify	-	m
noAttack	-	1−i−m

Fig. 4. HCSAN model of *CSPr*

available. After completion, if this activity succeeds in sending the request, the activity *Serv.rDoc* will be enabled. Otherwise, the request token will be put back in *req* to try again. The behavior of *recv* is similar to *send*. The only difference is the type of token they process. The two activities *intercept* and *modify* are added to the behavior model of *CSPr* to represent Man-in-the-Middle (MitM) attacks. In MitM attacks, an attacker establishes independent connections with the communicating parties and relays messages between them such that they

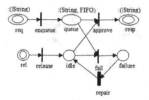

Activity	Distribution Function	Probability
approve	-	t
fail	-	1 - t
repair	exp (θ)	-

Fig. 5. HCSAN model of the hardware resources

believe that they are communicating directly over a private connection. But in fact, the connection is controlled by the attacker. As such, attacker will be able to intercept and modify the messages transferred between them.

For simplicity, the HCSAN models of the hardware resources are considered identical. As depicted in Fig. 5, the incoming requests which include the ID of the requesting activity are put in a queue and if at least one idle resource exists, one of the requests is approved probabilistically and its ID is put in the place resp. If the resource fails, it will be repaired. The order of processing requests is determined by the selection policy associated with the place queue i.e. FIFO. Whenever a timed activity releases a resource or the repair process completes, a token will be put in the place *idle*.

Now, to evaluate *reliability* as a dependability measure, the notion of system failure should be defined first. The GCS system fails when a token is put in the place *CApp.failure*. Therefore, the reliability of this system can be specified as:

$$C(a) = 0, \forall a \in A,$$
$$R(v) = \begin{cases} 1 & \text{if } v = \{(CApp.failure, 0)\} \\ 0 & \text{otherwise} \end{cases} \quad (4)$$

Performance measures can be evaluated in a similar way. For example, if we define the throughput of the GCS system during some interval $[t, t + \tau]$ as the number of documents successfully displayed for users in this interval, then the following reward structure can be used to specify throughput:

$$C(a) = \begin{cases} p & \text{if } a = CApp.display \text{ and } rdoc! = error \\ 0 & \text{otherwise} \end{cases}$$
$$R(v) = 0, \forall v \in \wp P(P, M) \quad (5)$$

where p is the success probability of the activity display and *rdoc* is the token that this activity has removed from the place *CApp.doc* (see Fig. 2).

To evaluate *confidentiality* as a security measure, we should determine in which states this attribute is compromised. The confidentiality of the GCS system is compromised whenever the content of a document is intercepted during transfer i.e. place *CApp.doc* is marked with a token whose value is *idoc*. Therefore, the confidentiality attribute can be specified using the reward structure

$$C(a) = 0, \forall a \in A,$$
$$R(v) = \begin{cases} 0 & \text{if } v = \{(CApp.doc, idoc)\} \\ 1 & \text{otherwise} \end{cases} \quad (6)$$

5   Conclusions and Future Work

Regarding the necessity of integrated and quantitative evaluation of software quality attributes, we proposed SANAM as a formal method for modeling software architectures and evaluating their quality attributes in a unified manner. As future work we intend to define transformation rules to extract SANAM models from software modeling notations (e.g. UML, PCM, etc.) and develop a software tool for automating the transformation and evaluation procedures.

References

1. Mairiza, D., Zowghi, D. Nurmuliani, N.: An investigation into the notion of non-functional requirements. In: ACM Sym. Applied Computing (SAC 2010), Sierra, Switzerland, pp. 311–317 (2010)
2. Bernardi, S., Merseguer, J., Petriu, D.C.: Model-driven dependability assessment of software systems. Springer, Heidelberg (2013)
3. Azgomi, M.A., Movaghar, A.: Coloured stochastic activity networks: preliminary definitions and behavior. In: 20th Annual UK Perf. Eng. Wksp., Bradford, UK, pp. 297–308 (2004)
4. Sedaghatbaf, A., Azgomi, M.A.: Attack modelling and security evaluation based on stochastic activity networks. J. Secur. Commu. Networks 7(4), 714–737 (2014)
5. Sanders, W.H., Meyer, J.F., Arbor, A.: A unified approach for specifying measures of performance, dependability, and performability. J. Computing 4, 215–237 (1991)
6. Movaghar, A.: Stochastic Activity Networks: a new definition and some properties. Sci. Iran. 8, 303–311 (2001)
7. Sharma, V.S., Trivedi, K.S.: Quantifying software performance, reliability and security: An architecture-based approach. J. Syst. Softw. 80, 493–509 (2007)
8. Cortellessa, V., Trubiani, C., Mostarda, L., Dulay, N.: An architectural framework for analyzing tradeoffs between software security and performance. In: First Int. Sym. Architecting Critical Syst., Prague, Czech Republic, pp. 1–18 (2010)
9. Sacanamboy, M., Cukic, M.: Combined performance and risk analysis for border management applications. In: Int. Conf. Dependable Syst. Networks, pp. 403–412 (2010)

Applicative Bisimulation and Quantum λ-Calculi[*]

Ugo Dal Lago[1,2] and Alessandro Rioli[1,2]

[1] Università di Bologna, Bologna, Italy
[2] INRIA, Sophia-Antipolis, France
{ugo.dallago,alessandro.rioli2}@unibo.it

Abstract. Applicative bisimulation is a coinductive technique to check program equivalence in higher-order functional languages. It is known to be sound — and sometimes complete — with respect to context equivalence. In this paper we show that applicative bisimulation also works when the underlying language of programs takes the form of a *linear* λ-calculus extended with features such as probabilistic binary choice, but also quantum data, the latter being a setting in which linearity plays a role. The main results are proofs of soundness for the obtained notions of bisimilarity.

1 Introduction

Program equivalence is one of the fundamental notions in the theory of programming languages. Studying the nature of program equivalence is not only interesting from a purely foundational point of view, but can also be the first step towards defining (semi)automatic techniques for program verification, or for validating compiler optimisations. As an example, conformance of a program to a specification often corresponds to the equivalence between the program and the specification, once the latter is written in the same formalism as the program.

If the language at hand is an higher-order functional language, equivalence is traditionally formalised as Morris' *context equivalence*: two programs are considered equivalent if and only if they have the same behavior in *every possible* context [15]. This makes it relatively easy to prove two programs to be *not* equivalent, since this merely amounts to finding *one* context which separates them. On the other hand, proving two terms to be equivalent requires one to examine their behaviour in *every possible* context.

Various ways to alleviate the burden of proving context equivalence have been proposed in the literature, from CIU theorems (in which the class of contexts is restricted without altering the underlying relation [14]) to adequate denotational semantics, to logical relations [17]. We are here interested in coinductive techniques akin to bisimulation. Indeed, they have been shown to be very powerful, to the point of not only being sound, but even complete as ways to prove terms to be context equivalent [16]. Among the various notions of bisimulation which are known to be amenable to higher-order programs, the simplest one is

---

[*] This work is partially supported by the ANR project 12IS02001 PACE.

© IFIP International Federation for Information Processing 2015
M. Dastani and M.Sirjani (Eds.): FSEN 2015, LNCS 9392, pp. 54–68, 2015.
DOI: 10.1007/978-3-319-24644-4_4

certainly Abramsky's applicative bisimulation [1], in which terms are seen as interactive objects and the interaction with their environment consists in taking input arguments or outputting observable results.

Applicative bisimulation is indeed well-known to be fully-abstract w.r.t. context equivalence when instantiated on plain, untyped, *deterministic* λ-calculi [1]. When the calculus at hand also includes a choice operator, the situation is more complicated: while applicative bisimilarity is invariably a congruence, thus sound for context equivalence, completeness generally fails [16,13], even if some unexpected positive results have recently been obtained by Crubillé and the first author [4] in a probabilistic setting. An orthogonal issue is the one of linearity: does applicative bisimulation work well when the underlying calculus has linear types? The question has been answered positively, but only for deterministic λ-calculi [3,2]. Finally, soundness does not hold in general if the programming language at hand has references [11].

In this paper, we define and study applicative bisimulation when instantiated on linear λ-calculi, starting with a purely deterministic language, and progressively extending it with probabilistic choice and quantum data, a setting in which linearity is an essential ingredient [19,20]. The newly added features in the language are shown to correspond to mild variations in the underlying transition system, which in presence of probabilistic choice becomes a labelled Markov chain. The main contributions of this paper are congruence results for applicative bisimilarity in probabilistic and quantum λ-calculi, with soundness with respect to context equivalence as an easy corollary. In all the considered calculi, Howe's technique [9,16] plays a key role.

This is the first successful attempt to apply coinductive techniques to quantum, higher-order, calculi. The literature offers some ideas and results about bisimulation and simulation in the context of quantum process algebras [8,7,6]. Deep relations between quantum computation and coalgebras have recently been discovered [10]. None of the cited works, however, deals with higher-order functions.

This paper is structured as follows. In Section 2, a simple linear λ-calculus, called ℓST_λ will be introduced, together with its operational semantics. This is a purely deterministic calculus, on top of which our extensions will be defined. Section 3 presents the basics of applicative bisimulation, instantiated on ℓST_λ. A probabilistic variation on ℓST_λ, called ℓPST_λ, is the subject of Section 4, which also discusses the impact of probabilities to equivalences and bisimilarity. Section 5 is about a quantum variation on ℓST_λ, dubbed ℓQST_λ, together with a study of bimilarity for it. Section 6 concludes the paper with a discussion about full-abstraction. An extended version of this paper with more details is available [5].

2   Linear λ-Calculi: A Minimal Core

In this section, a simple linear λ-calculus called ℓST_λ will be introduced, together with the basics of its operational semantics. *Terms* and *values* are generated by the following grammar:

$$e, f ::= v \mid ee \mid \text{if } e \text{ then } e \text{ else } e \mid \text{let } e \text{ be } \langle x, x \rangle \text{ in } e \mid \Omega;$$

$$v, w ::= x \mid \text{tt} \mid \text{ff} \mid \lambda x.e \mid \langle v, v \rangle.$$

Observe the presence not only of abstractions and applications, but also of value pairs, and of basic constructions for booleans. Pairs of arbitrary terms can be formed as follows, as syntactic sugar:

$$\langle e, f \rangle = (\lambda x.\lambda y.\langle x, y \rangle)ef.$$

Finally, terms include a constant Ω for divergence. b is a metavariable for truth values, i.e. b stands for either **tt** or **ff**. We need a way to enforce linearity, i.e., the fact that functions use their arguments *exactly* once. This can take the form of a linear type system whose language of *types* is the following:

$$A, B ::= \text{bool} \mid A \multimap A \mid A \otimes A.$$

The set $\mathcal{Y}$ includes all types. *Typing judgments* are in the form $\Gamma \vdash e : A$, where Γ is a set of assignments of types to variables. Typing rules are standard, and can be found in Figure 1. The set $\mathcal{T}_{\Gamma,A}^{\ell ST_\lambda}$ contains all terms e such that

$$\frac{}{x : A \vdash x : A} \qquad \frac{}{\vdash b : \text{bool}} \qquad \frac{\Gamma \vdash e : A \multimap B \qquad \Delta \vdash f : A}{\Gamma, \Delta \vdash ef : B} \qquad \frac{}{\Gamma \vdash \Omega : A}$$

$$\frac{\Gamma \vdash v : A \qquad \Delta \vdash w : B}{\Gamma, \Delta \vdash \langle v, w \rangle : A \otimes B} \qquad \frac{\Gamma, x : X, y : Y \vdash e : A \qquad \Delta \vdash f : X \otimes Y}{\Gamma, \Delta \vdash \text{let } f \text{ be } \langle x, y \rangle \text{ in } e : A}$$

$$\frac{\Gamma, x : A \vdash e : B}{\Gamma \vdash \lambda x.e : A \multimap B} \qquad \frac{\Gamma \vdash e : \text{bool} \qquad \Delta \vdash f : A \qquad \Delta \vdash g : A}{\Gamma, \Delta \vdash \text{if } e \text{ then } f \text{ else } g : A}$$

Fig. 1. Typing Rules

$\Gamma \vdash e : A$. $\mathcal{T}_{\emptyset,A}^{\ell ST_\lambda}$ is usually written as $\mathcal{T}_A^{\ell ST_\lambda}$. Notations like $\mathcal{V}_{\Gamma,A}^{\ell ST_\lambda}$ or $\mathcal{V}_A^{\ell ST_\lambda}$ are the analogues for values of the corresponding notations for terms.

Endowing ℓST_λ with call-by-value small-step or big-step semantics poses no significant problem. In the first case, one defines a binary relation $\rightarrow$ between closed terms of any type by the usual rule for β-reduction, the natural rule for the conditional operator, and the following rule: $\text{let } \langle v, w \rangle \text{ be } \langle x, y \rangle \text{ in } e \rightarrow e\{v, w/x, y\}$. Similarly, one can define a big-step evaluation relation $\Downarrow$ between closed terms and values by a completely standard set of rules (see [5] for more details). The expression $e \Downarrow$, as usual, indicates the existence of a value v with

$e \Downarrow v$. Subject reduction holds in the following sense: if $\emptyset \vdash e : A$, $e \to f$, and $e \Downarrow v$, then both $\emptyset \vdash f : A$ and $\emptyset \vdash v : A$.

The expressive power of the just-introduced calculus is rather poor. Nonetheless, it can be proved to be complete for first-order computation over booleans, in the following sense: for every function $F : \{\mathtt{tt}, \mathtt{ff}\}^n \to \{\mathtt{tt}, \mathtt{ff}\}$, there is a term which *computes* F, i.e. a term e_F such that $e_F \langle b_1, \ldots, b_n \rangle \Downarrow F(b_1, \ldots, b_n)$ for every $b_1, \ldots, b_n \in \{\mathtt{tt}, \mathtt{ff}\}^n$. Indeed, even if copying and erasing bits is not in principle allowed, one could anyway encode, e.g., duplication as the following combinator of type $\mathtt{bool} \multimap \mathtt{bool} \otimes \mathtt{bool}$: $\lambda x.\mathtt{if}\ x\ \mathtt{then}\ \langle \mathtt{tt}, \mathtt{tt} \rangle\ \mathtt{else}\ \langle \mathtt{ff}, \mathtt{ff} \rangle$. Similarly, if $\Gamma \vdash e : A$ and x is a fresh variable, one can easily find a term $\mathtt{weak}\ x\ \mathtt{in}\ e$ such that $\Gamma, x : \mathtt{bool} \vdash \mathtt{weak}\ x\ \mathtt{in}\ e : A$ and $\mathtt{weak}\ b\ \mathtt{in}\ e$ behaves like e for every $b \in \{\mathtt{ff}, \mathtt{tt}\}$.

But how could one capture program equivalence in an higher-order setting like the one we are examining? The canonical answer goes back to Morris [15], who proposed *context* equivalence (also known as *observational* equivalence) as the right way to compare terms. Roughly, two terms are context equivalent iff they behave the same when observed in any possible *context*, i.e. when tested against any possible *observer*. Formally, a context is nothing more than a term with a single occurrence of a special marker called the *hole* and denoted as $[\cdot]$ (see [5]). Given a context C and a term e, $C[e]$ is the term obtained by filling the single occurrence of $[\cdot]$ in C with e. For contexts to make sense in a typed setting, one needs to extend typing rules to contexts, introducing a set of rules deriving judgments in the form $\Gamma \vdash C[\Delta \vdash A] : B$, which can be read informally as saying that whenever $\Delta \vdash e : A$, it holds that $\Gamma \vdash C[e] : B$.

We are now in a position to define the context preorder: given two terms e and f such that $\Gamma \vdash e, f : A$, we write $e \leq_{\Gamma, A} f$ iff for every context C such that $\emptyset \vdash C[\Gamma \vdash A] : B$, if $C[e] \Downarrow$ then $C[f] \Downarrow$. If $e \leq_{\Gamma, A} f$ and $f \leq_{\Gamma, A} e$, then e and f are said to be *context equivalent*, and we write $e \equiv_{\Gamma, A} f$. What we have just defined, infact, are two *typed relations* $\leq$ and $\equiv$, that is to say two families of relations indexed by contexts and types, i.e. $\leq$ is the family $\{\leq_{\Gamma, A}\}_{\Gamma, A}$, while $\equiv$ is $\{\equiv_{\Gamma, A}\}_{\Gamma, A}$. If in the scheme above the type B is restricted so as to be $\mathtt{bool}$, then the obtained relations are the *ground* context preorder and *ground* context equivalence, respectively. Context equivalence is, almost by construction, a congruence. Similarly, the context preorder is easily seen to be a precongruence.

3 Applicative Bisimilarity and Its Properties

Context equivalence is universally accepted as the canonical notion of equivalence of higher-order programs, being robust, and only relying on the underlying operational semantics. Proving terms *not* context equivalent is relatively easy: ending up with a single context separating the two terms suffices. On the other hand, the universal quantification over all contexts makes proofs of equivalence hard.

A variety of techniques have been proposed to overcome this problem, among them logical relations, adequate denotational models and context lemmas.

As first proposed by Abramsky [1], coinductive methodologies (and the bisimulation proof method in particular) can be fruitfully employed. Abramsky's *applicative* bisimulation is based on taking argument passing as the basic interaction mechanism: what the environment can do with a λ-term is either evaluating it or passing it an argument.

In this section, we will briefly delineate how to define applicative bisimilarity for the linear λ-calculus ℓST_λ. We will do that in an unnecessarily pedantic way, defining a labelled transition system, and then playing the usual bisimulation game on top of it. This has the advantage of making the extensions to probabilistic and quantum calculi much easier.

A *labelled transition system* (LTS in the following) is a triple $\mathscr{L} = (\mathcal{S}, \mathcal{L}, \mathcal{N})$, where $\mathcal{S}$ is a set of *states*, $\mathcal{L}$ is a set of *labels*, and $\mathcal{N}$ is a subset of $\mathcal{S} \times \mathcal{L} \times \mathcal{S}$. If for every $s \in \mathcal{S}$ and for every $\ell \in \mathcal{L}$ there is *at most* one state $t \in \mathcal{S}$ with $(s, \ell, t) \in \mathcal{N}$, then $\mathscr{L}$ is said to be *deterministic*. The theory of bisimulation for LTSs is very well-studied [18] and forms one of the cornerstones of concurrency theory.

An applicative bisimulation relation is nothing more than a bisimulation on an LTS $\mathscr{L}_{\ell ST_\lambda}$ defined *on top of* the λ-calculus ℓST_λ. More specifically, the LTS $\mathscr{L}_{\ell ST_\lambda}$ is defined as the triple

$$(\overline{\mathcal{T}^{\ell ST_\lambda}} \uplus \overline{\mathcal{V}^{\ell ST_\lambda}}, \overline{\mathcal{E}^{\ell ST_\lambda}} \uplus \overline{\mathcal{V}^{\ell ST_\lambda}} \cup \{eval, \mathtt{tt}, \mathtt{ff}\} \cup (\mathcal{Y} \uplus \mathcal{Y}), \mathcal{N}_{\ell ST_\lambda}),$$

where:

- $\overline{\mathcal{T}^{\ell ST_\lambda}}$ is the set $\cup_{A \in \mathcal{Y}} (\mathcal{T}_A^{\ell ST_\lambda} \times \{A\})$, similarly for $\overline{\mathcal{V}^{\ell ST_\lambda}}$. On the other hand, $\overline{\mathcal{E}^{\ell ST_\lambda}}$ is $\cup_{A,B,E \in \mathcal{Y}} (\mathcal{T}_{x:A,y:B,E}^{\ell ST_\lambda} \times \{(A, B, E)\})$. Observe how any pair (v, A) appears twice as a state, once as an element of $\overline{\mathcal{T}^{\ell ST_\lambda}}$ and again as an element of $\overline{\mathcal{V}^{\ell ST_\lambda}}$. Whenever necessary to avoid ambiguity, the second instance will be denoted as $(\widehat{v}, A)$. Similarly for the two copies of any type A one finds as labels.

- The label *eval* models evaluation of terms, while the labels $\mathtt{tt}, \mathtt{ff}$ are the way a boolean constant declares its own value.

- The relation $\mathcal{N}_{\ell ST_\lambda}$ contains all triples in the following forms:

$$((\widehat{\mathtt{tt}}, \mathtt{bool}), \mathtt{tt}, (\widehat{\mathtt{tt}}, \mathtt{bool})); \qquad ((\widehat{\mathtt{ff}}, \mathtt{bool}), \mathtt{ff}, (\widehat{\mathtt{ff}}, \mathtt{bool}));$$
$$((\widehat{\lambda x.e}, A \multimap B), (v, A), (e\{v/x\}, B));$$
$$(((\widehat{\langle v, w \rangle}, A \otimes B), (e, (A, B, E)), (e\{v/x, w/y\}, E));$$
$$((e, A), A, (e, A)); \qquad ((\widehat{v}, A), \widehat{A}, (\widehat{v}, A)); \qquad ((e, A), eval, (\widehat{v}, A));$$

where, in the last item, we of course assume that $e \Downarrow v$.

Basically, values interact with their environment based on their types: abstractions take an input argument, pairs gives their two components to a term which can handle them, and booleans constants simply expose their value. The only way to interact with terms is by evaluating them. Both terms and values expose their type. As one can easily verify, the labelled transition system $\mathscr{L}_{\ell ST_\lambda}$ is deterministic. Simulation and bisimulation relations for $\mathscr{L}_{\ell ST_\lambda}$ are defined as for any other LTS. Notice, however, that both are binary relations on *states*, i.e., on elements of $\overline{\mathcal{T}^{\ell ST_\lambda}} \uplus \overline{\mathcal{V}^{\ell ST_\lambda}}$. Let us observe that:

- Two pairs (e, A) and (f, B) can be put in relation only if $A = B$, because each state makes its type public through a label. For similar reasons, states in the form (v, A) and $(\widehat{w}, B)$ cannot be in relation, not even if $A = B$.
- If (v, A) and (w, A) are in relation, then also $(\widehat{v}, A)$ and $(\widehat{w}, A)$ are in relation. Conversely, if $(\widehat{v}, A)$ and $(\widehat{w}, A)$ are in a (bi)simulation relation R, then $R \cup \{((v, A), (w, A))\}$ is itself a (bi)simulation.

As a consequence, (bi)similarity can be seen as a relation on terms, indexed by types. Similarity is denoted as $\preceq$, and its restriction to (closed) terms of type A is indicated with $\preceq_A$. For bisimilarity, symbols are $\sim$ and $\sim_A$, respectively. (Bi)similarity can be generalised to a typed relation by the usual open extension.

Example 1. An example of two distinct programs which can be proved bisimilar are the following:

$$e = \lambda x.\lambda y.\lambda z.\text{and } (xy) \text{ (or } z \text{ tt)}; \qquad f = \lambda x.\lambda y.\lambda z.x(\text{or } (\text{and } z \text{ ff}) \text{ } y);$$

where **and** and **or** are combinators computing the eponymous boolean functions. Both e and f can be given the type (bool $\multimap$ bool) $\multimap$ bool $\multimap$ bool $\multimap$ bool in the empty context. They can be proved bisimilar by just giving a relation $R_{e,f}$ which contains the pair (e, f) and which can be proved to be an applicative bisimulation. Another interesting example of terms which can be proved bisimilar are the term $e =$ if f then g else h and the term s obtained from e by λ-abstracting all variables which occur free in g (and, equivalently, in h), then applying the same variables to the obtained term. For more details, see [5].

Is bisimilarity sound for (i.e., included in) context equivalence? And how about the reverse inclusion? For a linear, deterministic λ-calculus like the one we are describing, both questions have already been given a positive answer [7]. In the next two sections, we will briefly sketch how the correspondence can be proved.

3.1   (Bi)similarity is a (Pre)congruence

A natural way to prove that similarity is included in the context preorder, (and thus that bisimilarity is included in context equivalence) consists in first showing that similarity is a *precongruence*, that is to say a preorder relation which is compatible with all the operators of the language.

While proving that $\preceq$ is a preorder is relatively easy, the naive proof of compatibility (i.e. the obvious induction) fails, due to application. A nice way out is due to Howe [9], who proposed a powerful and reasonably robust proof based on so-called precongruence candidates. Intuitively, the structure of Howe's method is the following:

1. First of all, one defines an operator $(\cdot)^H$ on typed relations, in such a way that whenever a typed relation R is a preorder, R^H is a precongruence.
2. One then proves, again under the condition that R is an equivalence relation, that R is included into R^H, and that R^H is substitutive.
3. Finally, one proves that $\preceq^H$ is itself an applicative simulation. This is the so-called Key Lemma [16], definitely the most difficult of the three steps.

Points 2 and 3 together imply that $\preceq$ and $\preceq^H$ coincide. But by point 1, $\preceq^H$, thus also $\preceq$, are precongruences. Points 1 and 2 do not depend on the underlying operational semantics, but on only on the language's constructs.

In Figure 2, one can find the full set of rules defining $(\cdot)^H$ when the underlying terms are those of ℓST_λ.

$$\frac{\emptyset \vdash cRt : A}{\emptyset \vdash cR^Ht : A} \qquad \frac{x : A \vdash xRt : A}{\emptyset \vdash xR^Ht : A}$$

$$\frac{\Gamma, x : B \vdash eR^Hh : A \qquad \Gamma \vdash (\lambda x.h)Rt : B \multimap A}{\Gamma \vdash (\lambda x.e)R^Ht : B \multimap A}$$

$$\frac{\Gamma \vdash eR^Hh : B \multimap A \qquad \Delta \vdash fR^Hs : B \qquad \Gamma, \Delta \vdash (hs)Rt : A}{\Gamma, \Delta \vdash (ef)R^Ht : A}$$

$$\frac{\begin{array}{c}\Gamma \vdash eR^Hh : \mathsf{bool}\\ \Delta \vdash fR^Hs : A \quad \Delta \vdash gR^Hr : A\\ \Gamma, \Delta \vdash (\mathtt{if}\ h\ \mathtt{then}\ s\ \mathtt{else}\ r)Rt : A\end{array}}{\Gamma, \Delta \vdash (\mathtt{if}\ e\ \mathtt{then}\ f\ \mathtt{else}\ g)R^Ht : A} \qquad \frac{\begin{array}{c}\Gamma \vdash eR^Hh : X \otimes Y\\ \Delta, x : X, y : Y \vdash fR^Hs : A\\ \Gamma, \Delta \vdash (\mathtt{let}\ h\ \mathtt{be}\ \langle x,y\rangle\ \mathtt{in}\ s)Rt : A\end{array}}{\Gamma, \Delta \vdash (\mathtt{let}\ e\ \mathtt{be}\ \langle x,y\rangle\ \mathtt{in}\ f)R^Ht : A}$$

$$\frac{\Gamma \vdash vR^Hu : A \qquad \Delta \vdash wR^Hz : B \qquad \Gamma, \Delta \vdash \langle u,z\rangle Re : A \otimes B}{\Gamma, \Delta \vdash \langle v,w\rangle R^He : A \otimes B}$$

Fig. 2. The Howe's Rules for ℓST_λ.

Theorem 1. *In ℓST_λ, $\preceq$ is included in $\leq$, thus $\sim$ is included in $\equiv$.*

4   Injecting Probabilistic Choice

The expressive power of ℓST_λ is rather limited, due to the presence of linearity. Nevertheless, the calculus is complete for first-order computations over the finite domain of boolean values, as discussed previously. Rather than relaxing linearity, we now modify ℓST_λ by endowing it with a form or probabilistic choice, thus obtaining a new linear λ-calculus, called ℓPST_λ, which is complete for probabilistic circuits. We see ℓPST_λ as an intermediate step towards ℓQST_λ, a quantum λ-calculus we will analyze in the following section.

The language of terms of ℓPST_λ is the one of ℓST_λ where, however, there is one additional binary construct $\oplus$, to be interpreted as probabilistic choice: $e ::= e \oplus e$. The set $\mathcal{Y}$ of types is the same as the one of ℓST_λ. An evaluation operation is introduced as a relation $\Downarrow \subseteq \mathcal{T}_{\emptyset,A}^{\ell PST_\lambda} \times \mathscr{D}_A^{\ell PST_\lambda}$ between the sets of closed terms of type A belonging to ℓPST_λ and the one of subdistributions of values of type A in ℓPST_λ. The elements of $\mathscr{D}_A^{\ell PST_\lambda}$ are actually subdistributions whose support is some finite subset of the set of values $\mathcal{V}_A^{\ell PST_\lambda}$, i.e., for each such $\mathscr{E}$, we have $\mathscr{E} : \mathcal{V}_A^{\ell PST_\lambda} \mapsto \mathbb{R}_{[0,1]}$ and $\sum_{v \in \mathcal{V}_A^{\ell PST_\lambda}} \mathscr{E}(v) \leq 1$. Whenever this does not cause ambiguity, subdistributions will be referred to simply as distributions. In Figure 3 a selection of the rules for big-step semantics in ℓPST_λ is given. Expressions in the form $\{v_i^{p_i}\}_{i \in I}$ have the obvious meaning, namely the distribution with support $\{v_i\}_{i \in I}$ which attributes probability p_i to each v_i.

As for the terms $e \in \mathcal{T}_A^{\ell PST_\lambda}$, the following lemma holds:

Lemma 1. *If $\emptyset \vdash e : A$, then there is a unique distribution $\mathscr{E}$ such that $e \Downarrow \mathscr{E}$.*

Lemma 1 only holds because the λ-calculus we are working with is linear, and as a consequence strongly normalising. If $e \Downarrow \mathscr{E}$, then the unique $\mathscr{E}$ from Lemma 1 is called the *semantics* of e and is denoted simply as $\llbracket e \rrbracket$.

$$\frac{}{v \Downarrow \{v^1\}} \qquad \frac{}{\Omega \Downarrow \emptyset} \qquad \frac{e \Downarrow \mathscr{E} \quad f \Downarrow \mathscr{F} \quad s\{w/x\} \Downarrow \mathscr{G}_{\lambda x.s,w}}{ef \Downarrow \sum_{\lambda x.s \in \mathfrak{S}(\mathscr{E}), w \in \mathfrak{S}(\mathscr{F})} \mathscr{E}(\lambda x.s) \mathscr{F}(w) \mathscr{G}_{\lambda x.s,w}}$$

$$\frac{e \Downarrow \mathscr{E} \quad f \Downarrow \mathscr{F} \quad g \Downarrow \mathscr{G}}{\text{if } e \text{ then } f \text{ else } g \Downarrow \mathscr{E}(\text{tt}) \mathscr{F} + \mathscr{E}(\text{ff}) \mathscr{G}} \qquad \frac{e \Downarrow \mathscr{E} \quad f \Downarrow \mathscr{F}}{e \oplus f \Downarrow \frac{1}{2} \mathscr{E} + \frac{1}{2} \mathscr{F}}$$

Fig. 3. Big-step Semantics of ℓPST_λ — Selection

Context equivalence and the context preorder are defined very similarly to ℓST_λ, the only difference being the underlying notion of observation, which in ℓST_λ takes the form of *convergence*, and in ℓPST_λ becomes the *probability* of convergence.

4.1 Applicative Bisimilarity

Would it be possible to define applicative bisimilarity for ℓPST_λ similarly to what we have done for ℓST_λ? The first obstacle towards this goal is the dynamics of ℓPST_λ, which is not deterministic but rather probabilistic, and thus cannot fit into an LTS. In the literature, however, various notions of probabilistic bisimulation have been introduced, and it turns out that the earliest and simplest one, due to Larsen and Skou [12], is sufficient for our purposes.

A *labelled Markov chain* (LMC in the following) is a triple $(\mathcal{S}, \mathcal{L}, \mathcal{P})$, where $\mathcal{S}$ and $\mathcal{L}$ are as in the definition of a LTS, while $\mathcal{P}$ is a *transition probability matrix*, i.e., a function from $\mathcal{S} \times \mathcal{L} \times \mathcal{S}$ to $\mathbb{R}_{[0,1]}$ such that for every s and for every ℓ, it holds that $\mathcal{P}(s, \ell, \mathcal{S}) \leq 1$ (where the expression $\mathcal{P}(s, \ell, X)$ stands for $\sum_{t \in X} \mathcal{P}(s, \ell, t)$ whenever $X \subseteq \mathcal{S}$). Given such a LMC $\mathcal{M}$, an equivalence relation R on $\mathcal{S}$ is said to be a *bisimulation* on $\mathcal{M}$ iff whenever $(s, t) \in R$, it holds that $\mathcal{P}(s, \ell, E) = \mathcal{P}(t, \ell, E)$ for every equivalence class E of $\mathcal{S}$ modulo R. A preorder R on $\mathcal{S}$ is said to be a *simulation* iff for every subset X of $\mathcal{S}$, it holds that $\mathcal{P}(s, \ell, X) \leq \mathcal{P}(t, \ell, R(X))$. With some efforts (see [5] for some more details) one can prove that there exist largest bisimulation and simulation, that we continue to call *similarity* and *bisimilarity*, respectively. Probabilistic (bi)simulation, despite the endeavor required to define it, preserves all fundamental properties of its deterministic sibling. As an example, a symmetric probabilistic simulation is a bisimulation. Moreover, bisimilarity is the intersection of similarity and co-similarity.

Labelled Markov chains are exactly the objects we need when generalising the construction $\mathscr{L}_{\ell ST_\lambda}$ to ℓPST_λ. The LMC $\mathscr{M}_{\ell PST_\lambda}$, indeed, is defined as the triple

$$(\overline{\mathcal{T}^{\ell PST_\lambda}} \uplus \overline{\mathcal{V}^{\ell PST_\lambda}}, \overline{\mathcal{E}^{\ell PST_\lambda}} \uplus \overline{\mathcal{V}^{\ell PST_\lambda}} \cup \{eval, \mathtt{tt}, \mathtt{ff}\} \cup (\mathcal{Y} \uplus \mathcal{Y}), \mathcal{P}_{\ell PST_\lambda})$$

where $\mathcal{P}_{\ell PST_\lambda}$ is the function assuming the following values:

$$\mathcal{P}_{\ell PST_\lambda}((\widehat{\mathtt{tt}}, \mathtt{bool}), \mathtt{tt}, (\widehat{\mathtt{tt}}, \mathtt{bool})) = 1; \qquad \mathcal{P}_{\ell PST_\lambda}((\widehat{\mathtt{ff}}, \mathtt{bool}), \mathtt{ff}, (\widehat{\mathtt{ff}}, \mathtt{bool})) = 1;$$
$$\mathcal{P}_{\ell PST_\lambda}((\widehat{\lambda x.e}, A \multimap B), (v, A), (e\{v/x\}, B)) = 1;$$
$$\mathcal{P}_{\ell PST_\lambda}((\widehat{\langle v, w \rangle}, A \otimes B), (e, (A, B, E)), (e\{v/x, w/y\}, E)) = 1;$$
$$\mathcal{P}_{\ell PST_\lambda}((e, A), A, (e, A)) = 1 \qquad \mathcal{P}_{\ell PST_\lambda}((\widehat{v}, A), \widehat{A}, (\widehat{v}, A)) = 1;$$
$$\mathcal{P}_{\ell PST_\lambda}((e, A), eval, (\widehat{v}, A)) = [\![e]\!](v);$$

and having value 0 in all the other cases. It is easy to realise that $\mathcal{P}_{\ell PST_\lambda}$ can indeed be seen as the natural generalisation of $\mathcal{N}_{\ell ST_\lambda}$: on states in the form $(\widehat{v}, A)$, the function either returns 0 or 1, while in correspondence to states like (e, A) and the label *eval*, it behaves in a genuinely probabilistic way.

As for ℓST_λ, simulation and bisimulation relations, and the largest such relations, namely similarity and bisimilarity, can be given by just instantiating the general scheme described above to the specific LMC modeling terms of ℓPST_λ and their dynamics. All these turn out to be relations on *closed* terms, but as for ℓST_λ, they can be turned into proper typed relations just by the usual open extension.

The question now is: are the just introduced coinductive methodologies sound with respect to context equivalence? And is it that the proof of precongruence for similarity from Section 3.1 can be applied here? The answer is positive, but some effort is needed. More specifically, one can proceed as in [4], generalising Howe's method to a probabilistic setting, which makes the Key Lemma harder to prove. By the way, the set of Howe's rules are the same as in ℓST_λ, except for a new one, namely

$$\frac{\Gamma \vdash e R^H h : A \qquad \Delta \vdash f R^H s : A \qquad \Gamma, \Delta \vdash (h \oplus s) R t : A}{\Gamma, \Delta \vdash (e \oplus f) R^H t : A}$$

Thus:

Theorem 2. *In ℓPST_λ, $\preceq$ is included in $\leq$, thus $\sim$ is included in $\equiv$.*

5   On Quantum Data

Linear λ-calculi with classical control and quantum data have been introduced and studied both from an operational and from a semantical point of view [20,7].

Definitionally, they can be thought of as λ-calculi in which ordinary, classic, terms have access to a so-called quantum register, which models quantum data.

A quantum register $\mathscr{Q}$ on a finite set of quantum variables $\mathcal{Q}$ is mathematically described by an element of a finite-dimensional Hilbert space whose computational basis is the set $\mathcal{SB}(\mathcal{Q})$ of all maps from $\mathcal{Q}$ to $\{\mathtt{tt}, \mathtt{ff}\}$ (of which there are $2^{|\mathcal{Q}|}$). Any element of this basis takes the form $|r_1 \leftarrow b_1, r_2 \leftarrow b_2, \cdots, r_n \leftarrow b_n\rangle$, where $\mathcal{Q} = \{r_1, \ldots, r_n\}$ and $b_1, \ldots, b_n \in \{\mathtt{tt}, \mathtt{ff}\}$. Elements of this Hilbert space, called $\mathcal{H}(\mathcal{Q})$, are in the form

$$\mathscr{Q} = \sum_{\eta \in \mathcal{SB}(\mathcal{Q})} \alpha_\eta |\eta\rangle, \tag{1}$$

where the complex numbers $\alpha_\eta \in \mathbb{C}$ are the so-called *amplitudes*, and must satisfy the *normalisation condition* $\sum_{\eta \in \mathcal{SB}(\mathcal{Q})} |\alpha_\eta|^2 = 1$. If $\eta \in \mathcal{SB}(\mathcal{Q})$ and r is a variable not necessarily in $\mathcal{Q}$, then $\eta\{r \leftarrow b\}$ stands for the substitution which coincides with η except on r where it equals b.

The interaction of a quantum register with the outer environment can create or destroy quantum bits increasing or decreasing the dimension of $\mathscr{Q}$. This shaping of the quantum register is mathematically described making use of the following operators:

- The probability operator $\mathtt{PR}_b^r : \mathcal{H}(\mathcal{Q}) \to \mathbb{R}_{[0,1]}$ gives the probability to obtain $b \in \{\mathtt{tt}, \mathtt{ff}\}$ as a result of the measurement of $r \in \mathcal{Q}$ in the input register:

$$\mathtt{PR}_b^r(\mathscr{Q}) = \sum_{\eta(r)=b} |\alpha_\eta|^2.$$

- If $r \in \mathcal{Q}$, then the projection operator $\mathtt{MS}_b^r : \mathcal{H}(\mathcal{Q}) \to \mathcal{H}(\mathcal{Q}-\{r\})$ measures the variable r, stored in the input register, destroying the corresponding qubit. More precisely $\mathtt{MS}_{\mathtt{tt}}^r(\mathscr{Q})$ and $\mathtt{MS}_{\mathtt{ff}}^r(\mathscr{Q})$ give as a result the quantum register configuration corresponding to a measure of the variable r, when the result of the variable measurement is $\mathtt{tt}$ or $\mathtt{ff}$, respectively:

$$\mathtt{MS}_b^r(\mathscr{Q}) = [\mathtt{PR}_b^r(\mathscr{Q})]^{-\frac{1}{2}} \sum_{\eta \in \mathcal{SB}(\mathcal{Q}-\{r\})} \alpha_{\eta\{r \leftarrow b\}} |\eta\rangle,$$

where $\mathscr{Q}$ is as in (1).
- If $r \notin \mathcal{Q}$, then the operator $\mathtt{NW}^r : \mathcal{H}(\mathcal{Q}) \to \mathcal{H}(\mathcal{Q} \cup \{r\})$ creates a new qubit, accessible through the fresh variable name r, and increases the dimension of the quantum register by one .

Qubits can not only be created and measured, but their value can also be *modified* by applying unitary operators to them. Given any such n-ary operator U, and any sequence of distinct variables $r_1, \ldots, r_n$ (where $r_i \in \mathcal{Q}$ for every $1 \leq i \leq n$), one can build a unitary operator $U_{r_1, \ldots, r_n}$ on $\mathcal{H}(\mathcal{Q})$.

5.1   The Language

We can obtain the quantum language ℓQST_λ as an extension of basic ℓST_λ. The grammar of ℓST_λ is enhanced by adding the following values:

$$e ::= U(v) \mid \texttt{meas}(v) \mid \texttt{new}(v); \qquad v ::= r;$$

where r ranges over an infinite set of quantum variables, and U ranges over a finite set of unitary transformations. The term $\texttt{new}(v)$ acting on boolean constant, returns (a quantum variable pointing to) a qubit of the same value, increasing this way the dimension of the quantum register. The term $\texttt{meas}(v)$ measures a value of type qubit, therefore it decreases the dimension of the quantum register.

Typing terms in ℓQST_λ does not require any particular efforts. The class of types needs to be sligthly extended with a new base type for qubits, called $\texttt{qbit}$, while contexts now give types not only to classical variables, but also to quantum variables. The new typing rules are in Figure 4.

$$\frac{\Gamma \vdash v : \texttt{qbit}}{\Gamma \vdash \texttt{meas}(v) : \texttt{bool}} \qquad \frac{\Gamma \vdash v : \texttt{bool}}{\Gamma \vdash \texttt{new}(v) : \texttt{qbit}}$$

$$\frac{\Gamma \vdash v : \texttt{qbit}^{\otimes n}}{\Gamma \vdash U(v) : \texttt{qbit}^{\otimes n}} \qquad \frac{}{r : \texttt{qbit} \vdash r : \texttt{qbit}}$$

Fig. 4. Typing rules in ℓQST_λ.

The semantics of ℓQST_λ, on the other hand, cannot be specified merely as a relation between terms, since terms only make sense computationally if coupled with a quantum register, namely in a pair in the form $[\mathcal{Q}, e]$, which is called a *quantum closure*. Analogously to what has been made for ℓPST_λ, small step reduction operator $\rightarrow$ and the big step evaluation operator $\Downarrow$ are given as relations between the set of quantum closures and of quantum closures distributions. In figures 5 and 6 the small-step semantics and big-step semantics for ℓQST_λ are given. Quantum closures, however, are not what we want to compare, since what we want to be able to compare are *terms*. Context equivalence, in other words, continues to be a relation on terms, and can be specified similarly to the probablistic case, following, e.g. [20].

5.2   Applicative Bisimilarity in ℓQST_λ

Would it be possible to have a notion of bisimilarity for ℓQST_λ? What is the underlying "Markov Chain"? It turns out that LMCs as introduced in Section 4.1 are sufficient, but we need to be careful. In particular, states of the LMC are not terms, but quantum closures, of which there are in principle nondenumerably many. However, since we are only interested in quantum closures which can be

$$[\mathscr{Q},(\lambda x.e)v] \rightarrow \{[\mathscr{Q}, e\{v/x\}]^1\}$$

$$\frac{[\mathscr{Q},e] \rightarrow \{[\mathscr{Q}_i, f_i]^{p_i}\}_{i \in I}}{[\mathscr{Q}, eg] \rightarrow \{[\mathscr{Q}_i, f_i g]^{p_i}\}_{i \in I}} \qquad \frac{[\mathscr{Q},e] \rightarrow \{[\mathscr{Q}_i, f_i]^{p_i}\}_{i \in I}}{[\mathscr{Q}, ve] \rightarrow \{[\mathscr{Q}_i, v f_i]^{p_i}\}_{i \in I}}$$

$$[\mathscr{Q},\texttt{if tt then } f \texttt{ else } g] \rightarrow \{[\mathscr{Q}, f]^1\} \qquad [\mathscr{Q},\texttt{if ff then } f \texttt{ else } g] \rightarrow \{[\mathscr{Q}, g]^1\}$$

$$\frac{[\mathscr{Q},e] \rightarrow \{[\mathscr{Q}_i, h_i]^{p_i}\}_{i \in I}}{[\mathscr{Q},\texttt{if } e \texttt{ then } f \texttt{ else } g] \rightarrow \{[\mathscr{Q}_i,\texttt{if } h_i \texttt{ then } f \texttt{ else } g]^{p_i}\}_{i \in I}}$$

$$[\mathscr{Q},\texttt{let } \langle v,w \rangle \texttt{ be } \langle x,y \rangle \texttt{ in } f] \rightarrow \{[\mathscr{Q}, f\{v/x, w/y\}]^1\}$$

$$\frac{[\mathscr{Q},e] \rightarrow \{[\mathscr{Q}_i, h_i]^{p_i}\}_{i \in I}}{[\mathscr{Q},\texttt{let } e \texttt{ be } \langle x,y \rangle \texttt{ in } g] \rightarrow \{[\mathscr{Q}_i,\texttt{let } h_i \texttt{ be } \langle x,y \rangle \texttt{ in } g]^{p_i}\}_{i \in I}}$$

$$[\mathscr{Q},\texttt{meas}(r)] \rightarrow \{[\mathrm{MS}^r_{\texttt{ff}}(\mathscr{Q}),\texttt{ff}]^{\mathrm{PR}^r_{\texttt{ff}}(\mathscr{Q})}, [\mathrm{MS}^r_{\texttt{tt}}(\mathscr{Q}),\texttt{tt}]^{\mathrm{PR}^r_{\texttt{tt}}(\mathscr{Q})}\}$$

$$[\mathscr{Q}, U\langle r_1,\ldots,r_n\rangle] \rightarrow \{[U_{r_1,\ldots,r_n}(\mathscr{Q}), \langle r_1,\ldots,r_n\rangle]^1\}$$

$$\frac{r \text{ fresh variable}}{[\mathscr{Q},\texttt{new}(b)] \rightarrow \{[\mathrm{NW}^r_b(\mathscr{Q}), r]^1\}} \qquad [\mathscr{Q}, \Omega] \rightarrow \emptyset$$

Fig. 5. Small-step Semantics of ℓQST_λ.

obtained (in a finite number of evaluation steps) from closures having an empty quantum register, this is not a problem: we simply take states as *those* closures, which we dub *constructible*. $\mathscr{M}_{\ell QST_\lambda}$ can be built similarly to $\mathscr{M}_{\ell PST_\lambda}$, where (constructible) quantum closures take the place of terms. The non zero elements of the function $\mathcal{P}_{\ell QST_\lambda}$ are defined as follows:

$$\mathcal{P}_{\ell QST_\lambda}(([\mathscr{Q},\widehat{\texttt{tt}}],\texttt{bool}),([\mathscr{W},e],A,\texttt{tt}),([\mathscr{Q}\otimes\mathscr{W},e],A)) = 1;$$
$$\mathcal{P}_{\ell QST_\lambda}(([\mathscr{Q},\widehat{\texttt{ff}}],\texttt{bool}),([\mathscr{W},e],A,\texttt{ff}),([\mathscr{Q}\otimes\mathscr{W},e],A)) = 1;$$
$$\mathcal{P}_{\ell QST_\lambda}(([\mathscr{Q},\widehat{\langle v,w\rangle}],A\otimes B),([\mathscr{W},e],(A,B,E)),([\mathscr{Q}\otimes\mathscr{W},e\{v/x,w/y\}],E)) = 1;$$
$$\mathcal{P}_{\ell QST_\lambda}(([\mathscr{Q},e],A),A,([\mathscr{Q},e],A)) = 1 \qquad \mathcal{P}_{\ell QST_\lambda}(([\mathscr{Q},\widehat{e}],A),A,([\mathscr{Q},\widehat{e}],A)) = 1;$$
$$\mathcal{P}_{\ell QST_\lambda}(([\mathscr{Q},e],A),eval,([\mathscr{U},v],A)) = [\![\mathscr{Q},e]\!]([\mathscr{U},v]).$$

Once we have a LMC, it is easy to apply the same definitional scheme we have seen for ℓPST_λ, and obtain a notion of applicative (bi)similarity. Howe's method, in turn, can be adapted to the calculus here, resulting in a proof of precongruence and ultimately in the following:

Theorem 3. *In* ℓQST_λ, $\preceq$ *is included in* $\leq$, *thus* $\sim$ *is included in* $\equiv$.

More details on the proof of this can be found in [5].

$$[\mathcal{Q}, v] \Downarrow \{[\mathcal{Q}, v]^1\} \qquad [\mathcal{Q}, \Omega] \Downarrow \emptyset \qquad \frac{r \text{ fresh variable}}{[\mathcal{Q}, \mathtt{new}(b)] \Downarrow \{[\mathtt{NW}_b^r(\mathcal{Q}), r]^1\}}$$

$$[\mathcal{Q}, U\langle r_1 \dots r_m\rangle] \Downarrow \{[U_{r_1,\dots,r_m}(\mathcal{Q}), \langle r_1,\dots,r_m\rangle]^1\}$$

$$[\mathcal{Q}, \mathtt{meas}(r)] \Downarrow \{[\mathtt{MS}_{\mathtt{ff}}^r(\mathcal{Q}), \mathtt{ff}]^{\mathrm{PR}_{\mathtt{ff}}^r(\mathcal{Q})}, [\mathtt{MS}_{\mathtt{tt}}^r(\mathcal{Q}), \mathtt{tt}]^{\mathrm{PR}_{\mathtt{tt}}^r(\mathcal{Q})}\}$$

$$\frac{\begin{array}{c} [\mathcal{Q}, e] \Downarrow \{[\mathcal{Q}_i, \lambda x.h_i]^{p_i}\}_{i \in I} \\ [\mathcal{Q}_i, f] \Downarrow \{[\mathcal{Q}_{i,h}, s_{i,h}]^{q_{i,h}}\}_{i,h \in \mathcal{H}} \\ [\mathcal{Q}_{i,h}, h_i\{s_{i,h}/x\}] \Downarrow \mathscr{E}_{i,h} \end{array}}{[\mathcal{Q}, ef] \Downarrow \sum_{i,h} p_i \cdot q_{i,h} \cdot \mathscr{E}_{i,h}} \qquad \frac{\begin{array}{c} [\mathcal{Q}, e] \Downarrow \{[\mathcal{Q}_{\mathtt{ff}}, \mathtt{ff}]^{p_{\mathtt{ff}}}, [\mathcal{Q}_{\mathtt{tt}}, \mathtt{tt}]^{p_{\mathtt{tt}}}\} \\ [\mathcal{Q}_{\mathtt{ff}}, g] \Downarrow \mathscr{E} \\ [\mathcal{Q}_{\mathtt{tt}}, f] \Downarrow \mathscr{F} \end{array}}{[\mathcal{Q}, \mathtt{if} \ e \ \mathtt{then} \ f \ \mathtt{else} \ g] \Downarrow p_{\mathtt{ff}}\mathscr{E} + p_{\mathtt{tt}}\mathscr{F}}$$

$$\frac{[\mathcal{Q}, e] \Downarrow \{[\mathcal{Q}_i, \langle v_i, w_i\rangle]^{p_i}\}_{i \in I} \qquad [\mathcal{Q}_i, f\{v_i/x, w_i/y\}] \Downarrow \mathscr{E}_i}{[\mathcal{Q}, \mathtt{let} \ e \ \mathtt{be} \ \langle x, y\rangle \ \mathtt{in} \ f] \Downarrow \sum_i p_i \cdot \mathscr{E}_i}$$

Fig. 6. Big-step Semantics of ℓQST_λ.

Example 2. An interesting pair of terms which can be proved bisimilar are the following two:

$$e = \lambda x.\mathtt{if} \ (\mathtt{meas} \ x) \ \mathtt{then} \ \mathtt{ff} \ \mathtt{else} \ \mathtt{tt}; \qquad f = \lambda x.\mathtt{meas}(X \ x);$$

where X is the unitary operator which flips the value of a qubit. This is remarkable given, e.g. the "non-local" effects entanglement could cause.

6   On Full-Abstraction

In the deterministic calculus ℓST_λ, bisimilarity not only is *included* into context equivalence, but *coincides* with it (and, analogously, similarity coincides with the context preorder). This can be proved by observing that in $\mathscr{L}_{\ell ST_\lambda}$, bisimilarity coincides with trace equivalence, and each linear test, i.e., each trace, can be implemented by a context. This result is not surprising, and has already been obtained in similar settings elsewhere [2].

But how about ℓPST_λ and ℓQST_λ? Actually, there is little hope to prove full-abstraction between context equivalence and bisimilarity in a linear setting if probabilistic choice is present. Indeed, as shown by van Breugel et al. [21], probabilistic bisimilarity can be characterised by a notion of test equivalence where tests can be *conjunctive*, i.e., they can be in the form $t = \langle s, p\rangle$, and t succeeds if both s and p succeeds. Implementing conjuctive tests, thus, requires *copying* the tested term, which is impossible in a linear setting. Indeed, it is easy to find a counterexample to full-abstraction already in ℓPST_λ. Consider the following two terms, both of which can be given type $\mathtt{bool} \multimap \mathtt{bool}$ in ℓPST_λ:

$$e = \lambda x.\mathtt{weak} \ x \ \mathtt{in} \ \mathtt{tt} \oplus \mathtt{ff}; \qquad f = (\lambda x.\mathtt{weak} \ x \ \mathtt{in} \ \mathtt{tt}) \oplus (\lambda x.\mathtt{weak} \ x \ \mathtt{in} \ \mathtt{ff}).$$

The two terms are not bisimilar, simply because tt and ff are not bisimilar, and thus also $\lambda x.$weak x in tt and $\lambda x.$weak x in ff cannot be bisimilar. However, e and f can be proved to be context equivalent: there is simply no way to discriminate between them by way of a linear context (see [5] for more details).

What one may hope to get is full-abstraction for extensions of the considered calculi in which duplication is reintroduced, although in a controlled way. This has been recently done in a probabilistic setting by Crubillé and the first author [4], and is the topic of current investigations by the authors for a non-strictly-linear extension of ℓQST_λ.

7   Conclusions

We show that Abramsky's applicative bisimulation can be adapted to linear λ-calculi endowed with probabilistic choice and quantum data. The main result is that in both cases, the obtained bisimilarity relation is a congruence, thus included in context equivalence.

For the sake of simplicity, we have deliberately kept the considered calculi as simple as possible. We believe, however, that many extensions would be harmless. This includes, as an example, generalising types to *recursive* types which, although infinitary in nature, can be dealt with very easily in a coinductive setting. Adding a form of controlled duplication requires more care, e.g. in presence of quantum data (which cannot be duplicated).

References

1. Abramsky, S.: The lazy λ-calculus. In: Turner, D. (ed.) Research Topics in Functional Programming, pp. 65–117. Addison Wesley (1990)
2. Bierman, G.M.: Program equivalence in a linear functional language. J. Funct. Program. 10(2), 167–190 (2000)
3. Crole, R.L.: Completeness of bisimilarity for contextual equivalence in linear theories. Electronic Journal of the IGPL 9(1) (January 2001)
4. Crubillé, R., Dal Lago, U.: On probabilistic applicative bisimulation and call-by-value λ-calculi. In: Shao, Z. (ed.) ESOP 2014 (ETAPS). LNCS, vol. 8410, pp. 209–228. Springer, Heidelberg (2014)
5. Dal Lago, U., Rioli, A: Applicative bisimulation and quantum λ-calculi (long version) (2014). http://arxiv.org/abs/1506.06661
6. Davidson, T.A.S., Gay, S.J., Mlnarik, H., Nagarajan, R., Papanikolaou, N.: Model checking for communicating quantum processes. IJUC 8(1), 73–98 (2012)
7. Deng, Y., Feng, Y.: Open bisimulation for quantum processes. CoRR, abs/1201.0416 (2012)
8. Simon, J.: Gay and Rajagopal Nagarajan. Communicating quantum processes. In: POPL, pp. 145–157 (2005)
9. Howe, D.J.: Proving congruence of bisimulation in functional programming languages. Inf. Comput. 124(2), 103–112 (1996)
10. Jacobs, B.: Coalgebraic walks, in quantum and turing computation. In: Hofmann, M. (ed.) FOSSACS 2011. LNCS, vol. 6604, pp. 12–26. Springer, Heidelberg (2011)

11. Koutavas, V., Levy, P.B., Sumii, E.: From applicative to environmental bisimulation. Electr. Notes Theor. Comput. Sci. 276, 215–235 (2011)
12. Larsen, K.G., Skou, A.: Bisimulation through probabilistic testing. Inf. Comput. 94(1), 1–28 (1991)
13. Lassen, S.B., Pitcher, C.: Similarity and bisimilarity for countable non-determinism and higher-order functions. Electr. Notes Theor. Comput. Sci. 10, 246–266 (1997)
14. Milner, R.: Fully abstract models of typed λ-calculi. Theor. Comput. Sci. 4, 1–22 (1977)
15. Morris, J.: Lambda Calculus Models of Programming Languages. PhD thesis, MIT (1969)
16. Andrew, M.: Pitts. Operationally-based theories of program equivalence. In: Semantics and Logics of Computation, pp. 241–298. Cambridge University Press (1997)
17. Plotkin, G.: Lambda definability and logical relations. In: Memo SAI-RM-4, School of Artificial Intelligence, Edinburgh (1973)
18. Sangiorgi, D.: Introduction to Bisimulation and Coinduction. Cambridge Universtity Press (2012)
19. Selinger, P., Valiron, B.: A Lambda Calculus for Quantum Computation with Classical Control. In: Urzyczyn, P. (ed.) TLCA 2005. LNCS, vol. 3461, pp. 354–368. Springer, Heidelberg (2005)
20. Selinger, P., Valiron, B.: On a fully abstract model for a quantum linear functional language. Electron. Notes Theor. Comput. Sci. 210, 123–137 (2008)
21. van Breugel, F., Mislove, M.W., Ouaknine, J., Worrell, J.: Domain theory, testing and simulation for labelled Markov processes. Theor. Comput. Sci. 333(1-2), 171–197 (2005)

Modeling and Efficient Verification of Broadcasting Actors

Behnaz Yousefi, Fatemeh Ghassemi, and Ramtin Khosravi

School of Electrical and Computer Engineering, University of Tehran, Iran
{b.yousefi,fghassemi,r.khosravi}@ut.ac.ir

Abstract. Many distributed systems use broadcast communication for various reasons such as saving energy or increasing throughput. However, the actor model for concurrent and distributed systems does not directly support this kind of communication. In such cases, a broadcast must be modeled as multiple unicasts which leads to loss of modularity and state space explosion for any non-trivial system. In this paper, we extend Rebeca, an actor-based model language, to support asynchronous anonymous message broadcasting. Then, we apply counter abstraction for reducing the state space which efficiently bypasses the constructive orbit problem by considering the global state as a vector of counters, one per each local state. This makes the model checking of systems possible without further considerations of symmetry. This approach is efficient for fully symmetric system like broadcasting environments. We use a couple of case studies to illustrate the applicability of our method and the way their state spaces are reduced in size.

Keywords: state space reduction, broadcast, Rebeca, actor-based language, model checking, verification.

1 Introduction

The actor model [2,13] is one of the pioneers in modeling of concurrent and distributed applications. It has been introduced as an agent-based language by Hewitt [13] and then extended by Agha as an object-based concurrent computation model [2]. An actor model consists of a set of actors that communicate through asynchronous message passing. Communication in actor models is based on unicast, i.e. in each message the receiver has to be specified. On the other hand, broadcast communication is a simple model of parallel computation [28] and a large number of algorithms in distributed networks use broadcast, such as consensus agreement [20,4,7,5,22], leader election [23,16,21], and max finding [9,17,27,18]. In addition, wireless channels have a broadcast nature as when a node sends a message, it can be received by any other node that lies within its communication range, which leads to power saving and throughput improvement [8]. Modeling these algorithms with actor model would cause some complexities both in modeling and analysis. In the modeling aspect, a broadcast has to be replaced with multiple unicasts, which leads to loss of modularity and cluttering of the model code. The (unnecessary) interleaving of these unicast messages

© IFIP International Federation for Information Processing 2015
M. Dastani and M.Sirjani (Eds.): FSEN 2015, LNCS 9392, pp. 69–83, 2015.
DOI: 10.1007/978-3-319-24644-4_5

causes state space explosion during analysis, the main obstacle in model checking of nontrivial systems. Using broadcasts instead of multiple unicasts, enables efficient use of counter abstraction technique [3] to overcome this problem.

In this paper, we extend the actor-based modeling language Rebeca [31] with broadcast communication. Rebeca is an operational interpretation of the actor model with the aim of bridging the gap between formal verification techniques and the real world software engineering of concurrent and distributed applications. This is achieved by its simple Java-like syntax and extensive tool support [1,32], including a modeling environment and a model checker employing well known reduction techniques [14]. The resulting modeling language provides a suitable framework to model mobile ad hoc networks (MANETs). Having broadcast as the main communication mechanism in the broadcasting actor language, we have applied counter abstraction to efficiently reduce the size of the state space. To the best of our knowledge, there is no actor-based language with direct support for broadcast communication. In [29], Rebeca is extended with *components* to provide a higher level of abstraction and encapsulation and broadcast has been used for communication between the components of actors and not within a component.

In the original actor model, message delivery is guaranteed and each actor has a mailbox to maintain messages while it is busy processing another message. However, due to unpredictability of networks, the arrival order of messages are assumed to be arbitrary and unknown [2]. To prevent state space explosion, Rebeca makes use of FIFO queues as a means of message storage [30] so that messages will be processed based on the order that they have been received. In our extended model, queues are replaced by *bags* (unordered multi-sets of messages).

The paper is structured as follows. Section 2 briefly introduces Rebeca and provides an overview on the counter abstraction technique. Section 3 presents our extension to Rebeca to support broadcast. In Section 4, we show how we have implemented counter abstraction to generate the state space compactly. To illustrate the applicability of our approach, we bring two case studies in Section 5. Finally, we review some related work in 6 before concluding the paper.

2   Preliminaries

2.1   Rebeca

Rebeca [31] is an actor- based modeling language which has been proposed for modeling and verification of concurrent and distributed systems. It aims to bring the formal verification techniques into the real world of software engineering by means of providing a Java-like syntax familiar to software developers and also providing tool support via an integrated modeling and verification environment [1]. A design principle behind Rebeca is to enable domain-specific extensions of the core language [30]. Examples of such extensions has been introduced in various domains such as probabilistic systems [33], real-time systems [25], and software product lines [26].

In Rebeca, actors are the units of computation, called rebecs (short for reactive objects) which are instances of the defined *reactive classes* in the model. Rebecs communicate with other rebecs only through message-passing which is fair and asynchronous. A rebec can send messages only to its *known rebecs* mentioned in its definition and also to itself using "self" keyword. The local state of a rebec is represented by its *state variables* as well as the contents of its message queue. The *message servers*, which indicate how received messages must be processed, are also other parts of a rebec definition. Each rebec has at least one message server called "initial" which acts as a constructor in object-oriented language and is responsible for initialization tasks, and it is always put in every rebec's queue initially.

A rebec is *enabled* if and only if there is at least one message in its queue. The computation takes place by removing a message from the head of the queue and executing its corresponding message server atomically, after which the rebec proceeds to process the next message in the queue (if exists). Processing a message may have the following consequences:

- the value of the state variables of the executing rebec may be modified,
- new rebecs may be created,
- some messages may be sent to other rebecs or the executing rebec itself.

Besides the definition of the reactive classes, the *main* part of a Rebeca model specifies the instances of the reactive classes initially created along with their known-rebecs. The parameters of initial message server, if there is any, will also be specified.

As an example, Fig.1 illustrates a simple leader election algorithm modeled in Rebeca, aiming to select a node with the highest id as the leader. The nodes are organized in a (directed) ring. Each node sends its id to its neighbor and upon receiving a message compares the received id with its own id. If it is greater than its own id, it passes the number to its neighbor. So, when a number passes through the ring and is received by the node which its id is equal to the received id, it means that node has the greatest id and will be elected as the leader.

2.2 Counter Abstraction

When analyzing complex systems, their state space is prone to grow exponentially in space, known as the state space explosion problem, which is common in the realm of model checking. Counter abstraction is one of the proposed approaches to overcome this difficulty [24,3]. Its idea is to record the global state of a system as a vector of counters, one per local state, tracking how many of the n components currently reside in that local state. In our work, "components" refer to actors in the system. Let n and m be the number of components and local states respectively. This technique turns the n-component model of a size exponential in n, i.e., m^n, into one of a size polynomial in n, i.e., $\binom{n+m-1}{m}$.

Counter abstraction can be seen as a form of symmetry reduction [10]. Two global states S and S' are identical up to permutation if for every local state

```
 1 │ reactiveclass Node                  22 │        if (num == myInt)
 2 │ {                                   23 │        {
 3 │     knownrebecs                     24 │            isLeader = true;
 4 │     {                               25 │            self.isLeader();
 5 │         Node neighbour;             26 │        }
 6 │     }                               27 │    }
 7 │     statevars                       28 │    msgsrv isLeader()
 8 │     {                               29 │    {
 9 │         boolean isLeader;           30 │        // elected as the
10 │         int myInt;                          leader,
11 │     }                               31 │        // continue the
12 │     msgsrv initial(int num)                    computation
13 │     {                               32 │    }
14 │         isLeader = false;           33 │ }
15 │         myInt = num;
16 │         neighbour.receiveInt(myInt) 35 │ main
17 │     }                               36 │ {
18 │     msgsrv receiveInt(int num)      37 │    Node node0(node1):(1);
19 │     {                               38 │    Node node1(node2):(2);
20 │         if (num > myInt)            39 │    Node node2(node0):(3);
21 │             neighbour.receiveInt(num); 40 │ }
```

Fig. 1. Simple leader election algorithm: an example of a Rebeca model

s, the same number of components reside in s is the same in the two states S and S', only the order of elements change through permutation. For example, consider a system which consists of 3 components each with only one variable v_i of type of Boolean. The global states of (T, T, F), (F, T, T) and (T, F, T) are equivalent and can be represented as $(2T, F)$.

3   Broadcasting Rebeca

In this section, we present a modeling language based on Rebeca, by replacing the unicast communication mechanism by broadcast. We name the language *bRebeca* and will describe its syntax and formal semantics in the following subsections.

3.1   Syntax

In bRebeca, rebecs communicate with each other only through broadcasting: the sent message will be received by all rebecs of the model (as specified in the main part). After taking a message from its bag, the receiving rebec simply discards the message if no corresponding message server is defined in its reactive class. Since every message will be received by all existing rebecs, unlike Rebeca, there is no need for declaring the known rebecs in the reactive class definitions. Furthermore, there is no need to specify the receiver of a message in a send statement. Every **initial** message server at least have one parameter, named

starter. The value of **starter** is only true for the rebec which initiates the algorithm by broadcasting the first message.

The grammar of bRebeca is presented in Fig. 2.

$$
\begin{aligned}
\text{Model} &::= \text{ReactiveClass}^+ \text{ Main} \\
\text{Main} &::= \textsf{main} \ \{\text{RebecDecl}^+ \ \} \\
\text{ReactiveClass} &::= \textsf{reactiveclass } C \ \{ \text{ StateVars MsgServer}^* \ \} \\
\text{StateVars} &::= \textsf{statevars } \{ \text{ VarDecl}^* \ \} \\
\text{MsgServer} &::= \textsf{msgsrv } M(< T \ V >^*) \ \{ \text{ Statement}^* \ \} \\
\text{VarDecl} &::= T \ V; \\
\text{Statement} &::= \text{Assign} \mid \text{Broadcast} \mid \text{Conditional} \\
\text{Assign} &::= V = Expr; \\
\text{Broadcast} &::= M(< V >^*); \\
\text{Conditional} &::= \textsf{if } (Expr)\{ \text{ Statement}^* \ \} \textsf{ else } \{ \text{ Statement}^* \ \} \\
\text{RebecDecl} &::= C \ R(< V >^*);
\end{aligned}
$$

Fig. 2. bRebeca language syntax: Angle brackets $(< \ >)$ are used as metaparentheses. Superscript ? denotes that preceding part is optional, superscript + is used for more than once repetition, and * indicates the zero or more times repetition. The symbols C, T, M, and V denote class, type, method and variable names respectively. The symbol E denotes an expression, which can be an arithmetic or Boolean expression.

3.2 Semantics

The formal semantics of bRebeca is expressed as a labeled transition system (LTS), defined by the quadruple $\langle S, \rightarrow, L, s_0 \rangle$, where S is a set of states, $\rightarrow$ a set of transitions between states, L a set of labels, and s_0 the initial state.

Let I denote the set of all existing rebec identifiers, ranged over $1..n$, V a set of all possible values for the state variables, and M the set of all message servers identifiers in the model. All rebecs of the model which execute concurrently form a closed model $R = \|_{i \in I} r_i$. Each rebec with identifier $i \in I$, is described by a tuple $r_i = \langle V_i, M_i \rangle$, where V_i is the set of its state variables and M_i the set of messages it can respond to. As said earlier, a rebec in bRebeca holds its received messages in an unordered bag (unlike Rebeca, in which maintains such messages in a FIFO queue).

Definition 1. *(Local State) The local state of a rebec r_i is an element of $S_i = Val_i \times Bag_i$, where Val_i is the set of all valuations for the state variables of r_i (functions from V_i into V), and Bag_i is the set of all possible bags of messages to rebec r_i.*

Definition 2. *(Global State) A global state S is defined as the combination of all local states of rebecs in the model:*

$$S = \prod_{i \in I} S_i$$

An initial state s_0 consists of all rebecs initial state, where all rebecs have executed their initial messages. In fact, an initial message server can be seen as a constructor in object-oriented languages.

To formally define the transitions between the states, we assume there are two sets of auxilary functions defined as follows:

- $Update_i(v_i, m) : V_i \times M_i \to V_i$ receives a valuation v_i for the state variables of r_i and a message m, and returns the updated valuation for the state variables of r_i. This function abstracts the effect of processing m by r_i on its state variables.
- $Sent_i(m) : M_i \to M$ specifies the set of messages broadcasted by r_i as a result of processing message m.

To keep our semantic description simple, we do not give the details of the above two functions, since the semantics of control statements and expressions are the same as those in Rebeca. We also ignore the parameters in the messages. For a detailed semantic description, the reader may refer to [31].

Definition 3. *(Transition Relation) Let L denote to the set of all messages which can be passed between rebecs in the model R, $L = \bigcup_{i \in I} M_i$. Also assume $s = \langle s_1, s_2, \ldots, s_n \rangle$ and $s' = \langle s'_1, s'_2, \ldots, s'_n \rangle$ be two states in S such that $s_i = \langle v_i, b_i \rangle$ and $s'_i = \langle v'_i, b'_i \rangle$. The transition relation $\to \subseteq S \times L \times S$ is defined such that $(s, m, s') \in \to$ (written as $s \xrightarrow{l} s'$) if and only if*

$$\exists i \in I \cdot m \in b_i \wedge$$
$$v'_i = Update_i(v_i, m) \wedge$$
$$b'_i = b_i \cup Sent_i(m) - \{m\} \wedge$$
$$(\forall j \in I, j \neq i \cdot v'_j = v_j \wedge b'_j = b_j \cup Sent_i(m)).$$

Note that in the definition above, the operators $\cup$ and $-$ are assumed to be applied to message bags, which are multi-sets. In other words, if m is already in b, $\{m\} \cup b$ adds another copy of m to b, and $b - \{m\}$ removes one instance of m from b.

4   Implementing Counter Abstraction

To apply the counter abstraction technique on bRebeca, we consider each global state as a vector of counters, one per each distinct local state, and keep track of how many rebecs have that local state: the same state variable values and bag.

The reduction takes place on-the-fly while constructing the state space. Whenever a new global state is reached, we create a temporary global state by comparing the local states and count how many are equal. Then the temporary global state is compared with existing temporary global states and if it is a new state, then it would be added to the set of the reached states. Fig. 3 shows an example of applying counter abstraction on a global state. The global state consists of three rebecs with only one state variable i and one update message The local states, i.e. the state variables and bags of rebecs r1 and r2 are equal and they can be considered the same while ignoring their identities.

Fig. 3. Example of applying counter abstraction on a global state

To implement the state space builder, we follow a model-driven approach implemented in C#. A reusable layer of abstract classes are defined to provide the basic entities and services needed to generate the state space, such as *State* and *Message*. Also, the basic mechanism of generating the state space using a Depth-First Search (DFS) is implemented in this layer (named *StateSpaceBuilder*). The DFS is implemented in a multi-threaded way to exploit multi-core processing power. This class takes the responsibility of handling nondeterminism in message scheduling: in each state, a separate task is created for scheduling each *enabled* rebec with distinct local state where rebecs are fairly run by keeping track of rebecs in each state.

The proposed model supports only broadcast communications, as rebecs have no ids to be distinguished from each other it would be impossible to add unicast to such a model. Though with some minor modifications of current model, as follows, very limited unicast would be feasible. A node can unicast a message only to itself or the sender of prepossessing message, otherwise it will jeopardize the soundness of counter abstraction technique by considering two states equal while they are not. In the other words, only relative addresses (i.e. the sender of a message) are allowed as ids have no absolute meaning.

We need to keep somehow the ids of rebecs instead of just counters in some level of state space exploration. While constructing the state space, by processing messages, we keep the ids of those rebecs together in a group which have the same local state, regardless of their ids. The resulting global state is called middle global state. To store reachable states, the final global states are computed from middle global states by counting the number of ids in each group.

To make unicast unconditionally possible we need to consider the permutation of ids and use the known-rebec concept like symmetry reduction[14].

For processing a bRebeca model, we use a bRebeca parser to generate a C# code from the source model. Each reactive class is translated into two basic classes: one subclass of *State* to represent the local states of the rebecs of that class, and another class which holds the implementation of the message servers. A translated message server, when executed, generates all possible "next states". Note that due to the existence of "non-deterministic assignment" in Rebeca, there may be more than one next state.

When generating a subclass of *State* for a rebec, the code generator is responsible for implementing an abstract *hash function*, which is used to compare the local states. This is essential to implement an efficient comparison for global states which is encoded as a mapping from (the polymorphic) State into integers, implemented by a Dictionary class in C#.

5   Case Studies

To illustrate the applicability of the proposed modeling language, two algorithms are modeled and the amount of reduction in state space size is shown.

5.1   Max-algorithm

Consider a network where every node stores an integer value and they are going to find the maximum value in the network in a distributed manner. The bRebeca code for the model is illustrated in Fig.4 for a simple network of three nodes.

The nodes in the network are modeled by the reactive class Node with two state variables my_i to store the node value and done which indicates whether the node has already sent its value or there is no need to send it, based on the values of the other nodes received so far. The goal is to find the maximum value of my_i among nodes. One node initiates the algorithm by broadcasting its value to other nodes. Upon receiving a value from others, each node compares its value with the received one. If its value is less than the received one, it updates its value to the received one and waits for receiving the next messages while giving up on sending by setting its done to true. Otherwise, it broadcasts its value to other rebecs, if it has not already and then sets its done to true. The algorithm terminates when there is no further message to be processed. It means that everyone has either transmitted its value or given up. In this case, all state variables have been updated to the maximum value. This algorithm is referred to as "Max-Algorithm" [17].

For a network consists of three rebecs, if we start with rebec rebec2 which has the maximum value (3), each node gives up transmitting after receiving the maximum and procedure has only one step. The reduced state space obtained from the execution of max-algorithm in this network is shown in Fig.5.

5.2   Leader Election

One way of electing leader in a distributed network is through flipping a coin [11]. The algorithm consists of several rounds. In each round, all competitors, nodes

```
 1 | reactiveclass Node                19 |    msgsrv send(int i)
 2 | {                                 20 |    {
 3 |    statevars                      21 |       if (i < my_i) {
 4 |    {                              22 |          if (!done) {
 5 |       int my_i;                   23 |             done = true;
 6 |       boolean done;               24 |             send(my_i);
 7 |    }                              25 |          }
                                      26 |       } else {
 9 |    msgsrv initial(int j,          27 |          my_i = i;
   |          boolean starter)         28 |          done = true;
10 |    {                              29 |       }
11 |       my_i = j;                   30 |    }
12 |       if(starter) {               31 | }
13 |          done = true;             32 | main
14 |          send(my_i);              33 | {
15 |       } else                      34 |       Node rebec0(1,false);
16 |          done = false;            35 |       Node rebec1(2,false);
17 |    }                              36 |       Node rebec2(3,true);
                                      37 | }
```

Fig. 4. Max-algorithm with 3 nodes

with coin value of true, participate by flipping their coin and broadcasting the observed results to the others. A round is completed whenever all competitors have flipped their coin and received other nodes' observation. At the end of each round:

- If there is only one node with coin value of true, then it is elected as the leader.
- If there is no node with coin value of true, it means that the round should be repeated. So all coin values of the previous competitors will be set to true.
- If the number of nodes with coin value of true is more than one, nodes with coin value of true will participate in the next round and flip the coin again.

Fig. 6 shows one execution scenario of the leader election algorithm in a network of five nodes.

The bRebeca code for this algorithm is represented in Fig. 7. There are two reactive classes, named Node and Barrier, in the model. We use Barrier to synchronize nodes before starting a new round, in order to prevent mixing up the messages between different rounds. The Barrier is to make sure that the current round is completed, and all nodes are aware of each other observation, and ready to start a new round. Reactive class Barrier has only one state variable which counts the number of nodes has completed their round. Whenever all nodes complete their round, it would broadcast start_next_round to all nodes to start a new round.

In reactive class Node, two state variables head and tail are used to store the number of heads and tails have been observed in the current round. The state variable comp indicates whether the node was a competitor in the previous

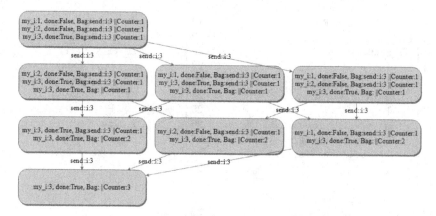

Fig. 5. max-algorithm state space

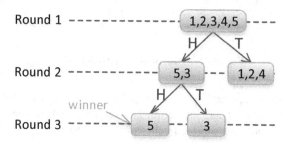

Fig. 6. An execution scenario of leader election algorithm with five nodes

round. Therefore if the number of competitors in the current round is equal to zero, no head observed in the previous round, we would be able to repeat the round by restoring the previous competitors (lines 32-35). In every round if currently there is more than one competitor and node is one them, its coin value is true, it flips its coin and after updating its counters accordingly broadcasts the result to the other nodes (lines 31-45). The number of previous and current competitors also need to be saved. Each node needs to keep the number of current competitors to decide when it has completed its round so it can inform the `Barrier` (line 46). The number of previous competitors is needed to specify when we can clean our counters and move to the next round (lines 25-30). Note that as the delivery order of messages is not guaranteed, a node may process its `rec_coin` message before `start_next_round` message. Hence, both message servers must check whether the counter variables, such as `head` and `tail`, belong to the previous round and need to be reset before using them.

```
 1 | reactiveclass Node {
 2 |     statevars {
 3 |         int head;
 4 |         boolean my_coin;
 5 |         int tail;
 6 |         int current_comp;
 7 |         int prev_comp;
 8 |         boolean comp;
 9 |         boolean is_leader;
10 |     }
   |
12 |     msgsrv initial(boolean starter) {
13 |         if(starter==true)
14 |             start_next_round();
15 |         my_coin=true;
16 |         head=3;
17 |         tail=0;
18 |         current_comp=3;
19 |         prev_comp=3;
20 |         comp=true;
21 |         is_leader=false;
22 |     }
   |
24 |     msgsrv start_next_round() {
25 |         if (head+tail == prev_comp) {
26 |             prev_comp = current_comp;
27 |             current_comp = head;
28 |             head = 0;
29 |             tail = 0;
30 |         }
31 |         if (current_comp != 1 &&
   |                 comp) {
32 |             if (current_comp == 0) {
33 |                 my_coin = true;
34 |                 current_comp =
   |                     prev_comp;
35 |             }
36 |             if (my_coin) {
37 |                 int ch=?(0,1);
38 |                 if (ch == 0) {
39 |                     my_coin = false;
40 |                     tail = tail+1;
41 |                 } else {
42 |                     my_coin=true;
43 |                     head=head+1;
44 |                 }
45 |                 rec_coin(my_coin);
46 |                 if (head+tail ==
   |                         current_comp)
```

```
47 |                     rec_barrier();
48 |             } else
49 |                 comp=false;
50 |         }
51 |         if (my_coin && current_comp
   |                 == 1)
52 |             is_leader = true;
53 |     }
   |
55 |     msgsrv rec_coin(boolean c) {
56 |         if (head + tail == prev_comp)
   |         {
57 |             prev_comp = current_comp;
58 |             current_comp = head;
59 |             head = 0;
60 |             tail = 0;
61 |         }
62 |         if (c)
63 |             head = head+1;
64 |         else
65 |             tail=tail+1;
66 |         if(head+tail == current_comp)
67 |             rec_barrier();
68 |     }
69 | }
   |
71 | reactiveclass Barrier {
72 |     statevars {
73 |         int barrier;
74 |     }
   |
76 |     msgsrv initial(boolean starter) {
77 |         barrier=0;
78 |     }
   |
80 |     msgsrv rec_barrier() {
81 |         barrier = barrier + 1;
82 |         if (barrier == 3) {
83 |             start_next_round();
84 |             barrier=0;
85 |         }
86 |     }
87 | }
88 | main {
89 |     Node rebec0(true);
90 |     Node rebec1(false);
91 |     Node rebec2(false);
92 |     Barrier bar(false);
93 | }
```

Fig. 7. Leader election algorithm

Table 1 compares the number of states resulted with and without applying counter abstraction. Note that with increasing the number of nodes, the opportunity of collapsing nodes together grows.

6   Related Work

In order to avoid state space explosion, different approaches have been proposed such as symbolic model checking [19], symmetry reduction [6], partial order reduction [12] and counter abstraction [3].

Table 1. Comparing the state spaces size with and without applying counter abstraction

	No. of nodes	No. of states	No. of states with reduction
Max-Algorithm	3	64	53
	4	3216	1675
	5	719,189	185,381
Leader election	3	3792	752
	4	308,553	15,905
	5	> 1,200,000	521,679

Counter abstraction has been studied in several other works (e.g., in [10,3,24]). The proposed approach in [24] aims to abstract an unbounded parameterized system into a finite-state system and then verify various liveness properties efficiently. The authors in [24] use limited abstracted variables to count for each local state of a process how many processes currently reside in. However, counters were saturated at a static value of c, meaning that c or more processes are at local state s. In [3], counter abstraction is used to achieve efficiency in BDD-based symbolic state space exploration of concurrent Boolean programs while unlike [24] it makes use of exact counters where in a global state only non-zero counters are stored. The idea of counting have also been used in [15] to record the local states of a biological system, in which each local state is represented as a vector of counters, each element denotes to the corresponding number of species.

In this paper counters are unbounded, similar to [3], to show the exact number of Rebecs having the specific local state, and abstracted local states are not limited either.

As mentioned before, there are several techniques for reducing the state space such as symmetry reduction which aims to reduce the state space by partitioning the state space into equivalence classes which are represented by one state[6] as their representative. Since finding the unique representative of state while exploring the state space, known as *constructive orbit problem*, is NP-Hard [6], some heuristics have been proposed to avoid this problem, which may result in multiple representatives. In [14], a polynomial-time heuristic solution is proposed to exploit symmetry in Rebeca, computing a representative state using the on-the-fly approach takes $O(n^4)$ in the worst-case. The complexity of the proposed algorithm is due to the role of "known rebecs" that should be preserved during the permutation. Since in the broadcast environment there is no notion of "known rebecs" and the system is fully symmetric, we can skip paying such a price by applying counter abstraction which is suitable for such systems. The complexity of finding the equivalent of each state is linear in the number of states.

7 Conclusion

In this paper we extended the syntax and semantics of Rebeca to support broadcast efficiently. On one hand, it makes modeling easier, by replacing a set of unicast statements by a single broadcast statement, there is no need to define each rebec as a known-rebec to every other rebec to make the broadcast possible. On the other hand, as all rebecs instantiated from one reactive class are identical, their indexes are irrelevant and can be ignored while constructing the state space. This property makes counter abstraction applicable which is more efficient in fully symmetry systems as discussed in section 6.

The broadcasting actors model provides a suitable framework to model wireless sensor (WSNs) and mobile ad hoc networks (MANETs). In these networks, broadcast is restricted by locality of nodes, meaning that a node receives a message if it is located close enough to a sender, so called connected. Connectivity of nodes defines the topology concept which should be modeled as a part of semantics. Due to energy consumption of nodes and their mobility, the underlying topology changes arbitrary. Therefore, to address local broadcast and topology changes, bRebeca can be extended at the semantics level to allow verification of WSNs and MANETs. To this aim, we pair the global state with the topology of networks and generate the state space for permutations of a topology. We merge states with identical structures of topology while applying counting abstraction which makes automatic verification of such networks susceptible.

References

1. Rebeca formal modeling language,
   http://www.rebeca-lang.org/wiki/pmwiki.php/Tools/Afra
2. Agha, G.A.: ACTORS - a model of concurrent computation in distributed systems. MIT Press series in artificial intelligence. MIT Press (1990)
3. Basler, G., Mazzucchi, M., Wahl, T., Kroening, D.: Symbolic counter abstraction for concurrent software. In: Bouajjani, A., Maler, O. (eds.) CAV 2009. LNCS, vol. 5643, pp. 64–78. Springer, Heidelberg (2009)
4. Bracha, G., Toueg, S.: Asynchronous consensus and broadcast protocols. Journal of the ACM 32(4), 824–840 (1985)
5. Cachin, C., Kursawe, K., Petzold, F., Shoup, V.: Secure and efficient asynchronous broadcast protocols. In: Kilian, J. (ed.) CRYPTO 2001. LNCS, vol. 2139, pp. 524–541. Springer, Heidelberg (2001)
6. Clarke, E.M., Emerson, E.A., Jha, S., Sistla, A.P.: Symmetry reductions in model checking. In: Computer Aided Verification, pp. 147–158. Springer (1998)
7. Correia, M., Veronese, G.S., Neves, N.F., Veríssimo, P.: Byzantine consensus in asynchronous message-passing systems: a survey. IJCCBS 2(2), 141–161 (2011)
8. Cui, T., Chen, L., Ho, T.: Distributed optimization in wireless networks using broadcast advantage. In: Decision and Control, pp. 5839–5844. IEEE (2007)
9. Dechter, R., Kleinrock, L.: Broadcast communications and distributed algorithms. Trans. Computers 35(3), 210–219 (1986)

10. Emerson, E.A., Trefler, R.J.: From asymmetry to full symmetry: New techniques for symmetry reduction in model checking. In: Pierre, L., Kropf, T. (eds.) CHARME 1999. LNCS, vol. 1703, pp. 142–157. Springer, Heidelberg (1999)
11. Fill, J.A., Mahmoud, H.M., Szpankowski, W.: On the distribution for the duration of a randomized leader election algorithm. Ann. Appl. Probab., 1260–1283 (1996)
12. Godefroid, P.: Partial-Order Methods for the Verification of Concurrent Systems. LNCS, vol. 1032. Springer (1996)
13. Hewitt, C.: Viewing control structures as patterns of passing messages. Artif. Intell. 8(3), 323–364 (1977)
14. Jaghoori, M.M., Sirjani, M., Mousavi, M.R., Khamespanah, E., Movaghar, A.: Symmetry and partial order reduction techniques in model checking Rebeca. Acta Informatica 47(1), 33–66 (2010)
15. Katoen, J.: Model checking: One can do much more than you think? In: Fundamentals of Software Engineering, pp. 1–14. Springer (2011)
16. Larrea, M., Raynal, M., Arriola, I.S., Cortiñas, R.: Specifying and implementing an eventual leader service for dynamic systems. IJWGS 8(3), 204–224 (2012)
17. Levitan, S.P., Foster, C.C.: Finding an extremum in a network. In: 9th International Symposium on Computer Architecture, pp. 321–325. ACM (1982)
18. Martel, C.U.: Maximum finding on a multiple access broadcast network. Inf. Process. Lett. 52(1), 7–15 (1994)
19. McMillan, K.L.: Symbolic model checking. Kluwer (1993)
20. Melliar-Smith, P.M., Moser, L.E., Agrawala, V.: Broadcast protocols for distributed systems. Trans. Parallel Distrib. Syst. 1(1), 17–25 (1990)
21. Mostéfaoui, A., Raynal, M., Travers, C.: Crash-resilient time-free eventual leadership. In: 23rd International Symposium on Reliable Distributed Systems, pp. 208–217. IEEE Computer Society (2004)
22. Okun, M., Barak, A.: Efficient algorithms for anonymous byzantine agreement. Theory Comput. Syst. 42(2), 222–238 (2008)
23. Ostrovsky, R., Rajagopalan, S., Vazirani, U.V.: Simple and efficient leader election in the full information model. In: Proceedings of the Twenty-Sixth Annual ACM Symposium on Theory of Computing, pp. 234–242. ACM (1994)
24. Pnueli, A., Xu, J., Zuck, L.D.: Liveness with (0, 1, infty)-Counter Abstraction. In: Brinksma, E., Larsen, K.G. (eds.) CAV 2002. LNCS, vol. 2404, pp. 107–122. Springer, Heidelberg (2002)
25. Reynisson, A.H., Sirjani, M., Aceto, L., Cimini, M., Jafari, A., Ingólfsdóttir, A., Sigurdarson, S.H.: Modelling and simulation of asynchronous real-time systems using Timed Rebeca. Sci. Comput. Program. 89, 41–68 (2014)
26. Sabouri, H., Khosravi, R.: Delta modeling and model checking of product families. In: Arbab, F., Sirjani, M. (eds.) FSEN 2013. LNCS, vol. 8161, pp. 51–65. Springer, Heidelberg (2013)
27. Shiau, S., Yang, C.: A fast maximum finding algorithm on broadcast communication. In: Li, M., Du, D.-Z. (eds.) COCOON 1995. LNCS, vol. 959, pp. 472–481. Springer, Heidelberg (1995)
28. Shiau, S., Yang, C.: A fast sorting algorithm and its generalization on broadcast communications. In: Du, D.-Z., Eades, P., Sharma, A.K., Lin, X., Estivill-Castro, V. (eds.) COCOON 2000. LNCS, vol. 1858, pp. 252–261. Springer, Heidelberg (2000)

29. Sirjani, M., de Boer, F.S., Movaghar, A., Shali, A.: Extended Rebeca: A component-based actor language with synchronous message passing. In: Fifth International Conference on Application of Concurrency to System Design, pp. 212–221. IEEE Computer Society (2005)

30. Sirjani, M., Jaghoori, M.M.: Ten years of analyzing actors: Rebeca experience. In: Agha, G., Danvy, O., Meseguer, J. (eds.) Formal Modeling: Actors, Open Systems, Biological Systems. LNCS, vol. 7000, pp. 20–56. Springer, Heidelberg (2011)

31. Sirjani, M., Movaghar, A., Shali, A., de Boer, F.S.: Modeling and verification of reactive systems using Rebeca. Fundam. Inform. 63(4), 385–410 (2004)

32. Sirjani, M., Shali, A., Jaghoori, M.M., Iravanchi, H., Movaghar, A.: A front-end tool for automated abstraction and modular verification of actor-based models. In: 4th International Conference on Application of Concurrency to System Design, pp. 145–150. IEEE Computer Society (2004)

33. Varshosaz, M., Khosravi, R.: Modeling and verification of probabilistic actor systems using pRebeca. In: Aoki, T., Taguchi, K. (eds.) ICFEM 2012. LNCS, vol. 7635, pp. 135–150. Springer, Heidelberg (2012)

A Theory of Integrating Tamper Evidence with Stabilization[*,**]

Reza Hajisheykhi[1], Ali Ebnenasir[2], and Sandeep S. Kulkarni[1]

[1] Computer Science and Engineering Department,
Michigan State University,
East Lansing, Michigan 48824, USA
{hajishey,sandeep}@cse.msu.edu
[2] Department of Computer Science,
Michigan Technological University,
Houghton, Michigan 49931, USA
aebnenas@mtu.edu

Abstract. We propose the notion of tamper-evident stabilization –that combines stabilization with the concept of tamper evidence– for computing systems. On the first glance, these notions are contradictory; stabilization requires that eventually the system functionality is fully restored whereas tamper evidence requires that the system functionality is permanently degraded in the event of tampering. Tamper-evident stabilization captures the intuition that the system will tolerate perturbation upto a limit. In the event that it is perturbed beyond that limit, it will exhibit permanent evidence of tampering, where it may provide reduced (possibly none) functionality. We compare tamper-evident stabilization with (conventional) stabilization and with active stabilization and propose an approach to verify tamper-evident stabilizing programs in polynomial time. We demonstrate tamper-evident stabilization with two examples and argue how approaches for designing stabilization can be used to design tamper-evident stabilization. We also study issues of composition in tamper-evident stabilization. Finally, we point out how tamper-evident stabilization can effectively be used to provide tradeoff between fault-prevention and fault tolerance.

Keywords: Self-stabilization, reactive systems, adversary, formal methods.

1 Introduction

In this paper, we introduce the notion of tamper-evident stabilizing systems, and study these systems in the context of composition, verification, and synthesis. The notion of tamper-evident stabilizing systems is motivated by the need for

---

[*] A brief announcement of this paper appears in SSS 2014.
[**] This work is supported by NSF CCF-1116546, NSF CNS 1329807, and NSF CNS 1318678.

© IFIP International Federation for Information Processing 2015
M. Dastani and M.Sirjani (Eds.): FSEN 2015, LNCS 9392, pp. 84–99, 2015.
DOI: 10.1007/978-3-319-24644-4_6

tamper-resistant systems that also stabilize. A tamper-resistant system ensures that an effort to tamper with the system makes the system less useful/inoperable (e.g., by zeroing out sensitive data in a chip or voiding the warranty). The notion of tamper resistance is contradictory to the notion of stabilization in that the notion of stabilization requires that in spite of any possible tampering the system inherently acquires its usefulness eventually.

Intuitively, the notion of tamper-evident stabilization is based on the observation that all tamper-resistant systems tolerate some level of tampering without making the system less useful/inoperable. For example, a tamper-resistant chip may have a circuitry that does some rudimentary checks on the input and discards the input if the check fails. A communication protocol may use CRC to ensure that most random bit-flips in the message are tolerated without affecting the system. However, if the tampering is beyond acceptable level then they become less useful/inoperable. Based on this intuition, we observe that a tamper-evident stabilizing system will recover to its legitimate state if its perturbation is within an acceptable limit. However, if it is perturbed outside this boundary, it will make itself inoperable. Moreover, when the system enters the mode of making itself inoperable, it is necessary that it cannot be prevented.

Thus, if the system is outside its normal legitimate states, it is in one of two modes: *recovery mode*, where it is trying to restore itself to a legitimate state, or *tamper-evident mode*, where it is trying to make itself inoperable. The recovery mode is similar to the typical stabilizing systems in that the recovery should be guaranteed after external perturbations stop. However, in the tamper-evident mode, it is essential that the system makes itself inoperable even if outside perturbations continue.

To realize the last requirement, we need to make certain assumptions about what external perturbations can be performed during tamper-evident mode. For example, if these perturbations could restore the system to a legitimate state then designing tamper-evident stabilizing systems is impossible. Hence, we view the system execution to consist of (1) program executions (in the absence of fault and adversary); (2) program executions in the presence of faults; and (3) program execution in the presence of *adversary*.

Faults are random events that perturb the system randomly and rarely. By contrast, the adversary is *actively* preventing the system from making itself inoperable. However, unlike faults, the adversary may not be able to perturb the system to an arbitrary state. Also, unlike faults, adversary may continue to execute forever. Even if the adversary executes forever, it is necessary that system actions have some fairness during execution. Hence, we assume that the system can make some number (in our formal definitions, we have this as strictly greater than 1) of steps between two steps of the adversary.

The contributions of the paper are as follows. We

- formally define the notion of tamper-evident stabilization;
- compare the notion of tamper-evident stabilization with (conventional) stabilization and active stabilization, where a system stabilizes in spite of the interference of an adversary [7];

- explain the cost of automated verification of tamper-evident stabilization;
- present some theorems about composing tamper-evident stabilizing systems;
- identify how methods for designing stabilizing programs can be used in designing tamper-evident stabilizing systems. We also identify potential obstacles in using those methods, and
- identify potential applications of tamper-evident stabilization and illustrate it with two examples.

Organization. The rest of the paper is organized as follows: In Section 2, we present the preliminary concepts on stabilization. We introduce the notion of tamper-evident stabilization, illustrate it with two examples, and compare it with (conventional) stabilization and active stabilization in Section 3. Section 4 represents an algorithm for automatic verification of tamper-evident stabilizing programs. We evaluate the composition of tamper-evident stabilizing systems in Section 5 and discuss a design methodology for tamper-evident stabilizing programs in Section 6. The relationship between tamper-evident stabilization and other stabilizing techniques is discussed in Section 7, and finally, Section 8 concludes our paper.

2   Preliminaries

Our program modeling utilizes standard approach for defining interleaving programs, stabilization [3, 11, 12], and active stabilization [7]. A program includes a finite set of variables with finite (or any finite abstraction of an infinite state system) domain. It also includes *guarded commands* (a.k.a. *actions*) [11] that update those program variables atomically. Since these internal variables are not needed in the definitions involved in this section, we describe a program in terms of its state space S_p, and its transitions $\delta_p \subseteq S_p \times S_p$, where S_p is obtained by assigning each variable in p a value from its domain.

Definition 1 (Program). *A program p is of the form $\langle S_p, \delta_p \rangle$ where S_p is the state space of program p and $\delta_p \subseteq S_p \times S_p$.*

Definition 2 (State Predicate). *A state predicate of p is any subset of S_p.*

Definition 3 (Computation). *Let p be a program with state space S_p and transitions δ_p. We say that a sequence $\langle s_0, s_1, s_2, ... \rangle$ is a computation iff*

- $\forall j \geq 0 :: (s_j, s_{j+1}) \in \delta_p$

Definition 4 (Closure). *A state predicate S of $p = \langle S_p, \delta_p \rangle$ is closed in p iff $\forall s_0, s_1 \in S_p :: (s_0 \in S \wedge (s_0, s_1) \in \delta_p) \Rightarrow (s_1 \in S)$.*

Definition 5 (Invariant). *A state predicate S is an invariant of p iff S is closed in p.*

Remark 1. Normally, the definition of invariant (legitimate states) also includes a requirement that computations of p that start from an invariant state are correct with respect to its specification. The theory of tamper-evident stabilization is independent of the behaviors of the program inside legitimate states. Instead, it only focuses on the behavior of p outside its legitimate states. We have defined the invariant in terms of the closure property alone since it is the only relevant property in the definitions/theorems/examples in this paper.

Definition 6 (Convergence). *Let p be a program with state space S_p and transitions δ_p. Let S and T be state predicates of p. We say that T converges to S in p iff*

- $S \subseteq T$,
- S *is closed in p,*
- T *is closed in p, and*
- *For any computation $\sigma = \langle s_0, s_1, s_2, ... \rangle$ of p if $s_0 \in T$ then there exists l such that $s_l \in S$.*

Definition 7 (Stabilization). *Let p be a program with state space S_p and transitions δ_p. We say that program p is* stabilizing *for invariant S iff S_p converges to S in p.*

Using the approach in [7, 15], we define the adversary as follows and define the notion of tamper-evident stabilization with respect to the capabilities of the given adversary in Section 3.

Definition 8 (Adversary). *We define an adversary for program $p = \langle S_p, \delta_p \rangle$ to be a subset of $S_p \times S_p$.*

Next, we define a computation of the program, say p, in the presence of the adversary, say *adv*.

Definition 9 ($\langle p, adv, k \rangle$-computation). *Let p be a program with state space S_p and transitions δ_p. Let adv be an adversary for program p and k be an integer greater than 1. We say that a sequence $\langle s_0, s_1, s_2, ... \rangle$ is a $\langle p, adv, k \rangle$-computation iff*

- $\forall j \geq 0 :: s_j \in S_p$, *and*
- $\forall j \geq 0 :: (s_j, s_{j+1}) \in \delta_p \cup adv$, *and*
- $\forall j \geq 0 :: ((s_j, s_{j+1}) \notin \delta_p) \Rightarrow (\forall l \mid j < l < j + k :: (s_l, s_{l+1}) \in \delta_p)$

Observe that a $\langle p, adv, k \rangle$-computation guarantees that there are at least $k - 1$ program transitions/actions between any two adversary actions for $k > 1$. Moreover, the adversary is not required to execute in a $\langle p, adv, k \rangle$-computation.

Remark 2 (Fairness among program transitions). The above definition and definition 3 only consider fairness between program actions and adversary actions. If a program requires fairness among its actions to ensure stabilization, they can be strengthened accordingly. For reasons of space, this issue is outside the scope of this paper.

Definition 10 (Convergence in the presence of adversary). *Let p be a program with state space S_p and transitions δ_p. Let S and T be state predicates of p. Let adv be an adversary for p and let k be an integer greater than 1. We say that T $\langle adv, k \rangle$-converges to S in p in the presence of adversary adv iff*

- $S \subseteq T$,
- S *is closed in* $p \cup adv$,
- T *is closed in* $p \cup adv$, *and*
- *For any* $\langle p, adv, k \rangle$*-computation* $\sigma = \langle s_0, s_1, s_2, ... \rangle$ *if* $s_0 \in T$ *then there exists l such that $s_l \in S$.*

Definition 11 (Active stabilization). *Let p be a program with state space S_p and transitions δ_p. Let adv be an adversary for program p and k be an integer greater than 1. We say that program p is k-active stabilizing with adversary adv for invariant S iff S_p $\langle p, adv, k \rangle$-converges to S in p.*

3   Tamper-Evident Stabilization

This section defines the notion of tamper-evident stabilization, illustrates it in the context of two examples, and compares it with the notion of (conventional) stabilization and active stabilization.

3.1   The Definition of Tamper-Evident Stabilization

In this section, we define the notion of tamper-evident stabilization.

Definition 12 (Tamper-evident stabilization).   *Let p be a program with state space S_p and transitions δ_p. Let adv be an adversary for program p. And, let k be an integer greater than 1. We say that program p is k-tamper-evident stabilizing with adversary adv for invariants $\langle S1, S2 \rangle$ iff there exists a state predicate T of p such that*

- T *converges to $S1$ in p*
- $\neg T$ $\langle adv, k \rangle$*-converges to $S2$ in p.*

From the above definition (especially closure of T and $\neg T$), it follows that $S1$ and $S2$ must be disjoint (See Figure 1(a)). In addition, tamper-evident stabilization provides no guarantees about program behaviors if the adversary executes in T.

Remark 3. Observe that in the above definition k must be greater than 1, as $k=1$ allows the adversary to prevent the program from executing entirely. In terms of permitted values of k, $k = 2$ provides the maximum power to the adversary. Hence, in most cases, in this paper we will consider $k=2$. In this case, we will omit the value of k. In other words *tamper-evident stabilizing* is the same as *2-tamper-evident stabilizing.*

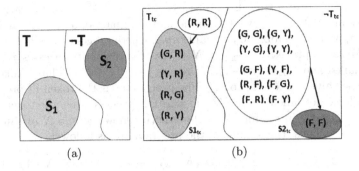

Fig. 1. (a) Structure of a tamper-evident stabilizing system, (b) Tamper-evident stabilizing traffic controller program

Remark 4. Based on the definition of convergence, in the above definition, $S1$ should be a subset of T. Given this constraint, if $S1 = T$ then it corresponds to a *pure tamper evident system*. If such a system is perturbed to a non-legitimate state then it is guaranteed to recover to $S2$ even in the presence of an adversary. And, if $T = S_p$, then it corresponds to a stabilizing program (cf. Theorem 3). Thus, tamper-evident stabilization captures a range of systems from the ones that are *pure tamper-evident* and that are *pure stabilizing*.

The notion of tamper-evident stabilization prescribes the behavior of the program from all possible states. In this respect, it is similar to the notion of stabilizing fault tolerance. In [3], authors introduce the notion of nonmasking fault tolerance; it only prescribes behaviors in a subset of states. We can extend the notion of tamper-evident stabilization in a similar manner. We do so by simply overloading the definition of tamper-evident stabilization.

Definition 13 (Tamper-evident stabilization in environment U). *Let p be a program with state space S_p and transitions δ_p. Let adv be an adversary for program p, and U be a state predicate. Moreover, let k be an integer greater than 1. We say that program p is k-tamper-evident stabilizing with adversary adv for invariants $\langle S1, S2 \rangle$ in environment U iff there exists a state predicate T such that*

- $S1, S2,$ and T are subsets of U,
- U is closed in $p \cup adv$,
- $U \Rightarrow$ $(T$ converges to $S1$ in $p)$,
- $U \Rightarrow$ $\neg T \langle adv, k \rangle$-converges to $S2$ in p.

Observe that if U equals *true* then the above definition is identical to that of Definition 12.

3.2 The Token Ring Program

This section describes the well-known token ring program [10] and then represent that this program is tamper-evident stabilizing. The program consists of N

processes arranged in a ring. Each process j, $0 \leq j \leq N-1$, has a variable $x.j$ with the domain $\{0, 1, \cdots, N-1\}$. To model the impact of adversary actions on a process j, we add an auxiliary variable $up.j$, where process j has failed iff $up.j$ is false. We say, a process j, $1 \leq j \leq N-1$, has the token iff processes j and $j-1$ have not failed and $x.j \neq x.(j-1)$. If process j, $1 \leq j \leq N-1$, has a token then it copies the value of $x.(j-1)$ to $x.j$. The process 0 has the token iff processes 0 and $N-1$ have not failed and $x.(N-1) = x.0$. If process 0 has the token then it increments its value in modulo N arithmetic (we show modulo N arithmetic by notation $+_N$). Thus, the actions of the program are as follows:

$$
\begin{aligned}
TR_0 :: \quad & up.0 \wedge up.(N-1) \wedge x.0 = x.(N-1) \quad \longrightarrow \quad x.0 := (x.(N-1) +_N 1) \\
TR_j :: \quad & up.j \wedge up.(j-1) \wedge x.j \neq x.(j-1) \quad \longrightarrow \quad x.j := x.(j-1);
\end{aligned}
$$

Adversary Action. The adversary can cause any process to fail. Hence, the adversary action can be represented as

$$
TR_{adv} :: up.j \quad \longrightarrow \quad up.j := false
$$

Tamper-evident Stabilization of the Program. To show that the token ring program TR is *tamper-evident stabilizing* in the presence of the adversary TR_{adv}, we define the predicate T_{tr} and invariants $S1_{tr}$ and $S2_{tr}$ as follows:

$$
\begin{aligned}
T_{tr} \ = \ & \forall j :: up.j \\
S1_{tr} = \ & T_{tr} \ \wedge \ (\forall j : 1 \leq j \leq N - 1 : (x.j = x.(j-1)) \vee (x.(j-1) = x.j +_N 1)) \\
& \wedge \ ((x.0 = x.(N-1)) \vee (x.0 = x.(N-1) +_N 1)) \\
S2_{tr} = \ & \neg T_{tr} \wedge \ (\forall j : 1 \leq j \leq N - 1 : (up.j \wedge up.(j-1)) \Rightarrow x.j = x.(j-1)) \\
& \wedge \ ((up.0 \wedge up.(N-1)) \Rightarrow (x.0 \neq x.(N-1)))
\end{aligned}
$$

Theorem 1. *The token ring program TR is tamper-evident stabilizing with adversary TR_{adv} for invariants $\langle S1_{tr}, S2_{tr} \rangle$.*

Proof. If T_{tr} is true then the program is essentially the same as the token ring program from [11] and, hence, it stabilizes to $S1_{tr}$. If T_{tr} is violated then the token cannot go past failed process(es). Hence, $S2_{tr}$ would eventually be satisfied. Note that for the second constraint, adversary action (that may fail a process) cannot prevent the program from reaching $S2_{tr}$.   □

3.3   Tamper-Evident Stabilizing Traffic Controller Program

This section describes another tamper-evident stabilizing program that illustrates a traffic light program that (1) recovers to normal operation from perturbations that do not cause the system to reach an unsafe state, and (2) permanently preserves the evidence of tampering if perturbations cause the system to reach an unsafe state. This example also illustrates why tamper-evident stabilization is desirable over (conventional) stabilization in some circumstances. Moreover, it can be used as a part of multiphase recovery [6] where a quick recovery is provided to safe states and complete recovery to legitimate states can be obtained later (or with human intervention).

Description of the Program. In this program, we have an intersection with two one-way roads [5]. Each road is associated with a signal that can be either green (G), yellow (Y), red (R), or flashing (F). As expected, in any normal state, at least one of the signals should be red to ensure that traffic accidents do not occur.

If such a system is perturbed by an adversary where an adversary can somehow affect the signal operation causing safety violations then it is crucial that such an occurrence is noted for potential investigation. (These adversary actions can be triggered with simple transient faults that reset clock variables. For simplicity, we omit the cause of such adversary actions and only consider their effects.) In this example, we consider the requirement that if both signals are simultaneously yellow or green then the system must reach a state where both signals are flashing to indicate a signal malfunction due to adversary.

Thus, this program consists of two variables sig_0 and sig_1. The program consists of five actions: The first two actions are responsible for normal operation where a signal changes from G to Y to R and back to G. The third action considers the case where the system is perturbed outside legitimate states (e.g., by transient faults) and it is desirable that the system recovers from that state. The fourth action considers the case where the adversary actions perturb the system beyond an acceptable level and, hence, it is necessary that the system enters the tamper-evident state. Thus, the program actions are as follows: (In this program, j is instantiated to be either 0 or 1, and k is instantiated to be $1 - j$.)

$$TC1_j :: (sig_j = G) \wedge (sig_k = R) \longrightarrow sig_j = Y$$
$$TC2_j :: (sig_j = Y) \wedge (sig_k = R) \longrightarrow (sig_j = R) \wedge (sig_k = G)$$
$$TC3_j :: (sig_j = R) \wedge (sig_k = R) \longrightarrow (sig_j = G)$$
$$TC4_j :: ((sig_j \neq R) \wedge (sig_k \neq R)) \vee (sig_k = F) \longrightarrow (sig_j = F)$$
$$TC5_j :: (sig_j = F) \wedge (sig_k = F) \longrightarrow \{notify\ the\ user\ that\ the\ system\ is\ in$$
$$S2\}$$

Adversary Actions. The adversary TC_{adv} can cause a red signal to become either yellow or green. Hence, the adversary actions can be represented as ($j = 0, 1$):

$$TC_{adv_1} :: sig_j = R \longrightarrow sig_j = Y$$
$$TC_{adv_2} :: sig_j = R \longrightarrow sig_j = G$$

Tamper-evident Stabilization of the Program. To show that the program TC is tamper-evident stabilizing in the presence of adversary TC_{adv}, we define the predicate T_{tc} and invariants $S1_{tc}$ and $S2_{tc}$ as follows:

$$T_{tc} = \langle ((G, R), (Y, R), (R, G), (R, Y)), (R, R) \rangle$$
$$S1_{tc} = \langle (G, R), (Y, R), (R, G), (R, Y) \rangle$$
$$S2_{tc} = \langle (F, F) \rangle$$

Theorem 2. *The traffic controller program TC is tamper-evident stabilizing with adversary TC_{adv} for invariants $\langle S1_{tc}, S2_{tc} \rangle$.*

Proof. If T_{tc} is true then the program is essentially the same as the traffic control program from [5] and, hence, it stabilizes to $S1_{tc}$. If the adversary TC_{adv} violates T_{tc}, the action $TC4$ can execute and one of the signals will be flashing. As a result, the other signal would eventually become flashing and $S2_{tr}$ would be satisfied (See Figure 1(b)).   □

3.4   Stabilization, Tamper-evident Stabilization, and Active Stabilization

In this section, we compare the notion of (conventional) stabilization, active stabilization and tamper-evident stabilization. Specifically, Theorem 3 considers the case where p is stabilizing and evaluates whether it is tamper-evident stabilizing, and Theorem 4 considers the reverse direction. Relation with active stabilization follows trivially from these theorems.

Theorem 3. *If a program p is* stabilizing *for* invariant S, *then p is* k-tamper-evident stabilizing *with adversary adv for* invariants $\langle S, \emptyset \rangle$, *for any adversary adv and* $k \geq 2$.

Proof. To prove tamper-evident stabilization, we need to identify a value of T. We set $T = true$, representing the state space of p. Now, we need to show that S_p converges to S in p and $\neg true$ $\langle adv, k \rangle$-converges to ϕ in p. Of these, the former is satisfied since p is stabilizing for invariant S, and the latter is trivially satisfied since $\neg true$ corresponds to the empty set.   □

Corollary 1. *If program p is* k-active stabilizing *with adversary adv and* $k \geq 2$ *for* invariant S, *then p is* k-tamper-evident stabilizing *with adversary adv for* invariants $\langle S, \emptyset \rangle$.

Note that, if there exists k and adv such that program p is k-active stabilizing with adversary adv for invariant S, then p is stabilizing for invariant S.

Theorem 4. *If program* $p = \langle S_p, \delta_p \rangle$ *is* k-tamper-evident stabilizing *with adversary adv for* invariants $\langle S1, S2 \rangle$, *then p is* stabilizing *for* invariant $(S1 \vee S2)$.

Proof. Since program p is tamper-evident stabilizing, the two constraints in the definition of tamper-evident stabilizing are true. If the program p starts from T, it converges to $S1$. If p starts from $\neg T$, in the presence or absence of adversary adv, it converges to $S2$. This completes the proof.   □

However, a similar result relating tamper-evident stabilization and active stabilization is not valid. In other words, it is possible to have a program p that is *k-tamper-evident stabilizing* with adversary adv for *invariants* $\langle S1, S2 \rangle$ but it is not *k-active stabilizing* with adversary adv for *invariant* $(S1 \vee S2)$. This is due to the fact that if the program begins in T then in the presence of the adversary, there is no guarantee that it would recover to $S1$.

4   Verification of Tamper-evident Stabilization

To prove tamper-evident stabilization of a given program, we need to determine the predicate T (from Definition 12). Based on Definition 12, from every state in $\neg T$, we must eventually reach a state in $S2$. Hence, from $\neg T$, we cannot reach a state in $S1$. Also, from every state in T, we must reach a state in $S1$. Thus, the only possible choice for T is the states from where the program can reach $S1$. Therefore, Algorithm 1 starts with the construction of T (Lines 1-3) and checking the closure property of predicates T and $\neg T$, and invariants $S1$ and $S2$ (Lines 4-6). Thereafter, we utilize CheckCycle() to detect if program p has cycles in $T - S1$. Notice that if there is a cycle in a state predicate Y, then the following is true for any state s_0 in the cycle: $\exists s_1 \in Y : (s_0, s_1) \in p$. As such, the absence of any cycles in Y would require the negation of the aforementioned expression to hold (see Line 16). This is the basic idea behind the CheckCycle routine (Lines 15-19). If any states in $T - S1$ is not removed, it implies that some of them form a cycle. If such a cycle exists then p is not tamper-evident stabilizing.

Utilizing the ideas in [7], we construct p_1 that considers the effect of adversary adv and checks for cycles of p_1 in $\neg T - S2$ (Line 8-9). In this construction, $reach(s_0, s_1, l)$ denotes that s_1 can be reached from s_0 by execution of exactly l transitions of $\neg T$. If such cycles of p_1 do not exist then p is tamper-evident stabilizing.

Algorithm 1. Verification of tamper-evident stabilization

Input: program $p = \langle S_p, \delta_p \rangle$, invariants $S1$ and $S2$, adversary adv.
Output: *true* or *false*.

1: $T = S1$
2: **repeat** $T1 = T$; $T = T1 \cup \{s_0 \mid (s_0, s_1) \in \delta_p \ \wedge \ s_1 \in T\}$
3: **until** $(T1 == T)$
4: **if** $\neg$(CheckClosure(T, p) $\wedge$ CheckClosure($\neg T$, p) $\wedge$ CheckClosure($S1$, p).$\wedge$ CheckClosure($S2$, p)) **then**
5:     **return** *false*
6: **end if**
7: **if** CheckCycle($T - S1, p$) $\neq \emptyset$ **then**   **return** *false*   **end if**
8: $p_1 = \{(s_0, s_1) \mid (\exists l : l \geq k - 1 : reach(s_0, s_1, l)) \ \vee \ (\exists s_2 : reach(s_0, s_2, l) \wedge (s_2, s_1) \in adv)\}$
9: **if** CheckCycle($\neg T - S2, p_1$) $\neq \emptyset$ **then**   **return** *false*   **end if**
10: **return** *true*

11: **function** CheckClosure(X, p)
12:     **if** $\forall s_0, s_1 \in S_p : (s_0 \in X \wedge (s_0, s_1) \in \delta_p) \ \Rightarrow \ (s_1 \in X)$ **then**   **return** *true*
13:     **else   return** *false*   **end if**
14: **end function**
15: **function** CheckCycle(Y, p)
16:     **repeat** $Y1 = Y$; $Y = Y_1 - \{s_0 \mid \forall s_1 \in Y : (s_0, s_1) \notin \delta_p\}$
17:     **until** $(Y1 == Y)$
18:     **return** Y
19: **end function**

Theorem 5. *The following problem can be solved in polynomial time in* $|S_p|$.[1]

Given a program p, adversary adv, and state predicates $S1$ and $S2$, is p tamper-evident stabilizing with adversary adv for invariants $\langle S1, S2 \rangle$?

---

[1] For reason of space, proofs appear in [17].

5   Composing Tamper-evident Stabilization

In this section, we evaluate the composition of tamper-evident stabilizing systems by investigating different types of compositions considered for stabilizing systems.

Parallel Composition.   A parallel composition of two programs considers the case where two independent programs are run in parallel on a weakly fair scheduler so that each program is guaranteed to execute its enabled actions. Weak fairness ensures that any action that is continuously enabled will be executed infinitely often. Thus, during the parallel execution, the behavior of one program does not affect the behavior of the other. Hence, if we have two programs p and q that do not share any variables such that p is stabilizing for S and q is stabilizing for R then parallel composition of p and q is stabilizing for $S \wedge R$.

Now, we consider the case where we have two programs p and q that are tamper-evident stabilizing for $\langle S1, S2 \rangle$ and $\langle S1', S2' \rangle$, and p and q do not share any variables. Is the parallel composition of p and q (denoted by $p[]q$) also tamper-evident stabilizing?

Theorem 6 (Parallel Composition). *Given programs p and q that do not share variables.*

p is tamper-evident stabilizing with adversary adv for $\langle S1, S2 \rangle$ $\wedge$
q is tamper-evident stabilizing with adversary adv for $\langle S1', S2' \rangle$
$\Rightarrow$
$p[]q$ is tamper-evident stabilizing with adversary adv for $\langle S1 \wedge S1', S2 \vee S2' \rangle$

Note that in parallel composition of two tamper-evident stabilizing programs, the first predicate is combined by conjunction whereas the second one is combined by disjunction. However, we could make $p[]q$ tamper-evident stabilizing for $\langle S1 \wedge S1', S2 \wedge S2' \rangle$ provided we add actions to p (respectively q) so that it checks if q (respectively, p) is in a state in $S2'$ (respectively, $S2$). Accordingly, p can change its own state to be in $S2$ (respectively, $S2'$).

Superposition.   We can also superpose two tamper-evident stabilizing systems in a similar manner. For example, consider the case where program p is superposed on program q, i.e., p has read-only access to variables of q and q does not have access to variables of p.

Theorem 7 (Superposition).

p is tamper-evident stabilizing with adversary adv for $\langle S1, S2 \rangle$ in $S1'$ $\wedge$
q is active stabilizing with adversary adv for $S1'$ $\wedge$
q is tamper-evident stabilizing with adversary adv for $\langle S1', S2' \rangle$ $\wedge$
q is silent in $S1'$, i.e., q has no transition (except self-loops) in $S1'$ $\wedge$
p is superposed on q
$\Rightarrow$
$p[]q$ is tamper-evident stabilizing with adversary adv for $\langle S1, S2 \vee S2' \rangle$.

Transitivity. Tamper-evident stabilization preserves transitivity in a manner similar to stabilizing programs. Specifically,

Theorem 8 (Transitivity 1).

p is tamper-evident stabilizing with adversary adv for $\langle S1, S2 \rangle$ in U $\wedge$
p is tamper-evident stabilizing with adversary adv for $\langle S1', S2' \rangle$ in $S1$
$\Rightarrow$
p is tamper-evident stabilizing with adversary adv for $\langle S1', S2 \rangle$ in U, and
p is tamper-evident stabilizing with adversary adv for $\langle S1', S2 \vee S2' \rangle$ in U.

We can also infer transitivity property by the following theorem.

Theorem 9 (Transitivity 2).

p is tamper-evident stabilizing with adversary adv for $\langle S1, S2 \rangle$ $\wedge$
$S1$ converges to $S1'$ in p $\wedge$
$S2$ $\langle adv, k \rangle$-converges to $S2'$ in p
$\Rightarrow$
p is tamper-evident stabilizing with adversary adv for $\langle S1', S2' \rangle$.

6 Designing Tamper-evident Stabilization by Local Detection and Global/Local Correction

In this section, we identify some possible approaches for designing tamper-evident stabilization. Specifically, we evaluate the use of some of the existing approaches for designing stabilization in designing tamper-evident stabilization.

Local Detection and Global Correction. One approach for designing stabilization is via local detection and global correction. In such a system, the invariant S of the system is of the form $\forall j : S.j$, where $S.j$ is a local predicate that can be checked by process j. Each process j is responsible for checking its own predicate. If the system is outside the legitimate state then the local predicate of at least one process is violated. Hence, this process is responsible for initiating a global correction (such as distributed reset [19]) to restore the system to a legitimate state.

A similar approach is also applicable for tamper-evident stabilization. For example, consider the case where the predicates involved in defining tamper-evident stabilization are $S1 = \forall j :: S1.j$, $S2 = \forall j :: S2.j$, and $T = \forall j :: T.j$. Based on the problem of tamper-evident stabilization, we have $\forall j :: (S1.j \Rightarrow T.j) \wedge (S2.j \Rightarrow \neg T.j) \wedge \neg(S1.j \wedge S2.j)$.

In this case, the actions of process j to obtain tamper-evident stabilization is as follows:

$\neg T.j \ \wedge \ \neg S2.j \longrightarrow$ *Satisfy $S2.j$*
$T.j \ \wedge \ \neg S1.j \longrightarrow$ *Initiate global correction to restore $S1$*

To utilize such an approach to design tamper-evident stabilization, we need to make some changes to global correction and put some reasonable constraints on what an adversary can do. In particular, the global correction to restore $S1$ involves changes to all processes. For tamper-evident stabilization, however, process j will execute its part in global correction only if $T.j$ is true. Also, if process j observes that $T.k$ is false for some neighbor k then j will satisfy $S2.j$. This will guarantee that if $T.j$ is false for some process then the program will eventually reach a state in $S2$. The definition of tamper-evident stabilization requires that $\neg T$ is closed in the adversary actions. This assumption is essential since if the adversary could move the system from a state in $\neg T$ to T then the system would have forgotten that it was tampered beyond acceptable levels. In the context of this example, it would be necessary that the adversary cannot cause the program to start in a state where $T.j$ is false for some process j and the adversary causes j to move to a state where $T.j$ is true.

Local Detection and Local Correction. We can also utilize the above approach in the context of local detection and local correction [3] to add tamper-evident-stabilization if invariant $S1$ is of the form $\forall j :: S1.j$, predicates of different processes are arranged in a partial order, and actions that correct $S1.j$ preserve all predicates that come earlier in the order. In such a system when process j finds that $T.j \wedge \neg S1.j$ is true it only locally satisfies $S1.j$. Given that we have a partial order, eventually we reach a state where $S.j$ is true in all states.

Effect of the Structure of the Predicate T. Intuitively, in tamper-evident stabilization, we have two convergence requirements. T converges to $S1$ and $\neg T$ converges to $S2$ in the presence of an adversary. If T is a conjunctive predicate then $\neg T$ is a disjunctive predicate. Hence, a reader may wonder what would happen if T were a disjunctive predicate instead of a conjunctive predicate. We argue that this is likely to be a harder problem than the case where T is a conjunctive predicate.

7   The Relationship between Tamper-evident Stabilization and other Stabilization Techniques

Starting with Dijkstra's seminal work [10] on stabilizing algorithms for token circulation, several variations of stabilizing algorithms have been proposed during the past decades. These algorithms can be classified into two categories: *stronger* stabilizing and *weaker* stabilizing algorithms.

The algorithms in the first category not only guarantee stabilization but also satisfy some additional properties. Examples of this category include fault-containment stabilization, byzantine stabilization, Fault-Tolerant Self Stabilization (FTSS), multitolerance, and active stabilization. Fault-containment stabilization (e.g., [14, 25]) refers to stabilizing programs that ensure that if one (respectively small number of) fault occurs then quick recovery is provided to the invariant. Byzantine stabilizing (e.g., [21, 22]) programs tolerate the scenarios where a subset of processes is byzantine. FTSS (e.g., [4]) covers stabilizing programs that tolerate permanent crash faults. Multitolerant stabilizing (e.g., [13, 19]) systems ensure that, in addition to stabilization, the program masks a certain class of faults. Finally, active stabilization [7] requires that the program should recover to the invariant even if it is constantly perturbed by an adversary.

By contrast, a stabilizing program satisfies the constraints of weaker versions of stabilization. However, a program that provides a weaker version of stabilization may not be stabilizing. Examples of this include weak stabilization, probabilistic stabilization, and pseudo stabilization. Weak stabilization (e.g., [9,16]) requires that starting from any initial configuration, there exists an execution that eventually reaches a point from which its behavior is correct. However, the program may execute on a path where such a legitimate state is never reached. Probabilistic stabilization [18] refers to problems that ensure that starting from any initial configuration, the program converges to its legitimate states with probability 1. Nonmasking fault tolerance (e.g., [1,2]) targets the programs where the program recovers from states reached in the presence of a limited class of faults. However, this limited set of states may not cover the set of all states. Pseudo stabilization [8] relaxes the notion of points in the execution from which the behavior is correct. In other words, every execution has a suffix that exhibits correct behavior, yet time before reaching this suffix is unbounded.

The aforementioned stabilizing algorithms consider several problems including mutual exclusion, leader election, consensus, graph coloring, clustering, routing, and overlay construction. However, none of them considers problem of tampering (e.g., [20,23,24]). In part, this is due to the fact that stabilization and tamper evidence are potentially conflicting requirements.

Tamper-evident stabilization is in some sense a weaker version of stabilization in that from Theorem 3 every stabilizing program is also tamper-evident stabilizing. In particular, a stabilizing program guarantees that from all states program would eventually recover to legitimate states. By contrast, tamper-evident stabilizing program gives the option of recovering to *tamper-evident* states. (Although Theorem 4 suggests that every tamper-evident stabilizing program can be thought of as a stabilizing program, the invariant of such a stabilizing program is of the form $\langle S1, S2 \rangle$, where $S2$ includes states that the system has no/reduced functionality.)

Tamper-evident stabilization is stronger than the notion of nonmasking fault tolerance. In particular, nonmasking fault-tolerance also has the notion of fault-span (similar to T in Definition 12) from where recovery to the invariant is provided. In tamper-evident stabilization, if the program reaches a state in $\neg T$, it is required that it stays in $\neg T$. By contrast, in nonmasking fault-tolerance, the program *may* recover from $\neg T$ to T.

Tamper-evident stabilization can be considered as a special case of nonmasking-failsafe multitolerance, where a program that is subject to two types of faults F_f and F_n provides (i) failsafe fault tolerance when F_f occurs, (ii) nonmasking tolerance in the presence of F_n, and (iii) no guarantees if both F_f and F_n occur in the same computation. We have previously identified [13] sufficient conditions for efficient stepwise design of failsafe-nonmasking multitolerant systems, where F_f and F_n do not occur simultaneously and their scopes of perturbation outside the invariant are disjoint. Based on the role of T in Definition 12, we can ensure that these conditions are satisfied (Due to reasons of space, this proof is beyond the scope of the paper) for tamper-evident stabilization. This suggests that efficient algorithms can be designed for tamper-evident stabilization based on the approach in [13].

8   Conclusion and Future Work

This paper introduces the notion of *tamper-evident stabilization* that captures the requirement that if a system is perturbed within an acceptable limit then it restores itself to legitimate states. However, if it is perturbed beyond this boundary then it permanently preserves evidence of tampering. Moreover, the latter operation is unaffected even if the adversary attempts to stop it. We formally defined tamper-evident stabilization and investigated how it relates to stabilization and active stabilization. We argued that tamper-evident stabilization is weaker than stabilization in that every stabilizing system is indeed tamper-evident stabilizing. Also, tamper-evident stabilization captures a spectrum of systems from *pure tamper-evident systems* to *pure stabilizing systems*. We also demonstrated two examples where we design tamper-evident stabilizing token passing and traffic control protocols. We identified how methods for designing stabilizing programs can be leveraged to design tamper-evident stabilizing programs. We showed that the problem of verifying whether a given program is tamper-evident stabilizing is polynomial in the state space of the given program. We note that the problem of adding tamper-evident stabilization to a given high atomicity program can be solved in polynomial time. However, the problem is NP-hard for distributed programs. Moreover, we find that parallel composition of tamper-evident stabilizing systems works in a manner similar to that of stabilizing systems. Nevertheless, superposition or transitivity requirements of tamper-evident stabilization are somewhat different than that for stabilizing systems.

We are currently investigating the design and analysis of tamper-evident stabilizing System-on-Chip (SoC) systems in the context of the IEEE SystemC language. Our objective here is to design systems that facilitate reasoning about what they do and what they do not do in the event of tampering. Second, we will leverage our existing work on model repair and synthesis of stabilization in automated design of tamper-evident stabilization. Third, we plan to study the application of tamper-evident stabilization in game theory (and vice versa).

References

1. Arora, A.: Efficient reconfiguration of trees: A case study in methodical design of nonmasking fault-tolerant programs. In: Langmaack, H., de Roever, W.-P., Vytopil, J. (eds.) FTRTFT 1994 and ProCoS 1994. LNCS, vol. 863, pp. 110–127. Springer, Heidelberg (1994)
2. Arora, A., Gouda, M., Varghese, G.: Constraint satisfaction as a basis for designing nonmasking fault-tolerant systems. Journal of High Speed Networks 5(3), 293–306 (1996)

3. Arora, A., Gouda, M.G.: Closure and convergence: A foundation of fault-tolerant computing. IEEE Transactions on Software Engineering 19(11), 1015–1027 (1993)
4. Beauquier, J., Kekkonen-Moneta, S.: On ftss-solvable distributed problems. In: WSS, pp. 64–79 (1997)
5. Bonakdarpour, B., Kulkarni, S.S.: Compositional verification of fault-tolerant real-time programs. In: EMSOFT, pp. 29–38 (2009)
6. Bonakdarpour, B., Kulkarni, S.S.: On the complexity of synthesizing relaxed and graceful bounded-time 2-phase recovery. In: Cavalcanti, A., Dams, D.R. (eds.) FM 2009. LNCS, vol. 5850, pp. 660–675. Springer, Heidelberg (2009)
7. Bonakdarpour, B., Kulkarni, S.S.: Active stabilization. In: Défago, X., Petit, F., Villain, V. (eds.) SSS 2011. LNCS, vol. 6976, pp. 77–91. Springer, Heidelberg (2011)
8. Burns, J.E., Gouda, M., Miller, R.E.: Stabilization and pseudo-stabilization. Distributed Computing 7(1), 35–42 (1993)
9. Devismes, S., Tixeuil, S., Yamashita, M.: Weak vs. self vs. probabilistic stabilization. In: ICDCS 2008, pp. 681–688 (2008)
10. Dijkstra, E.W.: Self-stabilizing systems in spite of distributed control. Communications of the ACM 17(11), 643–644 (1974)
11. Dijkstra, E.W.: A Discipline of Programming. Prentice-Hall (1990)
12. Dolev, S.: Self-Stabilization. MIT Press (2000)
13. Ebnenasir, A., Kulkarni, S.S.: Feasibility of stepwise design of multitolerant programs. TOSEM 21(1), 1–49 (2011)
14. Ghosh, S., Gupta, A.: An exercise in fault-containment: Self-stabilizing leader election. Information Processing Letters 59(5), 281–288 (1996)
15. Gouda, M.: Elements of security: Closure, convergence, and protection. Information Processing Letters 77(2-4), 109–114 (2001); In honor of Edsger W. Dijkstra
16. Gouda, M.: The theory of weak stabilization. In: Datta, A.K., Herman, T. (eds.) WSS 2001. LNCS, vol. 2194, pp. 114–123. Springer, Heidelberg (2001)
17. Hajisheykhi, R., Ebnenasir, A., Kulkarni, S.: Tamper-evident stabilization. Technical Report MSU-CSE-14-4 (June 2014)
18. Israeli, A., Jalfon, M.: Token management schemes and random walks yield self-stabilizing mutual exclusion. In: PODC, pp. 119–131 (1990)
19. Kulkarni, S., Arora, A.: Multitolerance in distributed reset. Chicago Journal of Theoretical Computer Science 1998(4) (December 1998)
20. Lie, D., Thekkath, C.A., Mitchell, M., Lincoln, P., Boneh, D., Mitchell, J.C., Horowitz, M.: Architectural support for copy and tamper resistant software. In: ASPLOS, pp. 168–177 (2000)
21. Malekpour, M.R.: A byzantine-fault tolerant self-stabilizing protocol for distributed clock synchronization systems. In: Datta, A.K., Gradinariu, M. (eds.) SSS 2006. LNCS, vol. 4280, pp. 411–427. Springer, Heidelberg (2006)
22. Nesterenko, M., Arora, A.: Tolerance to unbounded byzantine faults. In: SRDS, pp. 22–31 (2002)
23. Sean, W.: Smith and Steve Weingart. Building a high-performance, programmable secure coprocessor. Computer Networks 31(8), 831–860 (1999)
24. Suh, G.E., Clarke, D.E., Gassend, B., van Dijk, M., Devadas, S.: Aegis: architecture for tamper-evident and tamper-resistant processing. In: ICS, pp. 160–171 (2003)
25. Zhang, H., Arora, A.: Guaranteed fault containment and local stabilization in routing. Computer Networks 50(18), 3585–3607 (2006)

A Safe Stopping Protocol to Enable Reliable Reconfiguration for Component-Based Distributed Systems

Mohammad Ghafari, Abbas Heydarnoori, and Hassan Haghighi

DeepSE Group @ Politecnico di Milano, Italy
Sharif University of Technology, Iran
Shahid Beheshti University, Iran
mohammad.ghafari@polimi.it, heydarnoori@sharif.edu, h_haghighi@sub.ac.ir

Abstract. Despite the need for change, highly available software systems cannot be stopped to perform changes because disruption in their services may consequent irrecoverable losses. Current work on runtime evolution are either too disruptive, e.g., "blackouts" in unnecessary components in the *quiescence criterion* approach or presume restrictive assumptions such as the "black-box design" in the *tranquility* approach. In this paper, an architecture-based approach, called *SAFER*, is proposed which provides a better timeliness by relaxing any precondition required to start reconfiguration. We demonstrate the validity of the SAFER through model checking and a realization of the approach on a component model.

Keywords: Reconfiguration, Safe stopping, Consistency.

1   Introduction

Many software-intensive systems are required to be reconfigured to maintain the key functions while they face changes in user requirements and/or domain assumptions. In some special category of software systems, it may not be possible to simply shut down the software from functioning and then apply the changes. In this regard, runtime evolution[1] aims at adapting the system to changes without disrupting those parts of the system which are unaffected by the change [1]. The three most important issues which must be addressed in the runtime evolution are (i) reaching a safe application state, (ii) ensuring reliable reconfiguration, and (iii) transferring the internal state of entities which have to be replaced. Despite extensive research in component-based dynamic reconfiguration, and available component models which allow reconfiguration [2], safe reconfiguration is still an open problem, and existing approaches have made small steps in solving real world scenarios [3].

This paper focuses on the first two challenges of runtime evolution, i.e., reaching a safe application state and ensuring a reliable reconfiguration. It proposes

---

[1] Interchangeably in this paper, dynamic reconfiguration.

© IFIP International Federation for Information Processing 2015
M. Dastani and M.Sirjani (Eds.): FSEN 2015, LNCS 9392, pp. 100–109, 2015.
DOI: 10.1007/978-3-319-24644-4_7

an architecture-based reconfiguration approach, called $SAFER^2$, that provides a better timeliness by relaxing any preconditions required to start reconfiguration. The approach extends the notion of tranquility in a way that not only enjoys the low disruption of this proposal, but also works safely in both distributed and interleaved transactions. The paper presents the formalization of the proposed approach in Alloy [4] and the verification of its consistency by means of model checking in different architectural configurations and also for the most well known evolution scenarios [5]. Implementation of a running example on top of the Fractal [6] shows the applicability of this approach [5].

This paper is organized as follows. Section 2 gives an overview of the challenges posed by runtime evolution. SAFER, an approach for ensuring safe dynamic reconfiguration, is articulated in Section 3. Related work are then discussed in Section 4, and Section 5 concludes the paper. The verification and evaluation reports are available in the appendix.

2   Problem Setting

Existing approaches to safe dynamic reconfiguration try to put the elements of the running system that are subject to change at a specific state called safe state before performing the reconfiguration operations on them. Of most relevant work in this area, quiescence [1] causes a high disruption to the running system that is not acceptable in many critical systems [7]. To address this issue, Vandewoude et al. [8] proposed the concept of tranquility, as a low disruptive alternative to quiescence:

Definition 1 (Tranquility). *A component is tranquil if: (i) it is not currently engaged in a transaction that it initiated; (ii) it will not initiate new transactions; (iii) it is not actively processing a request; and (iv) none of its adjacent components are engaged in a transaction in which both of them have already participated and might still participate in the future.*

In [9], Ma et al. show that the tranquility criterion may not guarantee safe dynamic reconfiguration of distributed transactions. Moreover, when a component is used in an infinite sequence of concurrent interleaving transactions, it is not guaranteed that it will ever reach tranquility [8]. Also, tranquility criterion is not stable by itself. Once node N is in a tranquil state, all interactions between N and its environment should be blocked to assure that the tranquil state of that node is preserved [8]. In addition, tranquility does not guarantee consistency when deleting or detaching nodes [3]. Furthermore, both notions of quiescence and tranquility assume that a valid component substitution cannot be ensured if a transaction starts with an old version of a component and finishes with the new version [10]. These issues are thoroughly discussed in [7].

---

[2] SAFe runtimE Reconfiguration.

3   Safe Reconfiguration

In many critical cases, changes should be applied as soon as the software violates
a requirement, however, the consistency of changes is not guaranteed unless the
affected components of the system are in a safe state. Such a precondition is
not acceptable if changes in the running system are subject to very stringent
time constraints to react. This section extends the notion of tranquility, and
proposes *SAFER*, an approach to enable safe, low disruptive runtime evolution
in distributed contexts.

3.1   The Concept of Tranquility

The notion of tranquility is a necessary criterion, but not sufficient to guarantee
a safe reconfiguration [7]. In fact, the type of reconfiguration can also play an
important role in the system's consistency which has not been considered by existing approaches. Therefore, we extend tranquility to guarantee a more reliable
reconfiguration. To clarify the concept, the definitions of consistent reconfiguration and dependency violation are provided first:

Definition 2 (Consistent Reconfiguration). *A reconfiguration is consistent
if it applies desired changes in a way that it transfers the system from a consistent
configuration (before the evolution) to another consistent configuration (after the
evolution). More specifically, a consistent configuration is a state of the system
in which a component in a safe state can be changed without impacting both what
has been already executed and what has still to be executed in active transactions.*

Definition 3 (Dependency Violation). *Modification of a component may
have side effects on other components. Dependency violation is defined as the
removal or modification of a certain component that leads to malfunction or
failure in other component(s).*

Having these definitions in place, we define *e-tranquility*[3], an extension to
tranquility as follows:

Definition 4 (E-Tranquility). *(i) node N is in the tranquil state; (ii) the reconfiguration does not intend to delete or unlink the node; and (iii) the change
does not impose any dependency violation among the components.*

If one of these conditions is not satisfied, reaching e-tranquility delays until the
transaction which N belongs to, is accomplished completely (either committed
or rolled back). In the following section, we show that despite whether or not
e-tranquility is met, leveraging SAFER, relaxes any precondition to start the
evolution process. In other words, e-tranquility is only to indicate the time in
which an old component can be removed safely.

---

[3] Extended tranquility.

3.2   SAFER: An Approach to Safe Runtime Reconfiguration

The software architecture plays a central role in achieving a safe adaptation [11]. The behavioral and structural aspects of the architecture provide useful information like component dependencies. Here, we assume the availability of such information at runtime. This is not an infeasible assumption since reflective component models, e.g., Fractal [6], not only provide such an view by introspection but also allow changing them on-the-fly by intercession.

The concept of SAFER is established based on the idea that the transactions involving a component that will be updated should be separated from new transactions as soon as the update request is issued. This is operationalized as follows:

1. Whenever a component receives a change request, its new version is added to the system immediately. At this time, which is referred to as the *evolution time*, both the old and new versions of this component exist simultaneously.
2. As the second step, an event is published to dependent connectors (i.e., those which can initiate a transaction on the target component) to notify them about the start time of the evolution and the address of the new component.
3. When a connector receives a request, if the target is an evolved component N, the connector decides on the path to which the request should be routed, and the component which should serve the request (the old or the new version). In fact, the connector chooses the qualified component based on its knowledge about the undergoing evolution. The switching algorithm works based on the following rules: (i) if the request belongs to a transaction which has been initiated after the evolution time, it is directed to the new version of N; (ii) if the old version of N has not been used in the ongoing transaction, and reconfiguration is not resulted in a node deletion/unlinking or dependency violation, the new version is responsible for processing the request. Otherwise, the old version serves the request.
4. The switching policy continues till the old component reaches the e-tranquility. Finally, the old component will be removed completely from the system, and the completion of the evolution is notified to its dependent connectors. Accordingly, all subsequent requests will be processed by the reconfigured version.

According to SAFER, to guarantee that the old system and its related transactions will still work and that all functionalities and qualities are preserved during the reconfiguration, multiple versions of a component exist in the system until the component reaches the e-tranquility. In fact, each connector contains the intelligence necessary to manage the requests and is enriched by the information about the dependencies that exist among the components so that it can route messages to the proper version of a component.

In order to clarify SAFER, imagine a Message Delivery system as illustrated in Figure 1(a), it includes four main components which are connected by specific connectors (Cnn-*). Each component invoking a request to another component initiates a transaction. Each transaction as a unit of work may also need to use or collaborate with other neighboring components by initiating new transactions (sub-transactions). The completion of a transaction depends on its execution after the termination of its sub-transactions. We assume that transactions complete in a bounded time and that the initiator of a transaction is aware of its completion [1] . Respecting this definition, a behavioral scenario of the exemplary system specified in Figure 1(b) can be therefore described as follows:

"*Whenever a client requests* **Sender** *to send a message,* **Sender** *as the root transaction invokes a request to the* **(De)Compression** *in order to compress the message. Next, the compressed message is sent to* **Packer** *to encapsulate the message with a header (including the time-stamp, message type, and decompression key) required to extract the message later. As soon as the message is prepared, it is sent to* **Receiver**. *On the other side, once the message is received by the* **Receiver**, *it asks* **(De)Compression** *to decompress the message to obtain the original message*".

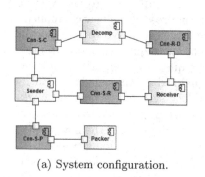

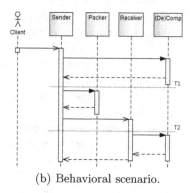

(a) System configuration.   (b) Behavioral scenario.

Fig. 1. Message Delivery System

To clarify SAFER, suppose a hypothetical situation where the (De)Compression component in the Message Delivery system needs to be replaced with a new version: Once an update request to (De)Compression is received, its new version will be added to the system. Thus, the dependent connectors of the (De)Compression (i.e., Cnn-S-C and Cnn-R-D) determine the component which should serve the incoming requests among a set of candidate components (the old or the new version). The coexistence of both of the versions of the (De)Compression continues until the old version finally reaches the e-tranquility. At this time, the old one can be removed safely from the system, and the new version of the (De)Compression is responsible for serving all corresponding requests. From the behavioral view of the system during the evolution, whenever Sender sends a request to use the compression service, since (De)Compression is under the evolution (two versions of this component coexist simultaneously), the request is mediated by Cnn-S-C to decide which version of (De)Compression should provide the service required by Sender. The target component is chosen based on considering both the initiation time of the transaction which the request belongs to and the history of using this component in the ongoing transaction.

Regarding the definition of tranquility and the behavior of the system depicted in Figure 1(b), although (De)Compression is tranquil at time T1, due to the dependency violation, changing this component leads the system toward a failure at time T2 where the compressed message needs to be decompressed. However, based on the e-tranquility, this component cannot be removed until the transactions involved with this component finish completely. As a result, when Receiver sends a decompression request at time T2, since the evolution is not completed yet, Cnn-R-D can still forward the request to the old version.

4 Related Work

Several work on software reconfiguration have been reported in literature, all of which tackle the problem from different perspectives. However, the most related approaches to deal with safe reconfiguration are considered here. These approaches fall into two major categories.

The first category of approaches is those addressing consistency through recovery. In these approaches, components can deal with the failures of an operation and recover from inconsistencies introduced during the reconfiguration. However, these approaches bring certain drawbacks: in one hand, it cannot be used in systems which do not use atomic actions. On the other hand, atomic actions are not suited to all application domains since they often result in reduced levels of concurrency in the target application. Besides, aborting transactions prior to reconfiguration is an expensive process. In contrast to the recovery approach, the second category focuses on preventing inconsistencies from occurring in the first place [8] [1] [9]. They try to put the elements of the running system that are subject to change at a specific state before performing reconfiguration operations on them. This category is of particular interest in this paper and is discussed more in the following.

Among existing approaches, a highly cited paper co-authored by Kramer and Magee [1], introduced quiescence as a reliable criterion to guarantee system consistency during the evolution. It works properly in interleaving transactions, guarantees to achieve a safe state in bounded time, and also is the only criterion which supports component removals. However, due to deactivation of all potentially related components before the reconfiguration to ensure consistency, it imposes high disruption to the running system. In order to reduce the disruption imposed by quiescence, tranquility criterion is proposed by Vandewoude et al. [8] which avoids unnecessary disturbances. Nevertheless, this criterion does not work safely in distributed transactions because of its assumption about black-box design. Moreover, there is no guarantee to achieve tranquility in bounded time in interleaving transactions [7]. In a recent work, Ma et al. [9] proposed a version-consistent approach that benefits dynamic component dependency model of the system. While it guarantees a safe dynamic reconfiguration in distributed contexts, the algorithm they propose seems to impose unnecessary processing time to maintain dynamic dependencies when the architecture model becomes large. The time is required to reach a safe state is bounded in most approaches, while it depends on a number of transactions for version-consistency. Both tranquility and version-consistent approaches assume that the interactions with the environment should remain blocked in order to remain stable. The more assumption a specific approach is based on, a narrower application area it would be applicable. Interested readers may consult with [7].

The idea of using multi-versioning is not a new concept. Cook et al. propose a framework, HERCULES, to improve the reliability of a system by keeping existing versions of the component running and only fully removing the old component when a determination is made that the new one fully satisfies its role [12]. The new version aims to correct deficiencies that have been detected in the old version and the old version offers an example of correct behavior outside of those deficiencies. Similarly, Miki-Rakic et al. [13] encapsulate the new and old components in a wrapper component named Multi-Versioning Connector. The wrapper serves as a connector between the encapsulated component versions and the rest of the system and is responsible for propagating the generated result(s).

5   Conclusions

In this paper, we promoted connectors for enabling a safe dynamic reconfiguration by addressing the shortcomings of tranquility in distributed contexts. We demonstrated that the proposed approach, called SAFER, not only impose low disruption, but also relaxes any preconditions required to start a reconfiguration that reduces the delay within which the system is being updated. To verify the consistency of SAFER, we specified it in Alloy and applied a model checking tool to examine SAFER in different architectural configurations and also possible evolution scenarios.

We implemented SAFER in a simple example and, we compared it with other approaches based on existing information. In order to objectively compare timeliness and the disruption introduced by this approach with existing approaches, different experiments with randomly generated system configurations, different levels of workloads, and even different component models are needed. This validation is beyond the scope of this paper and we leave it for future work.

Acknowledgments. The authors would like to acknowledge Hamidreza Moradi for his help in preparing the paper. This research has been funded by the European Commission, Programme IDEAS-ERC, Project 227977-SMScom.

Appendix

Verification Report

Dependability of runtime evolution is of major importance because any violations of consistency in running programs may lead to irreversible damages. To prevent this, reconfiguration safety should be ensured by performing appropriate (preferably formal) verification techniques. To achieve this goal, we have modeled our evolution procedure, i.e., SAFER, and its related definitions in Alloy [4] to verify whether if a consistent system is evolved using the SAFER, it still remains consistent. Due to space limitations, interested readers can refer to [5] for obtaining further details, including complete specifications of the structural, behavioral, and evolutional aspects of SAFER in Alloy

As stated earlier, a system is consistent if and only if all its transactions are consistent, and a transaction is consistent if and only if a specific version of each component is used during that transaction's lifecycle. In other words, all requests belonging to that transaction and its sub-transactions must be served by non-equivalent components.

pred consistent[t : Transaction, tm : Time]{
    *let exe = {e : t. * subTransactions.actions| e in ExeRequest and lte[e.pre, tm]}|*
      all disj e1, e2 : exe| equivalent[e1.to, e2.to] => e2.to in (e1.to).sysmetric
}

With respect to the above definition of consistent transactions, we executed the following assertion using the Alloy Analyzer to examine the reliability of SAFER for various configurations and the evolution scenarios in which we have corrective changes or node deletion/unlinkings.

assert algorithmPreservesConsistency{
    all t : Transaction, en : EndNotify| consistent[t, en.cause.pre] =>
                                 consistent[t, en.post]

}

More precisely, we let the Alloy Analyzer to consider all valid configurations of totally 12 components and connectors. The invariants which we have specified through the Alloy facts forced this tool to only instantiate valid configurations of our model. In addition, before analyzing the above assertion for generated configurations, we used more other assertions based on predicates some of which are given in [5] to show that our model was valid. After executing the assertion `algorithmPreservesConsistency` for all of the instantiated configurations, the tool reported no counterexamples, or in other words, it did not find any inconsistencies. Experience has shown that if a specification has a flaw, it can usually be demonstrated by a relatively small counterexample [14].

Evaluation Report

We claim that the proposed reconfiguration approach is promising in the sense that it covers the limitations of tranquility in distributed contexts. To evaluate the applicability of SAFER in practice, it is implemented as a tool to facilitate the evolution of our running example on top of the Fractal component model [6]. After realizing the SAFER, we put its functionalities in the Fractal components membrane as controller methods to be utilized in enabling a safe reconfiguration. Interested readers are referred to [5] for details of implementation and experimental setup.

The result of this preliminary evaluation shows that in situations that a reconfiguration results in deletion of a tranquil node, the node still remains in the system to guarantee if it may, at some point in the future, participate in an ongoing transaction, even if it has not yet participated. Accordingly, the connectors could still route requests from old transactions to the deleted node. Secondly, the behavior of a component and its environmental dependencies during its execution within a transaction remains consistent. Consequently, even a temporary dependency violation does not impose any inconsistency in distributed transactions while an ongoing transaction still could use the same version of a component. In addition, the simultaneous operation of both the old and the evolved version of components enhances the availability of the system in long reconfiguration plans that include a lot of actions which will take more time to be executed and increases unavailability. Likewise, it guarantees achieving tranquility in bounded time even in the case of interleaved transactions. This is addressed by bringing a new version of the component on line to service the new top-level transactions, while the old component gradually transitions to an inactive state. Indeed, since those transactions initiated after evolution time will use new version of the component intended to be evolved, the old version would not be involved in new transactions anymore and old transactions are isolated from new interleaved ones. Furthermore, on demand possibility of using the evolved entities by new transactions increases the reliability of system in the case of critical changes like security breaches in banking services. In other words, there is no need to wait for a safe state since it is only a precondition to safely remove the old components, but not to perform the change, e.g., adding a new component.

Although the results are promising, there is still space for improvements. Having the exact component dependency model in an adaptive system is not trivial especially when the system often goes under the evolution. One way of sidestepping the overhead imposed by SAFER to keep track of transactions and their log is to collect dependencies with the mining transaction log [15]. Moreover, the overhead of performing the evolution and memory consumption of multi-version existence of the same component might impose limitations in resource-poor scenarios, especially in cases with high workloads. A remedy to this problem would be deploying changes temporary on idle resources [16].

References

1. Kramer, J., Magee, J.: The evolving philosophers problem: Dynamic change management. IEEE Transactions on Software Engineering 16(11), 1293–1306 (1990)
2. Crnković, I., Sentilles, S., Vulgarakis, A., Chaudron, M.: A Classification Framework for Software Component Models. IEEE Transactions on Software Engineering 37(5), 593–615 (2011)
3. Costa, C., Ali, N., Pérez, J., Carsí, J.Á., Ramos, I.: Dynamic reconfiguration of software architectures through aspects. In: Oquendo, F. (ed.) ECSA 2007. LNCS, vol. 4758, pp. 279–283. Springer, Heidelberg (2007)
4. Jackson, D.: Alloy: A lightweight object modelling notation. ACM Transactions on Software Engineering and Methodology 11(2), 256–290 (2002)
5. Ghafari, M., Heydarnoori, A., Haghighi, H.: A safe stopping protocol to enable reliable reconfiguration for component-based distributed systems (2015), http://home.deib.polimi.it/ghafari/SAFER.html
6. Bruneton, E., Coupaye, T., Leclercq, M., Quéma, V., Stefani, J.B.: The FRACTAL component model and its support in Java: Experiences with auto-adaptive and reconfigurable systems. Software: Practice and Experience 36(11-12), 1257–1284 (2006)
7. Ghafari, M., Jamshidi, P., Shahbazi, S., Haghighi, H.: Safe stopping of running component-based distributed systems: Challenges and research gaps. In: 21st IEEE International Workshop on Enabling Technologies: Infrastructure for Collaborative Enterprises, pp. 66–71 (2012)
8. Vandewoude, Y., Ebraert, P., Berbers, Y., D'Hondt, T.: Tranquility: A low disruptive alternative to quiescence for ensuring safe dynamic updates. IEEE Transactions on Software Engineering 33(12), 856–868 (2007)
9. Ma, X., Baresi, L., Ghezzi, C., Panzica La Manna, V., Lu, J.: Version-consistent dynamic reconfiguration of component-based distributed systems. In: 19th ACM SIGSOFT Symposium and the 13th European Conference on Foundations of Software Engineering, pp. 245–255 (2011)
10. Banno, F., Marletta, D., Pappalardo, G., Tramontana, E.: Tackling consistency issues for runtime updating distributed systems. In: IEEE International Symposium on Parallel Distributed Processing, Workshops and PhD Forum, pp. 1–8 (April 2010)
11. Oreizy, P., Medvidovic, N., Taylor, R.N.: Runtime software adaptation: Framework, approaches, and styles. In: Companion of the 30th International Conference on Software Engineering, pp. 899–910 (2008)
12. Cook, J.E., Dage, J.A.: Highly reliable upgrading of components. In: 21st International Conference on Software Engineering, pp. 203–212 (1999)
13. Mikic-Rakic, M., Medvidovic, N.: Architecture-level support for software component deployment in resource constrained environments. In: IFIP/ACM Working Conference on Component Deployment, pp. 31–50 (2002)
14. Kim, J.S., Garlan, D.: Analyzing architectural styles. Journal of Systems and Software 83(7), 1216–1235 (2010)
15. Canavera, K.R., Esfahani, N., Malek, S.: Mining the execution history of a software system to infer the best time for its adaptation. In: 20th ACM SIGSOFT International Symposium on the Foundations of Software Engineering, pp. 1–11 (2012)
16. Ghafari, M., Heydarnoori, A.: Partial Scalability to Ensure Reliable Dynamic Reconfiguration. In: 7th IEEE International Conference on Self-Adaptation and Self-Organizing Systems Workshops, pp. 83–88 (September 2013)

Efficient Architecture-Level Configuration of Large-Scale Embedded Software Systems

Razieh Behjati[1] and Shiva Nejati[2]

[1] Certus Software V&V Center, Simula Research Laboratory, Norway
[2] SnT Centre, University of Luxembourg, Luxembourg
behjati@simula.no, shiva.nejati@uni.lu

Abstract. Configuration is a recurring problem in many domains. In our earlier work, we focused on architecture-level configuration of large-scale embedded software systems and proposed a methodology that enables engineers to configure products by instantiating a given reference architecture model. Products have to satisfy a number of constraints specified in the reference architecture model. If not, the engineers have to backtrack their configuration decisions to rebuild a configured product that satisfies the constraints. Backtracking configuration decisions makes the configuration process considerably slow. In this paper, we improve our earlier work and propose a backtrack-free configuration mechanism. Specifically, given a cycle-free generic reference architecture model, we propose an algorithm that computes an ordering over configuration parameters that yields a consistent configuration without any need to backtrack. We evaluated our approach on a simplified model of an industrial case study. We show that our ordering approach eliminates backtracking. It reduces the overall configuration time by both reducing the required number of value assignments, and reducing the time that it takes to complete one configuration iteration. Furthermore, we show that the latter has a linear growth with the size of the configuration problem.

Keywords: Model-based configuration, CSP, Backtracking, UML/OCL.

1 Introduction

Configuration is a recurring problem in many embedded software system domains such as energy, automotive, and avionics. In these domains, product-line engineering approaches [27,22] are largely applied to develop various configurations of a *reference architecture*. Briefly, a reference architecture provides a common, high-level, and customizable structure for all members of the product family [27] by specifying different types of components and configurable parameters, as well as, constraints capturing relationships between these parameters. Through configuration, engineers develop each product by creating component instances and assigning values to their parameters such that the constraints over parameters are satisfied.

© IFIP International Federation for Information Processing 2015
M. Dastani and M.Sirjani (Eds.): FSEN 2015, LNCS 9392, pp. 110–126, 2015.
DOI: 10.1007/978-3-319-24644-4_8

Normally, configuring embedded systems involves assigning values to tens of thousands of interdependent parameters, and ensuring their consistency. Typically, 15 to 20 percent of these parameters are interdependent. Finding consistent values for interdependent parameters without any automated support is challenging. Manual configuration – the common practice in many companies – is time-consuming and error-prone, especially for large-scale systems. During the last three decades, researchers have developed a large number of approaches to automate various configuration use cases [6]. Most of these approaches concern consistency of configuration decisions, and rely on constraint solvers (e.g., [13,23,19]) or SAT solvers (e.g., [20]) for ensuring consistency.

In our earlier work [4], we proposed an iterative approach for configuring large embedded systems where at each iteration the value for one parameter is specified. If at some point during configuration, a value assignment violates some constraints, then the engineers may have to *backtrack* some of their recent choices until they can find a configuration assignment consistent with the constraints in the reference architecture. Backtracking configuration decisions makes the configuration process considerably expensive.

In this paper, we extend our earlier work [4] and propose a new approach that eliminates backtracking during configuration by configuring parameters in a certain order. We explain how such an ordering is extracted from an acyclic[1] reference architecture model, and argue that if the ordering is followed, our algorithm generates consistent and complete configured products without any need to backtrack a decision. We argue that elimination of backtracking considerably improves the performance of our configuration approach. We show this by applying our approach to a simplified excerpt of an industrial case study from the oil and gas domain. The experiment shows that our ordering approach reduces the overall configuration time by both reducing the required number of value assignments, and reducing the time that it takes to complete one configuration iteration. Further, we demonstrate that in our backtrack-free configuration approach the time required for completing one configuration iteration grows linearly with the size of the configuration problem. In our original configuration approach, this time has a quadratic growth.

In the rest of the paper, we first present the related work and position our work in the literature. Section 3 provides an overview of the main concepts in product family modeling and configuration. Our ordering approach for eliminating backtracking, and the resulting backtrack-free configuration algorithm are presented in Section 4. In Section 5, we experimentally evaluate the efficiency and scalability of our approach. A discussion of the potentials and limitations of the work is presented in Section 6. Finally, we conclude the work in Section 7.

---

[1] In our approach, a reference architecture model consists of a component hierarchy, and a set of constraints (see Section 3.1). Such a reference architecture is acyclic if it neither contains any cycles in the component hierarchy nor in the constraints. This condition is required to ensure the termination of the configuration process as well as the complete elimination of backtracking (see Sections 4 and 6).

2 Related Work

Existing configuration approaches fall into two general categories, *non-interactive* and *interactive*. Most configuration approaches belong to the first category, where the objective is to produce some final configured products without requiring intermediate input from users. They may either find an optimized solution based on some given optimization criteria (e.g., [13,19]) or find all configuration solutions (e.g., [7,11,23]). The non-interactive approaches may either rely on meta-heuristic search approaches [14,16,21], or on systematic search techniques used in constraint solvers [9,10,18], or on symbolic decision procedures [8]. Among these, meta-heuristic search approaches are generally faster and require less memory. However, since meta-heuristic search is stochastic and incomplete, it cannot support an interactive process where engineers have to be provided with precise and complete guidance information at each iteration.

Interactive configuration methods (e.g., [17,20,30,31]) mostly rely on constraint solvers or symbolic reasoning approaches. Backtracking is required whenever an inconsistency arises, even though it may make the process considerably slower. In general, constraint solvers alleviate the drawbacks of backtracking by employing heuristics such as back-jumping [12], identifying no-goods constraints [1,2], and ordering the search [15]. None of these improvements, however, totally eliminates the possibility of backtracking. In addition, it is open whether these heuristics can be tailored to interactive configuration solutions.

Some more recent interactive configuration approaches [17,30] have eliminated backtracking by adding an offline preprocessing phase to configuration, during which all consistent configurations are computed and used to direct the user during the interactive phase, preventing the user to make any decision that gives rise to an inconsistency. These approaches only scale when the space of all consistent configurations can be encoded and computed within the available memory. In the case of large-scale embedded software systems, the complexity of constraints and the size of the configuration space is so large[2], making it impossible to compute the set of all possible configurations in an offline mode.

In our work, using information provided in reference architecture model, we identify an ordering over variables and show that by following this ordering, backtracking does not arise during the configuration of a single product. Our approach applies to architecture-level configuration of embedded software systems with architectural dependencies and constraints specified in First-Order Logic (FOL) [29]. Computation of ordering in our work is fast and performed based on static analysis of architectural models and the constraints syntax.

3 Preliminaries

The work presented in this paper is based on a model-based configuration framework presented in [4]. In this section, we present the reference architecture model,

---

[2] Creating a product usually involves configuring tens of thousands of parameters. The configuration space, which is in fact the combinatorial space created for these parameters is, as well, significantly large.

and exemplify the main concepts in modeling and configuration of embedded software systems. In addition, we propose the notion of a configuration tree.

3.1 The Reference Architecture Model

In our approach, a reference architecture model defines a hierarchy of component types. Each component has a number of configurable parameters, and may as well contain other *configurable elements*. We consider configurable parameters as one type of configurable elements. Furthermore, the reference architecture model specifies constraints among the configurable parameters. The SimPL methodology [5] is an approach for creating such reference architecture models. As mentioned earlier, during configuration, products are created by creating component instances and configuring their parameters. In the following, we explain components as the main building blocks of products, and constraints as they play a key role is ensuring the consistency of products. A complete specification of the reference architecture model and its formal semantics is given in [4].

3.1.1 Components

Each component in a product is an instance of a component type in the corresponding reference architecture. We define a component c as a tuple $(id, \mathcal{V})$, where id is a unique identifier, and $\mathcal{V}$ is a set of configurable elements. Each configurable element in $\mathcal{V}$ is a tuple $e = (id_e, t_e)$, where id_e is the name of the element, and t_e is the type of the element. Figure 1 gives a grammar for the types of elements in $\mathcal{V}$.

type	::= *single_type* | *arrayed_type* ;
single_type	::= **primitive_type** | **user_defined_type** | *referenced_type* ;
referenced_type	::= '&' **user_defined_type** ;
arrayed_type	::= *single_type* '[]' ;

Fig. 1. A simplified grammar for types.

In Figure 1, **primitive_type** represents a set of terminals for primitive types 'integer' and 'boolean' (we do not consider 'strings'), and **user_defined_type** denotes a set of terminals each corresponding to a component type defined in the reference architecture model.

Configurable elements of a primitive type or a referenced type represent configurable parameters. A configurable element of a user defined type represents a sub-component of c (i.e., the sub-component is a component $c' = (id', \mathcal{V}')$ itself).

3.1.2 Constraints

Let $c = (id, \mathcal{V})$ be a component. We use Φ_{id} to denote the set of constraints defined in the context of c (i.e., specifying relations among elements of c). Each member of the set Φ_{id} is a boolean expression denoting a constraint ϕ. A simplified grammar for the language of boolean expressions is given in Figure 2. This grammar maps to a subset of the Object Constraint Language (OCL) [26] that we use in the SimPL methodology. The grammar allows the basic OCL operators including for-all, exists, arithmetic, relational and logical operators. In Figure 2, FA represents the universal quantifier, which maps to OCL forAll operator. Similarly, EX represents the existential quantifier, which maps to OCL exists operator.

bool_ expr	::=	*bool_ term* (**OR** *bool_ term*)*;
bool_ term	::=	*bool_ factor* (**AND** *bool_ factor*)*;
bool_ factor	::=	**bool_ literal** | **bool_ qName** | **var** |
		'(' *bool_ expr* ')' | *rel_ expr* | **NOT** *bool_ factor* |
		FA '(' **var** 'in' **array_ qName** ',' *bool_ expr* ')' |
		EX '(' **var** 'in' **array_ qName** ',' *bool_ expr* ')' ;
rel_ expr	::=	*num_ expr* (**GT** | **LT** | **GEQ** | **LEQ** | **EQ** | **NEQ**) *num_ expr*;
num_ expr	::=	*num_ term* ((**PLUS** | **MINUS**) *num_ term*)*;
num_ term	::=	*num_ factor* ((**MUL** | **DIV**) *num_ factor*)*;
num_ factor	::=	**num_ literal** | **int_ qName** | **var** |
		'(' *num_ expr* ')' | **NEG** *num_factor*;

Fig. 2. A simplified grammar of boolean formulas.

Three types of qualified names (i.e., bool_qName, int_qName, and array_qName) are used in the production rules of the grammar given in Figure 2. Qualified names together with literals and operators create numerical, relational, and boolean expressions. Qualified names of numerical types (i.e., integer or a user defined enumeration) form one type of numerical factors and are used in creating relational expressions. Qualified names of type boolean form one type of boolean factors. Qualified names representing collections of items can be combined with set quantifiers (i.e., for all and exists) to form another group of boolean factors. In addition to these, variables (i.e., var) may be used as integer or boolean factors. Variables are used in combination with quantifiers.

3.1.3   A Configuration Example
Figure 3 is a class diagram showing an excerpt of a simplified reference architecture for a family of subsea oil production systems. It is part of a larger case study, which is presented in [5,4]. Each class in Figure 3 represents a component type, and each attribute in a class represents a configurable parameter. In addition, two OCL constraints are defined in the context of class ElectronicConnections.

To make a product, one has to create and configure an instance of a XmasTree. To do so, engineers have to specify the number of electronic boards on each of the Subsea Electronic Modules[3] (SEMs) by initializing the eBoards array in each

---

[3] A Subsea Electronic Module is an electronic unit, with software deployed on it. It is the main component in a subsea control system.

of the two SEMs (each XmasTree instance has two SEM instances) and assign a value to each item in those arrays, create a number of electronic connections by setting the size of array myConnections, and assigning values to relatedSEM, pinIndex and bIndex attributes of each ElectronicConnection instance.

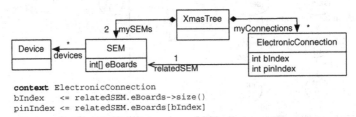

```
context ElectronicConnection
bIndex    <= relatedSEM.eBoards->size()
pinIndex <= relatedSEM.eBoards[bIndex]
```

Fig. 3. An excerpt of the reference architecture model of a subsea oil production system.

Example 1. Suppose that, at some point in the configuration of a product, a user configures an ElectronicConnection by first setting its bIndex to 5, then setting its pinIndex to 20, and finally setting its relatedSEM to one of the SEM instances. At this point, if the chosen SEM instance has less than 5 electronic boards, or its eBoards[5] is less than 20, an inconsistency happens. In this case, the user has to backtrack to fix the inconsistency, for example by changing the value of pinIndex or bIndex. Alternatively, to eliminate backtracking, the user can first configure relatedSEM, then assign a value to bIndex, and finally configure pinIndex.   ■

In this paper, based on a static analysis of the constraints, we propose an approach for identifying configuration orderings that eliminate backtracking.

3.2   The Configuration Tree

A product is usually represented by a *configuration tree*. We denote a configuration tree by a tuple (N, E), where N is the set of nodes, and E is the set of edges of the tree. In our approach, each node in a configuration tree has a type and a value, and each edge has a label. The type of a node belongs to the language of types in Figure 1. Based on this, we identify four types of nodes: *primitive nodes*, *component nodes* (if the node is typed by a user defined type), *reference nodes*, and *array nodes*. Figure 4 shows two example configuration trees.

Primitive nodes and reference nodes represent configurable parameters, and are always leaf nodes in the tree. The value of a leaf node must conform to its type. A missing value for a leaf node means that the corresponding configurable parameter is not yet configured. Nodes m13 and m15 in Figure 4-(b) are primitive and reference nodes, respectively. Both nodes are unconfigured.

Each array node has a child node of type 'int', which is connected to it by an edge labeled 'size()'. We refer to this node as the array's size node. An array node is called *uninitialized* if its size node does not have a value, and is called *initialized* otherwise. An initialized array node of size n, and type '*single_type*[]' has n additional child nodes. Each of these child nodes is typed by '*single_type*',

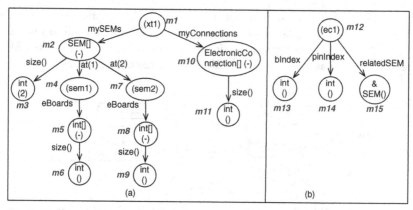

Fig. 4. Configuration subtrees representing two components. Text inside a circle represents the type and value (in parenthesis) of the node. The text next to a node is a unique name to refer to the node in our explanation of the approach. (a) an instance of XmasTree, and (b) an instance of ElectronicConnection.

and is connected to the array node via an edge labeled '$at(i)$', where i is an integer in $[1..n]$. Node m2 in Figure 4-(a) is an initialized array node of size two.

A component node represents a component. Such a node is typed by a user defined type, and its value is the identifier of the corresponding component. Let m be the component node representing the component $c = (id, \mathcal{V})$. For each $(id_e, t_e) \in \mathcal{V}$, there is a child node for m typed by t_e and connected to m via an edge labeled id_e. Node m1 in Figure 4-(a) is a component node of type XmasTree, representing a component with identifier xt1. To avoid cluttering, we have not shown the type of the component (i.e., XmasTree) in the text inside node m1. The subtree beneath m1 shows the configurable elements of xt1. None of these elements are configured in Figure 4-(a). One possible partial configuration is given in Figure 5.

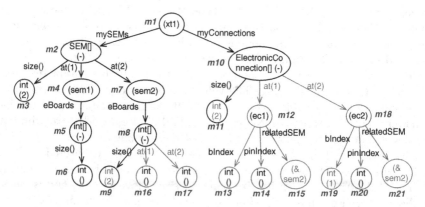

Fig. 5. One possible partial configuration of node *m1* in Figure 4-(a).

4   The Configuration Process

Our model-based configuration approach presented in [4] validates configuration decisions automatically and interactively. For this purpose, we use the configuration tree and the constraints defined in the reference architecture model to create a constraint network [24]. A constraint network is a finite set of variables, each associated with a finite domain of discrete values, and a number of constraints over those variables. The problem of finding a consistent configuration maps to a constraint satisfaction problem, where the objective is to find a consistent assignment of values to all the variables in the constraint network. Each configurable parameter (a leaf node in the configuration tree) maps to a variable in the constraint network. The domain of the variable corresponding to configurable parameter p is a finite set of literals that can be assigned to p. Each constraint in the reference architecture model is rewritten in terms of the variables in the constraint network, and is added to the constraint network. During configuration, new variables or constraints may be added to the constraint network. We call this the *dynamic growth* of the constraint network.

To ensure the consistency of configuration decisions, we use constraint propagation over finite domains [28]. Constraint propagation provides a sound approximation of consistency: it does not eliminate any consistent solution, but it may fail to identify all inconsistent value-assignments. In other words, constraint propagation prunes the search space, but it does not enumerate all possible solutions. The benefit of using constraint propagation is that it is fast, and therefore applicable in an interactive context. Its drawback is that it does not eliminate all inconsistent value-assignments, and therefore, backtracking may be needed to ensure consistency. This can be avoided by imposing some restrictions on the reference architecture model of the product family. In particular, the model of the product family should not contain any cyclic constraints.

Another reason for requiring backtracking in our original configuration approach is the dynamic growth of the constraint network. New constraints that are added to the constraint network may be inconsistent with some of the previously made decisions. To avoid this, we configure parameters in a particular order. In the following, before presenting our approach for ordering configuration decisions, we first present the notion of qualified names. Then, based on the proposed ordering approach, we present a backtrack-free configuration algorithm.

4.1   Qualified Names

Figure 6 shows a grammar for *qualified names*. A qualified name (e.g., int_qName) represents a typed variable (e.g., a configurable parameter) and may represent an individual item (e.g., int_qName) or a collection of items (i.e., array_qName). The last rule in Figure 6 is added to explicitly define int_qName and bool_qName as *primitive qualified names*. Primitive qualified names represent configurable parameters, and together with array qualified names are used in the grammar of boolean expressions in Figure 2.

A qualified name can be created by traversing a configuration tree. Let CT be a configuration tree, and n be a node representing a component $c = (id, \mathcal{V})$ in the configuration tree. Each node n' in the subtree rooted at n can be uniquely identified by a string created using id and edge labels. To do so, we start with string $str = \text{``}id\text{''}$, and follow the edges that bring us to n'. After traversing each edge, we concatenate str with ".l", where l is the label of the last traversed edge[4]. Using this approach each node in the tree may be represented by more than one string, depending on the starting node. A string should always start with the label of a component node.

```
1  int_ qName           ::= element_qName '.' int_prop_name |
2                            array_ qName '.' 'size()' |
3                            int_ array_qName '[' int_factor ']';
4  int_factor           ::= int_literal | int_qName;
5  int_ array_ qName     ::= element_qName '.' int_array_prop_name;
6  element_ qName        ::= component_id |
7                            element_qName '.' element_prop_name |
8                            element_ array_qName '[' int_factor ']';
9  element_ array_ qName ::= element_qName '.' element_array_prop_name;
10 bool_ qName          ::= element_qName '.' bool_prop_name |
11                           bool_ array_qName '[' int_factor ']';
12 bool_ array_ qName   ::= element_qName '.' bool_array_prop_name;
13 array_ qName         ::= int_ array_ qName | bool_array_ qName |
14                           element_ array_ qName;
15 primitive_ qName     ::= int_qName | bool_qName;
```

Fig. 6. The grammar of qualified names.

4.1.1 Semantically Valid Qualified Names

Let CT be a configuration tree representing a possibly partially-configured product derived from a given reference architecture. A subset of the qualified names created using the grammar in Figure 6 are semantically valid with respect to the configuration tree CT. We use $Q(CT)$ to denote this subset. A qualified name q belongs to $Q(CT)$ iff one of the following holds:

- q is the label of a component node in CT,
- $q = q1.t$, where $q1 \in Q(CT)$, and $q1$ represents a component $c = (id, \mathcal{V})$, such that t is the name of an element in $\mathcal{V}$,
- $q = q1[q2]$, where $q1 \in Q(CT)$, $q1$ represents an arrayed element, and $q2$ is either an integer literal or a semantically valid qualified name representing an integer parameter,
- $q = q1.size()$, where $q1 \in Q(CT)$, and $q1$ is an arrayed element.

---

[4] In the rest of this paper, for the sake of conciseness, we use $a[i]$ to denote $a.at(i)$, where a represents an array node in the configuration tree, and i is an integer literal.

4.1.2   Mapped and Unmapped Qualified Names

Let CT be a configuration tree, and q be a semantically valid qualified name in $Q(CT)$. If q corresponds to a node in CT, then we call q a *mapped* qualified name, otherwise, it is called an *unmapped* qualified name. A qualified name q is unmapped if any of the following conditions holds:

- a prefix of q maps to an unconfigured reference node,
- q is of the form $q1[q2]$, where $q2$ represents an unconfigured parameter,
- q is of the form $q1[q2]$, where $q1$ is an uninitialized array ($q1.size()$ is not configured).

In each case, a parameter is unconfigured. For a semantically valid unmapped qualified name q, we use $\mathcal{U}(q)$ to denote the set of all such unconfigured parameters. For a qualified name q mapped to a leaf node, we use $\mathcal{M}(q)$ to denote the corresponding configurable parameter.

Let CT be the configuration tree in Figure 5. Then xt1.mySEMs[1] is mapped, and sem1.eBoards[1] is an unmapped semantically valid qualified name in $Q(CT)$. An unmapped qualified name can become mapped as parameters are configured and the tree is expanded. For example, sem1.eBoards[1] becomes mapped after configuring the size of sem1.eBoards.

4.2   Ordering Configuration Decisions

Example 1 in Section 3.1.3 shows an example of inconsistencies that arise due to the dynamic growth. In this example, the two constraints in Figure 3 cannot be evaluated until relatedSEM is configured. This is because relatedSEM.eBoards, appeared in both constraints, is unmapped as it does not correspond to a unique node in the tree. By configuring relatedSEM both constraints become *ready-to-evaluate*, can be added to the constraint network, and can be used in constraint propagation to validate the values assigned to pinIndex and bIndex or to eliminate inconsistent values for them if they were not configured. We call a constraint that is not yet ready-to-evaluate, a *pending* constraint. Such a constraint contains one or more unmapped qualified names and is pending on one or more parameters to be configured. These parameters should be configured to make the unmapped qualified names mapped. For example, the constraints in *Example 1* are pending on relatedSEM to be configured. In each configuration iteration, each constraint is either pending or ready-to-evaluate. Figure 7 shows the state transition diagram of a constraint. As a consequence of configuring parameters, a pending constraint may become ready-to-evaluate. Only ready-to-evaluate constraints can be included in the constraint network.

Consider the ith step of configuration and let c be a pending binary constraint, containing two qualified names q_1 and q_2. Suppose that q_1 is unmapped, and q_2 is mapped to the configurable parameter p (i.e., $\mathcal{M}(q_2) = p$). This parameter cannot be configured until c becomes ready-to-evaluate (i.e., until q_1 becomes a mapped qualified name). We refer to such a parameter as a *pending* parameter. Let parameters $p_1, ..., p_n$ be the parameters that should be configured to make q_1

a mapped qualified name (i.e., $\mathcal{U}(q_1) = \{p_1, ..., p_n\}$). To eliminate backtracking, parameter p should be configured after all p_is are configured. This is shown in Figure 8. Before a parameter reaches the state ready, the set X, which is the set of all p_is as described above, should be empty. As shown in Figure 8, a parameter can be configured only when it is in state ready. Note that, as suggested by the formulation of X, in general p may be involved in more than one constraint.

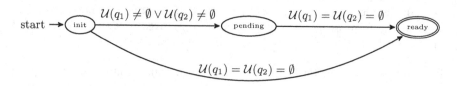

Fig. 7. States of constraint $c = \phi(q_1, q_2)$.

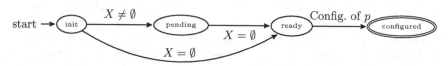

Fig. 8. States of parameter p. X is $\{p'|\exists c = \phi(q_1, q_2).p' \in \mathcal{U}(q_1) \wedge \mathcal{M}(q_2) = p\}$.

In other words, in each configuration iteration, the set of all unconfigured parameters is partitioned into two sets: pending and ready-to-configure parameters. This partitioning of parameters, together with the stepwise configuration, which in each iteration may add new unconfigured parameters to the system, imposes an ordering on the configuration decisions. Note that, in each iteration, there is no ordering among the ready-to-configure parameters. The acyclic property of the reference architecture model guarantees that every parameter eventually reaches the state ready.

4.3   Backtrack-Free Configuration

Algorithm 1 is our backtrack free configuration algorithm, which implements the ordering approach explained above. Input to the algorithm is a cycle-free reference architecture, which contains a class diagram and a set of constraints. The output is a configuration tree CT. We maintain three sets of parameters: configured (C), ready-to-configure (R), and pending parameters (P); and two sets of constraints: ready-to-evaluate (Φ), and pending (Φ') constraints. Using the input reference architecture model, we initialize all these sets and the configuration tree in line 1 of the algorithm.

Algorithm 1. BTFreeConfig

Input: A reference architecture RA
Output: a configuration tree CT
  1 $(CT, C, R, P, \Phi, \Phi') \leftarrow$ InitializeConfigurationProblem(RA)
  2 $D \leftarrow$ computeValidDomains(C, R, Φ)
  3 **while** $R \neq \emptyset$ **do**
  4   READ(i) $\triangleright$ i: index of the selected unconfigured parameter
  5   READ(v) $\triangleright$ value to be assigned to the selected parameter
  6      $\triangleright$ v must be in $D[i]$ (the domain of the selected parameter)
  7   **while not** $v \in D[i]$ **do**
  8   READ(v)
  9   applyConfiguration$(CT, C, R, P, \Phi, \Phi', i, tmp)$
 10    $D \leftarrow$ updateValidDomains(C, R, Φ)
 11   **if** some domains in D are empty **then**
 12   throwException$()$
 13 **return** CT

In line 2, domains of the unconfigured parameters are computed using the routine computeValidDomains. In this routine, we use a constraint solver to prune the domains by removing values that are inconsistent with one or more constraints in Φ or some values in C. Note that only the ready-to-evaluate constraints and their variables are considered when pruning the domains (i.e., P and Q are not included in the computation).

The while loop in lines 3–12 repeats while there are some ready-to-configure parameters (i.e., $R \neq \emptyset$). In each iteration, one parameter is configured. Both the parameter and its value are selected by the human user in lines 4 and 5 of the algorithm. Lines 7 and 8 guarantee that the selected value is within the domain of the selected parameter and is, therefore, consistent. As a result of assigning a value v to a parameter $R[i]$, one or more of the following may happen:

- new nodes may be added to the configuration tree, therefore new elements may be added to R and P
- if a constraint is pending on $R[i]$, it may become ready-to-evaluate, and
- some of the parameters that are pending on $R[i]$ may become ready for configuration. We move them to the set of ready-to-configure parameters R.

These actions are performed in line 9 by calling the routine applyConfiguration. The constraint solver is again invoked in line 10 to update the valid domains. If some domains become empty, the algorithm throws an exception in line 12. Otherwise, it continues to the next iteration. Eventually, a completely and consistently configured configuration tree is returned in line 13.

In [4], we showed that our original configuration algorithm produces complete and consistent products. A product is complete if it does not contain any unconfigured parameters, and is consistent if it satisfies all the constraints in the reference architecture model. In our technical report [3], we have shown that Algorithm 1 produces complete and consistent products, but without requiring backtracking. In other words, for any given acyclic reference architecture model, Algorithm 1 terminates without ever reaching line 12.

5   Evaluation

To evaluate the efficiency brought by our ordering approach, we performed an experiment using the reference architecture model presented in Figure 3. For this purpose, 1600 random configuration scenarios were created (800 scenarios for each of our original and backtrack-free configuration approaches). In each case, we started by configuring three parameters that identify the size of the configuration problem, then randomly configured the rest of the parameters. The first three parameters were configured as listed in Table 1. This is done merely to control the number of parameters in each case to simplify the analysis of the results. For each case in Table 1, we randomly generated 100 sample configuration scenarios using our original configuration approach, and 100 sample configuration scenarios using the backtrack-free configuration approach. Figure 9 shows the average response time in each iteration for both cases.

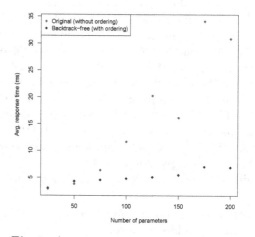

# Parameters	# Elec. Connections	# eBoards on SEMs
25	5	3,4
50	14	2,3
75	21	4,5
100	27	6,10
125	32	12,14
150	35	17,25
175	49	11,14
200	49	25,25

Table 1. Configuration settings.

Fig. 9. A comparison of the average response time for our original and backtrack-free configuration approaches.

In our original configuration approach, a complete configuration iteration, in addition to validating the decision and propagating it, may involve several decision roll-backs, and is therefore time consuming. On the other hand, a complete configuration iteration in the backtrack-free configuration approach involves validating and propagating the decision, and updating the ordering (i.e., updating lists of pending constraints and parameters). By using the ordering, we eliminate all the roll-backs and their costs. This explains why for most cases in Figure 9, an average iteration in the original configuration approach takes much longer than that in the backtrack-free configuration approach. This experiment shows that for configuration scenarios with more than 50 parameters, the time overhead of computing the ordering is negligible compared to the time that should otherwise be spent on rolling-back the decisions.

In our original configuration approach, for fixing an inconsistency, in addition to rolling back some of the decisions, new values must be assigned to the parameters that might have caused that inconsistency. In our experiment, on average 23.6 different values were tried per parameter to achieve a consistent configuration. This high number is a result of our current naive implementation of backtracking. By exploiting heuristics such as back jumping [12], this number can be reduced significantly. Table 2 shows the number of decisions that were needed to achieve a consistent configuration.

Table 2. Overhead of backtracking.

# Parameters	25	50	75	100	125	150	175	200
Avg. # Decisions	174.85	949.60	1773.49	2678.15	3426.29	2112.34	6301.47	3842.10
Avg. Ratio	6.99	18.99	23.65	26.78	27.41	14.08	36.00	19.21
Total Avg. Ratio (average number of decisions per parameter)						23.62		

To provide a better insight into the time complexity of our configuration approaches, we performed another experiment. The result of this experiment is shown in Figures 10 and 11. In each case, we measured the average response time for randomly generated configuration scenarios. Figure 10 shows that for our original approach the response time (i.e., the time that it takes to complete one configuration iteration) grows quadratically with the size of the configuration problem (i.e., the number of configurable parameters). On the other hand, as shown in Figure 11, in the case of our backtrack-free configuration approach, this growth is linear with the size of the configuration problem.

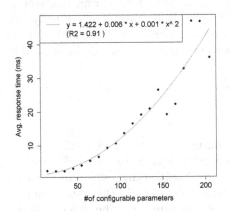

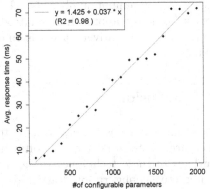

Fig. 10. Quadratic growth of the average response time in our original configuration approach.

Fig. 11. Linear growth of the average response time in our backtrack-free configuration approach.

Furthermore, Figure 11 gives an insight into the usability of our backtrack-free configuration approach. According to a study reported in [25], 0.1 second is about the limit for having the user feel that the system is reacting instantaneously. Figure 11 shows that our backtrack-free configuration approach can respond instantly even for configuration problems with up to 2000 parameters.

6   Discussion

Normally, backtracking is used to explore the search space, in order to resolve inconsistencies, or to find all solutions. In our configuration approach [4], we use backtracking to resolve inconsistencies that may arise while configuring a single product. Analyzing configuration scenarios shows that, in our approach, most of these inconsistencies are due to early configuration of parameters that are involved in some pending constraints. By delaying the configuration of such parameters, using our ordering approach, we can prevent inconsistent configurations. One should note that our approach cannot generally eliminate backtracking for every use-case, such as enumerating all configurations, or resolving inconsistencies that may arise due to cyclic constraints.

For our backtrack-free configuration approach to be able to produce consistent and complete products, the input reference architecture model must be cycle-free. In particular, to guarantee the termination of the configuration algorithm, the component hierarchy must be acyclic. Achieving this property for embedded software systems, where the software architecture follows, to a great extent, the architecture of hardware, is straightforward. To guarantee consistency, without requiring backtracking, the model should contain no cyclic constraints. Whether this restriction can negatively affect the applicability of our approach is a question that requires further investigation. Identifying the likelihood of embedded systems with cyclic constraints and proposing heuristics for ensuring their consistency with a minimum number of backtracks is left for future work. Finally, our proposed ordering approach may introduce some rigidity. Whether this rigidity affects usability negatively or not is an open questions that should be studied in future.

7   Conclusion

Constraint solving is generally used to ensure consistency of configurations, which are an essential part of software development in today's industries. A drawback of these techniques is the need for backtracking, which in the case of interactive configuration drastically hampers usability. In this paper, we proposed a partial ordering over the configurable parameters. The ordering is derived from a static analysis of the constraints between the parameters. Using the ordering approach, we have implemented a backtrack-free configuration tool. We performed a number of experiments using a case study from an industry partner. Results of our experiments show that our backtrack-free configuration tool ensures consistency, while preventing the need for backtracking. Furthermore, our approach significantly reduces the overall configuration time.

Acknowledgements. The first author acknowledges the Research Council of Norway (the ModelFusion Project - NFR 205606). The second author is funded by the National Research Fund - Luxembourg (FNR/P10/03 - Verification and Validation Laboratory).

References

1. Armstrong, A.A., Durfee, E.H.: Dynamic prioritization of complex agents in distributed constraint satisfaction problems. In: AAAI/IAAI (1997)
2. Bayardo, R.J., Miranker, D.P.: A complexity analysis of space-bounded learning algorithms for the constraint satisfaction problem. In: AAAI (1996)
3. Behjati, R., Nejati, S.: Backtrack-free consistent configuration of cyber-physical systems (2014), http://simula.no/publications/Simula.simula.2608
4. Behjati, R., Nejati, S., Briand, L.C.: Architecture-level configuration of large-scale embedded software systems. In: Accepted for publication in TOSEM (2014)
5. Behjati, R., Yue, T., Briand, L.C., Selic, B.: SimPL: a product-line modeling methodology for families of integrated control systems. In: Information and Software Technology (2013); Special Issue on Software Reuse and Product Lines
6. Benavides, D., Segura, S., Ruiz-Cortés, A.: Automated analysis of feature models 20 years later: A literature review. In: Inf. Syst. (2010)
7. Benavides, D., Segura, S., Trinidad, P., Ruiz Cortés, A.: FAMA: tooling a framework for the automated analysis of feature models. In: VaMoS (2007)
8. Bryant, R.E.: Graph-based algorithms for boolean function manipulation. IEEE Trans. Comput. (1986)
9. Carlsson, M., Mildner, P.: SICStus Prolog – the first 25 years. CoRR (2010)
10. Carlsson, M., Ottosson, G., Carlson, B.: An open-ended finite domain constraint solver. In: Hartel, P.H., Kuchen, H. (eds.) PLILP 1997. LNCS, vol. 1292, pp. 191–206. Springer, Heidelberg (1997)
11. Czarnecki, K., Kim, P.: Cardinality-Based Feature Modeling and Constraints: A Progress Report. In: Workshop on Software Factories at OOPSLA (2005)
12. Dechter, R., Frost, D.: Backjump-based backtracking for constraint satisfaction problems. Artif. Intell. 136(2) (2002)
13. Eames, B.K., Neema, S., Saraswat, R.: DesertFD: a finite-domain constraint based tool for design space exploration. Design Autom. for Emb. Sys. 14(2) (2010)
14. Fonseca, C.M., Fleming, P.J.: An overview of evolutionary algorithms in multiobjective optimization. In: Evolutionary Computation (1995)
15. Freuder, E.C.: A sufficient condition for backtrack-free search. Journal of the ACM (JACM) (1982)
16. Glover, F., Taillard, E.D.: A user's guide to tabu search. In: Annals OR (1993)
17. Hadzic, T., Subbarayan, S., Jensen, R.M., Andersen, H.R., Møller, J., Hulgaard, H.: Fast backtrack-free product configuration using a precompiled solution space representation. In: PETO (2004)
18. Hentenryck, P.V., Saraswat, V.A., Deville, Y.: Design, implementation, and evaluation of the constraint language cc(FD). In: Selected Papers from Constraint Programming: Basics and Trends (1995)
19. Horváth, Á., Varró, D.: Dynamic constraint satisfaction problems over models. Software and Systems Modeling (2010)

20. Janota, M., Botterweck, G., Grigore, R., Marques-Silva, J.: How to complete an interactive configuration process? In: van Leeuwen, J., Muscholl, A., Peleg, D., Pokorný, J., Rumpe, B. (eds.) SOFSEM 2010. LNCS, vol. 5901, pp. 528–539. Springer, Heidelberg (2010)
21. Kirkpatrick, S., Gelatt, C.D., Vecchi, M.P.: Optimization by simulated annealing. Science (1983)
22. Linden, F.J., Schmid, K., Rommes, E.: Software Product Lines in Action: The Best Industrial Practice in Product Line Engineering. Springer-Verlag New York, Inc. (2007)
23. Mazo, R., Salinesi, C., Diaz, D., Lora-Michiels, A.: Transforming attribute and clone-enabled feature models into constraint programs over finite domains. In: ENASE 2011 (2011)
24. Montanari, U.: Networks of constraints: Fundamental properties and applications to picture processing. Information Sciences 7, 95–132 (1974)
25. Nielsen, J.: Usability Engineering. Morgan Kaufmann Publishers Inc., San Francisco (1993)
26. OMG. OMG Object Constraint Language (OMG OCL), Version 2.3.1 (2012)
27. Pohl, K., Böckle, G., Linden, F.J.: Software Product Line Engineering: Foundations, Principles and Techniques. Springer-Verlag New York, Inc. (2005)
28. Rossi, F., van Beek, P., Walsh, T.: Handbook of Constraint Programming. Elsevier Science Inc., New York (2006)
29. Smullyan, R.M.: First-order logic. Springer (1968)
30. van der Meer, E.R., Wasowski, A., Andersen, H.R.: Efficient interactive configuration of unbounded modular systems. In: SAC (2006)
31. Xiong, Y., Hubaux, A., She, S., Czarnecki, K.: Generating range fixes for software configuration. In: ICSE 2012 (2012)

Benchmarks for Parity Games

Jeroen J.A. Keiren[1,2]

[1] Open University of the Netherlands
Faculty of Management, Science & Technology
Heerlen, The Netherlands
Jeroen.Keiren@ou.nl
[2] VU University Amsterdam
Theoretical Computer Science
Amsterdam, The Netherlands

Abstract. We propose a benchmark suite for parity games that includes the benchmarks that have been used in the literature, and make it available online. We give an overview of the parity games, including a description of how they have been generated. We also describe structural properties of parity games, and using these properties we show that our benchmarks are representative. With this work we provide a starting point for further experimentation with parity games.

1   Introduction

Parity games (see, *e.g.*, [24,55,78]) play an important role in model checking research. The μ-calculus model checking problem is polynomial time reducible to the problem of deciding the winner in parity games [73]. Other problems that are expressible in parity games are equivalence checking of labelled transition systems [73], as well as synthesis, satisfiability and validity of temporal logics [66].

Besides their practical interest for verification, solving (deciding the winner of) parity games is known to be in the complexity class $\mathsf{NP} \cap \mathsf{co} - \mathsf{NP}$, and more specifically in $\mathsf{UP} \cap \mathsf{co} - \mathsf{UP}$ [42]. Parity game solving is one of the few problems in this complexity class that is not known to be in P, yet there is hope that a polynomial time algorithm exists. In recent years this has led to the development of (1) a large number of algorithms for solving parity games, such as [44,67,68], all of which were recently shown to be exponential, and (2) the study of (polynomial time) reduction techniques for parity games [30,47,21,22].

So far, practical evaluation of parity game algorithms has been based on ad-hoc benchmarks, mainly consisting of random games or synthetic benchmarks. Friedmann and Lange observed in 2009 [30] that no standard benchmark set for parity games was available. They introduced a small benchmark set in the context of their comprehensive comparison of parity game solving algorithms and their related heuristics [30]. The set of benchmarks was extended in [47,21,22] using model checking and equivalence checking cases. To the best of our knowledge, the situation has not improved since then, and the benchmarks in these

M. Dastani and M.Sirjani (Eds.): FSEN 2015, LNCS 9392, pp. 127–142, 2015.
DOI: 10.1007/978-3-319-24644-4_9

papers still are the most comprehensive benchmarks included in a single paper. The number of games and the diversity of parity games in each set in isolation are however limited. The lack of standard benchmarks makes it hard to compare the different tools and algorithms presented in the literature.

To improve the current situation, in this paper we propose a set of parity games for benchmarking purposes that (1) is diverse, (2) contains games that originate from different verification problems, and (3) includes those games that have been used to experimentally evaluate algorithms in the literature.

In general, parity game examples in the literature can be classified as follows (we indicate their origins):

1. Encodings of problems such as model checking, equivalence checking and complementation of Büchi automata to parity games [53,54,75,47,21,22,30].
2. Synthetic parity games for which a certain solving algorithm requires exponential time [53,43,58,26,31,29,35].
3. Random games [6,49,68,69,30,31].

Our benchmarks include games from each of these categories.

Additionally, inspired by the properties for explicit state spaces in [60] we introduce a set of structural properties for parity games, and in the spirit of [61,62] we analyse our benchmarks. Among others, we introduce a novel notion of alternation depth for parity games.

The structure of the paper is as follows. We first introduce parity games and their structural properties in Section 2. Next we describe the benchmarks (Section 3) and the way in which they have been generated (Section 4). Finally we illustrate diversity of our benchmarks with respect to the structural properties in Section 5. This paper is based on the PhD thesis of the author [45, Chapter 5]; an extended version of this paper, including more detailed descriptions and analyses is available as [46]. We plan to keep [46] up-to-date when new benchmarks are added, and we invite the community to contribute benchmarks.

2 Parity Games and Their Structural Properties

A parity game is a two-player game played on a finite, directed graph by two players, *even* and *odd*, denoted $\Diamond$ and $\Box$, respectively. We use $\bigcirc \in \{\Diamond, \Box\}$ to denote an arbitrary player. Formally, a parity game is a structure $(V_\Diamond, V_\Box, \rightarrow, \Omega)$, where $V_\Diamond$ and $V_\Box$ are disjoint sets of vertices. We say that $\bigcirc$ owns v if $v \in V_\bigcirc$, we write V for $V_\Diamond \cup V_\Box$; $\rightarrow \subseteq V \times V$ provides the total edge relation—hence each vertex has a successor—and $\Omega: V \rightarrow \mathbb{N}$ assigns a non-negative integer priority to every vertex. The parity game is played by placing a token on some initial vertex, and then the players take turns moving the token: if the token is on a vertex $v \in V_\bigcirc$ then $\bigcirc$ plays the token to one of the successors of v. This way, an infinite play through the game is constructed. If the largest priority that occurs infinitely often on this play is *even* (resp. *odd*) then $\Diamond$ (resp. $\Box$) wins the play.

The time required for parity game solving and reduction algorithms depends on the structure of the game. Typically the algorithmic complexity of parity game algorithms are expressed in terms of the size of the game graph, *i.e.* the number of vertices and edges, and the number of priorities in the game. Although other structural properties may not affect the asymptotic running times of the algorithms, in general they do affect the actual running time. We therefore describe a number structural properties that could be used for the further study of parity games.

Sizes. As basic parity game properties, we consider the numbers of vertices $|V|$, $|V_\Diamond|$ and $|V_\Box|$, and the number of edges $|\to|$. We write $\Omega(V)$ for the set of priorities $\{\Omega(v) \mid v \in V\}$, and denote the number of priorities in the game by $|\Omega(V)|$. The number of vertices with priority k is represented by $|\Omega^{-1}(k)|$. The complexity of most parity game algorithms is expressed in these quantities. For parity games in which either $|V_\Box| = 0$ or $|V_\Diamond| = 0$, special polynomial time solving algorithms are available, see [30].

Degrees. Typical structural properties in the graph are the in- and out-degrees of vertices, *i.e.*, the number of incoming and outgoing edges of vertices. Formally, for vertex $v \in V$, $\mathsf{indeg}(v) = |\{u \in V \mid u \to v\}|$, $\mathsf{outdeg}(v) = |\{w \in V \mid v \to w\}|$, and $\mathsf{deg}(v) = |\{w \in V \mid v \to w \vee w \to v\}|$ are the in-degree, out-degree and degree of v. We consider the minimum, maximum and average of these values.

The degrees of vertices might have an effect on, *e.g.*, algorithms that use lifting strategies to propagate information between vertices. Examples of such algorithms are small progress measures [43] and the strategy improvement algorithm [68].

Strongly Connected Components. The strongly connected components (SCCs) of a graph are the maximal strongly connected subgraphs. More formally, a strongly connected component is a maximal set $C \subseteq V$ for which, for all $u, v \in C$, $u \to^* v$, *i.e.*, each vertex in C can reach every other vertex in C.

The strongly connected components in a graph induce a quotient graph. Let $\mathsf{sccs}(G)$ denote the strongly connected components of the graph. The quotient graph is the graph $(\mathsf{sccs}(G), \to')$ and for $C_1, C_2 \in \mathsf{sccs}(G)$, there is an edge $C_1 \to' C_2$ if and only if $C_1 \neq C_2$ and there exist $u \in C_1$ and $v \in C_2$ such that $u \to v$. Observe that the quotient graph is a directed acyclic graph.

We say that an SCC C is *trivial* if $|C| = 1$ and $C \not\to C$, *i.e.*, it only contains one vertex and no edges, and we say that C is *terminal* if $C \not\to'$, *i.e.*, its outdegree in the quotient graph is 0. The *SCC quotient height* of a graph is the length of the longest path in the quotient graph.

Parity game algorithms and heuristics can benefit from a decomposition into strongly connected components (SCCs). One prominent example of this is the global parity game solving algorithm presented by Friedmann and Lange [30], for which it was shown that SCC decomposition generally works well in practice.

Properties of Search Strategies. Given some initial vertex $v_0 \in V$, breadth-first search (BFS) and depth-first search (DFS) are search strategies that can be used to systematically explore all vertices in the graph. The fundamental difference between BFS and DFS is that the BFS maintains a queue of vertices that still need to be processed, whereas the DFS maintains a stack of vertices. We record the queue and stack sizes during the search.

Breadth-first search induces a natural notion of levels, where a vertex is at level k if it has least distance k to v_0. The *BFS height* of a graph is k if k is the maximal non-empty level of the BFS. For each level the number of vertices at that level is recorded. During a BFS, three kinds of edges can be detected, *viz.* edges that go to a vertex that was not yet seen, edges that go to a vertex that was seen, but has not yet been processed (*i.e.*, vertices in the queue) and edges that go back to a vertex on a previous level. This last type of edges is also referred to as a *back-level edge*. Formally it is an edge $u \to v$ where the level of u, say k_u is larger than the level of v, say k_v. The length of a back-level edge $u \to v$ is $k_u - k_v$.

Graph algorithms are typically based on a search strategy like BFS or DFS, given some initial vertex $v_0 \in V$. The characteristics of these search strategies are therefore likely to affect the performance of such graph algorithms.

Width-measures on Graphs. Width-measures of graphs are based on cops-and-robbers games [56,63], where different measures are obtained by varying the rules of the game. For various measures, specialised algorithms are known that can solve games polynomially if their width is bounded. Most of the measures have an alternative characterisation using graph decompositions.

The classical width notion for *undirected graphs* is *treewidth* [64,11]. Intuitively, the treewidth of a graph expresses how tree-like the graph is—the treewidth of a tree is 1. This corresponds to the idea that some problems are easier to solve for trees, or graphs that are almost trees, than for arbitrary graphs. For directed graphs, the treewidth is defined as the treewidth of the graph obtained by forgetting the direction of the edges. The complexity for solving parity games is bounded in the treewidth [57]; this means that, for parity games with a small, constant treewidth, parity game solving is polynomial.

Treewidth has been lifted to directed graphs in a number of different ways. For instance, *Directed treewidth* [41] is bounded by the treewidth [1]. *DAG-width* [7] describes how much a graph is like a directed acyclic graph. DAG-width bounds the directed tree width of a graph from above, and is at most the treewidth. The *Kelly-width* [40] is yet another generalitation of treewidth to directed graphs. If the Kelly-width of a graph is bounded, then also a bound on its directed treewidth can be given, however, classes of directed graphs with bounded directed treewidth and unbounded Kelly-width exist. *Entanglement* [9,10] is a graph measure that aims to express how much the cycles in a graph are intertwined. If an undirected graph has bounded treewidth or bounded DAG-with, then it also has bounded entanglement. Finally, *clique-width* [19] measures how close a graph is to a complete bipartite graph. For every directed graph with bounded treewidth an exponential upper bound on its clique-width can be given. Unlike the other width measures that we discussed clique-width does not have a characterisation in terms of cops-and-robbers games.

If a parity game is bounded to a constant in any of the measures introduced above, it can be solved in polynomial time.

Alternation Depth. Typically, the complexity of parity game algorithms is expressed in the number of vertices, the number of edges, and the number of priorities in the game. If we look at other verification problems, such as μ-calculus model checking, or solving Boolean equation systems, the complexity is typically expressed in terms of the *alternation depth*. Different versions of alternation depth (with varying precision) have been coined, see [14]. Intuitively, the alternation depth of a formula captures the number of alternations between different fixed point symbols.

Analogous to the definition of alternation depth for modal equation systems by Cleaveland *et al.* [18], our definition consists of two parts. First we define the nesting depth of a strongly connected component within a parity game, next we define the alternation depth of the parity game as the maximum of the nesting depths of its strongly connected components.

Definition 1. *Let* $G = (V_\Diamond, V_\Box, \rightarrow, \Omega)$ *be a parity game, and let* $\mathsf{sccs}(G)$ *be the set of strongly connected components of* G*. Let* $\mathcal{C} \in \mathsf{sccs}(G)$ *be a strongly connected component. The nesting depth of* v_i *in* $\mathcal{C}$ *is given by*

$$\mathsf{nd}(v_i, \mathcal{C}) \triangleq \max\{1,$$
$$\max\{\mathsf{nd}(v_j, \mathcal{C}) \mid v_j \rightarrow^*_{\mathcal{C}, \Omega(v_i)} v_i, v_j \neq v_i \text{ and } \Omega(v_i) \equiv_2 \Omega(v_j)\},$$
$$\max\{\mathsf{nd}(v_j, \mathcal{C}) + 1 \mid v_j \rightarrow^*_{\mathcal{C}, \Omega(v_i)} v_i \text{ and } \Omega(v_i) \not\equiv_2 \Omega(v_j)\}$$
$$\}$$

where $v_j \rightarrow_{\mathcal{C}, k} v_i$ *if* $v_j \rightarrow v_i$ *is an edge in the SCC* $\mathcal{C}$ *with* $\Omega(v_j) \leq k$ *and* $\Omega(v_i) \leq k$*. Intuitively, the nesting depth of a vertex* v *counts the number of alternations between even and odd priorities on paths of descending priorities in the SCC of* v*. Note that this is well-defined since we forbid paths between identical nodes.*

The nesting depth of an SCC $\mathcal{C} \in \mathsf{sccs}(G)$ is defined as the maximum nesting depth of any vertices in $\mathcal{C}$, i.e., $\mathsf{nd}(\mathcal{C}) \triangleq \max\{\mathsf{nd}(v, \mathcal{C}) \mid v \in \mathcal{C}\}$. The *alternation depth* of a parity game is defined as the maximal nesting depth of its SCCs.

Definition 2. *Let* $G = (V_\Diamond, V_\Box, \rightarrow, \Omega)$ *be a parity game, and let* $\mathsf{sccs}(G)$ *be the set of strongly connected components of* G*. Then the* alternation depth *of* G *is defined as* $\mathsf{ad}(G) \triangleq \max\{\mathsf{nd}(\mathcal{C}) \mid \mathcal{C} \in \mathsf{sccs}(G)\}$*.*

There are reasonable translations of the μ-calculus model checking problem into parity games, such that the alternation depth of the resulting parity game is at most the fixed point alternation depth of the μ-calculus formula as described by Emerson and Lei [25], see [45, Proposition 5.4]. Note that the alternation depth of a game can be smaller than the number of priorities in the game, and could provide an interesting alternative to the number of priorities in computing the complexity of parity game algorithms.

Other measures. When studying structural properties for labelled transition systems, other global measures such as *diameter* and *girth* have been considered. The diameter is the maximal length of a shortest path between any pair of vertices. The girth is the length of the shortest cycle in the graph. Also, local properties such as the *number of diamonds* and the *k-neighbourhood* were studied. These measures could be considered for parity games as well, but currently there is no clear indication that they are related to the performance of parity game algorithms. These measures and their analysis with respect to the games presented in the next section have been described in more detail in the extended version [46].

3   Benchmarks

For benchmarking parity game algorithms, it makes sense to distinguish three classes of parity games, (1) the games that are the result of encoding a problem into parity games, (2) games that represent hard cases for certain algorithms, and (3) random games. All three classes of games occur in the literature, and our benchmark set contains games from each of these classes. In the rest of this section we discuss our benchmarks. In the next section we briefly discuss these games with respect to the properties described in Section 2.

3.1   Encodings

A broad range of verification problems can be encoded as a parity game. The most prominent examples of these are the μ-calculus model checking problem—does a model satisfy a given property?—, equivalence checking problems—are two models equivalent?—, decision procedures—is a formula valid or satisfiable?— and synthesis—given a property, give a model that satisfies the property.

Model Checking. The model checking problems we consider are mainly selected from the literature. All of the systems are encodings that, given a model L of a system, and a property φ, encode the model checking problem $L \models \varphi$, *i.e.*, does L satisfy property φ. Most sensible encodings of model checking problems typically lead to a low number of priorities, corresponding to the low alternation depths of these properties. We verify fairness, liveness and safety properties. This set includes, but is not limited to, the model checking problems described in [54,75,30,21,22].

   We take a number of communication protocols from the literature, see, *e.g.*, [4,15,48,38]: two variations of the *Alternating Bit Protocol* (ABP), the *Concurrent Alternating Bit Protocol* (CABP), the *Positive Acknowledgement with Retransmission Protocol* (PAR), the *Bounded Retransmission Protocol* (BRP), the *Onebit* sliding window protocol, and the *Sliding Window Protocol* (SWP). All protocols are parameterised with the number of messages that can be sent, and the sliding window protocol is parameterised by the window size. For these protocols a number of properties of varying complexity was considered, ranging from alternation free properties, *e.g.* deadlock freedom, to fairness properties.

A *Cache Coherence Protocol* (CCP) [76] and a *wait-free handshake register* (Hesselink) [39] are considered. For the cache coherence protocol we consider a number of properties from [59] and for the register we consider properties from [39]. Additionally we consider a *leader election protocol* for which we verify whether it eventually stabilises.

To obtain parity games with a high degree of alternation between vertices owned by different players we also consider a number of two-player board games, *viz. Clobber* [2], *Domineering* [34], *Hex*, see *e.g.* [5,52], *Othello*, also known as reversi, see *e.g.* [65], and *Snake*. For these games we check for each of the players whether the player has a winning strategy starting from the initial configuration of the game. The games are parameterised by their board size.

Additionally, we consider a number of industrial model checking problems. The first is a system for lifting trucks (Lift) [37], of which we consider both a correct and an incorrect version. We verify the liveness and safety properties described in [37]. For the *IEEE 1394 Link Layer Protocol* (1394) we verify the properties from [51]. We translated the ACTL properties from [71] to the μ-calculus.

Finally, we check the *Elevator* described by Friedmann and Lange, in a version in which requests are treated on a first-in-first-out basis (FIFO), and on a last-in-first-out basis (LIFO). We then check whether, globally, if the lift is requested on the top floor, then it is eventually served. This holds for the FIFO version, but does not hold for the LIFO version of the model. The elevator model is parameterised by the strategy and the number of floors. Furthermore we consider the parity games generated using an encoding of an LTS with a μ-calculus formula, as well as the direct encoding presented in [30]. In a similar way we consider the Hanoi towers from [30] as well as our own version of this problem.

Equivalence Checking. Given two processes L_1, L_2, the problem whether $L_1 \equiv L_2$, for relations $\equiv$, denoting that L_1 and L_2 are equivalent under some process equivalence, can be encoded as a parity game [50,77]. We consider strong bisimulation, weak bisimulation, branching bisimulation and branching simulation equivalence in our benchmarks, using the approach described in [17]. The number of different priorities in these parity games is limited to 2, but they do include alternations between vertices owned by different players.

Here we again use the specifications of the communication protocols that we also used for model checking, *i.e.*, two ABP versions, CABP, PAR, Onebit and SWP. In addition we include a model of a buffer. We vary the capacity of the buffer, the number of messages that can be transmitted, and the window size in the sliding window protocol. We compare each pair of protocols using all four equivalences, resulting in both positive and negative cases. These cases are a superset of the ones described in [21,22].

In addition, we include a comparison of the implementation of the wait-free handshake register with a possible specification. The implementation is trace equivalent to the specification, but it is not equivalent with respect to the equivalences that we consider here.

Decision Procedures. Parity games can also be obtained from decision procedures for temporal logics such as LTL, CTL, CTL*, PDL and the μ-calculus. Friedmann *et al.* presented a decision procedure that is based on a combination of infinite tableaux in which the existence of a tableau is coded as a parity game [33]. For a given formula, it is checked whether it is (1) *valid*, *i.e.*, whether the formula holds in all models, or (2) *satisfiable*, *i.e.*, whether the formula is satisfiable in some model.

Our benchmark set includes a number of scalable satisfiability and validity problems that are provided as examples for the MLSolver tool [32]. In particular, we include the benchmarks used in [32]: encoding that a deterministic parity condition is expressible as a nondeterministic Büchi condition, and nesting Kleene stars in different logics. Additionally we consider formulas that involve encodings of a binary counter in various logics.

Synthesis. Another problem that involves solving parity games is the LTL synthesis problem. Traditional synthesis approaches convert a formula into a non-deterministic Büchi automaton, which is, in turn, transformed into a deterministic parity automaton using Safra's construction [66]. Emptiness of this deterministic parity automaton can then be checked using parity games with three priorities. Synthesis tools have been implemented that employ parity games internally, most notably GOAL [74] and Gist [16]. All synthesis tools that we are aware of, however, are research quality tools, of which we have not been able to obtain working versions on current computing platforms. As a result, our benchmark set currently does not include parity games obtained from the synthesis problem. We plan to extend our benchmarks with such games, and update [46] accordingly.

3.2 Hard Games

The interesting complexity of solving parity games, and its link to the model checking problem, have led to the conception of a large number of parity game solving algorithms. For most of these algorithms it has long been an open problem whether they have exponential lower bounds.

We consider the games described by Jurdziński that shows the exponential lower bound for small progress measures [43], the *ladder games* described by Friedmann [28] defeating strategy guessing heuristics, *recursive ladder games* that give a lower bound for the recursive algorithms, and *model checker ladder games* [27] for which the algorithm by Stevens and Stirling [72] behaves exponentially.

3.3 Random Games

The final class of games that is typically used in publications that empirically evaluate the performance of algorithms on parity games are random parity games [6,69,68,49,30]. We study three classes of random games. We expect that the structural properties of random games are, typically, different from parity games obtained in the previous classes. This class is, therefore, unlikely to give insights in the performance of parity game algorithms on practical problems.

4   Implementation

All games were generated on a 1TB main memory, 56-core Linux machine, where each core was running at 2.27GHz. Executions of tools generating and solving parity games, and tools collecting statistics about parity games, were limited to running times of 1 hour and their memory usage was limited to 32GB.

To systematically generate the benchmarks, we have implemented tooling that allows the parallel execution of individual cases. Here a case is either generating or solving a game, or collecting a single measure. Each individual case only uses a single core. The tools are implemented in an extensible way, *i.e.*, additional parity games, additional encodings, as well as additional measures can be added straightforwardly. The tools are available for download from https://github.com/jkeiren/paritygame-generator.

4.1   Generating Parity Games

For the generation of our benchmarks we rely on a number of external tools: version 3.3 of PGSolver [31] for generating random games, and games that prove to be hard for certain algorithms; version 1.2 of MLSolver to generate the games for satisfiability and validity problems [32]; and revision 11703 of the mCRL2 toolset [20] for the model checking and equivalence checking problems. For all games we have collected the information described in Section 2 to the extent in which this is feasible.

4.2   Collecting Statistics

We developed the tool pginfo for collecting structural information from parity games. The tool is available from https://github.com/jkeiren/pginfo and accepts parity games in the file format used by PGSolver. The tool reads a parity game, and writes statistics to a file in a structured way.

The implementation is built on top of the Boost Graph library [70], which provides data structures and basic algorithms for manipulating graphs. Computing the exact value for the width-measures is problematic: it is known to be NP-complete [3]. Approximation algorithms are known that compute upper- and lower bound for these measures; especially for treewidth these have been thoroughly studied [12,13]. To determine feasibility of computing width-measures for our benchmarks we have implemented three approximation algorithms. For computing upper and lower bounds on treewidth we implemented the greedy degree algorithm [12] and the minor min-width algorithm [36], respectively. For computing an upper bound of the Kelly-width we implemented the elimination ordering described in [40]. Even these approximation algorithms have proven to be impractical due to their complexity. Computing (bounds) on the other width measures is equally complex.

4.3   Availability of Parity Games

All parity games that are described in this paper are available for download from `http://www.github.com/jkeiren/paritygame-generator` in bzip2 compressed PGSolver format [31]. The dataset is approximately 10GB in size, and includes the structural information that was collected from these games.

5   Analysis of Benchmarks

We have presented benchmarks originating from different problems. Next we analyse them with respect to the measures described in Section 2. This analysis illustrates that our benchmarks exhibit a wide variety of properties. Furthermore, this gives us some insights in the characteristics of typical parity games. For each of the statistics, we only consider games for which that specific statistic could be computed within an hour, and we only include those statistics that can feasibly be computed for the majority of games, as a consequence the width measure are excluded from the analysis we present here. We used this selection to avoid timeouts for computing the measures that are expensive to compute. All graphs in this section are labelled by their class. Note that the satisfiability and validity problems are labelled by "mlsolver" and the games that are hard for some solving algorithms are labelled by "specialcases". The full data presented in this chapter is also available from `http://www.github.com/jkeiren/paritygame-generator`. Due to lack of space, we cannot present an analysis of all measures.

Our data set contains 1037 parity games that range from 2 vertices to 40 million vertices, and on average they have about 95,000 vertices. The number of edges ranges from 2 to 167 million, with an average of about 3.1 million. The 59 parity games are games in which all vertices are owned by a single player, the so-called solitaire games [8], the rest are parity games in which both players own non-empty sets of vertices. The parity games that we consider have differing degrees. There are instances in which the average degree is 1, the average degree is maximally 9999, but it is typically below 10. The ratio between the number of vertices and the number of edges is, therefore, relatively small in general. This can also be observed from Figure 1a, which displays the correlation between the two. The games in which these numbers coincide are on the line $x = y$, the other games lie around this line due to the log scale that we use. Our parity games generally contain a vertex with in-degree 0, which is the starting vertex. Most of the games contain vertices with a high in-degree—typically representing vertices that are trivially won by either of the players—, and vertices with a high out-degree.

In general, the SCC quotient height ranges up to 513 for the parity games that we consider with an average of around 14. The number of non-trivial SCCs can grow large, up to 1.4 million for our games.

We have included parity games with alternation depths up to 50,000 as shown in Figure 1b. Observe that the games for model checking and equivalence checking included in our benchmarks all have alternation depth at most 2. Model checking problems could be formulated that have a higher alternation depth—up

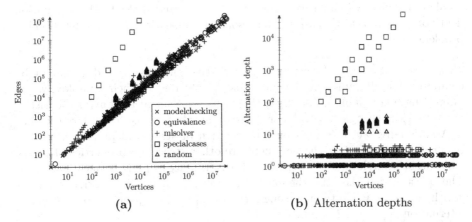

Fig. 1. Relation between number of vertices and (a) number of edges (b) alternation depth. The legend is the same for both plots.

to arbitrary numbers—however, in practice properties have limited alternation depth because they become too hard to understand otherwise. The satisfiability and validity properties have alternation depths between 1 and 4. The alternation depths of the random games are between 10 and 15. All parity games with more than 50 priorities represent special cases. Closer investigation shows that these special cases are the clique games and recursive ladder games.

To summarise, we have presented a large set of parity games. For a selection of the structural properties introduced in Section 2 we have shown that the games cover a large range of values. Due to space restrictions we have not covered all structural properties here, we refer to [46] for a more detailed analysis. Also observe that, for parity game specific properties such as alternation depth, higher values are only available for smaller games due to generation times. Unsurprisingly, the random games considered in this paper are not structurally similar to parity games that represent encodings of verification problems.

6 Closing Remarks

No standard benchmarks for parity game algorithms existed. As a consequence, it was virtually impossible to make a good comparison between algorithms and applications described in the literature. In this paper we have addressed this issue by presenting a comprehensive set of parity game benchmarks. Our benchmarks include the games that appear in the literature, and provides a first step towards standardising experimental evaluation of parity game algorithms. All games have been generated in an extensible way, and are available on-line.

We also presented a set of structural properties for parity games, and analysed our benchmarks with respect to these properties. Of particular interest is a new notion of alternation depth for parity games, that is always at most the number of priorities in a parity game, and that is bounded also by the alternation depth of μ-calculus formulae given a reasonable translation of the model checking problem.

Future work. Some of the structural properties, such as treewidth, cannot be computed for all games in the benchmark suite due to their complexity. An interesting algorithmic question is, therefore, whether algorithms or heuristics can be devised that can compute or approximate these measures for large graphs.

Additionally, we have presented a selection of structural properties in this paper. One can wonder whether there are other structural properties of parity games that are relevant to the practical performance of parity game algorithms. The question whether the theoretical complexity of existing parity game algorithms can be made tighter using structural properties, such as our notion of alternation depth is left open.

We believe our work also paves the way for a full-scale comparison of parity game algorithms and the effect of heuristics in the spirit of [30], including the comparison of alternative implementations of algorithms [20,23]. Here also the impact of the structural properties on the performance of implementations should be studied, since we have only scratched the surface of this aspect in this paper.

Finally, we welcome the addition of problems and properties to our benchmark suite to establish and maintain a corpus for experimentation with parity game algorithms. In particular parity games with a large number of priorities and a high alternation depth stemming from encodings of, *e.g.*, verification and synthesis problems form a welcome addition.

Acknowledgements For generating the parity games described in the paper, a large number of tools have been used. The author would like to thank the developers of, in particular, Gist, GOAL, mCRL2, MLSolver and PGSolver. Thanks also go to Wan Fokkink and Tim Willemse for helpful feedback on earlier versions of this paper, and remarks by anonymous reviewers that led to usability improvements of the benchmarks and tools presented.

References

1. Adler, I.: Directed tree-width examples. Journal of Combinatorial Theory, Series B 97(5), 718–725 (2007)
2. Albert, M.H., Grossman, J.P., Nowakowski, R.J., Wolfe, D.: An introduction to clobber. Integers 5(2) (2005)
3. Arnborg, S., Corneil, D.G., Proskurowski, A.: Complexity of finding embeddings in a k-tree. SIAM Journal on Algebraic Discrete Methods 8(2), 277–284 (1987)
4. Bartlett, K.A., Scantlebury, R.A., Wilkinson, P.T.: A note on reliable full-duplex transmission over half-duplex links. Communications of the ACM 12(5), 260–261 (1969)
5. Beck, A., Bleicher, M.N., Crowe, D.W.: Excursions into Mathematics: The Millennium Edition. CRC Press (2000)

6. Beffara, E., Vorobyov, S.G.: Adapting Gurvich-Karzanov-Khachiyan's algorithm for parity games. Technical report, Uppsala University, Sweden, Uppsala (2001)

7. Berwanger, D., Dawar, A., Hunter, P.W., Kreutzer, S., Obdržálek, J.: The DAG-width of directed graphs. Journal of Combinatorial Theory, Series B 102(4), 900–923 (2012)

8. Berwanger, D., Grädel, E.: Fixed-point logics and solitaire games. Theory of Computing Systems 37(6), 675–694 (2004)

9. Berwanger, D., Grädel, E.: Entanglement – A measure for the complexity of directed graphs with applications to logic and games. In: Baader, F., Voronkov, A. (eds.) LPAR 2004. LNCS (LNAI), vol. 3452, pp. 209–223. Springer, Heidelberg (2005)

10. Berwanger, D., Grädel, E., Kaiser, L., Rabinovich, R.: Entanglement and the complexity of directed graphs. Theoretical Computer Science 463, 2–25 (2012)

11. Bodlaender, H.L.: Treewidth: Algorithmic techniques and results. In: Privara, I., Ružička, P. (eds.) MFCS 1997. LNCS, vol. 1295, pp. 19–36. Springer, Heidelberg (1997)

12. Bodlaender, H.L., Koster, A.M.C.A.: Treewidth computations I. upper bounds. Information and Computation 208(3), 259–275 (2010)

13. Bodlaender, H.L., Koster, A.M.C.A.: Treewidth computations II. lower bounds. Information and Computation 209(7), 1103–1119 (2011)

14. Bradfield, J.C., Stirling, C.: Modal logics and mu-calculi: an introduction. In: Handbook of Process Algebra, pp. 293–330. Elsevier (2000)

15. Cerf, V., Kahn, R.E.: A protocol for packet network intercommunication. IEEE Transactions on Communications 22(5), 637–648 (1974)

16. Chatterjee, K., Henzinger, T.A., Jobstmann, B., Radhakrishna, A.: GIST: A solver for probabilistic games. In: Touili, T., Cook, B., Jackson, P. (eds.) CAV 2010. LNCS, vol. 6174, pp. 665–669. Springer, Heidelberg (2010)

17. Chen, T., Ploeger, S.C.W., van de Pol, J.C., Willemse, T.A.C.: Equivalence checking for infinite systems using parameterized Boolean equation systems. In: Caires, L., Vasconcelos, V.T. (eds.) CONCUR 2007. LNCS, vol. 4703, pp. 120–135. Springer, Heidelberg (2007)

18. Cleaveland, R., Klein, M., Steffen, B.: Faster model checking for the modal mu-calculus. In: Probst, D.K., von Bochmann, G. (eds.) CAV 1992. LNCS, vol. 663, pp. 410–422. Springer, Heidelberg (1993)

19. Courcelle, B., Olariu, S.: Upper bounds to the clique width of graphs. Discrete Applied Mathematics 101(1-3), 77–114 (2000)

20. Cranen, S., Groote, J.F., Keiren, J.J.A., Stappers, F.P.M., de Vink, E.P., Wesselink, J.W., Willemse, T.A.C.: An overview of the mCRL2 toolset and its recent advances. In: Piterman, N., Smolka, S.A. (eds.) TACAS 2013 (ETAPS 2013). LNCS, vol. 7795, pp. 199–213. Springer, Heidelberg (2013)

21. Cranen, S., Keiren, J.J.A., Willemse, T.A.C.: Stuttering mostly speeds up solving parity games. In: Bobaru, M., Havelund, K., Holzmann, G.J., Joshi, R. (eds.) NFM 2011. LNCS, vol. 6617, pp. 207–221. Springer, Heidelberg (2011)

22. Cranen, S., Keiren, J.J.A., Willemse, T.A.C.: A cure for stuttering parity games. In: Roychoudhury, A., D'Souza, M. (eds.) ICTAC 2012. LNCS, vol. 7521, pp. 198–212. Springer, Heidelberg (2012)

23. Di Stasio, A., Murano, A., Prignano, V., Sorrentino, L.: Solving parity games in Scala. In: Lanese, I., Madelaine, E. (eds.) FACS 2014. LNCS, vol. 8997, pp. 145–161. Springer, Heidelberg (2015)

24. Emerson, E.A., Jutla, C.S.: Tree automata, mu-calculus and determinacy. In: SFCS 1991: Proceedings of the 32nd Annual Symposium on Foundations of Computer Science, pp. 368–377. IEEE Computer Society (1991)
25. Emerson, E.A., Lei, C.L.L.: Efficient model checking in fragments of the propositional mu-calculus. In: Proceedings of LICS 1986, pp. 267–278. IEEE Computer Society (1986)
26. Friedmann, O.: A super-polynomial lower bound for the parity game strategy improvement algorithm as we know it. In: 2009 24th Annual IEEE Symposium on Logic In Computer Science, vol. 7, pp. 145–156 (2009)
27. Friedmann, O.: The Stevens-Stirling-algorithm for solving parity games locally requires exponential time. International Journal of Foundations of Computer Science 21(03), 277–287 (2010)
28. Friedmann, O.: An exponential lower bound for the latest deterministic strategy iteration algorithms. Logical Methods in Computer Science 7, 1–42 (2011)
29. Friedmann, O.: Recursive algorithm for parity games requires exponential time. RAIRO - Theoretical Informatics and Applications 45(4), 449–457 (2011)
30. Friedmann, O., Lange, M.: Solving parity games in practice. In: Liu, Z., Ravn, A.P. (eds.) ATVA 2009. LNCS, vol. 5799, pp. 182–196. Springer, Heidelberg (2009)
31. Friedmann, O., Lange, M.: The PGSolver collection of parity game solvers. Technical report, Institut für Informatik, Ludwig-Maximilians-Universität München, Germany (2010)
32. Friedmann, O., Lange, M.: A solver for modal fixpoint logics. In: Electronic Notes in Theoretical Computer Science, vol. 262, pp. 99–111. Elsevier (2010)
33. Friedmann, O., Latte, M., Lange, M.: A decision procedure for CTL* based on tableaux and automata. In: Giesl, J., Hähnle, R. (eds.) IJCAR 2010. LNCS, vol. 6173, pp. 331–345. Springer, Heidelberg (2010)
34. Gardner, M.: Mathematical games: Cram, crosscram and quadraphage: New games having elusive winning strategies. Scientific American 230, 106–108 (1974)
35. Gazda, M.W., Willemse, T.A.C.: Zielonka's recursive algorithm: dull, weak and solitaire games and tighter bounds. In: Proceedings GandALF 2013. EPTCS, vol. 119, pp. 7–20 (2013)
36. Gogate, V., Dechter, R.: A complete anytime algorithm for treewidth. In: Proceedings of the 20th Conference on Uncertainty in Artificial Intelligence, UAI 2004, pp. 201–208. AUAI Press (2004)
37. Groote, J.F., Pang, J., Wouters, A.G.G.: Analysis of a distributed system for lifting trucks. The Journal of Logic and Algebraic Programming 55(1-2), 21–56 (2003)
38. Groote, J.F., van de Pol, J.: A bounded retransmission protocol for large data packets. In: Nivat, M., Wirsing, M. (eds.) AMAST 1996. LNCS, vol. 1101, pp. 536–550. Springer, Heidelberg (1996)
39. Hesselink, W.H.: Invariants for the construction of a handshake register. Information Processing Letters 68, 173–177 (1998)
40. Hunter, P.W., Kreutzer, S.: Digraph measures: Kelly decompositions, games, and orderings. Theoretical Computer Science 399(3), 206–219 (2008)
41. Johnson, T., Robertson, N., Seymour, P.D., Thomas, R.: Directed tree-width. Journal of Combinatorial Theory, Series B 82(1), 138–154 (2001)
42. Jurdziński, M.: Deciding the winner in parity games is in UP ∩ co-UP. Information Processing Letters 68(3), 119–124 (1998)
43. Jurdziński, M.: Small progress measures for solving parity games. In: Reichel, H., Tison, S. (eds.) STACS 2000. LNCS, vol. 1770, pp. 290–301. Springer, Heidelberg (2000)

44. Jurdziński, M., Paterson, M., Zwick, U.: A deterministic subexponential algorithm for solving parity games. In: Proceedings of the Seventeenth Annual ACM-SIAM Symposium on Discrete Algorithm, SODA 2006, pp. 117–123 (2006)
45. Keiren, J.J.A.: Advanced Reduction Techniques for Model Checking. PhD thesis, Eindhoven University of Technology (2013)
46. Keiren, J.J.A.: Benchmarks for parity games (extended version). CoRR, abs/1407.3121 (2014)
47. Keiren, J.J.A., Willemse, T.A.C.: Bisimulation minimisations for Boolean equation systems. In: Namjoshi, K., Zeller, A., Ziv, A. (eds.) HVC 2009. LNCS, vol. 6405, pp. 102–116. Springer, Heidelberg (2011)
48. Koymans, C.P.J., Mulder, J.C.: A modular approach to protocol verification using process algebra. In: Applications of Process Algebra. Cambridge Tracts in Theoretical Computer Science, vol. 17, pp. 261–306 (1990)
49. Lange, M.: Solving parity games by a reduction to SAT. In: Proc. of the Workshop on Games in Design and Verification, GDV 2005 (2005)
50. Larsen, K.G.: Efficient local correctness checking. In: Probst, D.K., von Bochmann, G. (eds.) CAV 1992. LNCS, vol. 663, pp. 30–43. Springer, Heidelberg (1993)
51. Luttik, S.P.: Description and formal specification of the link layer of P1394. In: Workshop on Applied Formal Methods in System Design, pp. 43–56 (1997)
52. Maarup, T.: Hex - everything you always wanted to know about hex but were afraid to ask. Master's thesis (2005)
53. Mader, A.: Verification of Modal Properties Using Boolean Equation Systems. PhD thesis, Technische Universität München (1997)
54. Mateescu, R.: A generic on-the-fly solver for alternation-free Boolean equation systems. In: Garavel, H., Hatcliff, J. (eds.) TACAS 2003. LNCS, vol. 2619, pp. 81–96. Springer, Heidelberg (2003)
55. McNaughton, R.: Infinite games played on finite graphs. Annals of Pure and Applied Logic 65(2), 149–184 (1993)
56. Nowakowski, R., Winkler, P.: Vertex-to-vertex pursuit in a graph. Discrete Mathematics 43(2-3), 235–239 (1983)
57. Obdržálek, J.: Fast mu-calculus model checking when tree-width is bounded. In: Hunt Jr., W.A., Somenzi, F. (eds.) CAV 2003. LNCS, vol. 2725, pp. 80–92. Springer, Heidelberg (2003)
58. Obdržálek, J.: Algorithmic Analysis of Parity Games. PhD thesis, Laboratory for Foundations of Computer Science, School of Informatics, University of Edinburgh (2006)
59. Pang, J., Fokkink, W.J., Hofman, R., Veldema, R.: Model checking a cache coherence protocol of a Java DSM implementation. The Journal of Logic and Algebraic Programming 71(1), 1–43 (2007)
60. Pelánek, R.: Typical structural properties of state spaces. In: Graf, S., Mounier, L. (eds.) SPIN 2004. LNCS, vol. 2989, pp. 5–22. Springer, Heidelberg (2004)
61. Pelánek, R.: Web portal for benchmarking explicit model checkers. Technical Report FIMU-RS-2006-03, Faculty of Informatics Masaryk University Brno (2006)
62. Pelánek, R.: BEEM: benchmarks for explicit model checkers. In: Bošnački, D., Edelkamp, S. (eds.) SPIN 2007. LNCS, vol. 4595, pp. 263–267. Springer, Heidelberg (2007)
63. Quilliot, A.: Jeux et pointes fixes sur les graphes. PhD thesis, Université de Paris VI (1978)
64. Robertson, N., Seymour, P.D.: Graph minors. II. algorithmic aspects of tree-width. Journal of Algorithms 7(3), 309–322 (1986)

65. Rose, B.: Othello: A Minute to Learn... A Lifetime to Master (2005)
66. Safra, S.: On the complexity of omega-automata. In: 29th Annual Symposium on Foundations of Computer Science, pp. 319–327. IEEE (1988)
67. Schewe, S.: Solving parity games in big steps. In: Arvind, V., Prasad, S. (eds.) FSTTCS 2007. LNCS, vol. 4855, pp. 449–460. Springer, Heidelberg (2007)
68. Schewe, S.: An optimal strategy improvement algorithm for solving parity and payoff games. In: Kaminski, M., Martini, S. (eds.) CSL 2008. LNCS, vol. 5213, pp. 369–384. Springer, Heidelberg (2008)
69. Schewe, S.: Synthesis of Distributed Systems. Phd thesis, Universität des Saarlandes (2008)
70. Siek, J.G., Lee, L.Q., Lumsdaine, A.: The Boost Graph Library: User Guide and Reference Manual. Addison-Wesley (2002)
71. Sighireanu, M., Mateescu, R.: Verification of the link layer protocol of the IEEE-1394 serial bus (FireWire): An experiment with E-LOTOS. STTT 2(1), 68–88 (1998)
72. Stevens, P., Stirling, C.: Practical model checking using games. In: Steffen, B. (ed.) TACAS 1998. LNCS, vol. 1384, pp. 85–101. Springer, Heidelberg (1998)
73. Stirling, C.: Bisimulation, modal logic and model checking games. Logic Journal of IGPL 7(1), 103–124 (1999)
74. Tsay, Y.K., Chen, Y.F., Tsai, M.H., Chan, W.C., Luo, C.J.: GOAL extended: Towards a research tool for omega automata and temporal logic. In: Ramakrishnan, C.R., Rehof, J. (eds.) TACAS 2008. LNCS, vol. 4963, pp. 346–350. Springer, Heidelberg (2008)
75. van de Pol, J.C., Weber, M.: A multi-core solver for parity games. Electronic Notes in Theoretical Computer Science 220(2), 19–34 (2008)
76. Veldema, R., Hofman, R.F.H., Bhoedjang, R.A.F., Jacobs, C.J.H., Bal, H.E.: Source-level global optimizations for fine-grain distributed shared memory systems. ACM SIGPLAN Notices 36(7), 83–92 (2001)
77. Vergauwen, B., Lewi, J.: Efficient local correctness checking for single and alternating Boolean equation systems. In: Shamir, E., Abiteboul, S. (eds.) ICALP 1994. LNCS, vol. 820, pp. 304–315. Springer, Heidelberg (1994)
78. Zielonka, W.: Infinite games on finitely coloured graphs with applications to automata on infinite trees. Theoretical Computer Science 200(1-2), 135–183 (1998)

A Behavioural Theory
for a π-calculus with Preorders

Daniel Hirschkoff[1], Jean-Marie Madiot[1], and Xian Xu[2]

[1] ENS Lyon, Université de Lyon, CNRS, INRIA, France,
[2] East China University of Science and Technology, China

Abstract. We study the behavioural theory of πP, a π-calculus in the tradition of Fusions and Chi calculi. In contrast with such calculi, reduction in πP generates a preorder on names rather than an equivalence relation. We present two characterisations of barbed congruence in πP: the first is based on a compositional LTS, and the second is an axiomatisation. The results in this paper bring out basic properties of πP, mostly related to the interplay between the restriction operator and the preorder on names.

Consequently, πP is a calculus in the tradition of Fusion calculi, in which both types and behavioural equivalences can be exploited in order to reason rigorously about concurrent and mobile systems.

1 Introduction

The π-calculus expresses mobility via name passing, and has two binders: the input prefix binds the value to be received, and restriction is used to delimit the scope of a private name. The study of Fusions [16], Chi [8], Explicit Fusions [20] and Solos [13] has shown that using restriction as the only binder is enough to express name passing. In such calculi (which, reusing a terminology from [10], we shall refer to as *fusion calculi*), the bound input prefix, $c(x).P$, is dropped in favour of free input, $cb.P$, and communication involving two prefixes cb and $\bar{c}a$ generates the *fusion* of names a and b. This yields a pleasing symmetry between input and output prefixes; moreover, one can encode bound input in terms of free input as $(\nu x)cx.P$. Fusion calculi therefore promote *minimality* (keep only restriction as a binder) and *symmetry* (input and output prefixes play similar roles). Moreover, and most importantly, fusions act on restricted names, in contrast with the π-calculus, where restricted names can only replace names bound by input (and are thus treated like constants).

The behavioural theory of existing fusion calculi is generally simpler than in the π-calculus (in particular, bisimilarity is a congruence). Fusion calculi have notably been used to analyse concurrent constraints [19], to study distributed implementations of programming languages [9,5] and to establish connections with proof theory [7].

Symmetry comes however at a price. It has indeed been shown in [10] that i/o-types (input/output types, [17]) cannot be adapted to a fusion calculus. Such

© IFIP International Federation for Information Processing 2015
M. Dastani and M.Sirjani (Eds.): FSEN 2015, LNCS 9392, pp. 143–158, 2015.
DOI: 10.1007/978-3-319-24644-4_10

types go beyond the simple discipline of sorting, and can be useful, in particular, to reason using *typed behavioural equivalences* [17,18].

The intuitive reason of the incompatibility of i/o-types with fusions can be explained by considering the following structural congruence law in Explicit Fusions (but the point is essentially the same for other fusion calculi):

$$a(x).P \mid a{=}b \;\equiv\; b(x).P \mid a{=}b \ .$$

Process $a{=}b$ is an explicit fusion. The law says that in presence of $a{=}b$, an input on a can be viewed as the same input on b, *and vice-versa* (fusion processes are somehow akin to equators, in an asynchronous setting [12]). This shows that fusions define a symmetric relation on names; this is incompatible with a nontrivial (i.e., asymmetric) subtyping relation, which is necessary for i/o-types to make sense.

This observation has led in [10] to the introduction of πP, a π-calculus with name preorders. The most important difference between πP and existing name-passing calculi is that interaction does not have the effect of equating (or *fusing*) two names, but instead generates an *arc* process, as follows:

$$\bar{c}a.P \mid cb.Q \quad \longrightarrow \quad a/b \mid P \mid Q \ .$$

The arc a/b expresses the fact that anything that can be done using name b can be done using a as well (but not the opposite): we say that a is *above* b. Arcs induce a preorder relation on names, which can evolve along reductions.

Arcs can modify interaction possibilities: in presence of a/b, a is above b, hence a process emitting on b can also make an output transition along channel a. In general, an output on channel c can interact with an input on d provided c and d are *joinable*, written $c \curlyvee d$, which means that there is some name that is above both c and d according to the preorder relation. To formalise these observations, the operational semantics exploits *conditions* involving names, which are either of the form $b \prec a$ (a is above b), or $a \curlyvee b$ (a and b are joinable).

πP can be described as a variant of Explicit Fusions, in which arcs replace fusion processes. Beyond the possibility to define i/o-types and subtyping for πP [10], we would like to analyse the consequences of the novel aspects of πP, whose behaviour does not seem to be reducible to existing calculi.

In particular, name preorders have an impact on how processes express behaviours. Barbed congruence for πP, written $\simeq$, is defined in [10]. Some laws for $\simeq$ suggest that the behavioural theory of πP differs w.r.t. existing fusion calculi. As an illustration, consider the following *interleaving law*, which is valid in πP (and in π):

$$\bar{a}(x).\bar{b}(y).(\bar{x} \mid y) \;\simeq\; \bar{a}(x).\bar{b}(y).(\bar{x}.y + y.\bar{x}) \ .$$

$\bar{a}(x)$ is the emission of a fresh name x on a, and $\bar{x}$ (resp. y) stands for an output (resp. input) where the value being transmitted is irrelevant. In Fusions, unlike in the π-calculus, the process that creates successively two fresh names x and y cannot prevent the context from equating ("fusing") x and y. Hence, in order for the equivalence to hold, it is necessary to add a third summand on the right, $[x = y]\tau$. This example suggests that πP gives a better control on restricted names than existing fusion calculi. This issue also motivated the study of two variants of fusion calculi that have a refined notion of restriction [3,4].

The main purpose of the present work is to deepen the study of the behavioural theory of πP, in an untyped setting. We define a Labelled Transition System (LTS) for πP, and show that the induced notion of bisimilarity, written $\sim$, characterises $\simeq$ (Section 3). It can be noted that [10] presents a characterisation of barbed congruence, using an LTS that is rather ad hoc, because it is based on the definition of the reduction relation. Unlike the latter, the LTS we present here is *structural*.

The LTS reveals interesting aspects of interaction in πP. An important observation is related to the interplay between arcs and the restriction operator. It is for instance possible for a process to react to an input offer on some channel, say c, without being actually able to perform an output on c. This is the case for process $P_0 \triangleq (\nu a)(\overline{a}(x).0 \mid a/c)$. Because a is above c in the preorder, P_0 cannot do an output on c, although c is occurs free in P_0 (it could if the arc a/c was replaced with c/a). However, $P_0 \mid c(y).0$ can perform a reduction: intuitively, by extending the scope of (νa), the input at c can be moved to a, so that the communication takes place.

This phenomenon leads to the addition of a new type of labels in the LTS, corresponding to what we call *protected actions*: in the example P_0 can do a protected output at c, meaning that it can react to an input offer at c. Accordingly, we introduce *protected names*, which correspond to (usages of) names where a protected action occurs: intuitively, in P_0, name c is protected. As expected, protected actions correspond to observables in the reduction-based semantics supporting the definition of $\simeq$.

Arc processes do not have transitions, but they induce relations between names, which in turn influence the behaviour of processes. Accordingly, strong bisimilarity, $\sim$, not only tests transitions, but also has a clause to guarantee that related processes entail the same conditions.

Finally, the LTS also includes a label $[\varphi]\tau$, expressing "conditional synchronisation". Intuitively, process $\overline{a} \mid b$ is not able to perform a τ transition by itself, but it should be when the environment entails $a \curlyvee b$. Hence, in order for our LTS to be compositional, we include labels of the form $[\varphi]\tau$, interpreted as "τ under the condition φ".

In Section 4, we provide a second characterisation of barbed congruence, by presenting a set of laws that define an axiomatisation of $\simeq$. Algebraic laws help analysing the behaviour of the constructs of the calculus and their interplay. We present a sample of behavioural equalities, and explain how they can be derived equationally, in Section 4.1.

The axiomatisation we give is less simple than, say, the one for Fusions in [16], for two reasons: first, we manipulate preorders between names rather than equivalences. Second, the preorder is explicitly represented in processes, so that some equational laws must describe the interplay between processes and the preorder relation. On the contrary, such aspects are dealt with implicitly in Fusions—we sketch how our ideas can be adapted to Explicit Fusions in Section 4.3.

The axiomatisation exploits the idea that πP processes have a *state* component, corresponding to the preorder induced by arcs. Several laws in the axiomatisation express persistence of the state component (the state can only be extended along computation). Moreover, the restriction operator prevents the state from being globally shared in general: for instance, in process P_0 above, name a can be used instead of c, but is only known inside the scope of (νa). All in all, the handling of restriction in our axiomatisation requires more care than is usually the case, due to the necessity to express the "view" that subprocesses have on the preorder of names.

To present the axiomatisation, we renounce minimality. The syntax of the calculus in this paper differs from the one in [10]: we include bound prefixes and sums with conditions, as it is customary for axiomatisations for the π-calculus [15,18]. We compare the calculus from [10] with ours in Remark 3 and Proposition 11. We show that the differences are unimportant: the calculus from [10] can be encoded into ours and the behavioural equivalence is unaffected.

We focus in this paper on a finite calculus. This is sufficient to enlighten the main aspects of the behavioural theory of processes. We do not expect any unpredicted difficulty to arise, in the definition of labelled transitions and bisimilarity, from the extension of πP with a replication operator.

The paper describes our results and sketches the most important proofs. We refer to [11] for a more detailed presentation of the technical details. Related work is discussed along the paper, where it is relevant.

2 πP: Reduction-Based Semantics

The Calculus: Preorders and Processes. We consider a countable set of names $a, b, c, \ldots, x, y, \ldots$, and define conditions (φ), extended names (α, β), prefixes (π) and processes (P, Q) as follows:

$$\varphi ::= a \prec b \mid a \curlyvee b \qquad \alpha, \beta ::= a \mid \{a\} \qquad \pi ::= \alpha(x) \mid \overline{\alpha}(x) \mid [\varphi]\tau$$
$$P, Q ::= P \mid Q \mid (\nu a)P \mid a/b \mid \Sigma_{i \in I} \pi_i.P_i$$

There are two forms of conditions, ranged over with φ: $\varphi = a \prec b$ is read "b is above a" and $\varphi = a \curlyvee b$ is read "a and b are joinable". In both cases, we have $\mathsf{n}(\varphi) = \{a, b\}$. We explain below how we extend relations $\prec$ and $\curlyvee$ to extended names. When $\mathsf{n}(\varphi) = \{a\}$, we say that φ is *reflexive*, and abbreviate in this case prefix $[\varphi]\tau$ as τ. Condition $b \prec a$ is ensured by the arc process a/b.

In a prefix $\alpha(x)$ or $\overline{\alpha}(x)$, we say that extended name α is in subject position, while x is in object position. As discussed in Section 1, extended names include *protected names*, of the form $\{a\}$, which can be used in subject position only. We call *protected prefix* a prefix where the subject is a protected name. A prefix of the form $[\varphi]\tau$ is called a *conditional* τ, while other prefixes are called *visible*. Bound and free names for prefixes are given by: $\mathsf{bn}([\varphi]\tau) = \emptyset$ and $\mathsf{bn}(\alpha(x)) = \mathsf{bn}(\overline{\alpha}(x)) = \{x\}$, $\mathsf{fn}([\varphi]\tau) = \mathsf{n}(\varphi)$, $\mathsf{fn}(\alpha(x)) = \mathsf{fn}(\overline{\alpha}(x)) = \mathsf{n}(\alpha)$ with $\mathsf{n}(a) = \mathsf{n}(\{a\}) = \{a\}$.

In a sum process, we let I range over a finite set of integers. 0 is the inactive process, defined as the empty sum. We use S to range over sum processes of the form $\Sigma_{i \in I} \pi_i.P_i$, and write $\pi.P \in S$ if $\pi.P$ is a summand of S. We sometimes decompose sum processes using the binary sum operator, writing, e.g., $S_1 + S_2$ (in particular, $S + 0 = S$). We abbreviate $\pi.0$ as π, and write $\alpha(x).P$ simply as $\alpha.P$ when the transmitted name is not relevant, and similarly for $\overline{\alpha}$. In $(\nu a)P$, (νa) binds a in P, and prefixes $\alpha(x)$ and $\overline{\alpha}(x)$ bind x in the continuation process. The set of free names of P, $\mathsf{fn}(P)$, is defined in the usual way, and we work up to α-conversion of processes. $P\{^b/_a\}$ is the process obtained by substituting a with b in P, in a capture-avoiding way.

We use an overloaded notation, and define processes representing conditions:

$$a \curlyvee b \triangleq (\nu u)(u/a \mid u/b) \qquad a \prec b \triangleq b/a \ .$$

Below, Γ ranges over sets of conditions. We define $\Gamma \vdash \varphi$, meaning that Γ implies φ, and $P \triangleright \varphi$ (we write $P \triangleright \Gamma$ to express that P entails φ for all $\varphi \in \Gamma$):

$$\frac{}{\Gamma \vdash a \prec a} \qquad \frac{\varphi \in \Gamma}{\Gamma \vdash \varphi} \qquad \frac{\Gamma \vdash a \prec b \quad \Gamma \vdash b \curlyvee a}{\Gamma \vdash a \curlyvee b} \qquad \frac{\Gamma \vdash a \prec b \quad \Gamma \vdash b \prec c}{\Gamma \vdash a \prec c} \qquad \frac{\Gamma \vdash a \prec b \quad \Gamma \vdash c \prec b}{\Gamma \vdash a \curlyvee c} \qquad \frac{\Gamma \vdash a \prec b \quad \Gamma \vdash b \curlyvee c}{\Gamma \vdash a \curlyvee c}$$

$$\frac{}{a/b \triangleright b \prec a} \qquad \frac{P \triangleright \Gamma \quad \Gamma \vdash \varphi}{P \triangleright \varphi} \qquad \frac{P \triangleright \varphi}{P \mid Q \triangleright \varphi} \qquad \frac{Q \triangleright \varphi}{P \mid Q \triangleright \varphi} \qquad \frac{P \triangleright \varphi \quad a \notin \mathsf{n}(\varphi)}{(\nu a)P \triangleright \varphi}$$

As an example, the reader might check that $(\nu u)(u/a \mid u/b) \mid b/c \triangleright a \curlyvee c$.

Reduction Semantics and Barbed Congruence. The definition of structural congruence, $\equiv$, is standard. In particular, we have

$$\Sigma_{i \in I} \pi_i.P_i \ \equiv \ \Sigma_{i \in I} \pi_{\sigma(i)}.P_{\sigma(i)} \quad \text{if } \sigma \text{ is a permutation of } I \ .$$

Relations $\equiv$ and $\triangleright$ are used to define the reduction of processes. We rely on $\triangleright$ to infer that two processes interact on joinable (extended) names. This allows us to introduce reduction-closed barbed congruence, along the lines of [10].

Definition 1 (Reduction). *Relation* $\mapsto$ *is defined by the following rules:*

$$\frac{\overline{\alpha}(x).P \in S_1 \quad \beta(y).Q \in S_2 \quad R \triangleright \alpha \curlyvee \beta \quad x \neq y}{R \mid S_1 \mid S_2 \ \mapsto \ R \mid (\nu xy)(x/y \mid P \mid Q)} \qquad \begin{array}{l} \text{where:} \\ a \curlyvee \{b\} = \{b\} \curlyvee a = a \prec b \\ \{a\} \curlyvee \{b\} = \text{undefined} \end{array}$$

$$\frac{[\varphi]\tau.P \in S \quad R \triangleright \varphi}{R \mid S \ \mapsto \ R \mid P} \qquad \frac{P \mapsto P'}{P \mid R \mapsto P' \mid R} \qquad \frac{P \mapsto P'}{(\nu a)P \mapsto (\nu a)P'} \qquad \frac{P \equiv \mapsto \equiv P'}{P \mapsto P'}$$

Definition 2 (Barbs, barbed congruence). *We write* $P \downarrow_{\overline{a}}$ *if* $P \mid a(x).\omega \mapsto P'$, *where* P' *is a process in which* ω *is unguarded, and* ω *is a special name that does not appear in* P. *We define similarly the barb* $\downarrow_a$, *using the tester* $\overline{a}(x).\omega$.

Barbed congruence, $\simeq$, *is the largest congruence that satisfies:*

– *if* $P \downarrow_a$ *and* $P \simeq Q$ *then* $Q \downarrow_a$, *and similarly for* $\downarrow_{\overline{a}}$, *and*
– *if* $P \mapsto P'$ *and* $P \simeq Q$ *then for some* Q', $Q \mapsto Q'$ *and* $P' \simeq Q'$.

We can remark that $P_0 \downarrow_{\overline{c}}$, where P_0 is the process defined in Section 1.

The remainder of the paper is devoted to the presentation of two characterisations of $\simeq$. We first comment on the definition of $\pi\mathsf{P}$ given above.

One could consider an alternative version of reduction, called "eager", whereby arcs can rewrite prefixes in one step of computation, yielding, e.g., $d/c \mid c(x).P \mapsto d/c \mid d(x).P$. It appears in [10] that the present semantics is more compelling (for instance $a(x).a(y)$ would not be equivalent to $a(x) \mid a(y)$ in the eager version).

Remark 3 (Encodability of free and protected prefixes).

In πP, arcs act like "instantaneous forwarders". This allows us to define an encoding $[\cdot]_f$ from a calculus with free prefixes to a calculus with bound prefixes as follows (x is chosen fresh):

$$[ab.P]_f \triangleq a(x).([P]_f \mid x/b) \qquad [\bar{a}b.P]_f \triangleq \bar{a}(x).([P]_f \mid b/x) \ ,$$

where $[\cdot]_f$ preserves other operators of the calculi. We return to this encoding below (Proposition 11), and show that it allows us to reflect behavioural equivalence in [10] into our calculus.

We can also encode protected prefixes as follows (u is chosen fresh):

$$[\{a\}(x).P]_p \triangleq (\nu u)(u/a \mid u(x).[P]_p) \qquad [\{\bar{a}\}(x).P]_p \triangleq (\nu u)(u/a \mid \bar{u}(x).[P]_p) \ .$$

Although protected prefixes are in some sense redundant, we do not treat them as derived operators, to simplify the presentation (in particular in Section 4).

The results of this paper (Sections 3 and 4) can be adapted to a calculus featuring only free prefixes, and restriction as the only binder, like the calculus of [10]. This yields more complex definitions to handle bound prefixes and protected actions, in particular when defining sum processes. We discuss in [11] a presentation of transitions and bisimilarity based on free prefixes. It can be noted that the axiomatisation of Fusions given in [16] relies only on free input and output, and treats bound prefixes as derived operators. We think that, for πP, handling prefixes for bound and protected actions as derived operators would introduce further technical complications that would make the axiomatisation more obscure.

3   A Labelled Transition System for πP

3.1   LTS and Bisimilarity

The LTS defines transitions $P \xrightarrow{\mu} P'$, where the grammar for the labels, μ, is the same as the one for prefixes π. We comment on the rules, given in Figure 1.

The first two rules correspond to the firing of visible prefixes. The transition involves a fresh name x, upon which the participants in a communication "agree". Name y remains local, via the installation of an arc, according to the directionality of the prefix. (Adopting a rule with no arc installation would yield a more complex definition of $\sim$). The rule for the $[\varphi]\tau$ prefix is self explanatory. The rule describing communication follows the lines of the corresponding rule for $\mapsto$; no arc is installed (but arcs are introduced in the prefix rules).

The three rules mentioning $\triangleright$ are called *preorder rules*. The two preorder rules for visible actions exploit $\prec$, which is defined for extended names (as we did for $\curlyvee$ above). Note that the condition involving $\triangleright$ is *the same* in these two rules. To understand these rules, and the role of protected actions, we recall the

$$\frac{x \notin n(\alpha) \cup \{y\} \cup fn(P)}{\alpha(y).P \xrightarrow{\alpha(x)} (\nu y)(x/y \mid P)} \qquad \frac{x \notin n(\alpha) \cup \{y\} \cup fn(P)}{\overline{\alpha}(y).P \xrightarrow{\overline{\alpha}(x)} (\nu y)(y/x \mid P)} \qquad \frac{}{[\varphi]\tau.P \xrightarrow{[\varphi]\tau} P}$$

$$\frac{P \xrightarrow{\overline{\alpha}(x)} P' \quad Q \xrightarrow{\beta(x)} Q'}{P \mid Q \xrightarrow{[\alpha \curlyvee \beta]\tau} (\nu x)(P' \mid Q')} \qquad \frac{P \xrightarrow{[\varphi_2]\tau} P' \quad P \triangleright \Gamma \quad \Gamma, \varphi_1 \vdash \varphi_2}{P \xrightarrow{[\varphi_1]\tau} P'}$$

$$\frac{P \xrightarrow{\alpha(x)} P' \quad P \triangleright \alpha \prec \beta}{P \xrightarrow{\beta(x)} P'} \qquad \frac{P \xrightarrow{\overline{\alpha}(x)} P' \quad P \triangleright \alpha \prec \beta}{P \xrightarrow{\overline{\beta}(x)} P'} \qquad \begin{array}{l} a \;\prec\; \{b\} = a \curlyvee b \\ \{a\} \prec \{b\} = b \prec a \\ \{a\} \prec\; b \;= \text{undefined} \end{array}$$

$$\frac{P \xrightarrow{\mu} P' \quad a \notin fn(\mu) \cup bn(\mu)}{(\nu a)P \xrightarrow{\mu} (\nu a)P'} \qquad \frac{P \xrightarrow{\mu} P' \quad bn(\mu) \cap fn(Q) = \emptyset}{P \mid Q \xrightarrow{\mu} P' \mid Q} \qquad \frac{\pi_i.P_i \xrightarrow{\mu} P'}{\Sigma_i \pi_i.P_i \xrightarrow{\mu} P'}$$

Fig. 1. LTS for πP. Symmetric versions of the two rules involving $\mid$ are omitted.

basic intuition about arcs: an arc d/a can transform an interaction at a into an interaction at d. For instance, from $P \xrightarrow{a(x)} P'$ and $P \triangleright a \prec d$, we can derive $P \xrightarrow{d(x)} P'$. As a consequence, an input at a can synchronise with an output at b if both a and b can be "pulled upwards in the preorder", using arcs, to some name, say u, which is above a and b. Observe also that if, like in P above, the input at a is transformed into an input at d, then a name u' standing above d and b can be used to let the synchronisation happen (because u' would be above a and b).

If, on the contrary, we want to replace, in the input, name a with a name that sits below a, say c (like in process P_0 from Section 1), we are moving *downwards* in the preorder. Because of this, the action becomes protected, and we can derive for instance $P_0 \xrightarrow{\overline{(c)}(y)}$, because $\overline{a}(x).0 \mid a/c \triangleright c \curlyvee a$ (and hence $a \prec \{c\}$). By going downwards, we have somehow fixed the channel where the communication occurs (e.g., at a in $P f_x u 0$). Indeed, it is no longer the case that an output at b can synchronise with the protected input at c whenever some u is above b and c, because such u would not necessarily be above a (where the original input takes place) and b in the preorder. For this reason, we can only move further downwards in the preorder, and for instance deduce, from $P_0 \xrightarrow{\overline{(c)}(y)}$, that $P_0 \xrightarrow{\overline{(c_1)}(y)}$ as soon as $c_1 \prec c$ (which implies $\{c\} \prec \{c_1\}$).

The other preorder rule can be used to modify conditional τs involved in a transition. As an example, let $P_1 \triangleq (\overline{a}(x).Q \mid n/u) \mid (u(y).R \mid n/a)$. Process P_1 can perform a τ transition: the two arcs can, intuitively, let the output at a and the input at u interact at name n. Technically, this can be derived by inferring a $\xrightarrow{[a \curlyvee u]\tau}$ transition (from the output on the left and the input on the right), which can then be turned into a τ transition, exploiting the fact that *the whole process* entails $a \curlyvee u$. Finally, the congruence rules are as expected.

Definition 4 ($\sim$). *A symmetric relation $\mathcal{R}$ is a bisimulation if $P \mathcal{R} Q$ implies:*

- If $P \rhd \varphi$ then $Q \rhd \varphi$.
- If $P \xrightarrow{\alpha(x)} P'$, with $x \notin \text{fn}(Q)$, then there is Q' such that $Q \xrightarrow{\alpha(x)} Q'$ and $P' \mathcal{R} Q'$; we impose the same condition with $\overline{\alpha}$ instead of α.
- If $P \xrightarrow{[\varphi]\tau} P'$ then there is Q' such that $Q \xrightarrow{[\varphi]\tau} Q'$ and $P' \mid \varphi \mathcal{R} Q' \mid \varphi$.

Bisimilarity, written $\sim$, is the greatest bisimulation.

This definition can be related to the efficient bisimulation from [20]. In the last clause, we add φ in parallel, since the transition is fired only if φ is satisfied.

Remark 5. Our LTS does not have rules for opening and closing the scope of a restriction. Instead, we rely on arcs in πP to handle scope extrusion. To illustrate this, consider the following πP transition where a a private name c is emitted:

$$\overline{a}(c).P \xrightarrow{\overline{a}(x)} (\nu c)(c/x \mid P) \ .$$

Name x is visible in the label, and arc c/x is installed. Through x, the environment can affect c, so that πP actually *implements* scope extrusion via arcs, without the need to move restrictions. We have:

$$\overline{a}(c).P \mid a(y).Q \xrightarrow{\tau} (\nu x)((\nu c)(c/x \mid P) \mid (\nu y)(x/y \mid Q))$$
$$\simeq (\nu c)(\nu y)(P \mid c/y \mid Q) \ .$$

3.2   The Characterisation Theorem

Lemma 6. *If $P \equiv Q$ and $P \rhd \varphi$ then $Q \rhd \varphi$.*

Definition 7. *We define a relation $\sqsubseteq^\varphi$ between labels as follows: (i) $\alpha_1(x) \sqsubseteq^\varphi \alpha_2(x)$ and $\overline{\alpha}_1(x) \sqsubseteq^\varphi \overline{\alpha}_2(x)$ when $\varphi = \alpha_2 \prec \alpha_1$, and (ii) $[\varphi_1]\tau \sqsubseteq^\varphi [\varphi_2]\tau$ when $\varphi_1, \varphi \vdash \varphi_2$. We write $\sqsubseteq_P$ for the smallest preorder containing all $\sqsubseteq^\varphi$ when $P \rhd \varphi$.*

Intuitively, $\eta \sqsubseteq_P \mu$ means that label μ is less general than η, given some condition (φ above) entailed by P. For instance, we have $\{a\}(x) \sqsubseteq_0 a(x)$. This notion is used in the following lemma to reason about transitions of processes.

Lemma 8. *If $P \xrightarrow{\mu} P'$ and $\eta \sqsubseteq_P \mu$ then $P \xrightarrow{\eta} P'$. Conversely, whenever $P \xrightarrow{\eta} P'$, there exists μ such that $\eta \sqsubseteq_P \mu$ and $P \xrightarrow{\mu} P'$, of which there is a proof, not bigger than the one for $P \xrightarrow{\eta} P'$, that does not end with a preorder rule.*

Congruence for parallel composition is proved using Lemma 8, which gives:

Lemma 9. *Relation $\sim$ is a congruence.*

Theorem 10 (Characterisation). *$P \simeq Q$ iff $P \sim Q$.*

Proof (Sketch). The proof follows a standard pattern: soundness is a consequence of Lemma 9. For completeness, we have to show that contexts can express the conditions in the three clauses of Definition 4, and we define accordingly tester processes. The first clause about φ is handled using process $\overline{\alpha}.\overline{w_1} \mid \beta.\overline{w_2}$ where α and β are such that $\varphi = \alpha \curlyvee \beta$. For transitions (second clause), the counterpart of, e.g., $\xrightarrow{\{a\}(x)}$, is given by tester process $\overline{a}(y).(z/y \mid \overline{w} \mid w)$. We use process φ for the third clause, since $P \xrightarrow{[\varphi]\tau} Q$ iff $P \mid \varphi \xrightarrow{\tau} Q \mid \varphi$. □

As mentioned above, the calculus in [10] is a version of πP with prefixes for free input and output, and without the corresponding bound prefixes. Let us call that calculus πP$_1$. The encoding $[\cdot]_f$, which we introduced in Remark 3, allows us to embed πP$_1$ into πP in a faithful way:

Proposition 11. $P \simeq_{\pi P_1} Q$ *(in πP$_1$) iff $[P]_f \simeq [Q]_f$ (in πP).*

The proof of the above result exploits in a crucial way the fact that, although πP$_1$ does not feature sums and the $[\varphi]\tau$ prefix, those are not needed to prove the completeness of $\sim$.

4 Axiomatisation

4.1 Equational Laws for Strong Bisimilarity

Notations and Terminology. We use A to range over processes that consist of compositions of φ processes only, which we call *preorder processes*. We often view such processes as multisets of conditions. We use notation A, P to denote a process that can be written, *using the monoid laws for parallel composition*, as $A \mid P$, where P does not contain toplevel arcs. Note that A may contain restrictions, but only those corresponding to the definition of join processes (given in Section 2).

We write $\vdash P = Q$ whenever P and Q can be related by equational reasoning using the laws of Figure 2. We omit the standard laws expressing that $\mid$ and $+$ obey the laws of commutative monoids, and that $+$ is idempotent. We also omit the laws for equational reasoning (equivalence, substitutivity). We will reason up to these laws in the remainder.

Comments on the Laws. Before presenting the properties of the axiomatisation, we comment on the laws of Figure 2 and illustrate them on some examples.

As usual, expansion (L1) allows us to rewrite the parallel composition of two sum processes into a sum, the third summand describing synchronisation in πP.

Preorders. Laws L2-L5 express basic properties of relations $\prec$ and Υ, and actually provide an axiomatisation of $\sim$ for preorder processes.

Prefixes. Law L6 propagates φs in depth, expressing the persistence of condition processes (φ). Law L7 is the counterpart of the third clause of Definition 4, and describes the outcome of a $[\varphi]\tau$ transition. Similarly, laws L18-L19 correspond to the firing of visible transitions in the LTS (regarding these rules, see also the comments after Proposition 16).

α-conversion for input prefixes follows from laws L20 and L18, by deriving the following equalities (and similarly for the other visible prefixes):

$$a(y).P \stackrel{L18}{=} a(x).(\nu y)(x/y \mid P) \stackrel{L20}{=} a(x).(\nu y')(x/y' \mid P\{^{y'}/_y\}) \stackrel{L18}{=} a(y').P\{^{y'}/_y\}\,.$$

Expansion law (we can suppose $x \neq y$, $\mathsf{bn}(\pi_i) \notin \mathsf{fn}(T)$, $\mathsf{bn}(\rho_j) \notin \mathsf{fn}(S)$.)

L1 $\underbrace{\Sigma_i \pi_i.P_i}_{S} \mid \underbrace{\Sigma_j \rho_j.R_j}_{T} = \Sigma_i \pi_i.(P_i \mid T) + \Sigma_j \rho_j.(S \mid R_j)$

  $\qquad\qquad\qquad\qquad\qquad + \Sigma_{i,j}[\alpha \curlyvee \beta]\tau.(\nu xy)(x\!/\!y \mid P_i \mid R_j)$ when $\alpha \curlyvee \beta$ is defined. and $\{\pi_i, \rho_j\} = \{\overline{\alpha}(x), \beta(y)\}$

Laws for preorder processes

L2 $a \prec b \mid b \prec c = a \prec b \mid b \prec c \mid a \prec c$ L3 $a \prec b \mid c \prec b = a \prec b \mid c \prec b \mid a \curlyvee c$

L4 $a \prec b \mid b \curlyvee c = a \prec b \mid b \curlyvee c \mid a \curlyvee c$ L5 $a \prec a = 0$

Laws for prefixes   (the counterparts of laws L11-L13 for output are omitted)

L6 $\varphi, S + \pi.P = \varphi, S + \pi.(\varphi \mid P)$ L7 $[\varphi]\tau.P = [\varphi]\tau.(\varphi \mid P)$

L8 $[a \prec a]\tau.P = [b \curlyvee b]\tau.P$

L9 $[a \curlyvee b]\tau.P = [a \curlyvee b]\tau.P + [a \prec b]\tau.P$

L10 $[a \curlyvee b]\tau.P = [a \curlyvee b]\tau.P + [b \curlyvee a]\tau.P$

L11 $a(x).P = a(x).P + \{a\}(x).P$

L12 $b\!/\!a, S + a(x).P = b\!/\!a, S + a(x).P + b(x).P$

L13 $a\!/\!b, S + \{a\}(x).P = a\!/\!b, S + \{a\}(x).P + \{b\}(x).P$

L14 $b\!/\!a, S + [a \prec c]\tau.P = b\!/\!a, S + [a \prec c]\tau.P + [b \prec c]\tau.P$

L15 $a\!/\!b, S + [c \prec a]\tau.P = a\!/\!b, S + [c \prec a]\tau.P + [c \prec b]\tau.P$

L16 $b\!/\!a, S + [a \curlyvee c]\tau.P = b\!/\!a, S + [a \curlyvee c]\tau.P + [b \curlyvee c]\tau.P$

L17 $b\!/\!a, S + [a \curlyvee c]\tau.P = b\!/\!a, S + [a \curlyvee c]\tau.P + [c \prec b]\tau.P$

L18 $\alpha(y).P = \alpha(x).(\nu y)(x\!/\!y \mid P)$ if $x \notin \mathsf{fn}(P)$

L19 $\overline{\alpha}(y).P = \overline{\alpha}(x).(\nu y)(y\!/\!x \mid P)$ if $x \notin \mathsf{fn}(P)$

Laws for restriction   (the counterparts of laws L26 and L27 for output are omitted; $a \prec b \in A^{\neq}$ stands for $a \prec b \in A$ and $a \neq b$, and similarly for $a \curlyvee b$.)

L20 $(\nu b)P = (\nu a)(P\{^a\!/\!_b\})$ if $a \notin \mathsf{fn}(P)$ L21 $(\nu c)(\nu d)P = (\nu d)(\nu c)P$

L22 $P \mid (\nu a)Q = (\nu a)(P \mid Q)$ if $a \notin \mathsf{fn}(P)$ L23 $(\nu a)0 = 0$

L24 $(\nu a)A = \{b \prec c \mid b \prec a, \ a \prec c \in A^{\neq}\} \uplus \{b \curlyvee c \mid b \prec a, \ c \prec a \in A^{\neq}\}$
  $\qquad\qquad \uplus \{b \curlyvee c \mid a \curlyvee c, \ b \prec a \in A^{\neq}\} \uplus \{\varphi \in A \mid a \notin \mathsf{n}(\varphi)\}$

L25 $(\nu a)(A, \ S + \pi.P) \quad = (\nu a)\big(A, \ S + \pi.(\nu a)(A \mid P)\big)$ $a \notin \mathsf{n}(\pi)$

L26 $(\nu a)(A, \ S + a(x).P) \quad = (\nu a)\big(A, \ S + \Sigma_{a \prec b \in A^{\neq}} b(x).(\nu a)(A \mid P)$
  $\qquad\qquad\qquad\qquad\qquad\quad + \Sigma_{b \prec a \in A^{\neq}} \{b\}(x).(\nu a)(A \mid P)\big)$
  $\qquad\qquad\qquad\qquad\qquad \scriptstyle \nu a \curlyvee b \in A^{\neq}$

L27 $(\nu a)(A, \ S + \{a\}(x).P) = (\nu a)\big(A, \ S + \Sigma_{b \prec a \in A^{\neq}} \{b\}(x).(\nu a)(A \mid P)\big)$

L28 $(\nu a)(A, \ S + [a \prec c]\tau.P) = (\nu a)\big(A, \ S + \Sigma_{a \prec b \in A^{\neq}} [b \prec c]\tau.(\nu a)(A \mid P)\big)$ $a \neq c$

L29 $(\nu a)(A, \ S + [c \prec a]\tau.P) = (\nu a)\big(A, \ S + \Sigma_{b \prec a \in A^{\neq}} [c \prec b]\tau.(\nu a)(A \mid P)\big)$ $a \neq c$

L30 $(\nu a)(A, \ S + [a \curlyvee c]\tau.P) = (\nu a)\big(A, \ S + \Sigma_{a \prec b \in A^{\neq}} [b \curlyvee c]\tau.(\nu a)(A \mid P)$ $a \neq c$
  $\qquad\qquad\qquad\qquad\qquad\qquad\quad + \Sigma_{b \prec a \in A^{\neq}} [c \prec b]\tau.(\nu a)(A \mid P)\big)$
  $\qquad\qquad\qquad\qquad\qquad\qquad \scriptstyle \nu a \curlyvee b \in A^{\neq}$

Fig. 2. An axiomatisation of $\sim$

Laws L11-L17 can be used to expand process behaviours using the preorder: arcs can modify the subject of visible prefixes (L11-L13) and the condition in $[\varphi]\tau$ prefixes (L14-L17). Laws L9, L10 and L14-L17 rely on the defining properties of relations $\prec$ and $\curlyvee$. Finally, law L8 is used to equate all reflexive τ prefixes.

Restriction. Laws L20-L23 are standard. The other laws are used to "push" restrictions inside processes. Due to the necessity to handle the preorder component (A), they are rather complex.

Law L24 is used to eliminate a restriction on a name a in a preorder process, by propagating the information expressed by all φs that mention a.

Law L25 is rather self-explanatory, and shows how the A component prevents us from simply pushing the restriction downwards (under prefixes).

Laws L26-L30 describe a kind of "synchronous application" of the prefix laws seen above. For instance, the two summands in law L26 correspond to applications of laws L12-L13: as we push the restriction on a downwards, we make sure that all possible applications of these laws are taken into account.

Intuitively, L24 is applied after laws L25-L30 have been used to erase all prefixes mentioning the restricted name a, pushing the restriction on a inwards.

All in all, the set of laws in Figure 2 is rather lengthy. We make two comments on this. First, it can be remarked that axiomatisations often treat restriction separately, by first focusing on a restriction-free calculus. In πP, because of preorder processes, we cannot in general push restrictions on top of sum processes, so the situation is more complex (see also the discussion about [14] in Section 5).

Second, we could have presented the laws in a more compact way, by writing *schemas*. A uniform presentation for laws L8-L17 and L26-L30 is as follows:

$$\frac{\eta \sqsubseteq_A \mu \quad \mu.P \in S}{A, S = A, S + \eta.P} \qquad \frac{a \in \mathsf{fn}(\mu) \quad \forall \eta \sqsubseteq_A \mu \quad a \in \mathsf{fn}(\eta) \vee \exists \rho \ \eta \sqsubseteq_A \rho \wedge \rho.P \in S}{(\nu a)(A, \mu.P + S) = (\nu a)(A, S)}$$

(To remove $\mu.P$ from $\mu.P + S$, the second rule requires that some $\rho.P$ are in S. The second rule can be used to add those summands to S.) We prefer nevertheless to write all rules explicitly, since this is how they are handled in proofs.

Examples of Derivable Equalities. In the following examples, we sometimes switch silently to notation A, P to ease readability. We also allow ourselves to simplify some reasonings involving prefixes where the object is not important. We explain how the following derivable between πP processes can be derived:

$$(\nu a)(b/a \mid a/c) = b/c \qquad (\nu a)(S + a(x).P) = (\nu a)S$$
$$(\nu a)(a/b \mid a(x).P) = \{b\}(x).(\nu a)P \qquad \bar{a}(x).x = \bar{a}(x).\{x\} \qquad a(x).\{x\} = a(x).0$$

The first equality above is established using law L24: before getting rid of the restriction on a, we compute all conditions not involving a that can be deduced from $b/a \mid a/c$. In this case, this is only b/c.

The second equality is a direct consequence of law L26. Law L26 is also used for the third equality: only the second sum in the law is not empty, which gives $(\nu a)(a/b, a(x).P) = (\nu a)(a/b, \{b\}(x).(\nu a)P)$. Then, L22 allows us to restrict the scope of νa, and we can get rid of $(\nu a)a/b$ using law 24, which yields the result.

Another way to see the third equality is to observe that we can derive a/b, $a(x).P = a/b, a(x).P + \{a\}(x).P + \{b\}(x).P$ using laws L11 and L13. In the latter process, the sum is intuitively *expanded*, in the sense that all derivable toplevel summands have been made explicit. When considering the restricted version of both processes, it is sound to push the restriction on a downwards in the expanded process, to obtain the expected equality. In this sense, law L26 implements a "synchronous version" of this reasoning, so as to insure that when pushing a restriction downwards, the behaviour of the process is fully expanded.

The next two equalities illustrate the meaning of protected names. We reason as follows: $\overline{a}(x).x \stackrel{L19}{=} \overline{a}(x').(\nu x)(x/x', x) \stackrel{L26}{=} \overline{a}(x').(\nu x)(x/x', \{x'\}.(\nu x)(x/x' \mid 0))$. We then obtain the expected equality by getting rid of $(\nu x)x/x'$, twice, using laws L22 and L24. The reason why this equality holds is that fresh name x is emitted without the context having the ability to interact at x, since x will never be under another name in an arc. Therefore, the input at x is equivalent to a protected input.

In the last equality, because of the transition $a(x).\{x\} \xrightarrow{a(x')} (\nu x)(x'/x \mid \{x\})$, x will never be above another name, so that the prefix $\{x\}$ cannot be triggered, and is equivalent to 0. This equality is derived as follows:

$$a(x).\{x\} \stackrel{L18}{=} a(x').(\nu x)(x'/x \mid \{x\}) \stackrel{L27}{=} a(x').(\nu x)x'/x \stackrel{L24}{=} a(x').0 \ .$$

(we have explained above how $a(x').0 = a(x).0$ can be derived).

We leave it to the reader to check that the law for interleaving, presented in Section 1, can be derived using the expansion law, followed by the rules for prefixes and restriction to get rid of the summand $[x \curlyvee y]\tau.(\nu t, u)(t/u)$.

4.2   Soundness and Completeness of the Axioms

Lemma 12 (Soundness). *The laws of Figure 2 relate bisimilar processes.*

Proof (Sketch). For laws 24-30, we establish a "saturation property", expressing the fact that when erasing a preorder process φ or a prefix π that mentions a, we generate all processes φ or π could induce. The other laws are easy.   □

Auxiliary Results: Preorder Processes, Prefixes, Restriction.

In order to establish completeness, we first need some technical results, given by Propositions 13, 16 and 17.

First, laws L2-L5 can be used to *saturate* preorder processes:

Proposition 13. *If $A_1, S_1 \sim A_2, S_2$, then there exists $A^\star$ such that $\vdash A_i, S_i = A^\star, S_i$ ($i = 1, 2$), and $A^\star = \prod\{\varphi \mid \varphi$ not reflexive and $A_1 \rhd \varphi\}$.*

(Note that we could have picked A_2 instead of A_1 above.) We say that A is a *saturated preorder process* whenever $A^\star \equiv A$. We use $A^\star$ to range over such processes. We can remark that even if A contains only arcs, $A^\star$ may contain restrictions, because of induced conditions involving $\curlyvee$.

The next lemma relates transitions of sum processes and the laws for prefixes.

Lemma 14. *If* $A, S \xrightarrow{\mu} A, P$ *then* $\vdash A, S = A, S + \pi.Q$ *for some* π *and* Q *such that* μ *and* π *only differ in their bound names and* $\pi.Q \xrightarrow{\mu} P$.

Laws L9-L17 can be used to "saturate" the topmost prefixes in sums. We express this using the equivalence below, and rely on Lemma 14 to prove Prop. 16:

Definition 15 (Head sum normal form, $\asymp_h$). *Given two sum processes* S *and* T, *we write* $S \prec_h T$ *whenever for any summand* $\pi.P$ *of* S, *there exists a summand* $\pi.Q$ *of* T *with* $\pi.P \sim \pi.Q$. *We let* $S \asymp_h T$ *stand for* $S \prec_h T \wedge T \prec_h S$.

Proposition 16. *Whenever* $A^\star, S_1 \sim A^\star, S_2$, *where* S_1, S_2 *are two sum processes, there are* S_1', S_2' *s.t.* $\vdash A^\star, S_i = A^\star, S_i'$ *(for* $i = 1, 2$*) and* $S_1' \asymp_h S_2'$.

In the definition of $\prec_h$, we impose $\pi.P \sim \pi.Q$, and not simply $P \sim Q$. The equivalence induced by the choice of the latter condition would indeed be too discriminating. To see why, consider $Q_1 = a(x).c/x$ and $Q_2 = a(x).0$. Obviously, $c/x \not\sim 0$. On the other hand, we have $Q_1 \sim Q_2$: after a $\xrightarrow{a(y)}$ transition on both sides, we must compare $(\nu x)(c/x \mid y/x)$ and $(\nu x)(y/x)$, and both are bisimilar to 0. In order to derive $\vdash Q_1 = Q_2$, we rely on the following property, which explains the shape of laws L18, L19: $a(y).P \sim a(y).Q$ iff $(\nu y)(x/y \mid P) \sim (\nu y)(x/y \mid Q)$.

Proposition 17 expresses that restrictions can be pushed inwards in processes. It introduces a notion of measure on processes that is useful to reason by induction on processes in the completeness proof:

Proposition 17. *We define* $|P|$ *as follows:* $|\Sigma_i \pi_i.P_i| = \max_i (1 + |P_i|)$ $|(\nu a)P|$ $= |P|$, $|P \mid Q| = |P| + |Q|$, *and* $|a/b| = 0$.
  For any A, S, a, *there exist* A' *and* S' *such that* $\vdash (\nu a)(A, S) = A', S'$ *and* $|(\nu a)(A, S)| \geq |A', S'|$.

Establishing Completeness. The grammar $P ::= A, \Sigma_i \pi_i.P_i \mid (\nu a)P$ defines what we call $|$-*free processes*: only arcs are composed, and the non-preorder part of processes is a sum.

Proposition 18. *For all* $|$-*free processes* P *and* Q, $P \sim Q$ *iff* $\vdash P = Q$.

Proof (Sketch). The 'if' part follows from Lemmas 9 and 12. Suppose now $P \sim Q$; we reason by induction on $|P| + |Q|$. By Propositions 17, 13 and 16, we obtain $\vdash P = A^\star, S_1$ and $\vdash Q = A^\star, S_2$, for some A, S_1, S_2 such that $S_1 \asymp_h S_2$.
  We then consider $a(x).T_1 \in S_1$ and $a(x).T_2 \in S_2$ s.t. $a(x).T_1 \sim a(x).T_2$. The latter yields, by triggering the input transition, $(\nu x)(y/x \mid T_1) \sim (\nu x)(y/x \mid T_2)$. By induction we derive $\vdash (\nu x)(y/x \mid T_1) = (\nu x)(y/x \mid T_2)$ from which we get $\vdash a(x).T_1 = a(x).T_2$ by law L18.
  The other kinds of prefixes are handled similarly. This reasoning allows us to prove $\vdash S_1 = S_2$ and hence $\vdash P = Q$. $\qquad\square$

The expansion law yields the following result, which then gives Theorem 20.

Lemma 19. *For any* P, *there exists a* $|$-*free process* Q *s.t.* $\vdash P = Q$.

Theorem 20 (Axiomatisation of $\sim$). *For all P and Q, $P \sim Q$ iff $\vdash P = Q$.*

Remark 21 (Normal forms). The proofs of the results in this section suggest that we can define a strategy to apply the rules of Figure 2, in order to rewrite a πP process P to its *normal form*, $\mathsf{nf}(P)$, so that $P \sim Q$ iff $\mathsf{nf}(P) = \mathsf{nf}(Q)$. We leave the rigorous description of this normalisation procedure for future work.

4.3   Adapting our Axiomatisation to Explicit Fusions

We can reuse the ideas presented above to describe an axiomatisation for barbed congruence in Explicit Fusions (EF, [20]). EF feature *fusion processes*, of the form a=b, which can equate names via $\equiv$: we have a=$b \mid P \equiv a$=$b \mid P\{b/a\}$.

Like in πP, we work with three kinds of prefixes, $\bar{a}(x)$, $a(x)$ and $[a$=$b]\tau$, the latter being the counterpart of $[\varphi]\tau$ in πP (it appears, e.g., in [20]).

The "state component" of processes is simpler in EF than in πP, since fusions implement an equivalence relation on names. The laws of Figure 2 can be ported to EF, yielding an axiomatisation. We only discuss some relevant laws, and refer to [11] for a complete definition. The laws for fusion processes are

$$a\text{=}a = 0 \qquad a\text{=}b \mid a\text{=}c = a\text{=}b \mid a\text{=}c \mid b\text{=}c \qquad a\text{=}b = b\text{=}a \ ,$$

and the EF counterpart of (some of) the laws for prefixes in πP is given by

$$a\text{=}b \mid a(x).P = a\text{=}b \mid b(x).P \qquad a\text{=}b \mid [a\text{=}c]\tau.P = a\text{=}b \mid [b\text{=}c]\tau.P$$

(laws L6-L7 are inherited directly, φ denoting fusions). Because fusions satisfy transitivity, every fusion can be eliminated if one of its names is restricted, as $(\nu a)(a\text{=}b \mid P) \sim P\{b/a\}$. This makes the laws for restriction much simpler than in πP:

$$(\nu a)a\text{=}b = 0 \qquad (\nu a)\Sigma_i \pi_i.P_i = \Sigma_{i \mid a \notin \mathsf{n}(\pi_i)} \pi_i.(\nu a)P_i \ .$$

5   Conclusions and Future Work

Working with a preorder on names has an influence on the behavioural theory of πP, notably through the interplay between arcs and restrictions. The preorder relation is represented explicitly in πP processes, using arcs. We do not see any natural "implicit version" of πP, mimicking the relation between Explicit Fusions and Fusions, whereby the extension of the preorder along a communication would not generate an arc process.

The stateful nature of the preorder component of πP processes can be related to *frames* in the applied π-calculus [1] and Psi-calculi [2]. Arcs in πP can be seen in some sense as substitutions, but they differ from the active substitutions of applied π. The latter map variables to terms, while, in the tradition of fusion calculi, we only have (channel) names in πP. Moreover, several arcs acting on the same name are allowed in πP, while a substitution acts on at most one variable in applied π. For these reasons, the behavioural theories of πP and applied π are rather different. Liu and Lin's proof system for applied π [14] departs from our axiomatisation for πP, but has in common the stateful component of processes.

Psi-calculi can represent the active substitutions of applied π. It would be interesting to study whether arcs, and the preorder between names, can be represented in the setting of Psi-calculi. An important technical point to address in this perspective is whether transitivity of (generalised) channel equivalence in Psi-calculi would conflict with the fact that name joinability is not transitive in πP. Another important feature of Psi-calculi is that they come with a fully mechanised metatheory: this is clearly something that πP is lacking at the moment.

The behavioural theory of πP is based on an operational account. An intriguing question is the construction of a denotational model for πP, and the comparison with known models for π and Fusions. We would also like to study the weak version of behavioural equivalence.

The results of this work provide foundations for the behavioural theory of the πP calculus, which also has i/o-types (cf. [10]). As already mentioned, typed behavioural equivalence [17,6] can be used to establish fine behavioural properties of concurrent systems. We would like to find out whether it can be helpful to refine untyped analyses of systems where Fusions have been used.

Acknowledgements. We thank Davide Sangiorgi and Fu Yuxi for useful discussions about this work. This work has been supported by projects ANR 12IS02001 PACE, ANR 2010-BLAN-0305 PiCoq and NSF of China (61261130589).

References

1. Abadi, M., Fournet, C.: Mobile values, new names, and secure communication. In: Proc. of POPL, pp. 104–115. ACM (2001)
2. Bengtson, J., Johansson, M., Parrow, J., Victor, B.: Psi-calculi: Mobile processes, nominal data, and logic. In: LICS, pp. 39–48. IEEE (2009)
3. Boreale, M., Buscemi, M.G., Montanari, U.: D-fusion: A distinctive fusion calculus. In: Chin, W.-N. (ed.) APLAS 2004. LNCS, vol. 3302, pp. 296–310. Springer, Heidelberg (2004)
4. Boreale, M., Buscemi, M.G., Montanari, U.: A general name binding mechanism. In: De Nicola, R., Sangiorgi, D. (eds.) TGC 2005. LNCS, vol. 3705, pp. 61–74. Springer, Heidelberg (2005)
5. Carpineti, S., Laneve, C., Padovani, L.: PiDuce - A project for experimenting Web services technologies. Sci. Comput. Program. 74(10), 777–811 (2009)
6. Deng, Y., Sangiorgi, D.: Towards an algebraic theory of typed mobile processes. Theor. Comput. Sci. 350(2-3), 188–212 (2006)
7. Ehrhard, T., Laurent, O.: Acyclic solos and differential interaction nets. Logical Methods in Computer Science 6(3) (2010)
8. Fu, Y.: The χ-calculus. In: APDC, pp. 74–81. IEEE Computer Society (1997)
9. Gardner, P., Laneve, C., Wischik, L.: The fusion machine (Extended abstract). In: Brim, L., Jančar, P., Křetínský, M., Kučera, A. (eds.) CONCUR 2002. LNCS, vol. 2421, pp. 418–433. Springer, Heidelberg (2002)
10. Hirschkoff, D., Madiot, J.-M., Sangiorgi, D.: Name-passing calculi: From fusions to preorders and types. In: LICS, pp. 378–387. IEEE Computer Society (2013)
11. Hirschkoff, D., Madiot, J.-M., Xu, X.: Long version of this paper, http://madiot.org

12. Honda, K., Yoshida, N.: On reduction-based process semantics. Theor. Comp. Sci. 152(2), 437–486 (1995)
13. Laneve, C., Victor, B.: Solos in concert. Mathematical Structures in Computer Science 13(5), 657–683 (2003)
14. Liu, J., Lin, H.: Proof system for applied pi calculus. In: IFIP TCS. IFIP AICT, vol. 323, pp. 229–243. Springer, Heidelberg (2010)
15. Parrow, J., Sangiorgi, D.: Algebraic theories for name-passing calculi. Inf. Comput. 120(2), 174–197 (1995)
16. Parrow, J., Victor, B.: The fusion calculus: expressiveness and symmetry in mobile processes. In: LICS, pp. 176–185. IEEE (1998)
17. Pierce, B.C., Sangiorgi, D.: Typing and subtyping for mobile processes. Mathematical Structures in Computer Science 6(5), 409–453 (1996)
18. Sangiorgi, D., Walker, D.: The Pi-Calculus: a theory of mobile processes. Cambridge University Press (2001)
19. Victor, B., Parrow, J.: Concurrent constraints in the fusion calculus. In: Larsen, K.G., Skyum, S., Winskel, G. (eds.) ICALP 1998. LNCS, vol. 1443, pp. 455–469. Springer, Heidelberg (1998)
20. Wischik, L., Gardner, P.: Strong bisimulation for the explicit fusion calculus. In: Walukiewicz, I. (ed.) FOSSACS 2004. LNCS, vol. 2987, pp. 484–498. Springer, Heidelberg (2004)

Incremental Realization of Safety Requirements: Non-determinism vs. Modularity*

Ali Ebnenasir

Department of Computer Science,
Michigan Technological University, Houghton MI 49931, USA
aebnenas@mtu.edu

Abstract. This paper investigates the impact of non-determinism and modularity on the complexity of incremental incorporation of safety requirements while preserving liveness (a.k.a. the problem of *incremental synthesis*). Previous work shows that realizing safety in non-deterministic programs under limited observability is an NP-complete problem (in the state space of the program), where *limited observability* imposes read restrictions on program components with respect to the local state of other components. In this paper, we present a surprising result that synthesizing safety remains an NP-complete problem even for deterministic programs! The results of this paper imply that non-determinism is not the source of the hardness of synthesizing safety in concurrent programs; instead, limited observability has a major impact on the complexity of realizing safety. We also provide a roadmap for future research on exploiting the benefits of modularization while keeping the complexity of incremental synthesis manageable.

Keywords: Program Synthesis, Safety Specifications, Non-Determinism, Modularity.

1 Introduction

Understanding the complexity of realizing new (safety/liveness) properties is of paramount importance since today's systems often have to adapt to new requirements while preserving some existing functionalities. *Safety* stipulates that nothing bad ever happens (e.g., at most one process/thread accesses shared resources at any moment), and *liveness* states that something good will eventually occur (e.g., each process eventually gets access to shared resources). New requirements are raised due to changes in platform, environmental faults, design flaws, new user requirements (e.g., non-functional concerns), porting, etc. Thus, it is important to enhance our understanding of what complicates behavioral changes. Towards this end, this paper investigates the complexity of *redesigning* finite-state programs towards capturing new safety requirements while preserving liveness, called the *problem of incremental synthesis*.

---

* This work was sponsored in part by the National Science Foundation grant CCF-1116546.

© IFIP International Federation for Information Processing 2015
M. Dastani and M.Sirjani (Eds.): FSEN 2015, LNCS 9392, pp. 159–175, 2015.
DOI: 10.1007/978-3-319-24644-4_11

Several approaches exist for capturing safety most of which lack a thorough complexity analysis. For example, aspect-oriented approaches [5,17,16,10,13,6] provide a method for capturing and verifying cross-cutting functionalities. Control-theoretic techniques [25,12] realize new safety requirements by generating controllers that implement safety in different components of a system. Techniques based on transformation automata [24] enforce safety and/or security policies. Our previous work [7,3] shows that incremental synthesis for non-deterministic programs can be done in polynomial time (in the size of program state space) if we consider *unlimited observability*, where program components/processes can atomically read the state of other processes. Nonetheless, the authors of [4] demonstrate that incremental synthesis of safety in non-deterministic programs under limited observability is NP-complete (in the size of the program state space). *Limited observability* imposes restrictions on processes with regard to reading the state of other processes. Vechev *et al.* [27] present an exponential algorithm for synthesizing synchronization mechanisms under limited observability, but they provide no results on the general case hardness of synthesizing synchronization mechanisms. Now, the open questions are: *What role do non-determinism and observability/modularization play in the complexity of incremental synthesis? Is incremental synthesis of safety easier for deterministic programs?*

In this paper, we prove that non-determinism is not the major source of the complexity of incremental synthesis; rather it is modularization constraints that complicate the incremental synthesis of safety properties. We consider Alpern and Schneider's [1] definition of safety/liveness properties, where a *property* is a set of sequences of states. Their definition of a *safety* property P can be represented as a set of finite sequences that cannot be extended to be in P, which we call them *bad sequences*. We also investigate a special case of safety properties that can be specified as a set of *Bad Transitions* (BT) (introduced in [18]). The BT model is more general than the usual notion of *Bad States* (BS) in that every transition reaching a bad state is considered to be a bad transition, whereas not every bad transition reaches a bad state [20]. Previous work [7,3] shows that incremental synthesis of safety (for deterministic and non-deterministic programs) can be done in polynomial time (in the size of the state space) under unlimited observability. Nonetheless, we show that under limited observability the general case complexity of synthesizing safety in deterministic programs increases to NP-complete! Our results imply that limited observability has a major impact on the complexity of incremental synthesis of safety (see Figure 1) regardless of non-determinism/determinism. While modularity is a powerful design concept, *design for change* [22] is also an important goal. To achieve this goal, research should be focused on identifying the kind of modularization techniques that facilitate incremental synthesis.

Organization. Section 2 presents preliminary concepts. Section 3 formulates the problem of incremental synthesis of safety. Section 4 shows that the general case complexity of incremental synthesis of safety in deterministic programs increases to NP-complete if we assume limited observability. Finally, in Section 5, we make concluding remarks and present a roadmap for future research.

	Unlimited Observability	Limited Observability
Deterministic Programs	P	NP-complete*
Non-Deterministic Programs	P	NP-complete

Fig. 1. The impact of non-determinism and limited observability on the complexity of incremental synthesis (* depicts the contribution of this paper).

2   Preliminaries

In this section, we present formal definitions of finite-state programs, program components[1] The definition of specification is adapted from Alpern and Schneider [1]. We use a read/write model from [2,19].

Programs. A *program* $p = \langle V_p, C_p, \mathcal{I}_p, \mathcal{F}_p \rangle$ is a tuple of a finite set V_p of variables and a finite set C_p of computing components $C_1, \cdots, C_k$, where $k \geq 1$. Each variable $v_i \in V_p$, for $1 \leq i \leq N$, has a finite non-empty domain D_i. A *state s* of p is a valuation $\langle d_1, d_2, \cdots, d_N \rangle$ of program variables $\langle v_1, v_2, \cdots, v_N \rangle$, where $d_i \in D_i$. $\mathcal{I}_p$ denotes a finite set of initial states, and $\mathcal{F}_p$ represents a finite set of accepting/final states. For a variable v and a state s, $v(s)$ denotes the value of v in s. The *state space* $\mathcal{S}_p$ is the set of all possible states of p and $|\mathcal{S}_p|$ denotes the size of $\mathcal{S}_p$. A *state predicate* is a subset of $\mathcal{S}_p$. A *transition* is an ordered pair (s, s'), where s and s' are program states. A *component* C_j is a triple $\langle \delta_j, r_j, w_j \rangle$, where $1 \leq j \leq k$ and $\delta_j \subseteq \mathcal{S}_p \times \mathcal{S}_p$ denotes the *set of transitions* of C_j. We shall define r_j and w_j below. The set of transitions of a program p, denoted δ_p, is the union of the sets of transitions of its components; i.e., $\delta_p = \bigcup_{j=1}^{k} \delta_j$. A program p is *non-deterministic* iff (if and only if) the transition function δ_p is defined as $\mathcal{S}_p \to 2^{\mathcal{S}_p}$. A *deterministic* program is a special case where from each state there is *at most* one outgoing transition. That is, the set δ_p defines a *partial* (transition) function from $\mathcal{S}_p$ to $\mathcal{S}_p$. Thus, given a state $s \in \mathcal{S}_p$, δ_p returns *at most* one state $s' \in \mathcal{S}_p$. This is a property that each δ_j inherits from δ_p. *Notation.* For simplicity, we shall misuse p and δ_p interchangeably.

Read/Write Model. In order to model the access rights of each component C_j ($1 \leq j \leq k$) with respect to program variables, we define a set of variables that C_j is allowed to read, denoted r_j, and a set of variables that C_j can write, denoted w_j. Notice that, if a variable v of some component C_i is read/written through the *interface* of C_i, then v is considered readable/writable for the component that invokes the interface of C_i. We assume that $w_j \subseteq r_j$; i.e., a component cannot blindly write a variable it cannot read. The write restrictions of a component

---

[1] The term *component* can capture objects in object-oriented program, threads/processes in concurrent programming, nodes of network protocols, etc., computations and safety specifications.

C_j identify a set of transitions $\{(s, s') \mid \exists v : v \notin w_j : v(s) \neq v(s')\}$ that δ_j excludes, where v denotes a variable. For example, consider a program p_r with two components C_1 and C_2 and two binary variables v_1 and v_2. The component C_1 (respectively, C_2) can read and write the variable v_1 (respectively, v_2), but it cannot read (or write) v_2 (respectively, v_1). Let $\langle v_1, v_2 \rangle$ denote the state of the program p_r. A transition t_1, represented as $(\langle 0, 0 \rangle, \langle 1, 1 \rangle)$, does not belong to C_1 because $v_2 \notin w_1$ and the value of v_2 is being updated. For similar reasons, t_1 does not belong to C_2 either.

The effect of read restrictions is that, during the synthesis of safety, δ_j of a component C_j includes (respectively, excludes) a transition t iff a *group* of transitions associated with t is included (respectively, excluded) in δ_j [19,2]. In the aforementioned example, consider the transition t_2 as $(\langle 0, 0 \rangle, \langle 1, 0 \rangle)$. If C_1 includes only t_2, then the execution of t_2 can be interpreted as the atomic execution of the following if statement: 'if $(v_1 = 0) \wedge (v_2 = 0)$ then $v_1 := 1$'; i.e., C_1 needs to read v_2. Including both transitions $(\langle 0, 0 \rangle, \langle 1, 0 \rangle)$ and $(\langle 0, 1 \rangle, \langle 1, 1 \rangle)$ makes the value of v_2 irrelevant, thereby eliminating the need for reading v_2 by C_1. Thus, the component C_1 must either include or exclude both transitions as a group. Formally, a component C_j can include a transition (s, s') if and only if C_j also includes any transition (s_g, s'_g) such that for all variables $v \in r_j$, we have $v(s) = v(s_g)$ and $v(s') = v(s'_g)$, and for all variables $u \notin r_j$, we have $u(s) = u(s')$ and $u(s_g) = u(s'_g)$.

Computations. A *computation* of a program $p = \langle V_p, C_p, \mathcal{I}_p, \mathcal{F}_p \rangle$ is a sequence of states $\sigma = \ll s_0, s_1, \cdots \gg$, where each transition (s_i, s_{i+1}) in σ $(i \geq 0)$ belongs to some component C_j, $1 \leq j \leq k$, i.e., C_j *executes* the transition (s_i, s_{i+1}), and σ is *maximal*. That is, either σ is infinite, or if σ is finite and terminates in a state s_f, then there is no component of p that executes a transition (s_f, s) for any state s. A *computation prefix* of p is a finite sequence $\sigma = \ll s_0, s_1, \cdots, s_m \gg$ of states in which every transition (s_i, s_{i+1}), for $0 \leq i < m$, is executed by some component C_j, $1 \leq j \leq k$.

Properties and Specifications. Intuitively, a safety property/requirement states that nothing bad ever happens. Formally, we follow Alpern and Schneider [1] in defining a property as a set of sequences of states. A *safety* property $\mathcal{P}$ can be represented by a set of *finite* sequences of states, denoted $\mathcal{B}$, that cannot be extended to be in $\mathcal{P}$. Each sequence in $\mathcal{B}$ represents a scenario of the occurrence of something bad. For example, a safety property of a program with an integer variable x could stipulate that an increment of x must not *immediately* be followed by a decrement in the value of x. Such a safety property can be represented by a set of bad sequences of three states (i.e., two immediate transitions; one that increments x and the subsequent one that decrements x). In this paper, a liveness property states that something good eventually happens, including good things that occur infinitely often. Formally, a *liveness property*, denoted $\mathcal{L}$, is a set of sequences of states, where each sequence in $\mathcal{L}$ either terminates in a state belonging to a state predicate $\mathcal{F}$ (representing the good thing that should happen), or infinitely often visits some states in $\mathcal{F}$. This notion of liveness is sufficiently general to capture stutter-invariant Linear Temporal Logic (LTL) [8] properties [11,23]. Following Alpern and Schneider [1], we define a specification, denoted $spec$, as a set of safety and liveness properties. A computation $\sigma = \ll s_0, s_1, \cdots \gg$ of a program $p = \langle V_p, C_p, \mathcal{I}_p, \mathcal{F}_p \rangle$ *satisfies a specification spec from $\mathcal{I}_p$ iff* (1) $s_0 \in \mathcal{I}_p$, (2) no sequence of the safety of $spec$, denoted $\mathcal{B}$, appears in σ, and (3) if σ terminates in a state s_f, then $s_f \in \mathcal{F}_p$; otherwise, some states in $\mathcal{F}_p$ are reached infinitely often in σ. A *program p satisfies its specification spec from $\mathcal{I}_p$ iff* all computations of p satisfy $spec$ from any state in $\mathcal{I}_p$. Given a finite computation $\sigma = \ll s_0, s_1, \cdots, s_d \gg$, if no program component executes from s_d and $s_d \notin \mathcal{F}_p$, then σ is a *deadlocked computation* and s_d is a *deadlock state*. A computation $\sigma = \ll s_0, s_1, \cdots \gg$ of p is a *non-progress computation* iff σ does not infinitely often reach some state in $\mathcal{F}_p$ nor does it terminate in a state in $\mathcal{F}_p$. A deadlocked computation is an instance of a non-progress computation. Another example is the case where a computation of p includes a cycle in which no state belongs to $\mathcal{F}_p$, called a *non-progress cycle*. If a computation σ includes a sequence in $\mathcal{B}$, then σ is a *safety-violating computation*. A computation σ of p *violates spec* from a state s_0 iff σ starts at s_0 and σ is either a non-progress computation or a safety-violating computation. A program p *violates spec* from $\mathcal{I}_p$ iff there exists a computation of p that violates $spec$ from some state s_0 in $\mathcal{I}_p$.

Notation. Whenever it is clear from the context, we abbreviate 'p *satisfies spec from $\mathcal{I}_p$*' as 'p *satisfies spec*'.

Bad Transitions (BT) Model. Consider a special case in which safety specifications are modeled as a set of finite sequences of length 2; i.e., a sequence has only two states. That is, the safety specification rules out a set of transitions that must not appear in program computations, called *bad transitions* [18]. For instance, the safety specification of a program with an integer variable x may stipulate that x can be decremented only if its value is positive. Consider a state s_0, where $x(s_0) = -2$. State s_0 can be reached either by incrementing x from s_1, where $x(s_1) = -3$, or by decrementing x from s_2, where $x(s_2) = -1$. Observe that the transition (s_2, s_0) is a bad transition, whereas (s_1, s_0) is not. In this model, reaching s_0 does not necessarily violate safety and it depends on how s_0 is reached. Such a model of safety specification is a restricted version of the general model of safety specifications presented by Alpern and Schneider [1], but it is more general than the usual model of *bad states* often specified in the literature in terms of the *always* operator (or invariance properties) in temporal logic [8].

Remark. We investigate incremental synthesis under "no fairness".

3   Problem Statement

In this section, we formally define the problem of incremental synthesis of safety. Let $p = \langle V_p, C_p, \mathcal{I}_p, \mathcal{F}_p \rangle$ be a program that satisfies a specification $spec$. Moreover, let $\mathcal{B}$ denote the safety of $spec$, and $\mathcal{B}_{new}$ represent a new safety property (e.g., data race-freedom) that p does not satisfy. Our goal is to redesign p to a program

$p_r = \langle V_p^r, C_p^r, \mathcal{I}_p^r, \mathcal{F}_p^r \rangle$, such that p_r satisfies $\mathcal{B} \wedge \mathcal{B}_{new}$ and the liveness of *spec* from $\mathcal{I}_p^r$. For simplicity, during such redesign, we do not expand the state space of p; i.e., no new variables are added to V_p. Thus, we have $V_p^r = V_p$ and $\mathcal{S}_p^r = \mathcal{S}_p$. Since p_r must still satisfy *spec* from all states in $\mathcal{I}_p$, we should preserve all initial states of p. Thus, we require that $\mathcal{I}_p = \mathcal{I}_p^r$. We state the problem as follows:

Problem 1. **Incremental Synthesis of Safety**

- **Input:** A program $p = \langle V_p, C_p, \mathcal{I}_p, \mathcal{F}_p \rangle$ with its specification *spec*, its set of safety properties $\mathcal{B}$, a new safety property $\mathcal{B}_{new}$ and a set of read/write restrictions for all components in C_p.
    - *Input Assumptions:* The program p satisfies *spec* from $\mathcal{I}_p$, but p may not satisfy $\mathcal{B}_{new}$ from $\mathcal{I}_p$.
- **Output:** A *redesigned* program $p_r = \langle V_p^r, C_p^r, \mathcal{I}_p^r, \mathcal{F}_p^r \rangle$.
- **Constraints:**
    1. $V_p^r = V_p$ (i.e., $\mathcal{S}_p^r = \mathcal{S}_p$)
    2. $\mathcal{I}_p^r = \mathcal{I}_p$
    3. $\mathcal{F}_p^r \subseteq \mathcal{F}_p$ and $\mathcal{F}_p^r \neq \emptyset$
    4. The number of components and the read/write restrictions of each component in C_p remain the same in C_p^r, but δ_j of each component C_j may change in C_p^r
    5. $\delta_{p_r} \neq \emptyset$, and p_r satisfies $\mathcal{B} \wedge \mathcal{B}_{new}$ from $\mathcal{I}_p$
    6. Starting from any initial state $s_0 \in \mathcal{I}_p$, the revised program p_r satisfies its liveness specifications.

We now define the decision problem of incremental synthesis in the BT model.

Problem 2. **Decision Problem of Incremental Synthesis**

- **Instance:** A program $p = \langle V_p, C_p, \mathcal{I}_p, \mathcal{F}_p \rangle$ with its specification *spec*, its set of safety properties $\mathcal{B}$, a new safety property $\mathcal{B}_{new}$ and a set of read/write restrictions for all components in C_p, where $\mathcal{B}$ and $\mathcal{B}_{new}$ are specified in the BT model of safety.
- **Question:** Does there exist a program $p_r = \langle V_p^r, C_p^r, \mathcal{I}_p^r, \mathcal{F}_p^r \rangle$ that meets the constraints of Problem 1?

Significance of Problem 1. Several activities (e.g., debugging, porting, composition) during software development are instances of Problem 1. A few examples are as follows:

- **Debugging:** Consider the debugging of concurrent programs for data races between multiple threads. That is, multiple threads access shared data where at least one of them performs a write operation. Data race-freedom is a safety property whereas ensuring that each thread eventually gains access to the shared data (i.e., makes *progress*) is a liveness property. Eliminating data races while preserving the progress of each thread is a clear example of synthesizing safety [27].

- **Porting:** Consider a scenario in which a distributed application designed to be deployed on a traditional wireless network is considered for deployment on a wireless sensor network. The sensor nodes have a power-saving mode in which a node automatically turns off its radio (i.e., sleep mode) if no network activities are detected for a specific time interval. To port an existing wireless application to this new platform, one has to revise the application considering the sleep mode. That is, some of the activities would be forbidden in the sleep mode (e.g., sending messages). This is an additional safety constraint that should be met while preserving all other safety/liveness properties.
- **Composition and incremental development:** While in this paper we investigate Problem 1 in the same state space (i.e., no new variables are added while synthesizing safety), we will investigate the synthesis of safety under more relaxed conditions where the redesigned program may include new variables. Such a generalized formulation of Problem 1 captures software composition. Several approaches in software engineering (e.g. aspect-oriented programming [15]) rely on incremental design of software where modules/components that implement features/aspects are incrementally composed with an existing base system [15,14,26,16]. Moreover, there are numerous applications where software behaviors should evolve by composing plug-in components (e.g., Mozilla extensions) or by integrating mobile code (e.g., Java applets, composable proxy filters [21]). While some researchers have investigated type safety of compositions [26], dynamic safety properties of compositions are also of paramount importance.

4   Hardness of Incremental Synthesis

In this section, we illustrate that the general case complexity of synthesizing safety in deterministic programs increases significantly if program components have limited observability with respect to the state of other components. The intuition behind our complexity result lies in the difficulty of redesigning program computations towards capturing a new safety property while preserving liveness. Consider a computation $\sigma = \ll s_0, \cdots, s_{i-1}, s_i, \cdots \gg$, where $i > 0$, in a program p and a new safety property $\mathcal{B}_{new}$ that forbids the execution of the transition $t = (s_{i-1}, s_i)$; i.e., t must not be executed in the redesigned program. As such, we have to remove t. If $s_{i-1} \notin \mathcal{F}_p$, then σ becomes a deadlocked computation. To resolve the deadlock state s_{i-1}, we systematically synthesize a new sequence of states $\sigma_r = \ll s'_0, \cdots, s'_k \gg$, for $k \geq 0$, that is inserted between s_{i-1} and s_i to satisfy $\mathcal{B}_{new}$ (i.e., avoid executing t). Note that while a direct transition from s_{i-1} to s_i violates $\mathcal{B}_{new}$, there may be another sequence of states that can be traversed from s_{i-1} to s_i without violating $\mathcal{B}_{new}$. The same argument holds about building a computation prefix between any predecessor of s_{i-1} and any successor of s_i; there is nothing particular about s_{i-1} and s_i.

Additionally, the synthesized sequence σ_r must not preclude the reachability of the accepting states in σ. To meet this requirement, no transition (s, s') in σ_r should be grouped with a transition (s_g, s'_g) such that s_g is reachable in some computation of p_r and the execution of the transition (s_g, s'_g) causes one of the following problems: (1) s'_g is a deadlock state, (2) (s_g, s'_g) is a safety-violating transition that must not be executed, and (3) s'_g is a predecessor state of s_g in σ, thereby creating a non-progress cycle[2]. To ensure that the above cases do not occur, we should examine (i) all transitions selected to be in σ_r, (ii) all transitions used to connect σ_r to s_{i-1} and s_i along with their associated transition groups, and (iii) the transitions of other computations. Intuitively, this leads to exploring an exponential number of possible combinations of the safe transitions (and their transition groups) that can potentially be selected to be in σ_r. With this intuition, we prove that synthesizing safety in deterministic programs in the BT model of safety under limited observability is NP-complete (using a reduction from the 3-SAT problem [9]).

Problem 3. **The 3-SAT Decision Problem**
- **Instance:** A set of propositional variables, $x_1, x_2, ..., x_n$, and a Boolean formula $\Phi = C_1 \wedge C_2 \wedge ... \wedge C_m$, where $m, n > 1$ and each clause C_j $(1 \leq j \leq m)$ is a disjunction of exactly three literals. Wlog, we assume that the literals x_i and $\neg x_i$ do not simultaneously appear in the same clause $(1 \leq i \leq n)$.
- **Question:** Does there exist an assignment of truth values to $x_1, x_2, ..., x_n$ such that Φ is satisfiable?

In Subsection 4.1, we present a polynomial mapping from an arbitrary instance of 3-SAT to an instance of Problem 2. In Subsection 4.2, we illustrate that the instance of 3-SAT is satisfiable iff safety can be synthesized in the instance of Problem 2.

4.1   Polynomial Mapping from 3-SAT

In this section, we illustrate how for each instance of 3-SAT, we create an instance of Problem 2, which includes a program $p = \langle V_p, C_p, \mathcal{I}_p, \mathcal{F}_p \rangle$, and its safety specification $\mathcal{B}$ and the new safety property $\mathcal{B}_{new}$ that should be captured by the redesigned program. We build the instance of Problem 2 by considering states and transitions corresponding to each propositional variable and each clause in the instance of 3-SAT.

States and Transitions. Corresponding to each propositional variable x_i, where $1 \leq i \leq n$, we consider the states $a_i, a'_i, b_i, b'_i, c_i, c'_i$ and d_i (as illustrated in Figure 2). We also include an additional state a_{n+1}. For each variable x_i, the instance of Problem 2 includes the transitions $(a_i, d_i), (a_i, b_i), (b_i, a_i), (a_i, b'_i), (b_i, c_i), (b_i, c'_i), (b'_i, c'_i), (c'_i, b'_i), (c_i, a'_i), (c'_i, a'_i)$ and (d_i, a'_i).

Corresponding to each clause $C_r = x_i \vee \neg x_j \vee x_k$, where $1 \leq r \leq m$ and $1 \leq i, j, k \leq n$, program p includes 8 states $z_r, z_{ri}, z'_{ri}, z_{rj}, z'_{rj}, z_{rk}, z'_{rk}$ and z'_r, and 7 transitions $(z_r, z_{ri}), (z_{ri}, z'_{ri}), (z'_{ri}, z_{rj}), (z_{rj}, z'_{rj}), (z'_{rj}, z_{rk}), (z_{rk}, z'_{rk})$ and

---

[2] If s'_g is a successor of s_g in σ or is reachable in a different computation, then s_g should not have any other outgoing transition due to the determinism constraints.

(z'_{rk}, z'_r) depicted in Figure 3. Notice that the transitions in Figures 2 and 3 belong to different program components, which we shall explain later.

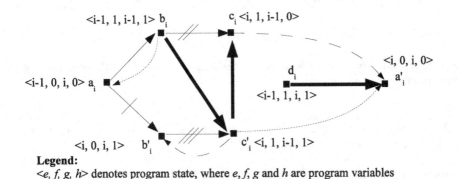

Legend:
$<e, f, g, h>$ denotes program state, where e, f, g and h are program variables

Fig. 2. The set of states and safe transitions corresponding to each propositional variable x_i in the instance of 3-SAT. Each state is annotated with the values assigned to program variables in that state.

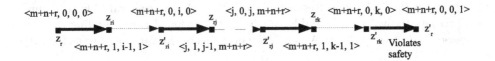

Fig. 3. States and transitions considered in the instance of Problem 2 corresponding to each clause $C_r = x_i \lor \neg x_j \lor x_k$ along with the values of variables.

Input program. The input program p includes the transitions (a_i, d_i) and (d_i, a'_i), for $1 \le i \le n$ and the transitions (a_n, a_{n+1}) and (a_{n+1}, a_1) (see Figure 4). Starting from a_1, the input program p executes transitions $(a_i, d_i), (d_i, a'_i)$ and (a'_i, a_{i+1}), where $1 \le i \le n$. From a_{n+1}, the program returns to a_1.

Initial and final states. The states a_1 and z_r $(1 \le r \le m)$ are initial states, and a_{n+1} is an accepting/final state. Moreover, the states z_{ri}, z_{rj}, z_{rk} and z'_r are accepting states, where $1 \le r \le m$ and $1 \le i, j, k \le n$. Starting from a_1, the final state a_{n+1} is infinitely often reached. Further, if the program starts at z_r then it will halt in the accepting state z'_r. Since all transitions $(a_i, d_i), (d_i, a'_i), (a'_i, a_{i+1})$ and (a_{n+1}, a_1) satisfy $\mathcal{B}$, the program p satisfies its safety and liveness specifications from a_1. In summary, we have

$$- \mathcal{I}_p = \{a_1\} \cup \{z_r | 1 \le r \le m\}$$

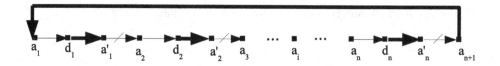

Fig. 4. States and transitions considered in the instance of Problem 2 corresponding to each propositional variable x_i.

- $\mathcal{F}_p = \{a_{n+1}\} \cup \{z_{ri}, z_{rj}, z_{rk}, z'_r |$ for each clause $C_r = x_i \vee \neg x_j \vee x_k$ in Φ, where $(1 \leq r \leq m) \wedge (1 \leq i, j, k \leq n)\}$

Safety Specifications. The safety specification $\mathcal{B}$ rules out any transition other than the transitions in Figures 2 and 3. Notice that while these transitions are permitted by the safety specification $\mathcal{B}$, the input program p does not necessarily include all of them. The new safety property $\mathcal{B}_{new}$ rules out the transitions (a_i, d_i) and (z'_{rk}, z'_r), where $1 \leq i, k \leq n$ and $1 \leq r \leq m$. Thus, in the revised version of the instance of Problem 2, denoted p_r, these transitions must not be executed.

Program variables. The instance of Problem 2, denoted p, has four variables e, f, g and h. We denote a program state by $\langle e, f, g, h \rangle$. Figure 2 illustrates the values of variables in the states included corresponding to each variable x_i. Figure 3 presents the values of variables in the states included corresponding to each clause $C_r = x_i \vee \neg x_j \vee x_k$. As such, the domains of the variables are as follows:

- The variable e has the domain $\{0, \cdots, n\} \cup \{m+n+1, \cdots, 2m+n\}$.
- The domain of variable f is equal to $\{0, 1\}$.
- The variable g has a domain of $\{0, \cdots, n+1\}$.
- The domain of the variable h is $\{0, 1\} \cup \{m+n+1, \cdots, 2m+n\}$.

Program components. The program p includes seven components C_1-C_7 whose transitions have been depicted in Figure 5. The read and write restrictions of each component are as follows:

- The first component C_1 includes the transitions (a_i, d_i) and (a_i, b_i), for all $1 \leq i \leq n$ (see Figures 2 and 5). The set of readable variables of C_1, denoted r_1, is equal to $\{e, f, g, h\}$ and its set of writable variables is $w_1 = \{f, g, h\}$.
- The set of transitions (a_i, b'_i) and (a'_i, a_{i+1}) comprises the component C_2 (see the arrow with a crossed line on it in Figures 2 and 5). We have $r_2 = \{e, f, g, h\}$ and $w_2 = \{e, g, h\}$.
- The component C_3 includes the transitions (b_i, c_i) for $1 \leq i \leq n$ (see the arrow with two parallel lines on it in Figures 2 and 5). We have $r_3 = \{e, f, g, h\}$ and $w_3 = \{e, h\}$.

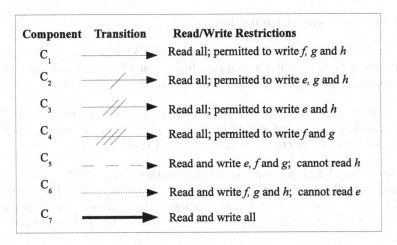

Component	Transition	Read/Write Restrictions
C_1		Read all; permitted to write f, g and h
C_2		Read all; permitted to write e, g and h
C_3		Read all; permitted to write e and h
C_4		Read all; permitted to write f and g
C_5		Read and write e, f and g; cannot read h
C_6		Read and write f, g and h; cannot read e
C_7		Read and write all

Fig. 5. Program components, their read/write restrictions and the annotation of their transitions.

- The fourth component, denoted C_4, includes transitions (b'_i, c'_i) for $1 \leq i \leq n$, $r_4 = \{e, f, g, h\}$ and $w_4 = \{f, g\}$ (see the arrow with three parallel lines on it in Figures 2 and 5).

- For component C_5, we have $r_5 = w_5 = \{e, f, g\}$; i.e., C_5 cannot read h. The component C_5 includes transition (c_i, a'_i), which is grouped with (c'_i, b'_i) and (z_{qi}, z'_{qi}), due to inability of reading h, where (z_{qi}, z'_{qi}) corresponds to a clause C_q in which the literal $\neg x_i$ appears (see the dashed arrow (z_{rj}, z'_{rj}) in Figure 3). Notice that in these three transitions, the values of the readable variables e, f and g are the same in the source states (and in the destination states) and the value of h does not change during these transitions because it is not readable for C_5.

- The sixth component C_6 can read/write $r_6 = w_6 = \{f, g, h\}$, but cannot read e. Its set of transitions includes $(c'_i, a'_i), (b_i, a_i)$ and (z_{ri}, z'_{ri}) (see Figures 2 and 3) that are grouped due to inability of reading e, where (z_{ri}, z'_{ri}) corresponds to a clause C_r in which the literal x_i appears.

- The component C_7 can read and write all variables and its set of transitions includes $(d_i, a'_i), (a_{n+1}, a_1), (b_i, c'_i)$ and (c'_i, c_i) for $1 \leq i \leq n$. Moreover, for each clause $C_r = x_i \lor \neg x_j \lor x_k$, where $1 \leq r \leq m$ and $1 \leq i, j, k \leq n$, component C_7 includes the following transitions: $(z_r, z_{ri}), (z'_{ri}, z_{rj}), (z'_{rj}, z_{rk})$ and (z'_{rk}, z'_r) (see Figure 3).

Theorem 1. *The complexity of the mapping is polynomial. (Proof is straightforward; hence omitted.)*

4.2   Correctness of Reduction

In this section, we show that the instance of 3-SAT is satisfiable iff the instance of Problem 2 (created by the mapping in Section 4.1) can be redesigned to meet the safety properties $\mathcal{B}$ and $\mathcal{B}_{new}$ while preserving its liveness.

Lemma 1. *If the instance of 3-SAT is satisfiable, then the instance of Problem 2, denoted p, can be redesigned to another program p_r for the safety property $\mathcal{B}_{new}$ such that p_r meets the requirements of Problem 1.*

Proof. If the 3-SAT instance is satisfiable, then there must exist a value assignment to the propositional variables $x_1, \cdots, x_n$ such that all clauses C_r, for $1 \le r \le m$, evaluate to true. Corresponding to the value assignment to a variable x_i, for $1 \le i \le n$, we include a set of transitions in the redesigned program as follows:

- If x_i is assigned *true*, then we include transitions $(a_i, b_i), (b_i, c_i), (c_i, a_i')$. Thus the computation prefix $\ll a_i, b_i, c_i, a_i', a_{i+1} \gg$ is synthesized between a_i and a_{i+1}. Since we have included the transition (c_i, a_i'), and transition (c_i, a_i') is grouped with (z_{qi}, z_{qi}'), where $1 \le q \le m$ for any clause C_q in which $\neg x_i$ appears, we must include (z_{qi}, z_{qi}') as well (see the dashed arrow (z_{rj}, z_{rj}') in Figure 3).
- If x_i is assigned *false*, then we include transitions $(a_i, b_i'), (b_i', c_i'), (c_i', a_i')$, thereby synthesizing the computation prefix $\ll a_i, b_i', c_i', a_i', a_{i+1} \gg$ between a_i and a_{i+1}. Due to the inability of reading e, including the transition (c_i', a_i') results in the inclusion of the transitions (z_{li}, z_{li}'), where $1 \le l \le m$, for any clause C_l in which x_i appears (see the dotted arrows (z_{ri}, z_{ri}') and (z_{rk}, z_{rk}') in Figure 3).
- For each clause $C_r = x_i \vee \neg x_j \vee x_k$, the transition (z_{ri}, z_{ri}') (respectively, (z_{rk}, z_{rk}')) is included iff x_i (respectively, x_k) is assigned *false*. The transition (z_{rj}, z_{rj}') is included iff x_j is assigned *true*.

Figure 6 depicts a partial structure of a redesigned program for the value assignment $x_1 = false$, $x_2 = true$ and $x_3 = true$ in an example clause $C_5 = x_1 \vee \neg x_2 \vee x_3$. Note that the bad transition (z_{53}', z_5') is not reached because $x_3 = true$ and the transition (z_{53}, z_{53}') is excluded.

Now, we illustrate that the redesigned program in fact meets the requirements of Problem 1. The state space remains obviously the same as no new variables have been introduced; i.e., $V_p = V_p^r$. During the selection of transitions based on value assignment to propositional variables, we do not remove any initial states. Thus, we have $\mathcal{I}_p = \mathcal{I}_p^r$.

Satisfying Safety Properties. Since the new safety property rules out transitions (a_i, d_i) and (z_{rk}', z_r'), we have to ensure that the redesigned program does not execute them. From a_i, the program either transitions to b_i or to b_i'. Thus, safety is not violated from a_i. Moreover, since all clauses are satisfied, at least one literal in each clause $C_r = x_i \vee \neg x_j \vee x_k$ must be true. Thus, at least one

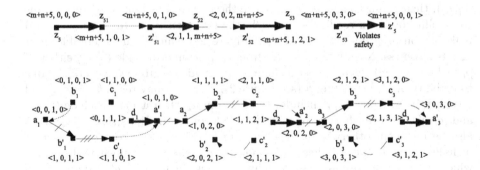

Fig. 6. A partial structure of the redesigned program corresponding to the value assignment $x_1 = false$, $x_2 = true$ and $x_3 = true$ for an example clause $C_5 = x_1 \vee \neg x_2 \vee x_3$.

of the three transitions $(z_{ri}, z'_{ri}), (z_{rj}, z'_{rj})$ or (z_{rk}, z'_{rk}) is excluded, thereby preventing the reachability of z'_{rk}; i.e., the safety-violating transition (z'_{rk}, z'_r) will not be executed.

Reachability of Accepting States (Satisfying Liveness Specifications).
While the accepting state z'_r is no longer reachable, the redesigned program halts in one of the accepting state z_{ri}, z_{rj} or z_{rk}. Moreover, the accepting state a_{n+1} is reached infinitely often due to the way we have synthesized the sequences of states $\ll a_i, b_i, c_i, a'_i, a_{i+1} \gg$ or $\ll a_i, b'_i, c'_i, a'_i, a_{i+1} \gg$ between a_i and a_{i+1}. That is, (non-)terminating computations remains (non-)terminating. Thus, starting from any initial state, some accepting states will be visited infinitely often; i.e., $\mathcal{F}^r_p \subseteq \mathcal{F}_p$. Therefore, if the instance of 3-SAT is satisfiable, then there exists a redesigned program for the instance of Problem 2 that satisfies the requirements of Problem 1.

Lemma 2. *If there exists a redesigned version of the instance of Problem 2 that meets the requirements of Problem 1, then the instance of 3-SAT is satisfiable.*

Proof. Let p_r be a redesigned version of the instance of Problem 2 that meets all the requirements of Problem 1. As such, the set of initial states $\mathcal{I}^r_p$ must be equal to the set $\{a_1\} \cup \{z_r | 1 \le r \le m\}$. Starting from a_1, p_r must execute a safe transition. Otherwise, we reach a contradiction; i.e., either a_1 is a deadlock state or the transition (a_1, d_1), which violates the new safety specification is executed. Thus, p_r either includes (a_1, b_1) or (a_1, b'_1), but not both (because p_r is a deterministic program). If p_r includes (a_1, b_1), then we set x_1 to *true* in the 3-SAT formula. If p_r includes (a_1, b'_1), then we set x_1 to *false*.

We assign truth values to each x_i, for $1 \le i \le n$, depending on the presence of (a_i, b_i) or (a_i, b'_i) at state a_i (similar to the way we assign a value to x_1). Such a value assignment strategy results in a unique truth-value assigned to each variable x_i. If p_r includes (a_i, b_i), then, from b_i, p_r includes either (b_i, c_i) or (b_i, c'_i) (see Figure 2), but not both (because of determinism). If p_r includes

(b_i, c_i'), then, from c_i', p_r must include either (c_i', c_i) or (c_i', a_i'). If p_r includes (c_i', a_i'), then it must include (b_i, a_i) since these two transitions are grouped due to inability of C_6 in reading e. As such, the two transitions (a_i, b_i) and (b_i, a_i) make a non-progress cycle in p_r (see Figure 2), which is unacceptable as it violates liveness. Now, we show that, from c_i', p_r cannot include (c_i', c_i) either. If p_r includes (c_i', c_i), then it must include (c_i, a_i'), which is grouped with (c_i', b_i') due to inability of C_5 in reading h (see Figure 2). Thus, p_r may reach b_i' from c_i' and deadlock in b_i'. Thus, if p_r includes (a_i, b_i) from a_i, then it must include (b_i, c_i) and (c_i, a_i'). In case where p_r includes (a_i, b_i') from a_i, the transition (b_i', c_i') must also be included; otherwise p_r deadlocks in b_i' (Figure 2). From c_i', p_r cannot include (c_i', c_i) because it has to include (c_i, a_i') that is grouped with (c_i', b_i'), which creates a non-progress cycle. Thus, p_r must include (c_i', a_i') from c_i'.

We also illustrate that each clause in the 3-SAT formula evaluates to *true*. Consider a clause $C_r = x_i \vee \neg x_j \vee x_k$. Starting from the initial state z_r, the transition (z_r, z_{ri}) must be present in p_r; otherwise z_r is a deadlock state. Moreover, from z_r, the safety-violating transition (z_{rk}', z_r') must not be executed. Thus, at least one of the transitions $(z_{ri}, z_{ri}'), (z_{ri}', z_{rj}), (z_{rj}, z_{rj}'), (z_{rj}', z_{rk})$ or (z_{rk}, z_{rk}') (see Figure 3) must be excluded in p_r. However, if one of the transitions (z_r, z_{ri}), $(z_{ri}', z_{rj}), (z_{rj}', z_{rk})$ or (z_{rk}', z_r') is excluded, then a reachable deadlock state could be created as their source states are not accepting states. Thus, if either z_{ri}' or z_{rj}' is reached from z_r, then the corresponding transition (z_{ri}', z_{rj}) or (z_{rj}', z_{rk}) must be present in p_r. Hence, at least one of the transitions (z_{ri}, z_{ri}'), (z_{rj}, z_{rj}') or (z_{rk}, z_{rk}') must be excluded in p_r; i.e., at least one literal in C_r must be *true*, thereby satisfying C_r.

Theorem 2. *Synthesizing safety (under limited observability) in deterministic programs in the BT model of safety specifications is NP-hard in $|\mathcal{S}_p|$. (Proof follows from Lemmas 1 and 2.)*

Theorem 3. *Synthesizing safety (under limited observability) in deterministic programs in the BT model of safety specifications is NP-complete (in $|\mathcal{S}_p|$).*

Proof. The proof of NP-hardness follows from Theorem 2. The proof of membership in NP is straightforward; given a revised program one can verify the constraints of Problem 1 (in the BT model) in polynomial time.

Theorem 4. *Synthesizing safety (under limited observability) in deterministic programs in the Bad State (BS) model of safety specifications is also NP-complete (in $|\mathcal{S}_p|$).*

Proof. The proof of NP-hardness works for the case where the safety specification rules out the reachability of states d_i and z_r' in the instance of Problem 2. The proof of NP membership is straightforward.

5   Conclusions and Future Work

This paper investigates the problem of capturing new safety requirements/properties while preserving existing safety and liveness properties, called *the problem of incremental synthesis.* Previous work [7,3] shows that incremental synthesis for non-deterministic programs can be done in polynomial time (in the size of program state space) under unlimited observability. Moreover, it is known [4] that the complexity of incremental synthesis of safety for non-deterministic programs would increase to NP-complete under limited observability. In this paper, we illustrated that even for deterministic programs the complexity of incremental synthesis of safety is NP-complete (in program state space). Our NP-hardness proof illustrates that the read inabilities of each component with respect to the local state of other components is a major cause of complexity. Such read inabilities are mainly created because of encapsulation/modularization of functionalities at early stages of design. On one hand, encapsulation/modularity enables designers to create good abstractions while capturing different functionalities. On the other hand, encapsulation exacerbates the complexity of behavioral changes [22] when new crosscutting requirements have to be realized across the components of an existing program. To facilitate change while reaping the benefits of modularization in design, we will extend the work presented in this paper in the following directions:

- *Sound polynomial-time heuristics.* We will concentrate on devising polynomial-time *heuristics* that reduce the complexity of synthesizing safety at the expense of completeness. That is, if heuristics succeed in generating a redesigned program, then the generated program will capture the new safety property while preserving liveness. However, such heuristics may fail to generate a redesigned program while one exists.
- *Sufficient conditions.* We will identify conditions under which safety can be synthesized in polynomial time. Specifically, we would like to address the following questions: (i) *What kinds of inter-component topologies (i.e., read/write restrictions) should a program have such that a new safety requirement can be captured in it efficiently?* (ii) *For which types of programs and safety specifications the complexity of synthesizing safety is polynomial?*
- *Backtracking.* We will implement a backtracking algorithm for synthesizing safety under limited observability. While we showed that it is unlikely that safety can efficiently be synthesized under limited observability, in many practical contexts the worst case exponential complexity may not be experienced. Thus, we expect that a backtracking algorithm can explore the entire state space in a reasonable amount of time. Moreover, we will implement a parallel version of the backtracking algorithm that will benefit from randomization for search diversification.
- *An extensible software framework.* We will develop a framework that provides automated assistance in synthesizing safety. Such a framework will include a repository of *reusable* heuristics that facilitate the synthesis of safety in an automated fashion. Two categories of users can benefit from our extensible framework, namely, (1) *developers of heuristics* who will focus on designing new heuristics and integrating them into our framework, and (2) *mainstream programmers* who will use the built-in heuristics to capture new safety properties in programs.

References

1. Alpern, B., Schneider, F.B.: Defining liveness. Information Processing Letters 21, 181–185 (1985)
2. Attie, P., Emerson, A.: Synthesis of concurrent programs for an atomic read/write model of computation. ACM Transactions on Programming Languages and Systems (TOPLAS) 23(2) (March 2001). An extended abstract appeared at the ACM Symposium on Principles of Distributed Computing (1996)
3. Bonakdarpour, B., Ebnenasir, A., Kulkarni, S.S.: Complexity results in revising UNITY programs. ACM Transactions on Autonomous and Adaptive Systems 4(1), 1–28 (2009)
4. Bonakdarpour, B., Kulkarni, S.S.: Revising distributed UNITY programs is NP-complete. In: Baker, T.P., Bui, A., Tixeuil, S. (eds.) OPODIS 2008. LNCS, vol. 5401, pp. 408–427. Springer, Heidelberg (2008)
5. Colcombet, T., Fradet, P.: Enforcing trace properties by program transformation. In: POPL 2000: Proceedings of the 27th ACM SIGPLAN-SIGACT Symposium on Principles of Programming Languages, pp. 54–66 (2000)
6. Djoko, S.D., Douence, R., Fradet, P.: Aspects preserving properties. In: ACM SIG-PLAN Symposium on Partial Evaluation and Semantics-based Program Manipulation (PEPM), pp. 135–145 (2008)
7. Ebnenasir, A., Kulkarni, S.S., Bonakdarpour, B.: Revising UNITY programs: Possibilities and limitations. In: Anderson, J.H., Prencipe, G., Wattenhofer, R. (eds.) OPODIS 2005. LNCS, vol. 3974, pp. 275–290. Springer, Heidelberg (2006)
8. Emerson, E.A.: chapter 16: Temporal and Modal Logics. In: Handbook of Theoretical Computer Science, vol. B, pp. 995–1067. Elsevier Science Publishers B.V (1990)
9. Garey, M., Johnson, D.: Computers and Interactability: A guide to the theory of NP-completeness. W.H. Freeman and Company (1979)
10. Goldman, M., Katz, S.: Maven: Modular aspect verification. In: Grumberg, O., Huth, M. (eds.) TACAS 2007. LNCS, vol. 4424, pp. 308–322. Springer, Heidelberg (2007)
11. Hansen, H., Penczek, W., Valmari, A.: Stuttering-insensitive automata for on-the-fly detection of livelock properties. Electronic Notes in Theoretical Computer Science 66(2), 178–193 (2002)
12. Iordache, M.V., Moody, J.O., Antsaklis, P.J.: Synthesis of deadlock prevention supervisors using Petri Nets. IEEE Transactions on Robotics and Automation 18(1), 59–68 (2002)
13. Khatchadourian, R., Dovland, J., Soundarajan, N.: Enforcing behavioral constraints in evolving aspect-oriented programs. In: Proceedings of the 7th Workshop on Foundations of Aspect-oriented Languages (FOAL), pp. 19–28 (2008)
14. Kiczales, G., Lamping, J., Mendhekar, A., Maeda, C., Lopes, C.V., Loingtier, J.-M., Irwin, J.: Aspect-oriented programming. In: Akşit, M., Matsuoka, S. (eds.) ECOOP 1997. LNCS, vol. 1241, pp. 220–242. Springer, Heidelberg (1997)
15. Kiczales, G., Rivieres, J.D.: The Art of the Metaobject Protocol. MIT Press, Cambridge (1991)
16. Krishnamurthi, S., Fisler, K.: Foundations of incremental aspect model-checking. ACM Transactions on Software Engineering and Methodology (TOSEM) 16(2), 7 (2007)
17. Krishnamurthi, S., Fisler, K., Greenberg, M.: Verifying aspect advice modularly. ACM SIGSOFT Software Engineering Notes 29(6), 137–146 (2004)

18. Kulkarni, S.S.: Component-based design of fault-tolerance. PhD thesis, Ohio State University, OH, USA (1999)

19. Kulkarni, S.S., Arora, A.: Automating the addition of fault-tolerance. In: Joseph, M. (ed.) FTRTFT 2000. LNCS, vol. 1926, pp. 82–93. Springer, Heidelberg (2000)

20. Kulkarni, S.S., Ebnenasir, A.: The effect of the safety specification model on the complexity of adding masking fault-tolerance. IEEE Transaction on Dependable and Secure Computing 2(4), 348–355 (2005)

21. McKinley, P.K., Padmanabhan, U.I., Ancha, N., Sadjadi, S.M.: Composable proxy services to support collaboration on the mobile internet. IEEE Transactions on Computers 52(6), 713–726 (2003)

22. Parnas, D.L.: Designing software for ease of extension and contraction. IEEE Transactions on Software Engineering 5(2), 128–138 (1979)

23. Salem, A.-E.B., Duret-Lutz, A., Kordon, F.: Model checking using generalized testing automata. Transactions on Petri Nets and Other Models of Concurrency 6, 94–122 (2012)

24. Smith, D.: Requirement enforcement by transformation automata. In: Sixth Workshop on Foundations of Aspect-Oriented Languages (FOAL), pp. 5–15 (2007)

25. Sreenivas, R.S.: On the existence of supervisory policies that enforce liveness in discrete-event dynamic systems modeled by controlled Petri Nets. IEEE Transactions on Automatic Control 42(7), 928–945 (1997)

26. Thaker, S., Batory, D.S., Kitchin, D., Cook, W.R.: Safe composition of product lines. In: 6th International Conference on Generative Programming and Component Engineering (GPCE), pp. 95–104 (2007)

27. Vechev, M., Yahav, E., Yorsh, G.: Inferring synchronization under limited observability. In: Kowalewski, S., Philippou, A. (eds.) TACAS 2009. LNCS, vol. 5505, pp. 139–154. Springer, Heidelberg (2009)

Analyzing Mutable Checkpointing via Invariants

Deepanker Aggarwal and Astrid Kiehn

Indraprastha Institute of Information Technology,
New Delhi, India
{deepanker10027,astrid}@iiitd.ac.in
http://www.iiitd.ac.in

Abstract. The well-known coordinated snapshot algorithm of mutable checkpointing [7,8,9] is studied. We equip it with a concise formal model and analyze its operational behavior via an invariant characterizing the snapshot computation. By this we obtain a clear understanding of the intermediate behavior and a correctness proof of the final snapshot based on a strong notion of consistency (reachability within the partial order representing the underlying computation). The formal model further enables a comparison with the blocking queue algorithm [13] introduced for the same scenario and with the same objective.
From a broader perspective, we advocate the use of formal semantics to formulate and prove correctness of distributed algorithms.

Keywords: snapshot, checkpointing, consistency, distributed computing.

1 Introduction

The on-the-fly calculation of a snapshot, a consistent global state, is a known means to enhance fault tolerance and system diagnosis of distributed systems. Coordinated snapshot algorithms exchange coordination messages to orchestrate the checkpointing. One of these is mutable checkpointing ([7,8,9]) which aims at a reduced coordination overhead - both in number of checkpoints to be taken and coordination messages to be sent. It is known from [7] that there is no algorithm which minimizes the number of checkpoints without blocking processes. To avoid the blocking, in mutable checkpointing, local checkpoints may be taken which may be discarded later. The presence of such checkpoints and an additional feature to further reduce the number of coordination messages hinder an easy analysis of the algorithm. With this paper we equip mutable checkpointing with a precise formal model and make it amenable to a formal analysis. We establish an invariant to obtain deeper insight into the intermediate behavior of the algorithm and prove consistency of the final snapshot. The model can further be used as a common ground for qualitative comparisons of snapshot algorithms. We give such a comparison with the conceptually different blocking queue algorithm [13] which, as mutable checkpointing, had been set up to reduce the coordination overhead.

© IFIP International Federation for Information Processing 2015
M. Dastani and M.Sirjani (Eds.): FSEN 2015, LNCS 9392, pp. 176–190, 2015.
DOI: 10.1007/978-3-319-24644-4_12

Unlike other coordinated snapshot algorithms (eg. Chandy/ Lamport's seminal algorithm [10]), mutable checkpointing algorithms do not monotonously build up the snapshot with the underlying computation. In mutable checkpointing, checkpoints of local states may be taken from which the underlying computation had already progressed. The computation of the snapshot, thus, involves forward and backward reasoning and the correctness of the algorithm, the consistency of the final snapshot, is not obvious. The proofs provided in the literature [7,8,9] are based on contradiction, use absence of orphans (messages recorded as received but not as being sent) as consistency notion, and lack a formal model. The formal proof provided in this paper is based on an invariant which characterizes the snapshot partially computed. We use a stronger but well-accepted notion of consistency [17]: reachability within the partial order representing the underlying distributed computation. It implies the absence of orphans.

In case of a snapshot algorithm the invariant should explain how the snapshot gradually builds up on course of the underlying computation. For a global state S of the underlying computation, the invariant should provide the snapshot calculated so far. We call the latter the *potential snapshot psn(S)* of S. For a snapshot algorithm which simply freezes local processes at certain points of their computation, the potential snapshot consists of these checkpoints and the current states of the none-frozen processes. In mutable checkpointing, local processes may be frozen to states – the so-called mutable checkpoints - from which they had already progressed. Reachability of $psn(S)$ can therefore not simply be obtained from a simultaneous progression of $psn(S)$ and S. We solve this problem by extracting a set of global states from S of which each corresponds to a different prediction of which of the mutable checkpoints will be frozen. These states collectively define the $psn(S)$. We then show how each of the states in $psn(S)$ progresses together with S, where the progress may be partial, only, due to the frozen processes. Using this result we provide a direct proof for the consistency of the final snapshot. The potential snapshot, however, – or more precisely the predicted states of it -, in general, are shown not to be consistent. This implies that if the run of a mutable checkpointing algorithm needs to be interrupted then the entire checkpointing needs to be started afresh.

The proof is based on the specification of the operational behavior of what we consider the essence of mutable checkpointing. We extracted it from the pseudocode given in [9] by removing all details not related to the basic concept of taking a mutable checkpoint upon receiving a flagged message for the first time (and before a checkpoint) – where the flag indicates that the sender had taken a checkpoint or a mutable checkpoint. In this way we obtained a concise description of the core of mutable checkpointing which we see as another contribution of this paper.

With this formal model and analysis we relate mutable checkpointing to the blocking queue algorithm introduced in [13]. In fact, this paper can be seen as a companion paper as it deploys the proof technique developed there (however, setting up the invariant for mutual checkpointing was a much more demanding task). Having fixed the underlying computation, the two snapshot algorithms can directly be compared due to the same underlying formal model. We show that the respective final snapshots, in general, are incomparable and discuss the differences between the algorithms.

The paper is structured as follows. Basic terminology is introduced in Section 2, followed by a short description of mutable checkpointing in Section 3. Section 4 specifies the operational behavior of the algorithm defined in terms of predicates and rules. The rules we deduced from the pseudocode of [9] where we abstracted away as many details as possible to get the essence of mutable checkpointing. In Section 5 we introduce the potential snapshot, show its progression with the underlying computation and prove the consistency of the final snapshot. Section 6 gives the comparison with the blocking queue algorithm of [13]. The conclusion is given in Section 7.

2   Preliminaries

We assume a finite number of processes P_1, ..., P_n which communicate solely by message passing via FIFO channels C_{ij}. Channel C_{ij} leads from P_i to P_j and for each pair of processes there is such a unidirectional channel. Channels are assumed not to lose or reorder messages. There is no assumption on the state space of processes.

A state $S = (p_1, \ldots, p_n, Chan)$ of a distributed computation is given by the histories (events performed so far) of the local processes and the current contents of the channels where $Chan : \{C_{ij} \mid i, j \leq n, i \neq j\} \to MSG^*$ and $p_i \in Events^*$. To ease readability, for a global state S we attach S as a superscript to the histories and channels and abbreviate $Chan(C_{ij})^S$ by C_{ij}^S. In the initial state S_0, $p_i^{S_0} = \varepsilon$, and $C_{ij}^{S_0} = \varepsilon$ for all i, j. A distributed computation is a sequence $\pi = S_0 \xrightarrow{e_1} S_1 \xrightarrow{e_2} S_2 \cdots \xrightarrow{e_k} S_k$ where each S_i is obtained from updating S_{i-1} according to the semantics of event e_i. We also write $\pi = S_0 \to^* S_k$ to mention the initial and final states of π, explicitly.

The notion of consistency of a state with a computation π is best understood in terms of π's space-time diagram (its partial order representation, see [14], [17] or [4]). A state is consistent with π if it is a cut of π closed under the *happens-before* ordering in the space-time diagram. Equivalently, a consistent state S of π can be characterized by that all local histories of S are prefixes of the corresponding histories of π's final state S_k, and if a message occurs as received in a history of S then it also needs to occur as having been sent in a history (that is there are no orphans).

Snapshot algorithms are superimposed on a distributed computation π on course of which a state consistent with π is to be calculated. We will only describe the behavior of the snapshot algorithm which, if it is non blocking, should allow for send and receive events induced by the underlying computation at any point of time. All other events of the snapshot algorithm are coordination events.

3   Mutable Checkpoint Algorithms

Mutable checkpoint algorithms are coordinated snapshot algorithms which reduce the coordination overhead (compared to [10]) by combining message flags (indicating whether messages have been sent before of after a checkpoint, cf. [15]) with the new concept of mutable checkpoints. Mutable checkpoints are taken on a tentative basis (on volatile storage) and are only finalized (on non-volatile storage) when the need for a local checkpoint has been confirmed.

The Algorithm in Short

The initiating process requests the processes it depends on (from which it had received a message) to take a checkpoint. Any process receiving such a request takes a checkpoint and propagates the request further to the – up to its knowledge – so far uninformed processes it itself depends on. After a process has taken a checkpoint all the messages sent out by this process carry a flag (bb=1). A process which hasn't received a checkpoint request but a message with flag (bb=1), takes a mutable checkpoint indicating that it must convert the current local state to a checkpoint, if in future it receives a checkpoint request. This is done before the received message is processed and only if it hadn't taken a mutable checkpoint earlier. Under certain progress assumptions, all processes which, in principle, need to take a checkpoint will finally have done so and this completes phase I of the algorithm. Phase II would deal with the confirmation that the checkpointing is complete and the dissemination of this information to the local processes. However, in this paper we only investigate phase I.

With minor modifications the algorithm has widely been published see [7,8,9], our reference algorithm is [9]. We specify the operational behavior of the algorithm in terms of predicates and transition rules which an implementation would need to satisfy. To be able to focus on the essence of mutable checkpointing, in the translation we omitted everything related to earlier checkpointing and a feature to reduce the number of coordination messages further (the $sent_i$ condition). We also assume that the initiating process is always P_1 and as in [9] do not consider concurrent checkpointing. Finally, all details relating to termination (the completion of taking checkpoints) of phase I are omitted.

The Algorithm in Detail

Rule numbers in brackets refer to corresponding rules given in the next section.

1. As part of their computations, processes send messages to each other which come attached with a flag (Rules 1.1 and 1.2). If the flag is set, this indicates that the sending process has already taken its checkpoint (instantly or belated via a mutable checkpoint).
2. Every process maintains a dependency vector which provides all the processes it depends on. A process P_i depends on process P_j if P_i has received a message from P_j. This is a dynamic notion of dependency as at the time

of initiation of the checkpointing all dependencies may not be known. The checkpointing will involve all processes which are dependent in a transitive way. Say at the time of initiation, the checkpointing process P_1 depends on P_2 and P_3, and P_3 depends on P_4. Then, P_4 needs to be included in the checkpointing.

3. The initiator takes its checkpoint and sends the checkpoint request to the processes it depends on using its dependency vector. It attaches the dependency vector to its request (Rule 3).

4. If a process P_j receives a checkpoint request from a process P_i then either of the following will happen:
   - If it has already taken a checkpoint (cp_taken_j is true), then the request is ignored (Rule 4.1).
   - If it has not taken a checkpoint but has taken a mutable checkpoint (mcp_taken_j is true), then by receiving the request it converts the mutable checkpoint into a checkpoint. This conversion is not explicitly modeled but from now on cp_taken_j will be true. Further, P_j propagates the checkpoint request to processes as follows. For each process P_k on which P_i does not depend on, but on which P_j depended when it took the mutable checkpoint, P_j sends a request to P_k (P_i has already sent a request to the processes on which it depends, Rule 4.2).
   - If it has neither taken a checkpoint or a mutable checkpoint, then it takes a checkpoint and propagates the request as in the previous case (Rule 4.3).

5. If a process P_j removes a message (with attached flag) from a channel then either of the following will happen:
   - If the received message has flag 0, then P_j processes the message (Rule 2.1, Rule 2.2). If this happens before a mutable checkpoint or checkpoint is taken, then P_j depends on P_i and the dependency vector might need to be updated (Rule 2.1).
   - If the flag is 1 and P_j has already taken a checkpoint, then P_j processes the message (Rule 2.3).
   - If the flag is 1 and P_j has neither taken a checkpoint nor mutable checkpoint, then it takes a mutable checkpoint and immediately after that processes the message (Rule 2.4). Taking the mutable checkpoint and processing the message is one atomic action.
   - If the flag is 1 and P_j has taken a mutable checkpoint but not a checkpoint, then P_j processes the message (Rule 2.5).

4   The Operational Behavior of Mutable Checkpointing

We specify the algorithm's behavior by a set of predicates and rules describing how the global state of the system changes with a transition. The rules of the following format:

Rule No.	Preconditions	Event	Postconditions

If a global state S satisfies the precondition of a rule, then the event may occur and S is updated to T as specified in the field of postconditions. The occurrence of event e is written as $S \xrightarrow{e} T$. So a distributed computation $\pi = S_0 \xrightarrow{e_1} S_1 \xrightarrow{e_2} S_2 \cdots \xrightarrow{e_k} S_k$ is a sequence of such events where each of the transitions is justified by one of the rules. In some of the rules (Rules 1.2 and 2.2) the preconditions are split into two rows. These should be read as a disjunction, that is, each of these rules presents two rules with the same event name and postconditions. The possible events and messages of the mutable checkpointing algorithm are given by the following table.

mcp_taken_i	process P_i takes a mutable checkpoint
cp_taken_i	P_i takes the checkpoint
$send_{ij}(.)$	P_i adds a message to channel C_{ij}
$rec_{ij}(.)$	P_j receives a message or
	checkpoint request from channel C_{ij}
$\langle cpr_i, dep \rangle$	the message that P_i has taken a checkpoint
	with attached dependency vector
$\langle msg, bb \rangle$	a message and attached flag

In the algorithm every local process maintains a dependency vector dep in which it keeps the dependencies to other processes: $dep_j(i) = 1$ if P_j has received a message from P_i before a mutable checkpoint has been taken. This dependency vector can be retrieved from the history of a process at any state. However, for clarity we explicitly mention it in the semantics.

The first element of a channel is at the rightmost position and provided by *first* and the remainder by *rem*. We use the simple dot to separate letters in a word. For the concatenation of words we use $\circ$. If an event occurs in the history of a process at state S then we state this as a predicate $event_i^S$. For example, $\neg mcp\_taken_i^S$ stands for that mcp_taken_i does not occur in the history p_i^S. It represents that P_i has not taken a mutable checkpoint so far. The $cp\_taken_i^S$ predicate, however, is more general as it also needs to cover the conversion of a mutable checkpoint to a (proper) checkpoint. Hence, $cp\_taken_i^S$ if and only if either cp_taken_i occurs in the history of P_i or $mcp\_taken_i^S$ and $rec_{ji}(\langle cpr_j, dep \rangle)^S$ for some j.

Rules are grouped according to their functionality.

5   Main Results

We here define the potential snapshot and show how it progresses with the underlying computation. With this invariant result we will show the reachability of the snapshot finally calculated.

As already discussed, in mutable checkpointing the potential snapshot $psn(S)$ extracted from an intermediate state S of the underlying computation cannot simply be a global state containing the current local checkpoints. At S there is no clarity whether a mutable checkpoint should be considered as a checkpoint or simply be discarded since the future computation steps cannot be foreseen.

Table 1. Rules 1.1, 1.2: A message can be sent at any time and the attached flag shows whether this happened before (bb=0) or after (bb=1) a checkpoint or mutable checkpoint was taken. Rules 2.1–2.5: A mutable checkpoint is taken if the flag of the received message is 1 and the receiving process has neither taken a checkpoint nor a mutable checkpoint so far. Rule 3: We assume that the checkpointing will always be initiated by P_1. It sends the checkpoint request to all the processes it depends on and takes the checkpoint as part of one atomic action. Rules 4.1–4.3: Receiving, setting and propagating a checkpoint request is modeled as one atomic event. This event comprises of removing the request from the channel, taking the checkpoint and propagating the request and causal dependencies to the concerned processes. These are the processes on which the receiving process depends but which are not listed in the dependency array received with the incoming request. In case a mutable checkpoint had been taken, it is converted to a permanent one (this, however, is not explicitly modeled).

No	Preconditions	Event	Postconditions
1.1	$\neg cp\_taken_i^S$ $\neg mcp\_taken_i^S$	$S \xrightarrow{send_{ij}(\langle msg,0 \rangle)} T$	$p_i^T = p_i^S.send_{ij}(\langle msg,0 \rangle)$ $C_{ij}^T = \langle msg,0 \rangle.C_{ij}^S$
1.2	$cp\_taken_i^S$ $mcp\_taken_i^S$	$S \xrightarrow{send_{ij}(\langle msg,1 \rangle)} T$	$p_i^T = p_i^S.send_{ij}(\langle msg,1 \rangle)$ $C_{ij}^T = \langle msg,1 \rangle.C_{ij}^S$
2.1	$first(C_{ij}^S) = \langle msg,0 \rangle$ $\neg mcp\_taken_j^S$ $\neg cp\_taken_j^S$	$S \xrightarrow{rec_{ij}(\langle msg,0 \rangle)} T$	$p_j^T = p_j^S.rec_{ij}(\langle msg,0 \rangle)$ $C_{ij}^T = rem(C_{ij}^S)$ $dep_j^T(i) = 1$
2.2	$first(C_{ij}^S) = \langle msg,0 \rangle$ $mcp\_taken_j^S$ $first(C_{ij}^S) = \langle msg,0 \rangle$ $cp\_taken_j^S$	$S \xrightarrow{rec_{ij}(\langle msg,0 \rangle)} T$	$p_j^T = p_j^S.rec_{ij}(\langle msg,0 \rangle)$ $C_{ij}^T = rem(C_{ij}^S)$
2.3	$first(C_{ij}^S) = \langle msg,1 \rangle$ $cp\_taken_j^S$	$S \xrightarrow{rec_{ij}(\langle msg,1 \rangle)} T$	$p_j^T = p_j^S.rec_{ij}(\langle msg,1 \rangle)$ $C_{ij}^T = rem(C_{ij}^S)$
2.4	$first(C_{ij}^S) = \langle msg,1 \rangle$ $\neg cp\_taken_j^S$ $\neg mcp\_taken_j^S$	$S \xrightarrow{rec_{ij}(\langle msg,1 \rangle)} T$	$p_j^T = p_j^S.mcp\_taken_j.rec_{ij}(\langle msg,1 \rangle)$ $C_{ij}^T = rem(C_{ij}^S)$
2.5	$first(C_{ij}^S) = \langle msg,1 \rangle$ $\neg cp\_taken_j^S$ $mcp\_taken_j^S$	$S \xrightarrow{rec_{ij}(\langle msg,1 \rangle)} T$	$p_j^T = p_j^S.rec_{ij}(\langle msg,1 \rangle)$ $C_{ij}^T = rem(C_{ij}^S)$
3	$\neg cp\_taken_1^S$	$S \xrightarrow{cp\_taken_1} T$	$p_1^T = p_1^S.cp\_taken_1$ $C_{1k}^T = \langle cpr_1, dep_1^S \rangle.C_{1k}^S$ for all $k > 1$ with $dep_1^S(k) = 1$
4.1	$first(C_{ij}^S) = \langle cpr_i, dep \rangle$ $cp\_taken_j^S$	$S \xrightarrow{rec_{ij}(\langle cpr_i, dep \rangle)} T$	$p_j^T = p_j^S.rec_{ij}(\langle cpr_i, dep \rangle)$ $C_{ij}^T = rem(C_{ij}^S)$
4.2	$first(C_{ij}^S) = \langle cpr_i, dep \rangle$ $\neg cp\_taken_j^S$ $\neg mcp\_taken_j^S$	$S \xrightarrow{cp\_taken_j} T$	$p_j^T = p_j^S.rec_{ij}(\langle cpr_i, dep \rangle).cp\_taken_j$ $C_{ij}^T = rem(C_{ij}^S)$ $C_{jk}^T = \langle cpr_j, dep \vee dep_j^S \rangle.C_{jk}^S$ for all k with $dep(k) = 0$, $dep_j^S(k) = 1$
4.3	$first(C_{ij}^S) = \langle cpr_i, dep \rangle$ $\neg cp\_taken_j^S$ $mcp\_taken_j^S$	$S \xrightarrow{rec_{ij}(\langle cpr_i, dep \rangle)} T$	$p_j^T = p_j^S.rec_{ij}(\langle cpr_i, dep \rangle)$ $C_{ij}^T = rem(C_{ij}^S)$ $C_{jk}^T = \langle cpr_j, dep \vee dep_j^S \rangle.C_{jk}^S$ for all k with $dep(k) = 0$, $dep_j^S(k) = 1$

In $psn(S)$ all options have to be simultaneously considered. Accordingly, $psn(S)$ is a set of global states of which each corresponds to a different prediction with respect to the final conversion of mutable checkpoints to (proper) checkpoints.

The formal definitions are given next. Note that all projection functions used in this paper are summarized in Figure 1. The freeze function allows one to cut down the history of individual processes to the point where they have taken a mutable checkpoint or a checkpoint. These points we call freeze points. In order to freeze a process P_i all events after the freeze point need to be deleted from the history. In general, the freezing of P_i may effect process P_j as the latter may have received a message from P_i sent after its freeze point. Processes that may be frozen are those in $MCP(S)$ while those in $CP(S)$ must be frozen if a freezing is to be conducted.

$$MCP(S) = \{P_i \mid mcp\_taken_i^S \text{ and } \neg cp\_taken_i^S\}$$
$$CP(S) = \{P_i \mid cp\_taken_i^S\}$$

Due to the various freezing options we obtain the set of potential snapshots:

$$PSN(S) = \{f(A,S) \mid CP(S) \subseteq A \subseteq MCP(S) \cup CP(S)\}$$

Each $f(A,S)$ provides a potential snapshot at state S of which the processes in A are frozen.

$$f(A,S) = < p_1^{f(A,S)}, p_2^{f(A,S)}, \ldots, p_n^{f(A,S)}, Chan^{f(A,S)} >$$

$$p_i^{f(A,S)} = \begin{cases} p_i^S \downarrow_{mcp,cp} & P_i \in A \\ p_i^S \mid_{rem\ bb=1}^A & P_i \notin A \end{cases}$$

$$Chan^{f(A,S)} = \{C_{ij}^{f(A,S)} \mid 1 \le i,j \le n \text{ and } i \ne j\}$$

$$C_{ij}^{f(A,S)} = \begin{cases} \widehat{C_{ij}^S}|_{bb=0} \text{ o } rev(p_j \uparrow_{mcp,cp,bb=0}^i) & P_i, P_j \in A \\ \widehat{C_{ij}^S}|_{bb=0} & P_i \in A, P_j \notin A \\ \widehat{C_{ij}^S} \text{ o } rev(p_j \uparrow_{mcp,cp}^i) & P_i \notin A, P_j \in A \\ \widehat{C_{ij}^S} & P_i \notin A, P_j \notin A \end{cases}$$

where $\widehat{C_{ij}}$ removes all the coordination messages from the channel and rev reverses the string. Note that we do not explicitly remove the flag (which are used for coordination reasons only) from a message, but this is implied whenever coordination messages are removed.

To show the simultaneous progression of $psn(S)$ with $S \xrightarrow{e} S'$ each of the states in $psn(S)$ needs to be considered with respect to its corresponding move. If a mutable checkpoint has to be frozen then those states in $psn(S)$ which had not predicted this are discarded. This means that the size of $psn(S)$ can shrink. It will, however, grow with every new mutable checkpoint taken as the concerned process will now have to be considered as progressing and as frozen, simultaneously. The next lemma describes this progression in detail.

$\downarrow_{mcp,cp}$ It is applied to the local history of a process and yields the string of send and receive events before mcp_taken or cp_taken in their respective order. Only one of the latter events can occur in a history.

$|_{rem\,bb=1}^{A}$ It is applied to the local history of a process not in A and removes all coordination messages and all messages with flag 1 received from a process in A.

$\uparrow_{mcp,cp}^{i}$ It is applied to the local history of a process P_j and yields the string of messages in $rec_{ij}(\langle msg, bb \rangle)$ events after mcp_taken or cp_taken in their respective order. Only one of the latter events can occur in a history.

$\uparrow_{mcp,cp,bb=0}^{i}$ It is applied to the local history of a process P_j and yields the string of messages in $rec_{ij}(\langle msg, 0 \rangle)$ events after mcp_taken or cp_taken in their respective order. Only one of the latter events can occur in a history.

$|_{sent}^{j}$ It is applied to the local history of a process P_i and yields the string of messages occurring in $send_{ij}(\langle msg, bb \rangle)$ events in their respective order.

$|_{bb=0}$ This projection is applied to strings of messages, only. It removes from the string all coordination messages and messages with attached flag 1.

Fig. 1. Projection functions used in this paper.

Lemma 1. *Let $S_0 \longrightarrow^* S$ and $S \xrightarrow{e} S'$ where e is an event of P_i, $i \in \{1, \ldots, n\}$. Then for all freeze sets A of S the following holds:*

1. $P_i \in A$ implies $f(A, S) = f(A, S')$
2. $P_i \notin A$ implies one of the following:
   (a) $e \notin \{cp\_taken_i, rec_{ji}(\langle cpr_j, dep \rangle), rec_{ji}(\langle msg, 1 \rangle) \mid j \in \{1, \ldots, n\}\}$, and $f(A, S) \xrightarrow{e} f(A, S')$
   (b) $e = rec_{ji}(\langle cpr_j, dep \rangle)$, $mcp\_taken_i^S$, and $f(A \cup \{P_i\}, S) = f(A \cup \{P_i\}, S')$
   (c) $e = cp\_taken_i$, $\neg mcp\_taken_i^S$, and $f(A, S) = f(A \cup \{P_i\}, S')$
   (d) $e = rec_{ji}(\langle msg, 1 \rangle)$, $P_j \notin A$, and
       i. $f(A, S) \xrightarrow{e} f(A, S')$
       ii. $f(A, S) = f(A \cup \{P_i\}, S')$ *if* $\neg mcp\_taken_i^S$
   (e) $e_i = rec_{ji}(\langle msg, 1 \rangle)$, $P_j \in A$, and
       i. $f(A, S) = f(A, S')$
       ii. $f(A, S) = f(A \cup \{P_i\}, S')$ *if* $\neg mcp\_taken_i^S$
3. $p_k^{f(A',S')} = p_k^{S'}$ if $P_k \notin A'$, $\neg mcp\_taken_k^{S'}$, $\neg cp\_taken_k^{S'}$ and A' is a freeze set of S'

where $A \cup \{P_i\}$ is a freeze set of the respective state whenever given as an argument to the freeze function.

Proof. By induction on the number of transitions leading from S_0 to S.

If there is no transition then $S_0 = S$ and $A = \emptyset$. Of item 2. only 2.(a) and 2.(c) apply which can be easily verified, and item 3. is trivial.

Now suppose the induction hypothesis applies to $S_0 \rightarrow^* S$ and there is one more transition $S \xrightarrow{e} S'$. We have to explore all freeze sets of the relevant state and all the possible transitions.

We sketch two cases, for all others we refer to [2].

Proof of item 2.(c) for Rule 4.2.

Rule 4.2 deals with the case $e = cp\_taken_i$, $first(C_{ji}^S) = \langle cpr_j, dep \rangle$, $\neg cp\_taken_i^S$ and $\neg mcp\_taken_i^S$. Let A be a freeze set of S.

$$
\begin{aligned}
p_i^{f(A \cup \{P_i\}, S')} &= p_i^{S'} \downarrow_{mcp,cp} \\
&= p_i^S.rec_{ji}(\langle cpr_j, dep \rangle.cp\_taken_i) \downarrow_{mcp,cp} \\
&= p_i^S && \text{def. } \downarrow_{mcp,cp} \\
&= p_i^{f(A,S)} && \text{ind. hyp. 3.}
\end{aligned}
$$

The proofs for the other p_k, $k \neq i$, and the channels are similar.

Proof of item 3. for Rule 4.2.

Let A' be a freeze set of S'. Then $A' \setminus \{P_i\}$ is a freeze set of S, and by induction hypthesis 2.(c), $f(A' \setminus \{P_i\}, S) = f(A', S')$. Let $P_k \notin A'$, $\neg mcp\_taken_k^S$ and $\neg cp\_taken_k^S$.

$$
\begin{aligned}
p_k^{f(A',S')} &= p_k^{f(A' \setminus \{P_i\}, S)} && \text{ind. hyp. 2.(c), already established} \\
&= p_k^S && \text{ind. hyp. 3.} \\
&= p_k^{S'}
\end{aligned}
$$

Note again, that in the lemma notationally we did not distinguish between a message with or without flag. However, in all events performed by a frozen process the flags have been removed. Similarly, in the next lemma $\sqsubseteq$ denotes the prefix relation up to messages with or without flags. We further do not distinguish between S_0 and $f(\emptyset, S)$. Lemma 2 summarizes the invariant property of reachable states relevant for the consistency proof of the final snapshot. It is an immediate corrollary of Lemma 1 and the basic definitions.

Lemma 2. *Let* $\pi : S_0 \to^* S$.

If A *is a freeze set of* S *then* $S_0 \to^* f(A,S)$ *and*

(1) $p_k^{f(A,S)} \sqsubseteq p_k^S$ *for* $P_k \in A$,

(2) $p_k^{f(A,S)} = p_k^S$ *for* $P_k \notin A$, $\neg mcp\_taken_k^S$ *and* $\neg cp\_taken_k^S$,

(3) $p_k^{f(A,S)} = p_k^S|_{rem\ bb=1}^A$ *for* $P_k \notin A$, $mcp\_taken_k^S$ *or* $cp\_taken_k^S$.

Lemma 2 shows that each $f(A, S)$ is reachable. This, however, does not mean that $f(A, S)$ is consistent with π since events of frozen processes are removed from the history and may create "holes". One may argue that the states to be considered here should be those with all none-frozen processes reset to their initial states. This would avoid the "hole" problem. For an arbitrary set of processes I, $I \subseteq \{P_1, \ldots, P_n\}$, the reset of I at S is defined by

$$
p_i^{r(I,S)} = \begin{cases} p_i^S & \text{if } P_i \notin I, \\ \varepsilon & \text{otherwise} \end{cases} \quad \text{and}
$$

$$
C_{ij}^{r(I,S)} = \begin{cases} C_{ij}^S & P_i, P_j \notin I, \\ p_i^S|_{sent}^j & P_j \in I, \\ \varepsilon & P_i \in I. \end{cases}
$$

In general, $r(I, S)$ is not a consistent state. This is always the case if a process in I had sent a message to a process not in I and this message had been received before the resetting. It would become an orphan.

This problem does not occur if S is the final state of a computation with completed checkpointing. The checkpointing is complete if there is no coordination message in any of the channels (recall that taking a checkpoint and propagating it further is an atomic event). The final snapshot T is defined by resetting all processes that have not taken a checkpoint at S to their starting point. So, in this case $I = \overline{CP(S)}$, the complement set of $CP(S)$.

Theorem 1. *Let π be a distributed computation from S_0 to S with completed checkpointing. Then the final snapshot T obtained by resetting to the initial state all processes that have not taken a checkpoint at S is consistent with π.*

Proof. The final snapshot is defined by $T := r(\overline{CP(S)}, f(CP(S), S))$. The histories of T are given by

$$p_i^T = \begin{cases} p_i^{f(CP(S),S)} & \text{if } P_i \in CP(S), \\ \varepsilon & \text{otherwise.} \end{cases}$$

By Lemma 2 we know that $f(CP(S), S)$ is reachable from S_0 as $CP(S)$ is a freeze set of S. So there is a computation

$$\pi' = S_0 \xrightarrow{e_1} U_1 \xrightarrow{e_2} \ldots \xrightarrow{e_m} U_m = f(CP(S), S).$$

Let I stand for $\overline{CP(S)}$. From π' we extract the computation which restricts to events performed by processes not in I, only.

$$S_0 \xrightarrow{\tilde{e}_1} r(I, U_1) \xrightarrow{\tilde{e}_2} \ldots \xrightarrow{\tilde{e}_m} r(I, U_m)$$

where $r(I, U_t) \xrightarrow{\tilde{e}_{t+1}} r(I, U_{t+1})$ stands for $r(I, U_t) = r(I, U_{t+1})$ if e_{t+1} is an event of a process in I, and for $r(I, U_t) \xrightarrow{\tilde{e}_{t+1}} r(I, U_{t+1})$ otherwise. For the former case there is nothing to prove, so consider the case e_{t+1} is performed by a process outside I. Again, if e_{t+1} is not of the form $rec_{ij}(msg)$ where $P_i \in I$, $P_j \in CP(S)$, the transition can obviously be performed. for the case $e_{t+1} = rec_{ij}(msg)$, $P_i \in I$, $P_j \in CP(S)$ we show that it cannot occur. So suppose there was such an event, then

$$p_j^{U_{t+1}} = p_j^{U_t}.rec_{ij}(msg)$$

$$p_j^{U_t}.rec_{ij}(msg) \sqsubseteq p_j^{f(CP(S),S)} \qquad \text{by Rule 2.1} \qquad (1)$$

$$p_j^{f(CP(S),S)} \sqsubseteq p_j^S \qquad \text{by Lemma 2} \qquad (2)$$

$$p_j^{f(CP(S),S)} = P_j^S \downarrow_{mcp,cp} \qquad \text{by definition} \qquad (3)$$

This implies $rec_{ij}(\langle msg, 0 \rangle)$ is in the history of p_j^S (by (1) and (2)) and occurs before $mcp\_taken_i^S$ or $cp\_taken_i^S$ (by (1) and (3)). Hence, by Rule 2.1, $dep_j^S(i) = 1$. Thus, since P_j had taken a checkpoint after the receive event it had also sent a cpr_j to P_i. Now, as $P_i \in I$, this event had not been received and must therefore be in C_{ji}^S. This, however, contradicts that the checkpointing was complete.

Table 2. Comparison of the two algorithms.

	Mutable Checkpointing	Blocking Queue Algorithm
blocking processes	no	no
delaying processing of messages	no	yes
PSN consistent	no	yes
Actions to be taken after phase I	discard unconverted mutable checkpoints	clear blocking queues
Autonomy of processes	no	yes

6   Comparison of Mutable Checkpointing with the Blocking Queue Algorithm

Like mutable checkpointing, the blocking queue algorithm in [13] aims at a reduced coordination overhead. It assumes the same system model. The main difference is that the receipt of flagged messages which would lead to mutable checkpoints are buffered in so-called blocking queues and are not processed until the necessary checkpoints have been taken. This can be viewed as blocking channels or blocking processes partially. Mutable checkpointing neither blocks channels nor processes but, in general, it takes mutable checkpoints which if not converted to checkpoints need to be discarded after completion of the checkpointing (i.e. after phase I). A garbage collection is not required in the blocking queue algorithm, but the blocking queues need to be cleared.

The snapshots determined by the two algorithms over the same underlying computation, in general, are incomparable. That is, it is not the case that a checkpoint taken in mutable computing is always equal or earlier than the corresponding checkpoint in the blocking queue setting, or vice versa. It may even happen that a process takes a checkpoint in one setting but not in the other. We discuss this next. It should be clear that a converted mutable checkpoint can be earlier than the corresponding checkpoint taken by the blocking queue algorithm. A computation in which a process takes a checkpoint in the blocking queue algorithm but not in mutable checkpointing is illustrated in Figure 2. We use M to depict a mutable checkpoint, $\underline{M}$ for a mutable checkpoint converted to a checkpoint, and $\otimes$ for a (regular) checkpoint. Arcs with numbers reflect messages and their flag. Checkpoint requests are indicated by *cpr*. In Figure 2, the checkpoint of P_i in the blocking queue algorithm has no counterpart in mutable checkpointing. Such checkpoints, however, can lead to earlier checkpoints in the blocking queue algorithms and in turn lead to fewer checkpoints than in mutable checkpointing.

With regard to the potential snapshots, it has been established in [13] that the potential snapshots of the blocking queue algorithm are always consistent, contrasting the general inconsistency of the potential snapshots of mutable checkpointing shown here. In particular, the former implies that one can always only reset those processes for which a checkpoint has been taken without losing consistency. In mutable checkpointing the processes not taking part in the checkpointing also need to be reset as they may have received messages sent out after

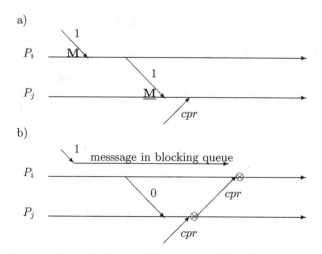

Fig. 2. a) Mutable checkpointing, b) blocking queue algorithm. Process P_i takes a checkpoint in in b), only.

a checkpoint. Similarly, the garbage collection after phase I does also involve the non-participating processes while for clearing the blocking queues it is sufficient for the participating processes to send a respective clearing message. For mobile computing environments the blocking queue algorithm seems therefore preferable, but it comes together with the temporary buffering and delaying of messages. The comparison is summed up in Table 2. Note, that we did not discuss autonomy of processes here as it is a feature present in [13] independent of the others (but it utilizes the blocking queues). In brief, it allows processes not to take a checkpoint immediately but to postpone it to a time more suitable.

7   Conclusions

We gave a concise specification of the operational behavior of mutable checkpointing, set up an invariant for the reachable states (Lemma 2) and utilized it for the correctness proof of the final snapshot. We extracted the specification of the operational behavior from the pseudo code in [9]. With our translation we omitted a feature not part of the mutable checkpointing concept (the $sent_i$ condition) and in this way obtained a more concise presentation of the algorithm. This feature, however, reduces the number of checkpoints further. It needs to be worked out how it reflects in the potential snapshot.

Taking aside the initial work [10] most papers on checkpointing prove correctness by contradiction. We believe that a direct approach provides more insight into an algorithm. It can also form the basis of a tool-supported proof as recently shown in [3] for Chandy/Lamport's snapshot algorithm (among others).

The set-up in [3] is based on the Event-B modelling language [6] and very similar to ours. Whether the proof given in this paper can be mechanized in a similar way is subject of future work.

A concise formal model can be the base of qualitative comparisons which would add to existing quantitative comparisons based on simulations, like [1,12]. We gave such a comparison with the blocking queue algorithm introduced in [13]. That algorithm is conceptually different – it employs partial buffering of channel contents – but the overall objective is the reduction of coordination overhead as for mutable checkpointing.

We further showed that for a given underlying computation the respective snapshots may be incomparable. The potential snapshots of [13] are always consistent unlike those of mutable checkpointing. Moreover, resetting processes and clearing blocking queues can be done in a localized way (that is involving only processes participating in the checkpointing). Hence, for computing environments in which the economic use of resources is crucial, the blocking queue algorithm seems preferable.

Recently, checkpointing has gained new attention in the area of high performance computing where fault tolerance techniques are essential [5,11,16]. As the reduction of the coordination overhead may help to improve the overall performance, the algorithm discussed in this paper may be of interest there.

References

1. Agbaria, A., Friedman, R.: Model-based performance evaluation of distributed checkpointing protocols. Performance Evaluation 65 (2008)
2. Aggarwal, D., Kiehn, A.: Analyzing Mutable Checkpointing via Invariants (full version). Technical Report IIIT Delhi, No IIITD-TR-2015-008 (2015)
3. Andriamiarina, M.B., Mery, D., Singh, N.K.: Revisiting snapshot algorithms by refinement-based techniques. Computer Science and Information Systems 11 (2014)
4. Babaoglu, Ö., Marzullo, K.: Consistent global states of distributed systems: Fundamental concepts and mechanisms. In: Distributed Systems. ACM Press/Addison-Wesley (1993)
5. Boutellier, A., Lemarinier, P., Krawezik, G., Cappello, F.: Coordinated checkpoint versus message log for fault tolerant MPI. In: IEEE Inernational Conference on Cluster Computing, Cluster 2013 (2012)
6. Cansell, D., Méry, D.: The Event-B modelling method - concepts and case studies. In: Bjorner, D., Henson, M. (eds.) Logics of Specification Languages, Springer, Heidelberg (2008)
7. Cao, G., Singhal, M.: On coordinated checkpointing in distributed systems. IEEE Transactions on Parallel and Distributed Systems 9(12), 1213–1225 (1998)
8. Cao, G., Singhal, M.: Mutable checkpoints: a new checkpointing approach for mobile computing systems. IEEE Transactions on Parallel and Distributed Systems 12(2), 157–172 (2001)
9. Cao, G., Singhal, M.: Checkpointing with mutable checkpoints. Theoretical Computer Science 290(2), 1127–1148 (2003)
10. Chandy, K.M., Lamport, L.: Distributed snapshots: determining global states of distributed systems. ACM Transactions on Computer Systems (TOCS) 3(1), 63–75 (1985)

11. Elliot, J., Kharbas, K., Fiala, D., Mueller, F., Ferreira, K., Engelmann, C.: Combining partial redundancy and checkpointing for HPC. In: IEEE Distributed Computing Systems, ICDCS 2012 (2012)
12. Jiang, Q., Luo, Y., Manivannan, D.: An optimistic checkpointing and message logging approach for consistent global checkpoint collection in distributed systems. Journal of Parallel Distributed Computing, 68 (2008)
13. Kiehn, A., Raj, P., Singh, P.: A causal checkpointing algorithm for mobile computing environments. In: Chatterjee, M., Cao, J.-n., Kothapalli, K., Rajsbaum, S. (eds.) ICDCN 2014. LNCS, vol. 8314, pp. 134–148. Springer, Heidelberg (2014)
14. Kshemkalyani, A.D., Singhal, M.: Distributed Computing: Principles, Algorithms, and Systems. Cambridge University Press (2008)
15. Lai, T.H., Tao, H.: Yang.: On distributed snapshots. Information Processing Letters 25 (1987)
16. Ljubuncic, I., Giri, R., Rozenfeld, A., Goldis, A.: Be kind, rewind: checkpoint & restore capability for improving reliability of large-scale semiconductor design. In: IEEE high Performance Extreme Computing Conference, HPEC 2014 (2014)
17. Raynal, M.: Distributed Algorithms for Message-Passing Systems. Springer (2013)

High Performance Computing Applications Using Parallel Data Processing Units

Keyvan Azadbakht, Vlad Serbanescu, and Frank de Boer

Centrum Wiskunde & Informatica, Amsterdam, The Netherlands
{k.azadbakht, vlad.serbanescu, f.s.de.boer}@cwi.nl

Abstract. Multicore processors are growing with respect to the number of cores on a chip. In a parallel computation context, multicore platforms have several important features such as exploiting multiple parallel processes, having access to a shared memory with noticeably lower cost than the distributed alternative and optimizing different levels of parallelism. In this paper, we introduce the Parallel Data Processing Unit (PDPU) which is a group of objects that benefits from the shared memory of the multicore configuration and that consists of two parts: a shared memory for maintaining data consistent, and a set of objects that are processing the data, then producing and aggregating the results concurrently. We then implement two examples in Java that illustrate PDPU behavior, and compare them with their actor based counterparts and show significant performance improvements. We also put forward the idea of integrating PDPU with the actor model which will result in an optimization for a specific spectrum of problems in actor based development.

Keywords: Multicore Processors, High Performance Computing, Actor Based Implementation, Shared Memory, Programming Construct, Data Management.

1 Introduction

In computer science research and industry, hardware development has always been progressing at a very fast rate in terms of performance and costs compared to the software adapted to run on it. Ever since the notion of parallel programming was first introduced, the demand for algorithms and models to support this paradigm has drastically increased. Very important issues like synchronization, concurrency and fine-grained task parallelism have been raised in a wide spectrum of domains requiring significant computing power and speed-up. Currently, chip manufacturers are moving from single-processor chips to new architectures that utilize the same silicon real estate for a conglomerate of multiple independent processors known as multicores, which is also the focus of our ongoing research in the UPSCALE European Project [25].

Throughout all of the mainstream languages, several libraries have been proposed with the objective to efficiently and reliably map tasks to these cores providing a high degree of parallelism to applications while avoiding race conditions and data inconsistency. At a lower level, compilers have also been adapted

© IFIP International Federation for Information Processing 2015
M. Dastani and M.Sirjani (Eds.): FSEN 2015, LNCS 9392, pp. 191–206, 2015.
DOI: 10.1007/978-3-319-24644-4_13

192 K. Azadbakht, V. Serbanescu, and F. de Boer

to ensure instruction-level parallelism on operations that do not depend on each other and these optimizations are completely transparent to the user. Our ongoing research in this project focuses on how to "lift" this transparency to a higher level, offering an abstraction of task-level parallelism that allows the user to specify how and which tasks are executed in parallel without the complexity of monitoring data dependencies. We present this approach in one of the main programming languages, namely the Java language, while avoiding the need to learn specific instructions of particular Java libraries and packages or forcing the programmer to adopt a certain "pattern" to developing highly concurrent applications.

In a parallel computation context, multicore platforms provide some features like exploiting several parallel processes and having access to a shared memory that enables us to propose new higher level software abstractions containing both parallel processes and the memory which is shared among them, and encapsulating the before-mentioned low level coordination issues as one solid entity. In this direction, we introduce the Parallel Data Processing Unit (PDPU) as the elementary effort towards the elaboration of this category of software abstractions. In a nutshell, we may have multiple PDPUs in a software, each of which has its own memory which is shared among constituent processes running in parallel. In addition, the synchronization considerations caused by concurrent access to the shared memory are managed as internal features and are hidden from the programmers.

Through this solution we offer designers a reliable and efficient framework for avoiding race conditions, deadlocks and managing critical sections in their programs. We also allow them to analyze their code and identify the exact degree of parallelism and cost of their parallel sections, while making a clear separation between sequential and concurrent parts of their programs. Finally our solution focuses on how to optimize memory accesses by separate processes in a MIMD architecture [23,24]. This is a crucial research question in the field of Computer Science as more and more computation intensive applications are moving to GRID environments or even further to CLOUD storage and resources. Therefore we formulate our main objective in this paper as follows: to introduce a new model for programming parallel data processing applications which encapsulates the multithreaded java programming model and its synchronization features. The model exposes an interface that is easy to use and transparent, while adding optimizations for efficient memory management and data consistency. In the rest of this paper, we first survey the related work in section 2. We then introduce the definition of PDPU in section 3. The implementation efforts and evaluation of PDPU will be addressed in section 4. In section 5, we put forward the idea of integrating PDPU with the actor model in order to take advantage of simplicity of higher level abstractions and better performance. Finally, we conclude the paper and present future works in section 6.

2   Related Work

In this section we look at several solutions proposed and developed in mainstream programming languages for adapting programs to run on multicores. We start from some of the basic concepts and examples that have been validated and used in research and industry for multicore programming. For each example we will look at what aspects are drawn into our solution, mainly the ease of use and readability of these solutions, as well as the drawbacks that we want to avoid in our approach. Furthermore, we look at some complex directions of research that are oriented towards memory management and mapping user-level threads to kernel-level threads and propose their integration into our model.

We first look into the kernel-level threads [22] which is a POSIX standard for programming in C, C++ and Fortran. The advantages of this standard are that, when implemented correctly, it is extremely efficient and fast, ensuring a high degree of parallelism that is specified by the user explicitly. The advantage of these threads is that they can be directly mapped to the kernel threads of an operating system making it very easy for the user to observe the load of each task and appropriately balance the computation amongst cores by correctly defining each thread's functionality and adjusting it according to its profiling results. It has been validated in numerous applications and has yielded the best scaling results among parallel programming solutions [17,21]. The drawbacks of this approach are centered around the fact that the user is responsible for synchronization, avoiding race conditions or deadlocks and managing critical sections and variables. The POSIX Library offers no warnings, compiler errors or exceptions when these issues occur. In our solution we use the thread mechanism due to its excellent performance and offer a certain degree of control to the user, however some of the basic synchronization issues are handled implicitly and due to our solution being specific to the Java language, it offers the user exceptions on these issues if they are violated.

Another contribution to our proposal is related to the OpenMP standard proposed in [20]. This solution is also specialized in shared-memory programming and parallelism is fully implicit. It comprises of a set of directives used to control repetitive instructions in particular and allow them to be scheduled on the available cores such that they can be executed in parallel. The directives offer limited control over scheduling options, the degree of parallelism and critical sections. What is the most important aspect that we draw from OpenMP is the transparency of the parallelism, as it does not have to be explicitly specified [16]. Basic instruction-level parallelism and, starting with the recently passed OpenMP 3.0 standard, task-level parallelism are achieved by adding the appropriate directive before a repetitive instruction or a code-block.

A significant research topic related to OpenMP is how to use this standard together with the well-known Message Passing Interface (MPI) standard for distributed programming [15]. This solution allows the user to explicitly model parallel processes at a much higher programming level than POSIX Threads while at the same time handling remote or local communication via messages. The communication is completely transparent to the user and avoids the implementation of sockets or remote method invocation. Essentially, every node is considered a separate entity with its own address space, a model which disregards shared memory. From a software engineering standpoint this standard is the easiest to use in the FORTRAN, C and C++ languages as it does not present any difficult language constructs and offers high level methods to handle, spawn, finalize and synchronize processes either on the same machine or on several computing entities. Communication transparency is the key feature that we introduce in our model from the MPI standard, but without affecting the shared memory model that an application may or may not be running on. A study in [19] has shown that a hybrid approach between OpenMP and MPI depending on the programming model can yield the best performance results and our solution is based on this hybrid approach.

Nobakht et al. [3] proposed a modeling language for leveraging performance and scheduling concepts to application level. The proposal introduces the notion of concurrent object groups (COGs) that isolates multiple objects into separate entities and exposes a user-friendly solution to set scheduling policies at a higher-programming level. As stated in our main objective, we model our solution for the Java language, therefore we needed to carefully study the parallel programming concepts introduced by the Java Platform[14]. The solutions for this programming language are similar to POSIX threads in the sense that the user is responsible for every step in the concurrent application's design. Although Java provides an abstraction for both Threads [13] and synchronization mechanisms [12] a programmer still has the difficult task of learning and using these new constructs being responsible for handling deadlocks, race conditions and data consistency. Our goal is to combine these solutions and their advantages to present a novel approach in multicore programming with a shared memory model. Our proposed setting is more general than coordination languages [31] in the sense that the data structures used for memory management can be customized and are not restricted to a specific tuple-space, with our aim being towards a more general data component.

3   The Definition of Parallel Data Processing Unit

Parallel Data Processing Unit (PDPU) is an abstract object (or unit) that puts together a group of objects so that they process the data in the shared memory concurrently. PDPU has two main constituents (Figure 1):

A group of processes: a frame that aggregates objects so that one can look at the group of objects as one solid entity. The group members and their corresponding details are abstracted away from the rest of the application (like a black box). Instead, PDPU provides one interface just like one coarse-grained object. There should be some reason that makes this frame meaningful e.g. conceptual coherence among active object classes. At least, all of them have one feature in common; they need a specific kind of data to process. From now on, we refer to the group members as processes since they process the data in shared memory,

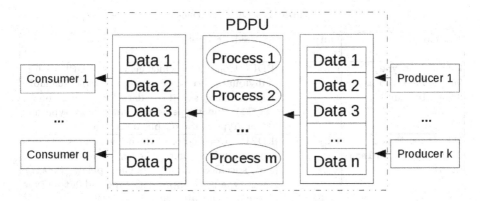

Fig. 1. General Perspective of PDPU

though they can also behave the same as producers by pushing data in the input shared memory through the interface.

Input and output shared memory: PDPU, as an individual object, has one input shared memory for storing data received from outside. This memory is shared within the processes, and the group processes the data from it. There is also an output shared memory which is filled with the data produced by processes. The processes do not share any memory except the input for reading and the output for writing. Furthermore, the data elements are just added or removed and they are immutable. We refer to those objects which are responsible to fill in the input shared memory as data producers. Producers are not a part of the PDPU, instead they use its interface in order to put the data. The output shared memory is also accessed by the objects called consumers through PDPU interface. Inside the PDPU, the shared memory is responsible for thread safety and data consistency when processes work with data concurrently.

3.1   PDPU Interface Description

As shown in Figure 1, there are a group of processes inside the PDPU. Each process must follow the following template:

```
Start Process ()
    Do
        data = retrieve()
        result = process(data)
        write(result)
    Until (data meets ending condition)
End Process
```

This abstract template shows how proactively processes obtain the data from the input shared memory and then process it based on their own logic. They

Table 1. PDPU interface

Method Name	Output Type	Method Description
`PDPU<InputType, OutputType>(Boolean, Runnable, int)`	Object	PDPU Consructor which generates PDPU with m individual processes from reproducible `Runnable` process and specified data retrieving policy (`isAll`). `InputType` is the input data type and `OutputType` is the output data type.
`PDPU<InputType, OutputType>(Boolean, List)`	Object	PDPU Consructor which generates PDPU with individual `Runnable` processes from `List` and specified data retrieving policy (`isAll`). `InputType` is the input data type and `OutputType` is the output data type.
`retrieve()`	InputType	Retrieve the data for process usage based on re-trieving policy
`add(InputType)`	Boolean	Add the data to the shared memory and return True if it is successful
`write(OutputType)`	Boolean	Write the data to the output shared memory and return True if it is successful
`read()`	OutputType	Return the data from output shared memory

may, if necessary, generate a result and put it in the output shared memory. In the above mentioned code, there are two functions which are provided by PDPU interface: *retrieve* and *write*. A brief description of the PDPU interface is given in Table 1. The "retrieve()" method provides the process with the next data element from input shared memory. It encapsulates which is the next data element and how the synchronization issues are handled. The process may generate some explicit result for processing each data element. In this case it uses "write(data)" to record them in the output shared memory. This function also encapsulates the synchronization issues for writing in the output shared memory as well. The process's result, however, may be produced implicitly through the "process()" method, as you will see in section 4. On the other hand, there has to be a data producer (or producers) which fills the input shared memory and consequently provides the processes with the data to be retrieved and processed. To this aim, the producer uses the interface method "add(data)" which adds the data to the shared memory. This function is propagated by PDPU interface.

In the definition of PDPU, there are two factors that impact the internal design of it and both should be specified based on user's problem requirements.

— *Initialization phase:* initial state and logic of the processes.
— *Memory access:* the way that the data in shared memory will be retrieved.

The processes may be instances of the same class and their internal state may be the same after initialization. We refer to this type of processes as Reproducible (R) and otherwise as Non-Reproducible (NR). If the process is reproducible, it is enough to initiate one process and to send it to the PDPU object along with its number of replicas. Otherwise, the programmer is supposed to make a list of processes with different initial states, and then to send the list to the PDPU object.

```
(1)    PDPU(isAll, process, m) //for Reproducible processes
(2)    PDPU(isAll, processList) // For Non-Reproducible processes
```

Furthermore, the data elements in the shared memory can have two different ways of being retrieved. The shared memory's data is targeted either to **all** processes or to **any** of them. In the first instance, it means all the m processes will retrieve one specific data, and in the second case it means that it is enough for the data to be processed just by one of the processes. An example of how PDPU is used is given in Listing 1.1. The processes inside PDPU retrieve the next data element as soon as they become idle. The start-up sequence of the processes is also based on which one retrieves data from the input shared memory earlier.

Listing 1.1. PDPU User Example

```
public class PDPUUser {

    Process [] process;
    PDPU<InputType, OuputType> pdpu;
    Input dataFlux = new input();
    //this can be a socketHandler
    //or anything which continuously receives Data

    public void Init(int m) {
        process = new process [m];
        pdpu = new PDPU<InputType, OuputType>("all", process
            );
        //the first parameter corresponds to how data is
            processed

        for (int i = 0 ; i < m; i++){
            process [i] = new Process();
            process [i].setPDPU(pdpu);
        }

        while(dataFlux.hasData())
            pdpu.add(dataFlux.getNewData());
            //The producer rule in the model

        for (int i = 1 ; i <= m; i++)
            pdpu.add(dataFlux.endData());
            // ending condition
    }
}

public class Process implements Runnable{

    PDPU<InputType, OutputType> pdpu;
```

```
public void setPDPU(PDPU<InputType, OutputType> pdpu){
    this.pdpu = pdpu;
}

public void run()    {
    InputType x;
    OuputType y;

    while (x != END_DATA){
        x = pdpu.retrieve(i);
        y = process(x);
        pdpu.write(y);
    }

    OutputType process(InputType x){}    // process
      related code
```
}

3.2 PDPU Scientific Impact

PDPUs bring about some advantages with respect to software engineering qualities, as they provide:

- *Ease of use*: some lower level implementation details are handled not by programmers, but by the PDPU; like allocating computation resources to the processes, allocating shared memory, and the thread-safety issues concerning access to the shared memory.
- *Understandability of system design and code*: PDPU as a coarse granular cohesive design component (or module) makes the design models of the system simpler and easier to understand.
- *Loose coupling*: the producer interacts only with PDPU interface instead of all processes.

Furthermore with respect to concurrent computation, PDPUs provide new abstract constructs for parallel programming languages and, more generally, they put forward a new paradigm of designing coarse grained objects which encapsulates both memory and multiple computation resources.

4 PDPU Implementation and Evaluation

In this section we present a technical explanation of the shared memory management. We illustrate the operation of PDPU through a case study with two examples in Java.

4.1   Memory Management

As explained in section 3 the PDPU hides all of the elements concerning synchronization, thread-safety and data consistency from the user. The memory can be customized to support retrieval of each data item by either **a single** process or **all** processes. In the first case, we implement the memory as a LinkedBlockingQueue[12] which translates to a classic producer-consumer [11] problem with the synchronization hidden from the user. The real issue appears in the second instance where the memory must take into account blocking all processes when new data is not available, releasing them for work when new data is added and cleaning up the input data when all processes have read it. This case maps to the classic readers/writers problem [10] with a garbage collection issue. We use a ConcurrentHashMap with an index for a key and a counter/data pair for a value. A CyclicBarrier is assigned to a separate counter (the current number of items that were added up to a moment) which blocks all processes when no new data is available. After each process reads an item from the hash map it increments the item's corresponding counter. The last process to read an item is responsible for eliminating the item based on the counter reaching the fixed number of processes. It is worth mentioning that because according to the definition of PDPU the data is immutable both in input and output shared memories, we use object cloning in order to have a copy of the data instead of reference to guarantee the immutability of the data.

4.2   Example 1: The Behavior of PDPU with Respect to Transferring Data

We first compare a Java program in the domain of actor based applications with its PDPU-based counterpart. In this example, there is no computation and the only important factor is delivering data elements to the processes. Figure 2 presents the PDPU in Object Oriented model. For implementing above mentioned actor based Java programs, we use ABS-API [7], an actor-model library implemented in JAVA 8 using the newly introduced feature of lambda expressions. We also run all the programs on SaraSURF cluster on a 16 core processor 2.70 GHz (Intel Xeon CPU E5-4650 0) with 128GB of memory[7] to have the same framework for comparison.

Let us assume a common actor based configuration in which there is a producer of data that provides multiple actors with a stream of data objects through message passing. The producer generates the data and sends it through asynchronous method invocation. Each data element will be processed by all of the actors. Therefore the producer composes and sends m messages for each data, where m is the number of actors receiving the message. Thus, for n data elements, the producer sends $m * n$ messages. However, instead of broadcasting each message to all actors, the PDPU alternative for this implementation involves having a PDPU which contains a fixed number of m processes. The producer is supposed to add each data element to the shared memory of the PDPU instance just once through calling "add(data)" and processes retrieve and process the data.

Therefore the producer adds the n data elements to the PDPU which starts m processes. It is clear that, in terms of transferring data to the processes, the computation complexities of producers are $O(nm)$ and $O(n+m)$ for the actor based and PDPU based implementations respectively. The difference is more clear, when we consider large m because of the future of multicore platforms, namely manycores, with thousands or even millions of cores on a chip. Figure 3 illustrates the advantage of PDPU in terms of performance. The important point of this plot is the behavior of these two approaches, disregarding the elapsed times. As you can see, the line corresponding to actor based implementation grows exponentially, when m is increased. The PDPU based implementation, however, grows at a linear rate. There are multiple factors other than computation complexity that impact on the elapsed time in the actor based configuration, namely, the resource consumption due to among others enqueueing and dequeueing the messages and generating the call stacks.

4.3   Example 2: The Concurrent Version of Sieve of Eratosthenes

In mathematics, the sieve of Eratosthenes, one of a number of prime number sieves, is a simple algorithm for finding all prime numbers up to any given limit. It does so by iteratively marking as composite (i.e. not prime) the multiples of each prime, starting with the multiples of 2 [6]. To model the algorithm in two different versions using actors [5] and PDPU, we use the well-known parallel algorithm which partitions the sequence of candidate numbers [2,1]. In this algorithm, the numbers are partitioned into smaller sequences of numbers with almost the same size. The size of each partition must be equal or greater than $\lfloor \sqrt{n} \rfloor$, and the number of partitions must be equal or less than $\lceil n/\lfloor \sqrt{n} \rfloor \rceil$, where n is the target number such that the first partition contains all of the prime numbers that sieve composites throughout all partitions. Therefore the first actor in the model, namely producer, will send asynchronous messages to the others that will invoke the sieving process. To this aim, each prime number must be sent m times to the m actors. This is where the PDPU based model affects the performance of the program. If prime numbers are processed on the

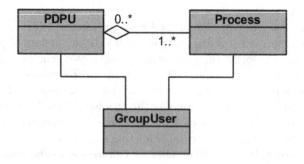

Fig. 2. The Object Oriented model containing PDPU

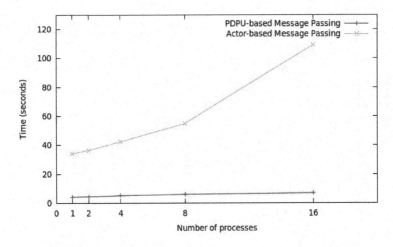

Fig. 3. The comparison between the behavior of Actor based and PDPU based Java programs. 10^6 data items are sent to each process.

same machine they can exploit PDPU abstraction which reads and writes the numbers in a shared data structure, with message passing being required only between the producer and remote partitions. So each prime number is produced and written in shared memory just once. The comparison of actor based and PDPU based implementations of prime sieve is shown in Figure 4. While both algorithms scale, PDPU based implementation outperforms the actor based one. However it is not because of theoretical analysis we have mentioned in Section 4.2, but because of practical overheads in ABS-API for receiving the messages containing data. In other words, when the producer is not the bottleneck, in opposite to example 1, then both programs performances are limited to the computations done in actors and processes. In this example, they behave the same, though there is some constant difference in performance. In contrast, if we consider just producers overheads and disregard other parts of programs, the PDPU based implementation significantly outperforms since the same reason mentioned in Section 4.2.

5   Discussion: Integrating PDPU with Actor Model

In previous sections, we introduced PDPU as a high abstraction level object that is orthogonal to both Java Threads and the actor model. PDPU enhances the Java language to obtain parallelism in processing data via encapsulating synchronization. In other words, it is simpler to implement a parallel data processing algorithm using PDPU than using Java Threads, and the programmer does not need to face synchronization issues, race conditions and so forth. We have also shown how PDPU outperforms actor based implementations and what is the reason behind it through the examples in section 4. In this section, we

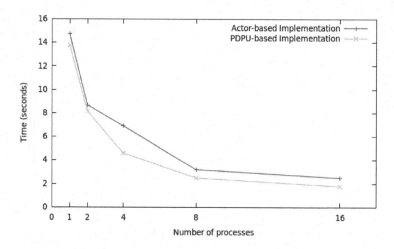

Fig. 4. The comparison between the behavior of Actor based and PDPU based implementations of Sieve of Eratosthenes. The target number for sieving is 10^9

explain how PDPU concept is integrated with actor model in such a way that the extended actor model exploits the strength points of both concepts.

Although it is achieved novel advantages in the area of actor model and asynchronous message passing, there are some downsides in practice e.g. the overhead of composing, sending and receiving messages and dealing with obtaining future results when their number is large. Sometimes the overhead is because of the nature of broadcasting mechanism — that is — broadcasting the same message to several actors which has both computation overhead, because of redundant repetitive actions for broadcasting message, and memory overhead, because of redundant queuing the same message by several actors. On the other hand, the actor model [7] provides the *actor* notion which is an entity with high abstraction level that leads to eliminating design and implementation complexities caused by the nature of parallel computation and programming. However, there can be higher abstract constructs or design patterns that still follow the actor concept and eliminate or lessen these cumbersome and confusing details in some specific circumstances.

This section puts forward the idea of a new abstract programming language construct, which is called **Active Group** in order to benefit from both actor based implementation and PDPU features. The general idea is that we have one actor-like component in a higher level abstraction. This component consists of one queue of runnable messages and one processing part which processes the messages. At lower abstraction level, similar to PDPU, the processing part contains multiple processes, i.e. actors, receiving messages. Instead of data elements in PDPU, here we will have runnable messages in the shared memory. You can see a simple scheme of Active Group in Figure 5. However we ignore some of its details, e.g. how actors have access to the shared queue. Here we briefly address

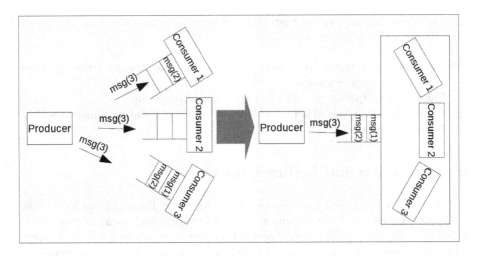

Fig. 5. Active Group (right side) and its extended actor based counterpart (left side)

some of these details as the main features of Active Groups. We use the same terminology as the definition of PDPU:

Proactive or Reactive Actors: The actor can proactively fetch one message from shared memory or wait for the next element to be prepared. In contrast, it may passively receive the message through an independent scheduler in the group, and process it. Thus the values for this feature are **Proactive** and **Reactive**. In the former case, there is no need for each individual actor to have a message queue.

Different Scheduling Policies: One of the advantages of the active group is to apply different scheduling policies. Data is usually received in a particular order, but if the policy is not FIFO, the group may process them in other orders. To this aim, data can be reordered based on, say, **Priority** or **Content**. Furthermore, if actors are not proactive, they are supposed to be managed as computation resources by schedulers. They may be selected as the target actor based on different policies like **Round Robin**.

Different Ways of Using the Shared Memory: In some applications of active groups, each message in the shared memory will be fetched by **one** actor and processed by it. So, in that case, the message is removed from shared memory (e.g. a queue of HTTP requests, each of which will be enough to be processed by one server). This type of shared memory is technically a queue. However, in some other applications, the message is used by **all** actors. In that case, the data is read from the shared memory but it is not removed since it will be used by others (e.g. in section 4.3, the messages containing prime numbers that are used by actors in concurrent version of sieve of Eratosthenes).

There can be several distinct versions of active group, each of which have different feature values. If we refer to the above-mentioned issues as customizable features of active group, then the ideal active group definition provides the user with all these features to be customizable with existing values. To reach this aim, there can be different ways:

1. Parameterizing the active group construct so that the user can initialize appropriate feature values.
2. Using polymorphism to refine the abstract active group.
3. Having distinct types of active groups so that their definition illustrates their features values.

6 Conclusion and Future Works

In this paper we proposed a coarser granular object, i.e. Parallel Data Processing Unit, which contains both computation and memory, and encapsulates efforts for synchronization issues to make parallel programming easier for programmers. Through case studies and complexity analysis, we have shown how it overcomes one of the drawbacks of actor model and significantly improves performance.

Reasoning about multi-threaded Java programs is notoriously hard (see [8]) because of its fine-grained interleaving. In contrast PDPUs allow for a compositional proof method along the lines of the proof method for monitors as introduced in [9]. Given an appropriate assertion language for describing the internal data structures of a PDPU such a proof method is based on the specification of these data structures by means of an *invariant*. The external proof obligations for the invariant are specified in terms of the implementations of the "add" and the "read" operation, given a precondition of the caller specifying the input parameter in case of an "add" operation. The internal proof obligations of the invariant are specified in terms of the implementations of the processes which involves the implementations of the "retrieve" and "write" operations.

We then put forward the idea of integrating this novel approach with the actor model by bridging the gap between their conceptual differences. To this aim, we have generalized PDPU as a new concept, called Active Group, which is based on actor model. It will make it possible for a broader types of problems to be implemented in Active Groups. As future work, we aim to extend the syntax and the operational semantics of ABS language [4] to have the new construct, namely Active Group, and also extend the ABS-API so that it contains support for defining and using Active Groups.

Acknowledgements. Partly funded by the EU project FP7-610582 ENVIS-AGE: Engineering Virtualized Services (http://www.envisage-project.eu). Partly funded by the EU project FP7-612985 UpScale: From Inherent Concurrency to Massive Parallelism through Type-based Optimizations (http://www.upscale-project.eu). This work was carried out on the Dutch national e-infrastructure with the support of SURF Foundation.

References

1. Pop, F., Potop-Butucaru, M.: Adaptive Resource Management and Scheduling for Cloud Computing
2. Serbanescu, V., et al.: Towards Type-Based Optimizations in Distributed Applications Using ABS and JAVA 8. In: Adaptive Resource Management and Scheduling for Cloud Computing, pp. 103–112. Springer International Publishing (2014)
3. Nobakht, B., et al.: Programming and deployment of active objects with application-level scheduling. In: Proceedings of the 27th Annual ACM Symposium on Applied Computing. ACM (2012)
4. Johnsen, E.B., Hähnle, R., Schäfer, J., Schlatte, R., Steffen, M.: ABS: A core language for abstract behavioral specification. In: Aichernig, B.K., de Boer, F.S., Bonsangue, M.M. (eds.) Formal Methods for Components and Objects. LNCS, vol. 6957, pp. 142–164. Springer, Heidelberg (2011)
5. Nobakht, B., de Boer, F.S.: Programming with actors in Java 8. In: Margaria, T., Steffen, B. (eds.) ISoLA 2014, Part II. LNCS, vol. 8803, pp. 37–53. Springer, Heidelberg (2014)
6. Bokhari, S.H.: Multiprocessing the sieve of Eratosthenes. Computer 20(4), 50–58 (1987)
7. SurfSara, https://surfsara.nl/
8. Brahm, E., et al.: An assertion-based proof system for multithreaded Java. Theoretical Computer Science 331(2), 251–290 (2005)
9. Hoare, C.A.R.: Monitors: An operating system structuring concept. Communications of the ACM 17(10), 549–557 (1974)
10. Andrews, G.R.: Concurrent programming: principles and practice. Benjamin/Cummings Publishing Company (1991)
11. Li, S., et al.: Analysis of the producer-consumer problem. Journal of Large-Scale Archetypes, 72–92 (2002)
12. Lea, D.: The java. util. concurrent synchronizer framework. Science of Computer Programming 58(3), 293–309 (2005)
13. Oaks, S., Wong, H.: Java threads. O'Reilly Media, Inc. (1999)
14. http://docs.oracle.com/javase/7/docs/api/overview-summary.html
15. Gropp, W., Lusk, E., Skjellum, A.: Using MPI: portable parallel programming with the message-passing interface, vol. 1. MIT press (1999)
16. Pop, A., Cohen, A.: OpenStream: Expressiveness and data-flow compilation of OpenMP streaming programs. ACM Transactions on Architecture and Code Optimization (TACO) 9(4), 53 (2013)
17. Briggs, E., et al.: DFT-Based Electronic Structure Calculations on Hybrid and Massively Parallel Computer Architectures. Bulletin of the American Physical Society (2014)
18. Asai, R., Vladimirov, A.: "Intel Cilk Plus for Complex Parallel Algorithms:" Enormous Fast Fourier Transform"(EFFT) Library." arXiv preprint arXiv:1409.5757 (2014)
19. Rabenseifner, R., Hager, G., Jost, G.: Hybrid MPI/OpenMP parallel programming on clusters of multi-core SMP nodes. In: 2009 17th Euromicro International Conference on Parallel, Distributed and Network-based Processing. IEEE (2009)
20. Dagum, L., Menon, R.: OpenMP: an industry standard API for shared-memory programming. IEEE Computational Science & Engineering 5(1), 46–55 (1998)
21. Gravvanis, G.A., et al.: A note on parallel finite difference approximate inverse preconditioning on multicore systems using POSIX threads. International Journal of Computational Methods 10(05) (2013)

22. Mueller, F.: A Library Implementation of POSIX Threads under UNIX. USENIX Winter (1993)
23. Snyder, L.: A taxonomy of synchronous parallel machines. Washington Univ. Seattle Dept. of Computer Science (1988)
24. Johnson, E.E.: Completing an MIMD multiprocessor taxonomy. ACM SIGARCH Computer Architecture News 16(3), 44–47 (1988)
25. UPSCALE European Project. http://www.upscale-project.eu/
26. Smith, T.F., Waterman, M.S.: Identification of Common Molecular Subsequences. J. Mol. Biol. 147, 195–197 (1981)
27. May, P., Ehrlich, H.C., Steinke, T.: ZIB Structure Prediction Pipeline: Composing a Complex Biological Workflow through Web Services. In: Nagel, W.E., Walter, W.V., Lehner, W. (eds.) Euro-Par 2006. LNCS, vol. 4128, pp. 1148–1158. Springer, Heidelberg (2006)
28. Foster, I., Kesselman, C.: The Grid: Blueprint for a New Computing Infrastructure. Morgan Kaufmann, San Francisco (1999)
29. Czajkowski, K., Fitzgerald, S., Foster, I., Kesselman, C.: Grid Information QServices for Distributed Resource Sharing. In: 10th IEEE International Symposium on High Performance Distributed Computing, pp. 181–184. IEEE Press, New York (2001)
30. Foster, I., Kesselman, C., Nick, J., Tuecke, S.: The Physiology of the Grid: an Open Grid Services Architecture for Distributed Systems Integration. Technical report, Global Grid Forum (2002)
31. Gelernter, D., Carriero, N.: Coordination languages and their significance. Communications of the ACM 35(2), 96 (1992)
32. National Center for Biotechnology Information. http://www.ncbi.nlm.nih.gov

Improved Iterative Methods for Verifying Markov Decision Processes

Jaber Karimpour, Ayaz Isazadeh, MohammadSadegh Mohagheghi,
and Khayyam Salehi

Department of Computer Science, University of Tabriz, Tabriz, Iran
{karimpour,isazadeh}@tabrizu.ac.ir, sadegh_rk@yahoo.com,
khayyam.salehi@gmail.com

Abstract. Value and policy iteration are powerful methods for verifying quantitative properties of Markov Decision Processes (MDPs). In order to accelerate these methods many approaches have been proposed. The performance of these methods depends on the graphical structure of MDPs. Experimental results show that they don't work much better than normal value/policy iteration when the graph of the MDP is dense. In this paper we present an algorithm which tries to reduce the number of updates in dense MDPs. In this algorithm, instead of saving unnecessary updates we use graph partitioning method to have more important updates.

Keywords: Markov decision processes, probabilistic model checking, value iteration, policy iteration, graph partitioning, variable ordering.

1 Introduction

Markov Decision Processes (MDPs) are transition systems that can be used for modeling both nondeterministic and stochastic behaviors of reactive systems. In this paper we mainly focus on the quantitative verification of MDPs and consider reachability probabilities, i.e., calculating the maximum (or minimum) probability of reaching some goal states.

In general there are some main classic methods to solve MDPs: value iteration [1], Gauss-Seidel, policy iteration, and linear programming approach [6]. Many researchers have tried to improve the performance of Value Iteration (VI) and Policy Iteration (PI) by reducing the number of updates of states [2,4,7–9]. Although the main focus of so-called papers is on dealing with some problems in learning, one can use those techniques for quantitative verification of MDPs [3,5].

Experimental results show that when the graph of an MDP is dense or in the situation where all states belong to only one Strongly Connected Component (SCC), Gauss-Seidel version of VI works better than other advanced methods. In addition, a good variable ordering can accelerate iterative methods, but finding the optimal variable ordering for cyclic MDPs is an NP-complete problem [9].

In this paper we concentrate on dense MDPs and consider maximum reachability probability problems (as defined in [1]). We present an algorithm that

© IFIP International Federation for Information Processing 2015
M. Dastani and M.Sirjani (Eds.): FSEN 2015, LNCS 9392, pp. 207–214, 2015.
DOI: 10.1007/978-3-319-24644-4_14

works faster than VI (and also faster than other methods). The main contribution is to present a prioritized algorithm for accelerating verification of dense MDPs.

The remainder of this paper is structured as follows. Section 2 formally defines MDPs and reviews PI algorithm. In Section 3 we present heuristics for variable reordering in both sparse and dense MDPs and then present a prioritized algorithm for dense MDPs. Section 4 summarises our experimental results and Section 5 presents conclusions and ideas for future research.

2   Preliminaries

In this section, we provide an overview of MDP and policy iteration method. Detailed definitions and topics are available in [1,5].

2.1   Markov Decision Processes (MDPs)

An MDP is a tuple $M = (S, Act, P, AP, L)$, where S is a countable set of states, Act is a finite set of actions, $P : S \times Act \times S \rightarrow [0,1]$ is the transition probability function such that for each state $s \in S$ and each action $\alpha \in Act : \sum_{s' \in S} P(s, \alpha, s') \in \{0, 1\}$, AP is a nonempty set of atomic propositions, and $L : S \rightarrow 2^{AP}$ is a labeling function.

For the sake of simplicity, we suppose that $AP = \{goal, non - goal\}$ and there is a unique start state s_0. For a state $s \in S$ and an enabled action $\alpha \in Act$, set of successors are defined as

$$Post(s, \alpha) = \{s' \in S | P(s, \alpha, s') > 0\} \text{ and } Post(s) = \cup_{\alpha \in Act} Post(s, \alpha).$$

A path in an MDP is a non-empty (finite or infinite) sequence of the form: $s_0 \xrightarrow{\alpha_0} s_1 \xrightarrow{\alpha_1} s_2 \xrightarrow{\alpha_2} \cdots$ where $s_i \in S$ and $s_{i+1} \in Post(s_i, \alpha)$ for each $i > 0$. We define $Paths_s$ as the set of infinite paths that start in s. To resolve nondeterministic choices in an MDP we require the notion of policy. A policy π selects an enabled action in each state based on the history of choices made so far (or simply the last state in memory-less policies). It restricts the behavior of the MDP to a set of paths $paths_s^\pi \subseteq paths_s$. One can define a probability space $Prob_s^\pi$ over the paths $Paths_s^\pi$ [1]. For an MDP M we use Π_M to denote the set of all policied of M.

MDPs can be used in the verification of systems (probabilistic verification). In this area, properties that should be verified against MDPs can be expressed using temporal logics such as PCTL [5]. In this paper, we concentrate on a limited yet important class of problems: maximum reachability probabilities, i.e. the maximum probability that a path through the MDP which starts from s_0 eventually reaches a goal state.

2.2   Quantitative Verification of MDPs

Model checking of PCTL formulas can be reduced to some important questions against MDPs. The maximum (or minimum) reachability probability is one of the most important questions against them. Given a set of goal states $G \subseteq S$, the maximum and minimum reachability probability can be defined as:

$$p_s^{min}(G) = \inf_{\pi \in \Pi_M} p_s^{\pi}(G) \text{ and } p_s^{max}(G) = \sup_{\pi \in \Pi_M} p_s^{\pi}(G),$$

where $p_s^{\pi}(G) = Prob_s^{\pi}(\{\omega \in Path_s^{\pi} | \exists i.\omega_i \in G\})$. As we have mentioned, there are some methods to compute reachability probabilities in MDPs but we only consider PI (because PI has better performance for dense MDPs).

2.3 Policy Iteration

Algorithm 1 describes the policy iteration method to calculate the values of p_s^{max}. This algorithm uses an array P to save the value $p_{s_i}^{max}$ for each state s_i. It first estimates a good policy (Line 8) and computes the value of states iteratively according to this policy (Lines 15-25). After reaching the threshold if the estimated policy is not optimal it will be improved and the iterative method continues. $Act[s_i]$ saves the best estimated action for each state s_i.

Algorithm1: *Policy Iteration*

```
1.  Set initial values: P[s_i] = 1 if {s_i ∈ G} and o.w.  P[s_i] = 0.
2.  diff1 := 1
3.  while diff1 > epsilon do
4.      diff1 := 0; temp := 0; diff2 := 1
5.      for i := 1 to    number_of_states do
6.          if P[s_i] < 1 then
7.              temp :=      max      Σ_{s'∈S} p(s_i, α, s') × P[s']
                          α∈enabled(s_i)
8.              Act[s_i] :=   arg max   Σ_{s'∈S} p(s_i, α, s') × P[s']
                          α∈enabled(s_i)
9.              if temp − P[s_i] > diff1 then
10.                  diff1 := temp − P[s_i] end if
11.          end if
12.      end for
13.      if diff1 < epsilon then
14.          return P[s_1] end if
15.      while diff2 > epsilon do
16.          diff2 := 0
17.          temp := 0
18.          for i:= 1 to number of states do
19.              if P[s_i] < 1 then
20.                  temp := Σ_{s'∈S} p(s_i, Act[s_i], s') × P[s']
21.                  if temp − P[s_i] > diff2 then
22.                      diff2 := temp − P[s_i] end if
23.              end if
24.          end for
25.      end while
26. end while
```

3   Accelerating VI and PI Algorithms

One of the main drawbacks of VI (and also PI) is that in every iteration it updates the values of all (nontrivial) states. Researchers proposed a range of methods to avoid unnecessary updates and speed up this algorithm. Some of these methods [4, 9] try to split the MDP to some SCCs and in every iteration only compute the new value for states in some SCCs. Another approach for accelerating iterative methods is to consider a better variable ordering [4, 5, 9].

We review the idea of variable reordering and propose a heuristic algorithm for variable reordering in dense MDPs.

3.1   Variable Ordering

The PI algorithm in Section 2 tries to use the update of states as soon as possible. In this case the order of updated states can influence the performance of algorithm. Let $StatesOrder[s_i]$ be the array that determines the (static) order of states for update. When the value of a state is updated the new value can be propagated to next computation if the values of next states depend on the value of the current state. There are some heuristics for variable ordering in previous works [3–5, 9], but none of them are useful for dense MDPs.

Here we propose an algorithm for variable reordering whose time complexity is linear in the size of the MDP. The idea of this algorithm is to select a state s for update where the most of states of $Post(s)$ have been updated before. The *for* loop in line 5 is used to guarantee the selection of all states.

Algorithm2: *VariableReordering*

```
1.  for i := 0 to n - 1
2.        Selected[i] := false;
3.  end for
4.  left := right := 0;
5.  for i := 0 to n - 1
6.        if Selected[i] = false then
7.              Selected[i] := true; StateOrder[left] := i;
8.              while left <= right and right < n do
9.                    j := StateOrder[left++];
10.                   for each s_k ∈ Post(s_j)
11.                         if Selected[k] = false then
12.                               Selected[k] := true;
13.                               StateOrder[right++] = k;
14.                         end if
15.                   end for
16.             end while
17.       end if
18. end for
```

Policy iteration algorithm should call this function before the beginning of inner *while* loop (line 15 of Algorithm 1). In this case the VariableReordering function uses $Post(s_j, Act[s_j])$ (line 10 of algorithm 2). The *for* loop of line 18 (of algorithm 1) should be in reverse order and the state s_i could be selected according to the *StateOrder* array:

```
for i := number_of_states down to 1
    s_i = StateOrder[i];
```

This algorithm is useful for sparse MDPs but in order to deal with dense MDPs we modify the Post set in line 10. Given $t < 1$ as a threshold, we define $Post(s_i, \alpha, t) = \{s_j | P(s_i, \alpha, s_j) \geq t\}$. The experimental results show that the good value for t is between 0.3 and 0.5. It causes the algorithm to consider more important transitions. Algorithm 2 is used as a precomputation for every policy modification and doesn't affect the correctness of the PI algorithm.

3.2 Prioritized Algorithm for PI

Prioritized algorithms [9] in general try to focus on regions of the problem space that are more important and have the maximum effect on the whole problem. In this section we propose an algorithm that uses a simple graph partitioning method for prioritizing state updates.

Inspiring from the idea of SCC-based methods [5] we propose an algorithm which uses a good heuristic to split the state space to some partitions and updates these states according to this partitioning. Let B be a partition. Define $AverageTrans(s_i, B) = \frac{\sum_{s_j \in B} P(s_i, Act(s_i), s_j)}{sizeof(B)}$. Our method tries to make partitions where for each state s_i and each partition B the value of $AverageTrans(s_i, B)$ is high if $s_i \in B$ and this value is low otherwise. In this case the partition that contains goal states is the most important and the frequency of updates for states of this partition should be more than the other two. We use this partitioning algorithm in the PI because for dense MDPs the performance of PI is usually better than the performance of VI.

We use an $O(n^2)$ heuristic for graph partitioning of the MDP because its overhead in the case of dense MDPs is negligible for most case studies. There are some options for the size of partitions. In this paper we define 3 partitions and suppose that the size of the first partition is 25% and the second partition is 35% of all state space. Algorithm 3 describes this partitioning method and because of page limitation, we only present the code for the first partition (with 25% of states).

Algorithm3: *Graph Partitioning*

```
1.  for i := 1 to number_of_states do
2.      Distance[i] := 0;
3.  end for
4.  for i := 1 to number_of_states do
5.      if s_i is a goal state then
6.          Selected[i] := true;
```

```
7.            for j := 1 to number_of_states do
8.                Distance[j] += P(s_j, Act[s_j], s_i);
9.            end for
10.     end if
11. end for
12. for i := 1 to 0.25×number_of_states do
13.        k := the index of non-selected state for which
               Distance[k] is maximum;
14.        Selected[k] := true;
15.        for j := 1 to number_of_states do
16.            if Selected[j] = false then
17.                Distance[j] += P(s_k, Act[s_k], s_j) + P(s_j, Act[s_j], s_k);
18.            end if
19.        end for
20. end for
```

This algorithm should be called before the second *while* loop (Line 15) in Algorithm 1. In order to use the result of this algorithm we modify Algorithm 1 and add the following statements after Line 18:

```
if i % 7 = 0
    update states of partition #3
else if i % 7 = 2 or i % 7 = 5
        update states of partition #2
    else
        update states of partition #1
    end if
end if
```

4   Experiments

We implemented the proposed and original iterative algorithms in C++ using MS Visual Studio 2010 and ran it on an Intel Core i3 processor with 4GB memory. In the sections that follow we first consider the proposed algorithm of Section 3.1 and then consider the algorithm of Section 3.2.

4.1   Results for the Variable Ordering Algorithm

We tested our modified ordering algorithm on some dense MDPs. These models are randomly generated problems with 100 states and 3 actions per state and a parameter λ. We created these MDPs such that for each state s_i, the average of maximum value of $P(s_i, \alpha, s_{i+1})$ is λ with standard deviation of 0.1. Table 1 shows results of running Policy Iteration with best and worst variable ordering and also a random variable ordering. For simplicity we only present number of iterations for the execution of PI with $\epsilon = 10^{-6}$.

The impact of variable ordering for these case studies is considerable where the λ parameter is more than 30%.

Table 1. Results of Variable Ordering for Some Dense MDPs

λ	0.9	0.7	0.5	0.3	0.2	0.1
Random ordering	11.6K	5.5K	3.7K	2.9K	2.6K	2.5K
Best ordering	1.7K	1.9K	2K	2.1K	2.2K	2.2K
Worst ordering	20.5K	9.2K	5.6K	3.8K	3.2K	2.9K
Best/random	0.147	0.364	0.568	0.758	0.846	0.88

4.2   Results for Partitioning-Based Algorithms

SysAdmin problem [9] is a good example of real problems that have dense MDPs. Because of relatively high number of actions per state, the performance of PI algorithm is better than VI and Gauss-Seidel. We used an implementation for the MDP of this problem that is developed by the authors of [9].

We also defined one other MDP: M1 is a model that the probability of reaching to 20% of its states is about 8 times more than the probability of reaching other 80% of states. This model has 400 states where average number of actions per state is 3.

It has been shown that the performance of SCC-based methods is lower than standard iterative method for dense MDPs [9]. Hence, we don't compare our algorithm with SCC-based methods. To compare it with learning based ones, we use the implementation of learning algorithms that the authors of [3] proposed.

Table 2 shows the results of running normal VI and PI methods and, our prioritized algorithm (PI with algorithm 3). We called our algorithm Prioritized PI (PPI). Because of high average number of actions per state, the running time of PI is less than VI. The results show that our prioritized algorithm reduces the running time for all models. While prioritized methods of [9] could not improve the performance of iterative methods for SysAdmin, our algorithm accelerates iterative computations for these models.

Table 2. Results for our prioritized algorithm

Model	Number of States	Time in VI	Time in PI	Time in Learning-based	Time in PPI
SysAdmin6	64	< 0.1	< 0.1	2.6	< 0.1
SysAdmin8	256	0.7	0.19	11.5	0.16
SysAdmin9	512	4.5	0.76	24.3	0.63
SysAdmin10	1023	27.2	2.45	49	1.96
M1	410	1.11	0.95	8.5	0.49

The main reason that the performance of learning based algorithms for dense MDP's is so low is that these methods doesnt usually propose good variable ordering for this class of MDPs.

5   Conclusions and Future Research

The main contribution of this paper is that we present a prioritized algorithm for dense MDPs and show that it can reduce the running time of iterative methods for solving probabilistic reachability problems of this class of MDPs.

An approach for future works is to use a good variable ordering in each partition in our prioritized algorithm. In addition, one can propose a better prioritized algorithm that outperforms other prioritized ones in both dense and sparse models.

While many of previous works focus on VI, we believe that variable reordering can improve the performance when it is used in PI. One can also improve the performance of PI for both dense and sparse MDPs and outperform the VI approach by using advanced methods for selection of good policies (like action elimination.)

References

1. Baier, C., Katoen, J.P.: Principles of model checking. MIT press Cambridge (2008)
2. Barto, A.G., Bradtke, S.J., Singh, S.P.: Learning to act using real-time dynamic programming. Artificial Intelligence 72(1), 81–138 (1995)
3. Brázdil, T., Chatterjee, K., Chmelík, M., Forejt, V., Křetínský, J., Kwiatkowska, M., Parker, D., Ujma, M.: Verification of markov decision processes using learning algorithms. In: Cassez, F., Raskin, J.-F. (eds.) ATVA 2014. LNCS, vol. 8837, pp. 98–114. Springer, Heidelberg (2014)
4. Dai, P., Mausam, J.G., Weld, D.S., Goldsmith, J.: Topological value iteration algorithms. J. Artif. Intell. Res(JAIR) 42, 181–209 (2011)
5. Kwiatkowska, M., Parker, D., Qu, H.: Incremental quantitative verification for markov decision processes. In: 2011 IEEE/IFIP 41st International Conference on Dependable Systems & Networks (DSN), pp. 359–370. IEEE (2011)
6. Puterman, M.L.: Markov decision processes: discrete stochastic dynamic programming. John Wiley & Sons (1994)
7. Sanner, S., Goetschalckx, R., Driessens, K., Shani, G.: Bayesian real-time dynamic programming. In: IJCAI, pp. 1784–1789. Citeseer (2009)
8. Smith, T., Simmons, R.: Focused real-time dynamic programming for mdps: Squeezing more out of a heuristic. In: AAAI, pp. 1227–1232 (2006)
9. Wingate, D., Seppi, K.D.: Prioritization methods for accelerating mdp solvers. Journal of Machine Learning Research, 851–881 (2005)

A Pre-congruence Format for XY-simulation

Harsh Beohar[1] and Mohammad Reza Mousavi[1,*]

Center for Research on Embedded Systems
Halmstad University, Sweden
{harsh.beohar,m.r.mousavi}@hh.se

Abstract. XY-simulation is a generalization of bisimulation that is parameterized with two subsets of actions. XY-simulation is known in the literature under different names such as modal refinement, partial bisimulation, and alternating simulation. In this paper, we propose a pre-congruence rule format for XY-simulation. The format allows for checking compositionality of XY-simulation for an arbitrary language with structural operational semantics, by performing very simple checks on the syntactic shape of the rules. We apply our format to derive concrete compositionality results for different notions of behavioral pre-order with respect to different process calculi in the literature.

1 Introduction

XY-simulation is a generalization of bisimulation that is parameterized by two subsets of actions: X and Y [1]. The idea is to weaken the transfer property of a bisimulation relation in the following way: the actions in X are simulated from left to right, while the actions in Y are simulated from right to left. XY-simulation is well-known in the literature, albeit under different names, such as modal refinement [16], partial bisimulation [6], and alternating simulation [4].

An essential property for any notion of behavioral pre-order and hence, also for XY-simulation, is the so-called pre-congruence property. This property allows for compositional verification and reasoning about processes under arbitrary contexts. The pre-congruence property has been studied in the literature for some instances of XY-simulation and for a fixed set of well-known operators from the field of process algebras (see [6,16] for instance). In this paper, we generalize these results by providing generic sufficient conditions for compositionality of XY-simulation with respect to any arbitrary set of operators with a Structural Operational Semantics (SOS) [21]. We do so by restricting the syntactic shape of the SOS rules to ensure pre-congruence. The result of this paper provides a unified account of existing results and is instantiated to generate new results. Furthermore, the proposed rule format can serve as a yardstick for language designers to check the compositionality of their operators while defining their semantics.

* The research of M.R. Mousavi has been partially supported by the Swedish Research Council within the EFFEMBAC (Effective Model-Based Testing of Concurrent Systems) grant.

M. Dastani and M.Sirjani (Eds.): FSEN 2015, LNCS 9392, pp. 215–229, 2015.
DOI: 10.1007/978-3-319-24644-4_15

To develop our rule format, we employ the modal decomposition approach proposed in [9,13] in combination with an existing modal characterization of XY-simulation, due to [11]. We devise a modal decomposition that specifies when an open term satisfies a modal formula in terms of the modal formulae that are to be satisfied by its variables. This modal decomposition is then directly employed in generating a pre-congruence rule format for XY-simulation. The obtained format is an elegant and simple one; the only specific checks required are simple checks on the labels of the transition formulae, with respect to their inclusion in X or Y. As we demonstrate by some examples in this paper, the format is applicable to various notions of behavioral pre-order and to various process calculi in the literature.

The rest of this paper is structured as follows. In Section 2, we recall the basic definitions that will be used throughout the paper. Then, in Section 3, we first formulate and prove the modal decomposition theorem and using that, derive our pre-congruence rule format. In Section 4, we apply the obtained rule format to various examples from the literature. In Section 5, we show that the syntactic conditions on the rule format cannot be trivially relaxed. Finally, in Section 6, we conclude the paper and present the direction of our ongoing research.

2   Preliminaries

In this section, we first quote the basic definition of labeled transition systems and XY-simulation and some of their properties. Subsequently, we recall a formalization of SOS, and building upon this formalization, we define the basic rule formats that will form the foundations of our results in this paper.

2.1   Transition Systems and XY-simulation

We start by recalling below the well-known notion of labeled transition systems.

Definition 1 (Labeled Transition Systems). *A labeled transition system (LTS) is a triple* $(\mathbb{P}, \mathcal{A}, \rightarrow)$, *where* $\mathbb{P}$ *is the set of* processes, $\mathcal{A}$ *is the set of actions, and* $\rightarrow \subseteq \mathbb{P} \times \mathcal{A} \times \mathbb{P}$ *is the transition relation. We denote* $(p, a, q) \in \rightarrow$ *by* $p \xrightarrow{a} q$.

The following definition formalizes the notion of XY-simulation, originally due to [1].

Definition 2 (XY-simulation). *Let* $X, Y \subseteq \mathcal{A}$. *A binary relation* $\mathcal{R} \subseteq \mathbb{P} \times \mathbb{P}$ *is an* XY-simulation *relation iff the following transfer conditions are satisfied:*

1. $\forall_{p,a,q,p'} \ (p \xrightarrow{a} p' \wedge p\mathcal{R}q \wedge a \in X) \ \Rightarrow \ \exists_{q'} \ q \xrightarrow{a} q' \wedge p'\mathcal{R}q'$.
2. $\forall_{p,a,q,q'} \ (q \xrightarrow{a} q' \wedge p\mathcal{R}q \wedge a \in Y) \ \Rightarrow \ \exists_{p'} \ p \xrightarrow{a} p' \wedge p'\mathcal{R}q'$.

Two processes $p, q \in \mathbb{P}$ *are* XY-similar *, denoted by* $p \preceq_{X,Y} q$, *iff there is an* XY-simulation relation $\mathcal{R}$ such that $p\mathcal{R}q$.

It is worth noting that in [2], XY-simulation relations are called *covariant-contravariant simulation* relations.

The following lemma lists some of the intuitive properties of XY-similarity.

Lemma 1. *Consider an arbitrary LTS $(\mathbb{P}, \mathcal{A}, \rightarrow)$ and assume that $X, Y, X', Y' \subseteq \mathcal{A}$; the following statements hold.*

1. *Relation $\preceq_{X,Y}$ is a pre-order.*
2. *If $X \subseteq X'$, then $\preceq_{X',Y} \subseteq \preceq_{X,Y}$.*
3. *If $Y \subseteq Y'$, then $\preceq_{X,Y'} \subseteq \preceq_{X,Y}$.*
4. *$\preceq_{Y,X} = \preceq_{X,Y}^{-1}$.*

Proof. **1.** It is straightforward to verify that the identity relation is an XY-simulation relation. To prove transitivity, let $p \preceq_{X,Y} p'$ and $p' \preceq_{X,Y} p''$ with $\mathcal{R}$ and $\mathcal{R}'$ their witnessing XY-simulation relations, respectively. It remains to show that $\mathcal{R} \circ \mathcal{R}' = \{(p, p'') \mid \exists_{p'} \ p\mathcal{R}p' \wedge p'\mathcal{R}'p''\}$ is an XY-simulation relation. We distinguish the following cases:

- Let $p \xrightarrow{a} q$, for some $a \in X$, and $p\mathcal{R} \circ \mathcal{R}'p''$. By the definition of relation composition, there exists some p' such that $p\mathcal{R}p'$ and $p'\mathcal{R}'p''$. Since $\mathcal{R}$ and $\mathcal{R}'$ are XY-simulation relations, we have $p' \xrightarrow{a} q'$, $p'' \xrightarrow{a} q''$, and $q\mathcal{R} \circ \mathcal{R}'q''$, for some q', q''.
- Let $p'' \xrightarrow{a} q''$, for some $a \in Y$, and $p\mathcal{R} \circ \mathcal{R}'p''$. Similar to the previous case.

The proof of Items **2.**, **3.**, and **4.** are straightforward from Definition 2.   □

Definition 3 (Modal Characterization of XY-simulation). *Let $\Phi_{X,Y}$ be the set of modal formulas generated by the following grammar:*

$$\Phi_{X,Y} ::= \bigwedge_{i \in I} \varphi_i \mid \bigvee_{i \in I} \varphi_i \mid \langle a \rangle \varphi \mid [b]\varphi \qquad (a \in X, b \in Y).$$

The semantics of a formula $\varphi \in \Phi_{X,Y}$ is inductively defined in the standard way, i.e.,

$$p \models \bigwedge_{i \in I} \varphi_i \iff \forall_{i \in I} \ p \models \varphi_i \qquad\qquad p \models \bigvee_{i \in I} \varphi_i \iff \exists_{i \in I} \ p \models \varphi_i$$

$$p \models \langle a \rangle \varphi \iff \exists_q \ p \xrightarrow{a} q \wedge q \models \varphi \qquad p \models [a]\varphi \iff \forall_q \ p \xrightarrow{a} q \Rightarrow q \models \varphi \ .$$

Note that $\top = \bigwedge_\emptyset$ and $\bot = \bigvee_\emptyset$. Furthermore, we let $\Phi = \Phi_{\mathcal{A},\mathcal{A}}$ and $\varphi_1 \vee \varphi_2 = \bigvee_{i \in \{1,2\}} \varphi_i$. For any two formulas $\varphi, \varphi' \in \Phi$, we define $\varphi \Rightarrow \varphi' = neg(\varphi) \vee \varphi'$, where $neg : \Phi \rightarrow \Phi$ is a function that encodes negation in the logic, by pushing negation through conjunction, disjunction, and the modalities in the standard way.

Theorem 1. $p \preceq_{X,Y} q \iff \forall_{\varphi \in \Phi_{X,Y}} \ p \models \varphi \Rightarrow q \models \varphi.$

Proof. Standard (see [11]).   □

2.2   Transition System Specifications

In this section, we recall some basic concepts that are used in the meta-theory of SOS. Regarding the notions treated in this section and the next one, we refer to [3,19] for more details, examples and results.

Definition 4 (Terms and Signatures). *Let $\mathbb{V}$ be an infinite set of variables with $|\mathbb{V}| \geq |\mathcal{A}|$. A signature is a collection Σ of function symbols $f \notin \mathbb{V}$ equipped with a function $ar : \Sigma \to \mathbb{N}$ denoting their arity. The set $\mathbb{T}(\Sigma)$ of terms over signature Σ is defined as follows:*

- *$\mathbb{V} \subseteq \mathbb{T}(\Sigma)$,*
- *if $f \in \Sigma$ and $t_1, \cdots, t_{ar(f)} \in \mathbb{T}(\Sigma)$ then $f(t_1, \cdots, t_{ar(f)}) \in \mathbb{T}(\Sigma)$.*

A *constant* term $c()$ is denoted by c. Let $\mathbf{var}(t)$ denote the set of variables that occur in term t. Let $T(\Sigma) = \{t \mid \mathbf{var}(t) = \emptyset\}$ denote the set of *closed* terms. A *(closed) Σ-substitution* σ is a total function from the set of variables $\mathbb{V}$ to (closed) terms $(T(\Sigma))$ $\mathbb{T}(\Sigma)$.

Definition 5 (Transition System Specifications). *Let Σ be a signature. A positive Σ-literal is an expression of the form $t \xrightarrow{a} t'$ with $t, t' \in \mathbb{T}(\Sigma)$ and $a \in \mathcal{A}$. A negative Σ-literal is an expression of the form $t \xrightarrow{a}\!\!\!\!\!/\;\; $ with $t \in \mathbb{T}(\Sigma)$ and $a \in \mathcal{A}$. A transition rule (or simply a rule) over Σ is an expression of the form $\frac{H}{\alpha}$ with H a set of Σ-literals (whose elements are called the premises of the rule) and α a Σ-literal (called the conclusion of the rule). Furthermore, the left- and the right-hand side (if any) of the conclusion of a rule are called the source and the target of the rule, respectively. A transition system specification (TSS) over Σ is a collection of rules over Σ. A TSS is standard if all its rules have positive conclusions and positive if moreover all premises of its rules are also positive.*

For each literal α of the form $t \xrightarrow{a} t'$ $(t \xrightarrow{a}\!\!\!\!\!/\;\;)$, the action label of α, denoted by $action(\alpha)$, is defined to be a. For each two terms t, t', literals $t \xrightarrow{a} t'$ and $t \xrightarrow{a}\!\!\!\!\!/\;\; $ deny each other.

A TSS is meant to define an LTS; however, in the presence of negative literals, this is not straightforward. To start with, we first recall the definition of irredundant proof, by Bloom et al. [9], which corresponds to the intuitive notion of proof from a given set of hypotheses.

Definition 6 (Irredundant Proof). *Let P be a TSS over a signature Σ. An irredundant proof of a transition rule $\frac{H}{\alpha}$ from P is a well-founded, upwardly branching tree with the nodes labeled by Σ-literals, and some of the leaves marked as "hypotheses", such that:*

- *the root is labeled by α.*
- *H is the set of labels of the hypotheses, and*
- *if β is the label of a node $\star$ which is not a hypothesis and K is the set of labels of the nodes directly above $\star$, then there is a transition rule $\frac{K'}{\beta'}$ in P and substitution σ such that $\sigma(K') = K$ and $\sigma(\beta') = \beta$.*

A proof of $\frac{K}{\alpha}$ from P is an irredundant proof of $\frac{H}{\alpha}$ from P with $H \subseteq K$.

Note that the term "irredundant" highlights that the set of literals marked as hypotheses in the proof corresponds exactly to the set of premises of the proven rule. In other words, irredundantly provable rules contain no junk literals (i.e., literals not used in the proof tree) among their premises.

Next, we use the notion of irredundant proof to define the LTS associated with a TSS. This is achieved through the following notion of well-supported proof [23].

Definition 7. *Let P be a standard TSS over a signature Σ. A* well-supported proof *of a closed literal α from P is a well-founded, upwardly branching tree with the nodes labeled by closed Σ-literals, such that the root is labeled by α and if β is the label of a node $\star$ and K is the set of labels of the nodes directly above $\star$, then*

- *either there is a rule $\frac{K'}{\beta'}$ from P and closed substitution σ such that $\sigma(K') = K \wedge \sigma(\beta') = \beta$,*
- *or β is negative and for every set N of closed negative literals such that $\frac{N}{\gamma}$ is irredundantly provable from P for γ a closed literal denying β, a literal in K denies one in N.*

A well-supported proof *of α from P (if it exists) is denoted by $P \vdash_{ws} \alpha$.*

In order to unequivocally define an LTS, a TSS has to be complete, as defined below.

Definition 8 (Complete TSSs). *A standard TSS is* complete *if and only if for any closed literal $t \xrightarrow{a}$, either $P \vdash_{ws} t \xrightarrow{a} t'$ for some closed term t', or $P \vdash_{ws} t \xnrightarrow{a}$.*

It is often possible to establish completeness by using a syntactic measure on rules, called stratification [10]. All practical examples of TSSs are standard and complete and hence, almost all SOS meta-theorems are formed around complete TSSs. In this paper, we also follow this tradition and formulate our results for complete TSSs.

2.3   Rule Formats

The goal of a rule format is to establish a semantic property via syntactic constraints on rules. One of the most important semantic properties addressed by rule formats is compositionality or (pre-)congruence, defined below.

Definition 9 (Pre-congruence). *Let P be a TSS over signature Σ. A preorder $\sqsubseteq \subseteq T(\Sigma) \times T(\Sigma)$ on closed terms is a* pre-congruence *if and only if for all operators $f \in \Sigma$ and closed terms $t_1, t'_1, \cdots, t_{ar(f)}, t'_{ar(f)} \in T(\Sigma)$, we have that $t_i \sqsubseteq t'_i$ (for $i \in [1, ar(f)]$) implies $f(t_1, \cdots, t_{ar(f)}) \sqsubseteq f(t'_1, \cdots, t'_{ar(f)})$.*

A rule format that establishes pre-congruence for simulation (and congruence for bisimulation) is the following ntyft/ntyxt format [14].

Definition 10 (ntyft/ntyxt format). *An* ntytt *rule is a transition rule in which the right-hand sides of positive premises are variables that are all distinct and do not occur in the source of the conclusion. An ntytt rule is an* ntyxt *rule if the source of its conclusion is a variable and an* ntyft *rule if the source of its conclusion contains exactly one function symbol applied to distinct variables. An ntytt rule (resp. an ntyft rule) is an* nxytt *rule (resp. an* nxyft *rule) if the left-hand sides of its premises are variables. A TSS is in the* ntyft/ntyxt *format if it contains only ntyft and ntyxt rules.*

The ready simulation format, defined below, guarantees pre-congruence for ready simulation. Moreover, it is the basis of the modal decomposition technique presented in [9,13] and hence, also serves as the basis of our approach.

Definition 11 (Ready simulation format). *A transition rule has no* looka-head *if the variables occurring in the right-hand sides of its positive premises do not occur in the left-hand sides of its premises. A TSS is in the* ready sim-ulation format *if it is in the ntyft/ntyxt format and its transition rules have no lookahead.*

SOS rules are meant to define a flow of variable valuations from the source of the conclusion to the premises and eventually to the target of the conclusion. However, some rules may feature free variables whose valuations do not depend on the source of the conclusion. Rules without free variables and lookahead are called decent [9].

Definition 12 (Decent rule). *A variable occurring in a transition rule is* free *iff it does not occur in the source of the conclusion nor in the right-hand sides of the positive premises of the rule. A transition rule is* decent *if it has no lookahead and does not contain free variables.*

Rules with free variables can always be replaced with infinitely many decent rules, by replacing the free variables with all their possible closed valuations. The following lemma captures this intuition. According to the following lemma, focusing on decent rules in the proofs does not impose any extra theoretical constraint.

Lemma 2 ([9]). *Let P be a standard TSS in the ready simulation format. Then there is a TSS P^+ in the decent ntyft format such that any closed literal α is provable from P^+ if and only if $P \vdash_{ws} \alpha$.*

Definition 13. *A P-ruloid is a decent nxytt rule that is irredundantly provable from P^+. Lastly, the set of all P-ruloids of a given TSS P is denoted by $\bar{P}$.*

For the results to come, we need the following lemma. Intuitively, it states that for any TSS P in the ready simulation format, there is a well-supported proof of a positive closed literal α if and only if there is an irredundant proof of a P-ruloid such that the closed literal α is a closed substitution instance of the ruloid.

Lemma 3 ([9]). *Let P be a TSS in the ready simulation format. For any term $t \in \mathbb{T}(\Sigma)$, closed term t', and a closed substitution σ, we have $P \vdash_{ws} \sigma(t) \xrightarrow{a} t'$ iff there are a P-ruloid $\dfrac{H}{t \xrightarrow{a} u}$ and a closed substitution σ' such that $P \vdash_{ws} \sigma'(\alpha)$ (for every $\alpha \in H$), $\sigma'(t) = \sigma(t)$, and $\sigma'(u) = t'$.*

3   Deriving a Pre-congruence Format

The basic machinery developed in [9] to derive a pre-congruence format works in two steps. First, a modal formula $\varphi \in \Phi$ for an open term t is decomposed into a choice of modal formulas $\psi(x)$ for variables x such that $\sigma(t)$ satisfies φ if and only if for one of those ψ's and all the variables x in t, $\sigma(x)$ satisfies $\psi(x)$ (Theorem 2). This is achieved by considering the provable transition rules for term t (given that such rules are in a given rule format.) Secondly a pre-congruence format for a pre-order is devised such that if a modal formula belongs to characterizing logic of the pre-order, then the resulting decomposed modal formulas also belong to the same characterizing logic (Theorem 3).

3.1   Modal Decomposition

Definition 14. *Let P be a standard TSS over Σ in the ready simulation format. The decomposition function $\cdot^{-1} : \mathbb{T}(\Sigma) \to (\Phi \to 2^{V \to \Phi})$ for a term is defined in the following way:*

1. $\psi \in t^{-1}(\langle a \rangle \varphi)$ iff

$$\psi(x) = \bigvee_{\frac{H}{t \xrightarrow{a} u} \in \bar{P}} \bigvee_{\chi \in u^{-1}(\varphi)} \left(\chi(x) \wedge \bigwedge_{(x \xrightarrow{c} \!\!\!/\,) \in H} [c] \bot \wedge \bigwedge_{(x \xrightarrow{b} y) \in H} \langle b \rangle \chi(y) \right),$$

   whenever $x \in \mathbf{var}(t)$. For $x \notin \mathbf{var}(t)$, we let $\psi(x) = \top$.

2. $\psi \in t^{-1}([a]\varphi)$ iff $\psi(x)$ (for $x \in \mathbf{var}(t)$) is defined to be

$$\bigwedge_{\frac{H}{t \xrightarrow{a} u} \in \bar{P}} \left[\left(\bigwedge_{(x \xrightarrow{c} \!\!\!/\,) \in H} [c] \bot \wedge \bigwedge_{(x \xrightarrow{b} y) \in H} \langle b \rangle \top \right) \Rightarrow \right.$$
$$\left. \left(\bigvee_{\chi \in u^{-1}(\varphi)} \chi(x) \wedge \bigwedge_{(x \xrightarrow{b} y) \in H} [b] \bigvee_{\chi \in u^{-1}(\varphi)} \chi(y) \right) \right].$$

   As in the previous case, we let $\psi(x) = \top$ for $x \notin \mathbf{var}(t)$.

3. $\psi \in t^{-1}(\bigwedge_{i \in I} \varphi_i)$ iff $\psi(x) = \bigwedge_{i \in I} \psi_i(x)$, where $\psi_i \in t^{-1}(\varphi_i)$ for $i \in I$.

4. $\psi \in t^{-1}(\bigvee_{i \in I} \varphi_i)$ iff $\psi(x) = \bigvee_{i \in I} \psi_i(x)$, where $\psi_i \in t^{-1}(\varphi_i)$ for $i \in I$.

Note that item **2.** has not been treated in the past decomposition approaches [9,13]. It concerns the semantic clause of the box modality $[a]\varphi$, i.e., for any closed terms t, t', if there is a transition $t \xrightarrow{a} t'$, then t' must satisfy φ.

Theorem 2. *Let P be a complete TSS in the ready simulation format over the signature Σ. Then, for any term $t \in \mathbb{T}(\Sigma)$, closed substitution σ, and a formula $\varphi \in \Phi$, we have $\sigma(t) \models \varphi \iff \exists_{\psi \in t^{-1}(\varphi)} \forall_{x \in \mathbf{var}(t)} \; \sigma(x) \models \psi(x)$.*

Proof. By structural induction on φ. In the remainder, we only consider the case when $\varphi = [a]\varphi'$. The proof of the remaining cases is the same as the proof given in [13, Theorem 2].

($\Leftarrow$) Let $\sigma(t) \xrightarrow{a} t'$ for some closed term t'. We need to show that $t' \models \varphi'$. We begin by using Lemma 3 to find a P-ruloid of the form:

$$\frac{\{x \xrightarrow{b_i} y_i \mid i \in I_x \wedge x \in \mathbf{var}(t)\} \cup \{x \xrightarrow{c_j} \mid j \in J_x \wedge x \in \mathbf{var}(t)\}}{t \xrightarrow{a} u} \tag{1}$$

and a closed substitution σ' such that $\sigma(t) = \sigma'(t)$, $P \vdash_{\mathrm{ws}} \sigma'(H)$, and $\sigma'(u) = t'$. Since $\exists_{\psi \in t^{-1}(\varphi)} \forall_{x \in \mathbf{var}(t)} \; \sigma(x) \models \psi(x)$, by Definition 14, we have (for every $x \in \mathbf{var}(t)$):

$$\sigma(x) \models \left(\bigwedge_{j \in J_x} [c_j]\bot \wedge \bigwedge_{i \in I_x} \langle b_i \rangle \top \right) \Rightarrow \left(\bigvee_{\chi \in u^{-1}(\varphi')} \chi(x) \wedge \bigwedge_{i \in I_x} [b_i] \bigvee_{\chi \in u^{-1}(\varphi')} \chi(y) \right). \tag{2}$$

We claim that $\forall_{z \in \mathbf{var}(u)} \; \sigma'(z) \models \bigvee_{\chi \in u^{-1}(\varphi')} \chi(z)$. Let $z \in \mathbf{var}(u)$. We distinguish the following cases depending on the position of z in the decent P-ruloid:

- Let $z = x$ for some $x \in \mathbf{var}(t)$. Using $\sigma(x) = \sigma'(x)$ and $P \vdash_{\mathrm{ws}} \sigma'(H)$ in (2) we get $\sigma'(x) \models \bigvee_{\chi \in u^{-1}(\varphi')} \chi(x)$.
- Let $z = y_i$ for some $i \in I_x$ and $x \in \mathbf{var}(t)$. Then, using $\sigma(x) = \sigma'(x)$ and $P \vdash_{\mathrm{ws}} \sigma'(H)$ in (2) we have $\sigma'(x) \models [b_i] \bigvee_{\chi \in u^{-1}(\varphi')} \chi(y_i)$ and $P \vdash_{\mathrm{ws}} \sigma'(x) \xrightarrow{b_i} \sigma'(y_i)$. Therefore, from the semantics of box modality we obtain $\sigma'(y_i) \models \bigvee_{\chi \in u^{-1}(\varphi')} \chi(y_i)$.

This proves the claim. Fix $\bar{\chi}(z) = \bigvee_{\chi \in u^{-1}(\varphi')} \chi(z)$ for every $z \in \mathbf{var}(u)$. Since Definition 14 is closed under arbitrary disjunctions, we know that $\bar{\chi} \in u^{-1}(\varphi')$. Moreover, we have $\sigma'(z) \models \bar{\chi}(z)$ (for every $z \in \mathbf{var}(u)$). Thus, by the induction hypothesis we obtain $\sigma'(u) \models \varphi'$.

($\Rightarrow$) Let $\sigma(t) \models [a]\varphi'$. Suppose there are no P-ruloids of the form $\frac{H}{t \xrightarrow{a} u}$. Then, by Definition 14 we have $\psi(x) = \bigwedge_\emptyset = \top$ for every $x \in \mathbf{var}(t)$. Since every closed term satisfies $\top$, we have $\sigma(x) \models \psi(x)$ for every $x \in \mathbf{var}(t)$ as required.

Now suppose there is a P-ruloid of the form given in (1). It suffices to show that the condition in (2) holds. Assume that $\sigma(x) \models \bigwedge_{j \in J_x} [c_j]\bot \wedge \bigwedge_{i \in I_x} \langle b_i \rangle \top$. Then, the completeness of P together with the semantics of box modality guarantee that $P \vdash_{\mathrm{ws}} \sigma(x) \xrightarrow{c_j}$ (for every $j \in J_x$). Furthermore, from the semantics of diamond modality, for every $i \in I_x$, we find some closed term t_i such that $P \vdash_{\mathrm{ws}} \sigma(x) \xrightarrow{b_i} t_i$. Thus, we can define a closed substitution σ' such that $\sigma(x) = \sigma'(x)$ (for $x \in \mathbf{var}(t)$), $\sigma'(y_i) = t_i$ (for $i \in I_x$). Note that σ' is well-defined because the P-ruloids have no lookahead and all y_i's are distinct (i.e., $\forall_{i,i' \in I_x} \; i \neq i' \Rightarrow$

$y_i \neq y_{i'}$). By Lemma 3, we obtain $\sigma(t) \xrightarrow{a} \sigma'(u)$. Thus, $\sigma'(u) \models \varphi'$ because $\sigma(t) \models [a]\varphi'$. From the induction hypothesis we obtain

$$\exists_{\chi \in u^{-1}(\varphi')} \forall_{z \in \mathbf{var}(u)} \; \sigma'(z) \models \chi(z). \tag{3}$$

From (3) we have, for every $x \in \mathbf{var}(t)$, $\sigma(x) \models \bigvee_{\chi \in u^{-1}(\varphi')} \chi(x)$. Thus, it suffices to show that, for every $x \in \mathbf{var}(t)$, we have $\sigma(x) \models \bigwedge_{i \in I_x} [b_i] \bigvee_{\chi \in u^{-1}(\varphi')} \chi(y_i)$.

Let $\sigma(x) \xrightarrow{b_i} t''$ for some $i \in I_x$. Then, we define a closed substitution σ'' such that $\sigma(t) = \sigma''(t)$, $\sigma''(y_i) = t''$, and $\sigma''(y_{i'}) = \sigma'(y_{i'})$ (for $i' \in I_x$ such that $i \neq i'$). By repeating the same arguments (from above) to derive $P \vdash_{\mathrm{ws}} \sigma(t) \xrightarrow{a} \sigma'(u)$, we can find $P \vdash_{\mathrm{ws}} \sigma(t) \xrightarrow{a} \sigma''(u)$. Thus, $\sigma''(u) \models \varphi'$ because $\sigma(t) \models [a]\varphi'$. We can again instantiate the induction hypothesis to find a $\chi'' \in u^{-1}(\varphi')$ such that $\forall_{z \in \mathbf{var}(u)} \sigma''(z) \models \chi''(z)$. Therefore, $\sigma''(y_i) \models \bigvee_{\chi \in u^{-1}(\varphi')} \chi(y_i)$ and we can conclude that $\sigma(x) \models [b_i] \bigvee_{\chi \in u^{-1}(\varphi')} \chi(y_i)$.

We have shown for every P-ruloid $\dfrac{H}{t \xrightarrow{a} u}$ and for every $x \in \mathbf{var}(t)$, if $\sigma(x) \models \bigwedge_{(x \xrightarrow{c}\!\!\!/) \in H} [c] \bot$ and $\sigma(x) \models \bigwedge_{(x \xrightarrow{b} y) \in H} \langle b \rangle \top$ then $\sigma(x) \models \bigvee_{\chi \in u^{-1}(\varphi')} \chi(x)$ and $\sigma(x) \models \bigwedge_{x \xrightarrow{b} y \in H} [b] \bigvee_{\chi \in u^{-1}(\varphi')} \chi(y)$. Therefore, the formula $\psi(x)$ as defined in Definition 14(2) is satisfied by $\sigma(x)$. $\qquad\square$

3.2 XY-simulation Format

Definition 15. *Given a set H of premises, we write H^+ and H^- to denote the set of all positive and negative literals in H, respectively. A rule $\dfrac{H}{t \xrightarrow{a} u}$ is in the XY-simulation format iff it is in the ready simulation format and the following conditions hold:*

1. *If $a \in X$ then*
   (a) *$\forall_\alpha \, (\alpha \in H^+ \Rightarrow action(\alpha) \in X)$*
   (b) *$\forall_\alpha \, (\alpha \in H^- \Rightarrow action(\alpha) \in Y)$*
2. *If $a \in Y$ then*
   (a) *$\forall_\alpha \, (\alpha \in H^+ \Rightarrow action(\alpha) \in Y)$*
   (b) *$\forall_\alpha \, (\alpha \in H^- \Rightarrow action(\alpha) \in X)$*

A TSS is in the XY-simulation format iff all its rules are in the XY-simulation format.

Lemma 4. *If a TSS is in the XY-simulation format, then all its P-ruloids are.*

Due to space limitations, we do not present the complete poof of Lemma 4. It goes by an induction on the depth of the irredundant proof for the P-ruloid at hand.

Theorem 3. *Let P be a standard TSS in the XY-simulation format and Σ be its signature. If $t \in \mathbb{T}(\Sigma)$, $\varphi \in \Phi_{X,Y}$, and $\psi \in t^{-1}(\varphi)$ then $\forall_{x \in \mathbf{var}(t)} \psi(x) \in \Phi_{X,Y}$.*

Proof. We prove this theorem by structural induction on φ and consider the cases when $\varphi = \langle a \rangle \varphi'$ and $\varphi = [a]\varphi'$. In the following, due to Lemma 4, we use the fact that every derived P-ruloid is in the XY-simulation format, whenever P is in the XY-simulation format.

(1) Let $\varphi = \langle a \rangle \varphi'$ for some $a \in X$. By Definition 14, we have

$$\psi(x) = \left(\chi(x) \wedge \bigwedge_{(x \xrightarrow{c}\!\!\!\!\!/\;)\in H} [c]\bot \wedge \bigwedge_{(x \xrightarrow{b} y)\in H} \langle b \rangle \chi(y) \right) ,$$

for some P-ruloid $\frac{H}{t \xrightarrow{a} u}$ and a decomposition function $\chi \in u^{-1}(\varphi')$. Hence, by the induction hypothesis $\chi(z) \in \Phi_{X,Y}$ (for $z \in \mathbf{var}(u)$). It suffices to show that $\forall_{(x \xrightarrow{c}\!\!\!\!\!/\;)\in H}\, c \in Y$ and $\forall_{x \xrightarrow{b} y \in H}\, b \in X$.

- Let $(x \xrightarrow{c}\!\!\!\!\!/\;) \in H$. Then, Definition 15(1b) ensures that $c \in Y$.
- Let $x \xrightarrow{b} y \in H$. Then, Definition 15(1a) ensures that $b \in X$.

(2) Let $\varphi = [a]\varphi'$ for some $a \in Y$. By Definition 14, we have (for $x \in \mathbf{var}(t)$):

$$\psi(x) = \bigwedge_{\frac{H}{t \xrightarrow{a} u} \in \bar{P}} \left(\bigvee_{(x \xrightarrow{c}\!\!\!\!\!/\;)\in H} \langle c \rangle \top \vee \bigvee_{(x \xrightarrow{b} y)\in H} [b]\bot \vee \right.$$
$$\left. \left(\bigvee_{\chi \in u^{-1}(\varphi')} \chi(x) \wedge \bigwedge_{(x \xrightarrow{b} y)\in H} [b] \bigvee_{\chi \in u^{-1}(\varphi')} \chi(y) \right) \right).$$

By the induction hypothesis we have, for every $\chi \in u^{-1}(\varphi'), z \in \mathbf{var}(u)$, that $\chi(z)$ is a formula in $\Phi_{X,Y}$; therefore $\bigvee_{\chi \in u^{-1}(\varphi')} \chi(z)$ is a formula in $\Phi_{X,Y}$. Thus, it suffices to show that $\forall_{x \xrightarrow{b} y \in H}\, b \in X \Rightarrow b \in Y$ and $\forall_{(x \xrightarrow{c}\!\!\!\!\!/\;)\in H}\, c \in Y \Rightarrow c \in X$, which follow directly from conditions (2a) and (2b) of Definition 15, respectively. $\square$

Corollary 1 (Main Result). *Let P be a complete TSS in the XY-simulation format over the signature Σ. Then, for any term $t \in \mathbb{T}(\Sigma)$ and closed substitutions σ, σ' we have:* $\forall_{x \in \mathbf{var}(t)}\, \sigma(x) \preceq_{X,Y} \sigma'(x) \implies \sigma(t) \preceq_{X,Y} \sigma'(t).$

Proof. It suffices to show that if $\sigma(t) \models \varphi$ then $\sigma'(t) \models \varphi$, for all $\varphi \in \Phi_{X,Y}$.

$$\sigma(t) \models \varphi \implies \exists_{\psi \in t^{-1}(\varphi) \cap \Phi_{X,Y}} \forall_{x \in \mathbf{var}(t)}\, \sigma(x) \models \psi(x) \quad \text{(Theorem 2 and 3)}$$
$$\implies \exists_{\psi \in t^{-1}(\varphi) \cap \Phi_{X,Y}} \forall_{x \in \mathbf{var}(t)}\, \sigma'(x) \models \psi(x) \quad (\because \forall_{x \in \mathbf{var}(t)}\, \sigma(x) \preceq_{X,Y} \sigma'(x))$$
$$\implies \sigma'(t) \models \varphi \quad \text{(Theorem 2).}$$

4   Applications

In this section, we review the different incarnations of XY-simulation relation present in the literature and assert their pre-congruence property with respect to some well-known operators from the field of process algebra. To start with, through the following proposition, we establish a link between XY-similarity and some other notions of behavioral pre-order and equivalence.

Proposition 1. *Let* $(\mathbb{P}, \mathcal{A}, \rightarrow)$ *be an arbitrary LTS. Then, the following statements hold:*

1. *Relation* $\preceq_{\mathcal{A},\mathcal{A}}$ *is the bisimilarity relation in the sense of [20].*
2. *Relation* $\preceq_{\mathcal{A},\emptyset}$ *is the similarity relation in the sense of [18].*
3. *If* $X \subseteq \mathcal{A}$, *then the relation* $\preceq_{\mathcal{A},X}$ *is the partial bisimilarity relation in the sense of [6].*
4. *If the set of actions are partitioned into two sets of may actions* $\mathcal{A}_\Diamond$ *and must actions* $\mathcal{A}_\Box$, *then the relation* $\preceq_{\mathcal{A}_\Diamond,\mathcal{A}_\Box}$ *is the modal refinement relation in the sense of [16].*
5. *If the set of actions are partitioned into two sets of input actions* $\mathcal{I}$ *and output actions* $\mathcal{O}$, *then the relation* $\preceq_{\mathcal{O},\mathcal{I}}$ *is the alternating similarity relation in the sense of [4].*

In the following subsection, we show how our rule format can be applied to obtain compositionality results for various process calculi.

4.1 Partial Bisimulation

In [6], Baeten et al. used the partial bisimulation pre-order to define controllability of nondeterministic processes. (Controllability is a central notion in the supervisory control theory.) To this end, they defined a basic sequential process algebra $\mathrm{BSP}_|(\mathcal{A}_\downarrow, B)$ (for some fixed subset $B \subseteq \mathcal{A}$ and $\mathcal{A}_\downarrow = \mathcal{A} \uplus \{\downarrow\}^1$) and provided a ground-complete axiomatization of partial bisimulation pre-order. The signature of process terms Σ in $\mathrm{BSP}_|(\mathcal{A}_\downarrow, B)$ is given below:

$$\Sigma = \{\ (\mathbf{0}, 0)\ ,\ (\mathbf{1}, 0)\ ,\ (a., 1)_{a \in \mathcal{A}}\ ,\ (+, 2)\ ,\ (|, 2)\ \}.$$

Constant $\mathbf{0}$, called *inaction*, denotes that no actions can be performed and can only deadlock, whereas constant $\mathbf{1}$ denotes successful termination. The family of unary operators $a.\_$ (for $a \in \mathcal{A}$), called *action prefix* operator, expresses that a process can initially perform a and then the argument process takes over. Binary operator $\_ + \_$, known as the *alternative composition* operator, specifies the choice between two process terms. Lastly, the *synchronization parallel composition* is denoted by $\_|\_$ and specifies that the two arguments synchronize on common actions. The formal semantics for each operator in Σ is given in Table 1 by means of a standard TSS that is in the ready simulation format.

By a quick inspection of the labels, we note that all rules in Table 1 are in the $\mathcal{A}_\downarrow B$-simulation format, the $\mathcal{A}_\downarrow \emptyset$-simulation format, and the $\mathcal{A}_\downarrow \mathcal{A}_\downarrow$-simulation format. Therefore, we obtain the following (pre-)congruence results for free.

Corollary 2. *Partial bisimilarity pre-order* $\preceq_{\mathcal{A}_\downarrow, B} \subseteq T(\Sigma) \times T(\Sigma)$ *is a pre-congruence relation for all closed terms in process algebra* $\mathrm{BSP}_|(\mathcal{A}_\downarrow, B)$. *Moreover, similarity pre-order* $\preceq_{\mathcal{A}_\downarrow, \emptyset}$ *and bisimilarity equivalence* $\preceq_{\mathcal{A}_\downarrow, \mathcal{A}_\downarrow}$ *are also pre-congruence and congruence relations, respectively, for all constructs of process algebra* $\mathrm{BSP}_|(\mathcal{A}_\downarrow, B)$.

---

[1] We employ $\downarrow$ (by a coding proposed by Baeten and Verhoef in [7]) as a special action label modeling successful termination.

Table 1. Operational rules of $BSP_|(\mathcal{A}_\downarrow, B)$, where $a \in \mathcal{A}, a_\downarrow \in \mathcal{A} \cup \{\downarrow\}$.

$$1 \xrightarrow{\downarrow} 1 \quad (1) \qquad a.x \xrightarrow{a} x \quad (2) \qquad \frac{x \xrightarrow{a_\downarrow} x'}{x + y \xrightarrow{a_\downarrow} x'} \quad (3)$$

$$\frac{y \xrightarrow{a_\downarrow} y'}{x + y \xrightarrow{a_\downarrow} y'} \quad (4) \qquad \frac{x \xrightarrow{a_\downarrow} x' \quad y \xrightarrow{a_\downarrow} y'}{x|y \xrightarrow{a_\downarrow} x'|y'} \quad (5)$$

4.2 Modal Refinement

Next, we consider the framework of modal specifications [15,16]. Let Act be the set of action labels ranged over by $\mathbf{a}, \mathbf{b}, \cdots$. Construct the set of *may* and *must* actions as: $\mathcal{A}_\Diamond = Act \times \{\Diamond\}$ and $\mathcal{A}_\Box = Act \times \{\Box\}$. We write $\mathbf{a}_\Diamond$ and $\mathbf{a}_\Box$ to denote the elements $(\mathbf{a}, \Diamond) \in \mathcal{A}_\Diamond$ and $(\mathbf{a}, \Box) \in \mathcal{A}_\Box$, respectively. Let $\mathcal{A} = \mathcal{A}_\Diamond \cup \mathcal{A}_\Box$ and consider the following signature:

$$\Sigma_m = \{ \ (\mathbf{0}, 0) \ , \ (a., 1)_{a \in \mathcal{A}} \ , \ (+, 2) \ , \ (|, 2) \ , \ (\vee, 2) \ , \ (\wedge, 2) \ \}.$$

The formal semantics of the operators in $\Sigma \cap \Sigma_m$ remains the same in this new setting, whereas the semantics of conjunction and disjunction is given by the rules in Table 2.

Table 2. Operational rules for $\vee$ and $\wedge$, taken from [15]

$$\frac{x \xrightarrow{\mathbf{a}_\Diamond} x'}{x \vee y \xrightarrow{\mathbf{a}_\Diamond} x'} \quad (6) \qquad \frac{y \xrightarrow{\mathbf{a}_\Diamond} y'}{x \vee y \xrightarrow{\mathbf{a}_\Diamond} y'} \quad (7) \qquad \frac{x \xrightarrow{\mathbf{a}_\Box} x' \quad y \xrightarrow{\mathbf{a}_\Box} y'}{x \vee y \xrightarrow{\mathbf{a}_\Box} x' \vee y'} \quad (8)$$

$$\frac{x \xrightarrow{\mathbf{a}_\Box} x'}{x \wedge y \xrightarrow{\mathbf{a}_\Box} x'} \quad (9) \qquad \frac{y \xrightarrow{\mathbf{a}_\Box} y'}{x \wedge y \xrightarrow{\mathbf{a}_\Box} y'} \quad (10) \qquad \frac{x \xrightarrow{\mathbf{a}_\Diamond} x' \quad y \xrightarrow{\mathbf{a}_\Diamond} y'}{x \wedge y \xrightarrow{\mathbf{a}_\Diamond} x' \wedge y'} \quad (11)$$

Note that the process terms induced by our operational rules are not admissible (consistent) in the sense of [16], i.e., the set of must transitions are not necessary included in the set of may transitions. In essence, the transition system induced by our algebra corresponds to the mixed transition system, where the consistency assumption is dropped.

By inspection we note that all the rules in Table 1 and Table 2 are in $\mathcal{A}_\Diamond\mathcal{A}_\Box$-simulation format. Therefore, we obtain the following pre-congruence result for free.

Corollary 3. *The modal refinement pre-order $\preceq_{\mathcal{A}_\Diamond, \mathcal{A}_\Box} \subseteq T(\Sigma_m) \times T(\Sigma_m)$ is a pre-congruence relation. Moreover, the $\mathcal{A}_\Diamond\mathcal{A}_\Box$-simulation format subsumes the static constructor format given by Larsen and Thomsen [16, Section 4].*

Next consider the following modified operational rules of conjunction $\wedge'$ taken from [17]. Note that, in [17], the conjunction is defined between any two arbitrary interface automata [12] and we interpret the input actions as must actions and the output actions as may actions.

$$\frac{x \xrightarrow{\mathbf{a}\square} x' \quad y \xrightarrow{\mathbf{a}\square} \!\!\!\!\!\!\diagup}{x \wedge' y \xrightarrow{\mathbf{a}\square} x'} \quad (9') \qquad\qquad \frac{y \xrightarrow{\mathbf{a}\square} y' \quad x \xrightarrow{\mathbf{a}\square} \!\!\!\!\!\!\diagup}{x \wedge' y \xrightarrow{\mathbf{a}\square} y'} \quad (10')$$

$$\frac{x \xrightarrow{\mathbf{a}\square} x' \quad y \xrightarrow{\mathbf{a}\square} y'}{x \wedge' y \xrightarrow{\mathbf{a}\square} x' \wedge' y'} \quad (11') \qquad\qquad \frac{x \xrightarrow{\mathbf{a}\diamond} x' \quad y \xrightarrow{\mathbf{a}\diamond} y'}{x \wedge' y \xrightarrow{\mathbf{a}\diamond} x' \wedge' y'} \quad (11'')$$

Clearly, rules $(9')$ and $(10')$ are not in the $\mathcal{A}_\diamond\mathcal{A}_\square$-simulation format because they violate condition (2b) of Definition 15. Next, by a counterexample, we show that the modal refinement pre-order is not a pre-congruence for the modified conjunction operator $\wedge'$.

Example 1. Consider the following process terms: $t = \mathbf{a}_\square.\mathbf{b}_\square.0$, $t' = \mathbf{a}_\square.\mathbf{c}_\square.0$, and $\bar{t} = t + t'$. Clearly, $\bar{t} \preceq_{\mathcal{A}_\diamond,\mathcal{A}_\square} t$ and $\bar{t} \preceq_{\mathcal{A}_\diamond,\mathcal{A}_\square} t'$. However, $\bar{t} \wedge' \bar{t} \npreceq_{\mathcal{A}_\diamond,\mathcal{A}_\square} t \wedge' t'$.

5   Adequacy of XY-simulation Format

In this section, with the help of the following counterexamples, we motivate why the conditions of XY-simulation format are essential for the pre-congruence result. In particular, we show how dropping each of the conditions is sufficient for breaking pre-congruence.

Example 2. Consider the synchronous parallel composition parameterized with a partial function $\gamma : \mathcal{A} \times \mathcal{A} \to \mathcal{A}$ (called as *communication* function [5]) such that rule 5 is substituted by the following rules:

$$\frac{x \xrightarrow{a} x' \quad y \xrightarrow{b} y' \quad \gamma(a,b) \text{ is defined}}{x|_\gamma y \xrightarrow{\gamma(a,b)} x'|_\gamma y'} \quad (5') \qquad \frac{x \xrightarrow{\downarrow} x' \quad y \xrightarrow{\downarrow} y'}{x|_\gamma y \xrightarrow{\downarrow} x'|_\gamma y'} \quad (5'').$$

Let $\mathcal{A} = \{a, b\}$ and the communication function γ be defined as: $\gamma(b,b) = a$ and undefined otherwise. Clearly, the inequation $b.0 \preceq_{\{a\},\{b\}} a.0$ holds; however, $b.0|_\gamma b.0 \npreceq_{\{a\},\{b\}} a.0|_\gamma a.0$. We note that rule 5 of $|_\gamma$ violates Definition 15(1a). Similarly, by defining a communication function γ' as $\gamma(a,a) = b$ and undefined otherwise, we can see that $b.0|_{\gamma'} b.0 \npreceq_{\{a\},\{b\}} a.0|_{\gamma'} a.0$. Furthermore, we now note that rule 5 of $|_{\gamma'}$ violates Definition 15(2a).

Example 3. This example concerns negative premises. Consider the unary operator θ (called the *priority* operator) from TCP [5], which also comes with a partial ordering $<$ on the set of actions $\mathcal{A}$. Intuitively, the priority operator can execute an a-transition if the operand can execute an a-transition and no action with priority over a can be executed.

$$\frac{x \xrightarrow{a} x' \quad x \xrightarrow{b} \quad \text{for all } b \text{ with } a < b}{\theta(x) \xrightarrow{a} \theta(x')} \quad (12)$$

Clearly, the above rule is in the ready simulation format. Let $\mathcal{A} = \{a, b\}$ with $a < b$ and consider the process terms $a.\mathbf{0}, a.\mathbf{0} + b.\mathbf{0}$. It holds that $a.\mathbf{0} \preceq_{\mathcal{A}, \emptyset} a.\mathbf{0} + b.\mathbf{0}$; however, $\theta(a.\mathbf{0}) \npreceq_{\mathcal{A}, \emptyset} \theta(a.\mathbf{0} + b.\mathbf{0})$. We note that rule 12 of θ violates Definition 15(1b). Furthermore, since $\preceq_{\emptyset, X} = \preceq_{X, \emptyset}^{-1}$, the above counterexample also highlights the violation of Definition 15(2b).

6   Conclusions

In this paper, we proposed a pre-congruence rule format for XY-simulation. The rule format guarantees that once the SOS rules of a given language satisfy certain syntactic conditions, then XY-simulation is pre-congruence for the constructs of the language. We showed that the format is applicable to obtain compositionality results for different behavioral pre-orders and for different process calculi. We also showed that dropping each of the syntactic conditions imposed by the rule format can jeopardize compositionality.

We intend to exploit the results of this paper in order to obtain a rule format for input-output conformance (ioco) testing [22], which is a behavioral pre-order widely used as a basis for model-based testing. This will generalize the earlier compositionality results reported in [8], which only address a particular synchronization operator and the hiding (abstraction) operator.

References

1. Aarts, F., Vaandrager, F.W.: Learning I/O automata. In: Gastin, P., Laroussinie, F. (eds.) CONCUR 2010. LNCS, vol. 6269, pp. 71–85. Springer, Heidelberg (2010)
2. Aceto, L., Fábregas, I., de Frutos Escrig, D., Ingólfsdóttir, A., Palomino, M.: Relating modal refinements, covariant-contravariant simulations and partial bisimulations. In: Arbab, F., Sirjani, M. (eds.) FSEN 2011. LNCS, vol. 7141, pp. 268–283. Springer, Heidelberg (2012)
3. Aceto, L., Fokkink, W.J., Verhoef, C.: Structural operational semantics. In: Handbook of Process Algebra, Chapter 3, pp. 197–292. Elsevier (2001)
4. Alur, R., Henzinger, T.A., Kupferman, O., Vardi, M.Y.: Alternating refinement relations. In: Sangiorgi, D., de Simone, R. (eds.) CONCUR 1998. LNCS, vol. 1466, pp. 163–178. Springer, Heidelberg (1998)
5. Baeten, J.C.M., Basten, T., Reniers, M.A.: Process Algebra: Equational Theories of Communicating Processes. Cambridge University Press (2009)
6. Baeten, J.C.M., van Beek, D.A., Luttik, B., Markovski, J., Rooda, J.E.: A process-theoretic approach to supervisory control theory. In: American Control Conference (ACC), pp. 4496–4501 (June 2011)
7. Baeten, J.C.M., Verhoef, C.: A congruence theorem for structured operational semantics with predicates. In: Best, E. (ed.) CONCUR 1993. LNCS, vol. 715, pp. 477–492. Springer, Heidelberg (1993)

8. van der Bijl, M., Rensink, A., Tretmans, J.: Compositional testing with ioco. In: Petrenko, A., Ulrich, A. (eds.) FATES 2003. LNCS, vol. 2931, pp. 86–100. Springer, Heidelberg (2004)

9. Bloom, B., Fokkink, W., van Glabbeek, R.J.: Precongruence formats for decorated trace semantics. ACM ToCL 5(1), 26–78 (2004)

10. Bol, R., Groote, J.F.: The meaning of negative premises in transition system specifications. J. ACM 43(5), 863–914 (1996)

11. Boudol, G., Larsen, K.G.: Graphical versus logical specifications. TCS 106(1), 3–20 (1992)

12. de Alfaro, L., Henzinger, T.A.: Interface automata. In: Proc. of ESEC/FSE-9, pp. 109–120. ACM (2001)

13. Fokkink, W.J., van Glabbeek, R.J., de Wind, P.: Compositionality of hennessy-milner logic by structural operational semantics. TCS 354(3), 421–440 (2006)

14. Groote, J.F.: Transition system specifications with negative premises. TCS 118(2), 263–299 (1993)

15. Larsen, K.G.: Modal specifications. In: Sifakis, J. (ed.) CAV 1989. LNCS, vol. 407, pp. 232–246. Springer, Heidelberg (1990)

16. Larsen, K.G., Thomsen, B.: A modal process logic. In: Proceedings of the Third Annual Symposium on Logic in Computer Science, pp. 203–210 (1988)

17. Lüttgen, G., Vogler, W.: Modal interface automata. In: Baeten, J.C.M., Ball, T., de Boer, F.S. (eds.) TCS 2012. LNCS, vol. 7604, pp. 265–279. Springer, Heidelberg (2012)

18. Milner, R.: An algebraic definition of simulation between programs. In: Proceedings of the 2nd International Joint Conference on Artificial Intelligence, IJCAI, pp. 481–489. Morgan Kaufmann Publishers Inc. (1971)

19. Mousavi, M.R., Reniers, M.A., Groote, J.F.: SOS rule formats and meta-theory: 20 years after. TCS 373, 238–272 (2007)

20. Park, D.: Concurrency and automata on infinite sequences. In: Proceedings of the 5th GI-Conference on TCS. LNCS, vol. 104, pp. 167–183. Springer, Heidelberg (1981)

21. Plotkin, G.D.: A structural approach to operational semantics. JLAP 60, 17–139 (2004)

22. Tretmans, J.: Model based testing with labelled transition systems. In: Hierons, R.M., Bowen, J.P., Harman, M. (eds.) FORTEST. LNCS, vol. 4949, pp. 1–38. Springer, Heidelberg (2008)

23. van Glabbeek, R.J.: The meaning of negative premises in transition system specifications II. JLAP 60-61, 229–258 (2004)

Tooled Process for Early Validation
of SysML Models Using Modelica Simulation

Jean-Marie Gauthier, Fabrice Bouquet,
Ahmed Hammad, and Fabien Peureux

Institut FEMTO-ST – UMR CNRS 6174, University of Franche-Comté
16, route de Gray, 25030 Besançon, France
{jmgauthi,fbouquet,ahammad,fpeureux}@femto-st.fr

Abstract. The increasing complexity and heterogeneity of systems require engineers to consider the verification and validation aspects in the earliest stages of the system development life cycle. To meet these expectations, Model-Based Systems Engineering (MBSE) is identified as a key practice for efficient system development while simulation is still widely used by engineers to evaluate the performance and conformance of complex systems regarding requirements. To bridge the gap between high-level modeling (from requirements) and simulation, the present paper proposes a Model-Driven Engineering (MDE) tooled approach to automate the system requirements validation using SysML models and Modelica simulation. The implementation of the related toolchain has been officially adopted by the OMG SysML-Modelica working group.

Keywords: Requirements Validation, SysML Models, Modelica Simulation, Model Transformation, Code Generation, OMG Standard.

1 Introduction

Over the last years, the complexity of physical and hybrid systems has considerably grown since these systems integrate an increasing number of heterogeneous components (electrical, mechanical, software, etc). At the same time, system engineers always have to achieve the following objectives: building the right system correctly, reducing costs and ensuring delivery date. Designing the right system is still a challenge for engineers. Bad design choices or bugs, which are not discovered during early design stages, may indeed be very expensive. Therefore, it is today crucial to be able to validate a system design as soon as possible, even before the development has started and a single line of code has been written. Moreover, despite the increasing complexity of the system requirements, a consistent understanding of the project scopes between all the involved engineer teams is required to ensure the conformity to requirements, and to provide adapted guidance for their production and development choices. Hence, it entails the necessity of adopting and sharing an overall view of system development, especially during the early design stages (in particular during conceptual design, system design and rapid prototyping).

© IFIP International Federation for Information Processing 2015
M. Dastani and M.Sirjani (Eds.): FSEN 2015, LNCS 9392, pp. 230–237, 2015.
DOI: 10.1007/978-3-319-24644-4_16

In the last decade, to overcome these challenges, Model-Based System Engineering (MBSE) methodologies have emerged on the sharing and standardization of embedded software technologies [1]. MBSE deals with the definition of system models that could be exploited during all the system development life cycle, such as the System Modeling Language (SysML) [2]. This approach puts a strong emphasis on the use of models at the different steps of the system specification. As reported by the International Council on Systems Engineering (INCOSE), validation of system requirements using modeling and simulation is today a common method for system analysis and evaluation. Replacing the traditional document centric approach by MBSE approaches entails to use models as the core of the requirements definition, design, analysis, verification and validation activities. In this MBSE context, the communication and cooperation between all the project stakeholders are necessary, and it is thus stimulating to design a first overall system model from requirements. A model may describe expected requirements, behaviours and structure of the designed system. It may be used to validate some parts or the whole designed system regarding functional as well as non-functional requirements. To achieve that, different kinds of analysis can be performed: this can be abstract formal analysis methods (e.g., using analytic techniques) as well as simulation-based analysis (e.g., using SystemC hardware models). Formal analysis allows to cover and guarantee corner cases of the system behaviours while the simulation computation time is in general much smaller. Nevertheless, some components may be too complex for economical formal verification. In these cases, formal analysis may be done on an abstract functional level whereas the implementation or detailed internal behaviours have to be checked via accurate simulation models. However, in some cases, simulation models are the only possibility to estimate timed behaviours of software-hardware interactions.

To address mechatronic systems and embedded systems modeling, high-level design using SysML is on the rise. SysML allows to graphically specify all aspects of physical systems (mixing software and hardware parts) including requirements, structural and behavioural aspects. Moreover, using SysML improves the communication since it eases the interaction between different teams of multi-domain engineers. But SysML is not executable: there is neither an action language nor a simulation framework to evaluate SysML models containing equations. To overcome this issue, we propose a tooled approach to automatically generate Modelica[1] simulation code from SysML models.

The contributions of this paper are threefold. First, it relies on the SysML-Modelica Transformation specification [3], provided by the Object Management Group (OMG), to integrate Modelica concepts in SysML models. Second, we propose a Model-Driven Engineering (MDE) approach to automatically translate such high-level SysML models into executable Modelica code. The obtained simulation results are then compared with the initial system requirements to assess them. Thirdly, to evaluate this whole process, experiments have been conducted within the Smart Blocks project in the mechatronic domain.

---

[1] http://www.modelica.org/ [Last visited: Jan. 2015]

The paper is structured as follows. Section 2 introduces the integration of Modelica constructs into SysML models and describes the process of Modelica code generation from such models. Section 3 discusses the relevance of the tooled approach. Finally, after surveying related work in Sect. 4, we conclude and outline the future work in Sect. 5.

2   From SysML Models to Modelica Code

SysML and Modelica are two complementary languages: their joint use enables the integration of Modelica simulation constructs to complete architectural SysML models. This integration, based on existing recommendations provided by the OMG, has been implemented as the SysML4Modelica profile, which defines the practical contribution of the present paper. Then, we describe the process of Modelica code generation from SysML models using model-driven engineering techniques. The implementation of this whole process is available to the community[2] (demos, examples and source code).

2.1   The Gap between SysML and Modelica

To support MBSE principles, OMG has developed and promotes the System Modeling Language (SysML) that enables systems engineers to specify all aspects of a complex system using graphical constructs. SysML is built on the well-known Unified Modeling Language (UML) by bringing adapted semantics to the system engineering field: SysML is implemented as a UML profile. Using SysML enables the adoption of a Model-Based approach to represent, specify and manage knowledge at the early stage of the design. However, SysML is a semi-formal language and it lacks of structures for requirements and model validation. To tackle this issue, the Modelica language is a convincing candidate: it is a non-proprietary, object-oriented and equation-based language for complex physical systems simulation. Moreover, OMG promotes a dedicated standard (SysML-Modelica Transformation standard) to integrate Modelica semantics into SysML.

The objectives of the SysML-Modelica Transformation specification are to enable a bi-directional transformation between the both modeling languages. The specification defines an extension to SysML, called SysML4Modelica, which proposes matching semantics between the SysML4Modelica constructs and the Modelica language. The integration of Modelica concepts into SysML is based on a profiling approach. Basically, the SysML4Modelica constructs enable to stereotype elements that are part of the Block Definition Diagram (BDD) and the Internal Block Diagram (IBD) of SysML (the BDD is analogous to the UML class diagram whereas the IBD permits to represent physical or logical interactions between component instances via input and output FlowPorts). Thus, BDD and IBD (and optionally the requirements diagram) are the SysML diagrams that are addressed by the approach.

---

[2] https://github.com/SysMLModelicaIntegration/ [Last visited: Jan. 2015]

This SysML4Modelica profile is therefore used to bridge the gap between the two modeling language: SysML, which is a non executable graphical high-level modeling language, and Modelica, which is used as simulation language for complex and heterogeneous systems. The next step of the proposed process is to perform Modelica code generation from SysML models profiled with SysML4Modelica. Thus, the next subsections describe this process and its implementation using Model Driven Architecture (MDA) approach.

2.2 Model to Model Transformation

Model transformation and code generation are the backbone of the Model Driven Architecture approach [4]. In the context of MBSE, this approach helps to bring the analysis of specifications and the rapid prototyping closer. Considering that SysML enables system modeling from specifications, MDA offers techniques to obtain executable Modelica prototypes from SysML models. The next paragraphs give details of this process, which is depicted in Fig. 1.

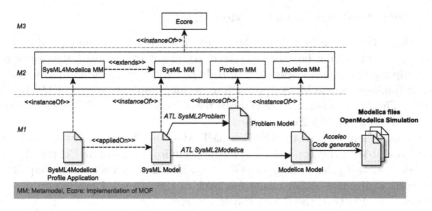

Fig. 1. Modelica Generation Process

The starting point of this translation process consists of manually giving Modelica semantics to SysML models using SysML4Modelica constructs. After verifying that the SysML model contains the correct Modelica constructs, using the automated SysML2Problem verification, a model transformation, based on the ATLAS Transformation Language (ATL) framework, is performed from the SysML4Modelica metamodel to the Modelica metamodel. ATL [5] is a model transformation language inspired by the OMG standard QVT[3]. It makes it possible to implement model transformation rules and to run transformation process. ATL matched rules are the heart of the transformation process as they describe how output elements (that conform to the output metamodel) are produced from input elements (that conform to the input metamodel). For instance, Fig. 2 shows an example of such ATL matched rule.

---

[3] http://www.omg.org/spec/QVT/1.1/ [Last visited: Jan. 2015]

```
rule Block2ModelicaModel{
  from
      sysmlBlock: MMuml!Class(
      sysmlBlock.isBlockStereotyped() and
      sysmlBlock.isModelicaModelStereotyped()
  )
  to
      modelicaModel: MMmodelica!Model()
}
```

Fig. 2. ATL Matched Rule

Within this approach, ATL is used to automatically verify the correctness of SysML4Modelica constructs (`SysML2Problem`) and to translate SysML models into Modelica models (`SysML2Modelica`). The Modelica metamodel is built with Eclipse Modeling Framework (EMF) as an `ecore` file. The generated Modelica model defines the entry point of Modelica code generation, which is described in the next subsection.

2.3 From Modelica Model to Modelica Code

To perform the generation of the Modelica code from the generated Modelica models, the approach is based on the Acceleo technology. Acceleo[4], developed by the company Obeo, is an open source code generator from the Eclipse foundation. It implements the MDA approach to develop application from EMF based models. The Acceleo language is an implementation of the MOF Models to Text Transformation (MOFM2T) standard.

The implementation of the OMG SysML-Modelica Transformation specification is available for the Topcased and Papyrus environments as an Eclipse plugin. It is adopted and promoted by the OMG SysML-Modelica working group. The next section discusses experiments feedback of the proposed process on a concrete case study about the Smart Blocks system.

3   Discussion and Lessons Learned from Experiments

The following discussion is based on the obtained results and lessons learned from the experiments of our prototype for carrying out the Smart Blocks[5] case study (results are presented in [6]). Basically, the goal of this project consists to empirically evaluate the reliability and the scalability of our approach, and finally to answer the following questions regarding the proposed tooled process:

(A) How appropriate and convenient is the SysML4Modelica profile?
(B) Is our prototype efficient enough to support large systems modeling and simulation?
(C) Does it fit the need to validate a high-level SysML design and requirements at the soonest?

---

[4] http://www.eclipse.org/acceleo/ [Last visited: Jan. 2015]
[5] http://smartblocks.univ-fcomte.fr/ [Last visited: Jan. 2015]

3.1   Using SysML4Modelica

At the first sight, the relevance of the proposed approach to early validate system design using SysML models to perform Modelica simulation, instead of writing directly Modelica code for simulation, is debatable. SysML is indeed a high-level modeling language, traditionally used to specify all aspects of a complex system at the earliest stage of the development, whereas Modelica is used later in the development life cycle for rapid prototyping. However, the integration of the both notations enables to fulfill validation challenges and offers new perspectives.

On the one hand, software developers as well as software architects are experienced in using modeling methodology, but they usually lack knowledge to perform hardware related coding and setup of variables to support compilers and simulation platform. The proposed approach allows them to initiate the simulation validation process (in collaboration with engineers) and therefore guarantees the continuous validation of the modeled expected requirements. On the other hand, from robotics engineers point of view and feedback, the advantages of using SysML over using Modelica directly are also significant since the proposed approach attempts to bring closer system modeling from requirements using SysML and allows rapid prototyping using Modelica simulation.

Nevertheless, the gap between SysML and Modelica being quite important at business-level, the cost to perform simulation from SysML model can be also important since design teams have to learn two languages. One important key for the adoption success of this approach by the industry would be to provide reverse-engineering tools that enable to automate the generation of SysML models from existing simulation code. It should also be underlined that the SysML4Modelica profile can be applied to existing SysML models without changing the structure of the model. Incomplete model can also be handled: we could generate the structure of Modelica code without considering all the behavioural rules (e.g., equations, algorithms).

3.2   Scalability of the Approach

The Smart Blocks case study is not very large. To evaluate the scalability of the proposed approach, we have applied it on a large and complex energy manager of a new generation of helicopter type. Basically, this system is composed of an energy source that emulates a permanent power source (alternator coupled with a turbine or a fuel cell system), an accumulators battery and a battery of super-capacitors. Each source is connected with a controller that gives managing strategies. The SysML model of this energy manager system contains 20 blocks, 30 properties, 37 constraints, 30 instances, 109 flow ports and 62 connectors. This case study allows to assess the scalability of the proposed approach regarding modeling effort and automatic Modelica code derivation (the transformation process takes less than one second to generate 23 Modelica files). For confidentiality reasons, experiments results and report about this case study are not presented in this paper.

3.3   Validation of a Design at the Soonest

High-level SysML model validation over requirements was the main motivation of the proposed approach. The Smart Blocks case study is managed by strong requirements concerning the velocity and the acceleration of different kind of tiny objects. Therefore, the SysML model of the system had to meet these requirements. The results obtained with several simulations with different initial conditions gave some clues on future design choices. Moreover, structural modeling error are immediately detected and reported by the SysML2Problem checking.

4   Related Work

This section discusses related work investigating the integration of Modelica into UML and SysML models in the context of MBSE.

In [7, 8], the authors propose techniques to apply the ModelicaML profile on UML models to generate Modelica code. An Eclipse plugin for the Papyrus modeler has been developed, but it is not based on the OMG SysML-Modelica specification and it does not take into account SysML models. Schramm et al. [9] introduce the *MDRE4BR* profile (Model Driven Requirement Engineering for Bosch Rexroth), which aims to perform verification of the design against the requirements using an executable model. This profile extends the current SysML requirements constructs and is linked with ModelicaML to translate analytical models into executable Modelica models. However, this work focuses on the SysML requirements diagram only. Nytsch-Geusen [10] also proposes to use a special format of UML, named *UMLH*, for the modeling of hybrid systems. Modelica code can be produced automatically from UMLH models. However, the generated code has to be manually completed with the physical equations of the system to allow simulations.

A representation of Modelica models in SysML is introduced by Johnson et al. in [11]. This work explores the definition of continuous dynamics models in SysML and the use of triple graph grammar to maintain a bidirectional mapping between SysML and Modelica constructs. A mapping between SysML and Modelica considering a smaller subset of the Modelica language has been proposed by Vasaiely [12]. This work does not use the OMG specification, but uses its own mapping between SysML parametric diagrams and Modelica equations.

5   Conclusion and Future Work

The present paper proposes a tooled MDE approach to validate requirements of complex systems at the earliest stages of design process. This approach consists to generate Modelica simulation code from SysML models. To address this issue, the OMG SysML-Modelica Transformation specification has been implemented as a UML profile for SysML called SysML4Modelica. The model transformations are based on ATL and Acceleo rules, and use a dedicated Modelica metamodel that verifies Modelica syntax. The constraints defined in the OMG specification are thus verified and ensure the SysML model consistency. The approach has been experimented and validated within several industrial case studies.

We are now investigating a novel SysML modeling approach that could allow both to generate test cases and to simulate the system under test from a unique SysML model. This innovative approach could be used within Hardware-In-the-Loop process since the simulation could play two key roles: simulating a system component and providing test cases and oracles for its concrete product. Finally, depending on the OMG standards evolution, we will update the proposed prototype, which is officially promoted by the OMG SysML-Modelica group.

Acknowledgment. This project is supported by the Smart Blocks project (contract ANR-2011-BS03-005) and the Labex ACTION program (contract ANR-11-LABX-0001-01) – see http://www.labex-action.fr/en.

References

1. Estefan, J.: Survey of Model-Based Systems Engineering (MBSE) Methodologies. INCOSE, Survey TD-2007-003-01.B (June 2008)
2. Moore, A., Steiner, R., Friedenthal, S.: A Practical Guide to SysML: The Systems Modeling Language. Morgan Kaufmann (2009) ISBN 9780123743794
3. SysML-Modelica Transformation specification V1.0, Object Management Group (November 2012). http://www.omg.org/spec/SyM/1.0/
4. MDA Guide Version 1.0.1, Object Management Group (May 2003). http://www.omg.org/mda/mda_files/MDA_Guide_Version1-0.pdf
5. Bézivin, J., Breton, E., Dupé, G., Valduriez, P.: The ATL transformation-based model management framework. University of Nantes, Tech. Rep. (August 03, 2003)
6. Gauthier, J.-M., Gendreau, D., Hammad, A., Bouquet, F.: Modeling and simulation of modular complex system: Application to air-jet conveyor. In: Proc. of the IEEE/ASME Int. Conference on Advanced Intelligent Mechatronics (AIM 2014), pp. 1194–1199. IEEE CSP, Besançon (July 2014)
7. Pop, A., Akhvlediani, D., Fritzson, P.: Towards unified system modeling with the modelicaml UML profile. In: Proc. of the 1st Workshop on Equation-Based Object-Oriented Modeling Languages and Tools, EOOLT 2007, pp. 13–24. Linköping Univ. Electronic Press, Berlin (2007)
8. Schamai, W., Fritzson, P., Paredis, C., Pop, A.: Towards unified system modeling and simulation with ModelicaML: modeling of executable behavior using graphical notations. In: Proc. of the 7th Modelica Conference, pp. 612–621. Linköping Univ. Electronic Press, Como (2009)
9. Ji, H., Lenord, O., Schramm, D.: A model driven approach for requirements engineering of industrial automation systems. In: Proc. of the 4th Workshop on Equation-Based Object-Oriented Modeling Languages and Tools (EOOLT 2011), pp. 9–18. Linköping Univ. Electronic Press, Switzerland (2011)
10. Nytsch-Geusen, C.: The use of the UML within the modeling process of modelica-models. In: Proc. of the 1st Workshop on Equation-Based Object-Oriented Modeling Languages and Tools (EOOLT 2007), pp. 1–11. Linköping Univ. Electronic Press, Berlin (2007)
11. Johnson, T., Kerzhner, A., Paredis, C.J., Burkhart, R.: Integrating models and simulations of continuous dynamics into SysML. Journal of Computing and Information Science in Engineering 12(1), 13–24 (2012)
12. Vasaiely, P.: Interactive simulation of sysml models using modelica. Bachelor Thesis, Dept Computer Science, Hamburg University of Applied Sciences (2009)

Can High Throughput Atone for High Latency in Compiler-Generated Protocol Code?

Sung-Shik T.Q. Jongmans and Farhad Arbab

Centrum Wiskunde & Informatica, Amsterdam, The Netherlands

Abstract. High-level concurrency constructs and abstractions have several well-known software engineering advantages when it comes to programming concurrency protocols among threads in multicore applications. To also explore their complementary performance advantages, in ongoing work, we are developing compilation technology for a high-level coordination language, Reo, based on this language's formal automaton semantics. By now, as shown in our previous work, our tools are capable of generating code that can compete with carefully hand-crafted code, at least for some protocols. An important prerequisite to further advance this promising technology, now, is to gain a better understanding of how the significantly different compilation approaches that we developed so far, which vary in the amount of parallelism in their generated code, compare against each other. For instance, to better and more reliably tune our compilers, we must learn under which circumstances parallel protocol code, with high throughput but also high latency, outperforms sequential protocol code, with low latency but also low throughput.

In this paper, we report on an extensive performance comparison between these approaches for a substantial number of protocols, expressed in Reo. Because we have always formulated our compilation technology in terms of a general kind of communicating automaton (i.e., constraint automata), our findings apply not only to Reo but, in principle, to any language whose semantics can be defined in terms of such automata.

1 Introduction

Context. A promising application domain for coordination languages is programming protocols among threads in multicore applications. One reason for this is a classical software engineering advantage: coordination languages typically provide high-level constructs and abstractions that more easily compose into correct—with respect to programmers' intentions—protocol specifications than do conventional lower-level synchronization mechanisms (e.g., locks or semaphores). However, not only do coordination languages simplify programming protocols, but their high-level constructs and abstractions also leave more room for compilers to perform optimizations that conventional language compilers cannot apply. Eventually, sufficiently smart compilers for coordination languages should be capable of generating code (e.g., in Java or in C) that can compete

© IFIP International Federation for Information Processing 2015
M. Dastani and M.Sirjani (Eds.): FSEN 2015, LNCS 9392, pp. 238–258, 2015.
DOI: 10.1007/978-3-319-24644-4_17

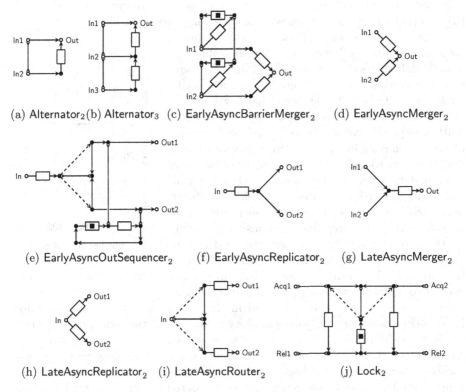

(a) Alternator₂ (b) Alternator₃ (c) EarlyAsyncBarrierMerger₂ (d) EarlyAsyncMerger₂

(e) EarlyAsyncOutSequencer₂ (f) EarlyAsyncReplicator₂ (g) LateAsyncMerger₂

(h) LateAsyncReplicator₂ (i) LateAsyncRouter₂ (j) Lock₂

Fig. 1. Example connectors (ordered alphabetically)

with carefully hand-crafted code. Preliminary evidence for feasibility of this goal appears elsewhere [13]. A crucial step toward adoption of coordination languages for multicore programming, then, is the development of such compilers.

To study the performance advantages of using coordination languages for multicore programming, in ongoing work, we are developing compilation technology for the coordination language Reo [1,2]. Reo facilitates compositional construction of protocol specifications manifested as *connectors*: channel-based mediums through which threads can communicate with each other. Figure 1 shows a number of example connectors in their usual graphical syntax. Briefly, a connector consists of one or more *channels*, through which data items flow, and a number of *nodes*, on which channel ends coincide. Reo features an open-ended set of channels, which means that programmers can define their own channels with custom semantics. Figure 1, for instance, includes standard synchronous channels (normal arrows) and asynchronous channels with a 1-capacity buffer (rectangle-decorated arrows), among others. Nodes, in contrast, have fixed semantics. Threads can perform blocking I/O operations—put and get—on the named *public nodes* of a connector, while a connector uses its anonymous *private nodes* only for internal routing. Section 2 provides a more detailed overview of Reo; Section 4 explains the behavior of the connectors in Figure 1.

Figure 2 shows one of our most promising achievements in developing compilation technology so far [13]. It shows the performance of three k-producer-single-consumer protocol implementations in C, for $k \in \{2^i \mid 2 \le i \le 9\}$: one naive hand-written implementation (continuous line), one optimized hand-written implementation (dashed line), and one implementation compiled from a Reo connector (dotted line). In every round of this protocol, every producer sends one data item to the consumer. Once the consumer has received a data item from every producer, in any order, it sends an acknowledgement to the producers, thereby signaling that the consumer is ready for the next round. (The Reo connector for this protocol, for $k = 2$, resembles EarlyAsyncBarrierMerger$_2$ in Figure 1c.) This example shows that already our current compilation technology is capable of generat-

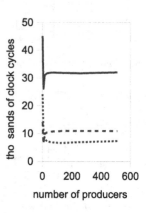

Fig. 2. Earlier results [13]

ing code that can compete with—and in this case even outperform—carefully hand-crafted code. Surely, our technology is not yet mature enough to achieve similarly positive results in *every* multicore application, for *every* connector. Nevertheless, this example offers preliminary evidence that programming protocols among threads using high-level constructs and abstractions can result in equally good—or better—performance as compared to conventional low-level, manual techniques.

Problem. Despite our encouraging first results, a long road still lies ahead of us before we reach the point at which our tools can compile every connector into high-performance code, the following step of which we try to take in this paper.

In the Reo literature, three different approaches for compiling Reo connectors exist [11]. In the *distributed approach*, a compiler implements the behavior of each of the k constituents of a connector (i.e., its nodes and its channels) and runs these k implementations in parallel as a distributed system; in the *centralized approach*, a compiler computes the behavior of a connector as a whole, implements this behavior, and runs this implementation sequentially as a centralized system. The distributed approach has maximal parallelism, and it has the advantage of fast compilation at build-time and high throughput at run-time. However, this comes at the cost of higher latency at run-time (because of a necessary distributed consensus algorithm). In contrast, the centralized approach has maximal sequentiality, and it has the advantage of low latency at run-time. However, this comes at the cost of slower compilation and lower throughput. Moreover, centralized-approach compilers may generate an amount of code exponential in k, which may make their output prohibitively large and the time to produce it prohibitively long. Proença et al. observe that a partially-distributed, partially-centralized *hybrid approach*, where a compiler splits a connector into parts, implements those parts according to the centralized approach, and runs those implementations according to the distributed approach, is generally ideal [16,17]: a hybrid approach strikes a middle ground between latency and throughput at run-time while achieving reasonably fast compilation at build-time.

We started developing a centralized-approach compiler and gradually moved to a hybrid-approach version, mainly motivated by the latter's advantages at build-time. Before this paper, however, we had only little understanding of the implications with respect to run-time performance. Moreover, in recent work [11], we found a case where hybrid-approach compilation actually took much longer than centralized-approach compilation. This made us realize that we *must* improve our understanding of the differences between the centralized approach and the hybrid approach to advance our compilation technology.

Contribution & Organization. In this paper, we compare centralized-approach compilation and execution with hybrid-approach compilation and execution. For this, we use nine different connector "families" (i.e., connectors parametric in the number of the coordinated threads), "members" of which Figure 1 shows. Our comparison reveals previously unknown strengths and weaknesses of the approaches under investigation. These new insights are imperative for the future development of our compilation technology and, consequently, for evidencing the performance merits of high-level constructs and abstractions for multicore programming, complementary to their classical software engineering advantages.

Although framed in the context of Reo, our technology works at the level of Reo's formal automaton semantics. This means that we have formulated and implemented our compilers in terms of a general kind of communicating automaton. Therefore, our findings apply to compilation technology not only for Reo but for any high-level model or language whose semantics one can define in terms of such automata (e.g., some process calculi). We expect this generality to make our work interesting to a larger audience, beyond the Reo community.

In Section 2, we discuss preliminaries on Reo and its automaton semantics. In Section 3, we present a centralized-approach and a hybrid-approach compiler for Reo, which we implemented from scratch (though conceptually based on earlier implementations). In Section 4, we explain our experimental setup. In Sections 5 and 6, we discuss our experimental results: in Section 5, we discuss results related to the *compilation* of our experimental connectors, while in Section 6, we discuss results related to their *execution*. Section 7 concludes this paper.

2   Preliminaries

Reo is a language for compositional construction of concurrency protocols, manifested as connectors [1,2]. Connectors consist of channels and nodes, organized

Table 1. Graphical syntax and informal semantics of common channels

Syntax	Semantics
$e_1 \longrightarrow e_2$	Synchronously takes a data item d from its source end e_1 and writes d to its sink end e_2.
$e_1 \dashrightarrow e_2$	Synchronously takes a data item d from its source end e_1 and nondeterministically either writes d to its sink end e_2 or loses d.
$e_1 \rangle\!\!-\!\!\langle e_2$	Synchronously takes data items from both its source ends and loses them.
$e_1 \;\boxed{}\; e_2$ x	Asynchronously [takes a data item d from its source end e_1 and stores d in a buffer x], then [writes d to its sink end e_2 and clears x].

in a graph-like structure. Every channel consists of two ends and a constraint that relates the timing and the content of the data-flows at those ends. A channel end has one of two types: *source ends* accept data (i.e., a source end of a channel connects to that channel's data source/producer), while *sink ends* dispense data (i.e., a sink end of a channel connects to that channel's data sink/consumer). Reo makes no other assumptions about channels and allows, for instance, channels with two source ends. Table 1 shows four common channels.

Channel ends coincide on nodes. Contrasting channels, every node behaves in the same way: repeatedly, it nondeterministically selects an available data item out of one of its coincident sink ends and replicates this data item into each of its coincident source ends. A node's nondeterministic selection and its subsequent replication constitute one atomic execution step; nodes cannot temporarily store, generate, or lose data items. Threads can perform blocking I/O operations on the *public nodes* of a connector: put operations enable threads to send data, while get operations enable threads to receive data. In Figure 1, we distinguish the white, named public nodes of a connector from its shaded, anonymous *private nodes*. Before a connector makes a global execution step, usually instigated by pending I/O operations, its channels and its nodes must have reached consensus about their behavior to guarantee mutual consistency of their local execution steps (e.g., a node should not replicate a data item into a channel with an already full buffer). Afterward, connector-wide data-flow emerges.

Through *composition*, programmers can construct arbitrarily complex connectors out of simpler ones. As Reo supports both synchronous and asynchronous channels, connector composition enables mixing synchronous and asynchronous communication within the same protocol.

Our compilers generate code for Reo connectors based on their *constraint automaton* (CA) semantics [4]. Constraint automata are a general formalism for modeling concurrent systems, better suited for modeling Reo connectors—and their composition in particular—than classical automata or traditional process calculi. For Reo, a CA specifies *when* during execution of a connector *which* data items flow *where* (i.e., through which channel ends). Structurally, every CA

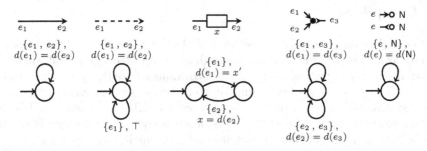

Fig. 3. Constraint automata for the channels in Table 1 (first three from the left), for a private node with two incoming and one outgoing channel (fourth from the left), and for two public nodes, each with either one incoming or one outgoing channel (fifth from the left). The latter CA is defined not only over the names of its coincident channel ends but also over its own name. (Threads use node names—not channel end names—to perform I/O operations on, and therefore, public node names must explicitly occur in their CA semantics.)

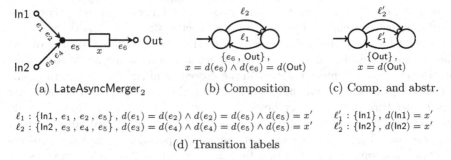

(a) LateAsyncMerger$_2$ (b) Composition   (c) Comp. and abstr.

$\ell_1 : \{In1, e_1, e_2, e_5\}, d(e_1) = d(e_2) \wedge d(e_2) = d(e_5) \wedge d(e_5) = x'$ $\ell'_1 : \{In1\}, d(In1) = x'$
$\ell_2 : \{In2, e_3, e_4, e_5\}, d(e_3) = d(e_4) \wedge d(e_4) = d(e_5) \wedge d(e_5) = x'$ $\ell'_2 : \{In2\}, d(In2) = x'$

(d) Transition labels

Fig. 4. Composition and abstraction of LateAsyncMerger$_2$ in Figure 1g

consists of finite sets of states and transitions, which model a connector's internal configurations and atomic execution steps. Every transition has a label that consists of two elements: (i) a set with the names of those channel ends that have synchronous data-flow (ii) and a logical formula that specifies which particular data items may flow through which of those ends. In such formulas, $d(e_1) = d(e_2)$ means that the same data item flows through e_1 and e_2. In practice, we associate every node and every channel with an elementary CA for its behavior. Figure 3 shows example CAs. A *product operator* on CAs subsequently models connector composition: to obtain the "big" CA for a whole connector, one can incrementally form the product of the "small" CAs for its constituent nodes and channels. Afterward, one can abstract away private nodes' coincident channel ends with a *hide operator* on CAs [4], which also eliminates internal transitions involving only such ends. Figure 4 shows the composite CA of LateAsyncMerger$_2$.

3   Compilers

Our compilers operate fully at the level of Reo's CA semantics. Our focus on Reo so far in this paper is therefore misleading: we use Reo's graphical, channel-based abstractions, just as *a*—not *the*—programmer-friendly syntax for exposing CA-based protocol programming. Different syntax alternatives for CAs may work equally well or yield perhaps even more user-friendly languages. For instance, we know how to translate UML sequence/activity diagrams and BPMN to CAs [3,7,15]. Algebras of Bliudze and Sifakis [6], originally developed for BIP [5], also have a straightforward interpretation in terms of CAs, thereby offering an interesting alternative possible syntax. Due to their generality, CAs can thus serve as an intermediate format for compiling specifications in many different languages and models of concurrency, by reusing the core of our compilers. This makes the development of our compilation technology relevant beyond Reo.

For our performance comparison, based on earlier implementations [10,14], we developed two Reo/CA-to-Java compilers as mentioned already in Section 1: a centralized-approach one, henceforth referred to as $\texttt{Compiler}_{\texttt{centr}}$, and a hybrid-approach one, henceforth referred to as $\texttt{Compiler}_{\texttt{hybr}}$. (Both compilers are available on request.) Both compilers generate shared-memory Java code, geared toward multicore execution. On input of a connector, $\texttt{Compiler}_{\texttt{centr}}$ (i) first finds a small CA for every channel and every node that this connector consists of, (ii) then forms the product of all those CAs to get a big CA for the whole connector, abstracting away all internal details in the process, and (iii) finally generates one piece of sequential code for that big CA. At run-time, this piece of code logically has its own thread. (Physically, however, we can optimize this "protocol thread" away by letting "computation threads" perform its work.) Essentially, the construction of a big CA in this way corresponds to parallel expansion in process algebra [8]. $\texttt{Compiler}_{\texttt{hybr}}$ also first finds a set of small CAs, but in contrast to $\texttt{Compiler}_{\texttt{centr}}$, it does not form their product to get a big CA. Instead, it computes an m-size *partition* of this set. By doing so, $\texttt{Compiler}_{\texttt{hybr}}$ effectively splits a connector into a number of "regions" (i.e., connected subconnectors), each of which has a corresponding subset in the partition. After computing a partition, $\texttt{Compiler}_{\texttt{hybr}}$ forms products on a per-region basis, which results in m "medium" CAs, and generates a piece of sequential code for each of them. At run-time, every such piece of code has its own thread. These threads use shared-memory (plus concurrency protection) to synchronize their actions whenever necessary.

$\texttt{Compiler}_{\texttt{hybr}}$'s partitioning algorithm iterates over the set of small CAs and incrementally extends its computed partition (starting from an empty one) [9,14]. For every small CA α, the algorithm decides either to add $\{\alpha\}$ to the partition (as a new singleton subset) or to add α to one or more existing parts. (In the latter case, the algorithm subsequently merges all extended subsets into one new subset.) Jongmans et al. formulated the condition based on which the algorithm makes this decision generally, in terms of CAs and their transitions. In the context of Reo, however, this partitioning algorithm precisely coincides with the identification of *synchronous/asynchronous regions* of a connector [17] (each of which gets a corresponding subset in the partition). The asynchronous regions of a

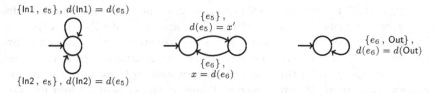

$\{\mathsf{In1}, e_5\}, d(\mathsf{In1}) = d(e_5)$

$\{\mathsf{In2}, e_5\}, d(\mathsf{In2}) = d(e_5)$

$\{e_5\},$
$d(e_5) = x'$

$\{e_6\},$
$x = d(e_6)$

$\{e_6, \mathsf{Out}\},$
$d(e_6) = d(\mathsf{Out})$

Fig. 5. Medium CAs that result from applying the partitioning algorithm to LateAsyncMerger$_2$ (see also Figure 4. The middle CA represents the asynchronous channel in the middle (i.e., one asynchronous region). The leftmost CA represents the synchronous region left of the asynchronous channel (i.e., three nodes, two channels). It repeatedly makes a choice between its two inputs and passes the data item from that input into the asynchronous channel (i.e., into buffer x). The rightmost CA represents the synchronous region right of the asynchronous channel (i.e., only one node). It repeatedly passes a data item from the asynchronous channel (i.e., from buffer x) to its output.

connector are its smallest connected subconnectors that have only asynchronous data-flow (e.g., the fourth channel in Table 1). By removing the asynchronous regions from a connector, its pairwise disconnected synchronous regions remain: connected subconnectors with synchronous data-flow. Intuitively, asynchronous regions decouple synchronous regions. Such decoupling enables synchronous regions to run independently of each other: communication between synchronous regions always proceeds in an asynchronous fashion, through a shared asynchronous region. Figure 5 shows the medium CAs that result from applying the previous partitioning algorithm to LateAsyncMerger$_2$, composing CAs on a per-subset basis, and abstracting away private nodes (see also Figure 4). Note that a connector without asynchronous regions consists of one comprehensive synchronous region. For such connectors, Compiler$_{\text{hybr}}$ reduces to Compiler$_{\text{centr}}$.

Notably, a connector represents the logic behind—not the architecture of—the data-flow in a protocol. For instance, even though Lock$_2$ in Figure 1j, which represents a classical lock, consists of a mix of synchronous, asynchronous, and lossy channels, its compiler-generated code uses neither physical hardware channels nor virtual software channels to realize its desired behavior.

4   Experimental Setup

Practical details. To study under which circumstances code generated by Compiler$_{\text{hybr}}$ outperforms code generated by Compiler$_{\text{centr}}$, we performed a number of experiments. In every experiment, we compared the performance of centralized and hybrid implementations of a k-parametric connector family, for $k \in \{2, 4, 6, 8, 10, 12, 14, 16, 32, 48, 64\}$. Figure 1 shows the $k = 2$ members of the nine connector families that we investigated. (One can extend these $k = 2$ members to their $k > 2$ versions in a similar way as how we extended Figure 1a to Figure 1b.) We selected these families because each of them exhibits different behavior in terms of (a)synchrony, exclusion, nondeterminism, polarity, sequentiality, and parallelism, thereby aiming for a balanced comparison. In total, thus, we investigated 99 different connectors and twice as many Java implementations. We ran every implementation nine times on a machine with 24 cores (two Intel E5-2690V3 processors with twelve physical cores statically at 2.6 GHz in two sockets, hyperthreading disabled) and averaged our measurements. In every run, we warmed up the JVM for thirty seconds before starting to measure the number of "rounds" that an implementation could finish in the subsequent four minutes. What constitutes one round differs per connector; see below.

Primarily, we wanted to study and measure the overhead of the synchronization algorithm between the protocol threads in the hybrid implementations (which increases their latency) relative to those implementations' increased parallelism (which increases their throughput). To focus our measurements on only that particular aspect, we needed to eliminate as much as possible all other, orthogonal sources of computation inside compiler-generated code. One notable such source is data processing: although both our compilers support compilation of *data-sensitive connectors*, whose behavior may depend on the particular data items that pass through them, we nevertheless compiled all connectors in a data-insensitive fashion. This ensured that no data processing occurred at run-time during our experiments, which would have constituted a substantial source of sequential, unoptimized computation, even though we already know of ways to significantly improve this. If we would have enabled data processing, its irrelevant—at least to this comparison—overhead would have polluted our measurements. Perhaps even worse, our results would become obsolete the moment we implement our upcoming data processing optimizations.

For convenience, we divided the connector families under study—except Lock— over two categories: k-producer-single-consumer and single-producer-k-consumer. Both of these categories consist of four families. The k-producer-single-consumer category contains LateAsyncMerger (cf. Figure 1g), EarlyAsyncMerger (cf. Figure 1d), EarlyAsyncBarrierMerger (cf. Figure 1c), and Alternator (cf. Figures 1a and 1b); the single-producer-k-consumer category contains LateAsyncReplicator (cf. Figure 1h), EarlyAsyncReplicator (cf. Figure 1f), LateAsyncRouter (cf. Figure 1i), and EarlyAsyncOutSequencer (cf., Figure 1e).

Connectors. Next, we explain the behavior of the connectors in Figure 1. We start with explaining the k-producer-single-consumer connector families. With LateAsyncMerger$_k$ (cf. Figure 1g), whenever producer i puts a data item on its local node Ini, the connector stores this data item in its only buffer (unless this buffer is already filled by another producer, in which case the put suspends until the buffer becomes empty). The relieved producer can immediately continue, possibly before the consumer has completed a get for its data item (i.e., communication between a producer and the consumer transpires asynchronously). Whenever the consumer gets a data item from its local node Out, the connector empties the previously full buffer. The consumer gets data items in the order in which producers put them (i.e., communication between a producer and the consumer transpires transactionally, i.e., undisrupted by other producers). Every round consists of a put by a producer and a get by the consumer; in every round, two transitions fire.

With EarlyAsyncMerger$_k$ (cf. Figure 1d), whenever a producer i puts a data item on its local node Ini, the connector stores this data item in its corresponding buffer. The relieved producer can immediately continue, possibly before the consumer has completed a get for its data item (i.e., communication between a producer and the consumer transpires asynchronously). Whenever the consumer gets a data item from its local node Out, the connector empties one of the previously full buffers, selected nondeterministically. The consumer does not necessarily get data items in the order in which producers put them (i.e., communication between a producer and the consumer transpires not necessarily transactionally). Every round consists of a put by a producer and a get by the consumer; in every round, two transitions fire.

Connectors in the EarlyAsyncBarrierMerger family work in largely the same way as those in the EarlyAsyncMerger family, except that the former enforce a barrier on the producers: no producer can put its n-th data item until all other producers have put their $(n-1)$-th data items. The consumer may still get data items in an order different from the order in which the producers put them. Every round consists of a put by every producer and k gets by the consumer, one for every producer; in every round, $2k$ transitions fire.

With Alternator$_k$ (cf. Figures 1a and 1b), whenever a producer i attempts to put a data item on its local node Ini, this operation suspends until both (1) the consumer attempts to get a data item from its local node Out, and (2) every other producer j attempts to put a data item on its local node Inj (i.e., the producers can put only synchronously). Once each of the producers and the consumer attempt to put/get, the consumer gets the data item sent by the top producer (i.e., communication between the top producer and the consumer transpires synchronously), while the connector stores the data items of the other producers in their corresponding buffers (i.e., communication between the other producers and the consumer transpires asynchronously). Afterward, the consumer gets the remaining buffered data items in the spatial top-to-bottom order of the producers. Every round consists of a put by every producer and k gets by the consumer, one for every producer; in every round, k transitions fire.

We proceed with explaining the single-producer-k-consumer connector families. With EarlyAsyncReplicator$_k$ (cf. Figure 1f), whenever the producer puts a data item on its local node In, the connector stores this data item in its only buffer. The relieved producer can immediately continue, possibly before the consumers have completed gets for its data item (i.e., communication between the producers and a consumer transpires asynchronously). Whenever a consumer i attempts to get a data item from its local node Out$i$, this operation suspends until both (1) the buffer has become full, and (2) every other consumer attempts to get a data item (i.e., the consumers can get only synchronously). Once the buffer has become full and each of the consumers attempts to get, every consumer gets the data item in the buffer, while the connector empties that buffer. Every round consists of a put by the producer and a get by every consumer; in every round, two transitions fire.

With LateAsyncReplicator$_k$ (cf. Figure 1h), whenever the producer **puts** a data item on its local node In, the connector stores a copy of this data item in each of its buffers. The relieved producer can immediately continue, possibly before the consumers have completed **gets** for its data item (i.e., communication between the producers and a consumer transpires asynchronously). Whenever a consumer i **gets** a data item from its local node Out$i$, the connector empties its corresponding full buffer. Every round consists of a **put** by the producer and a **get** by every consumer; in every round, $k + 1$ transitions fire.

With LateAsyncRouter$_k$ (cf. Figure 1i), whenever the producer **puts** a data item on its local node In, the connector stores this data item in exactly one of its buffers (instead of a copy in each of its buffers as LateAsyncReplicator$_k$ does), selected nondeterministically. The relieved producer can immediately continue, possibly before the consumer of the selected buffer has completed a **get** for its data item (i.e., communication between the producer and a consumer transpires asynchronously). Whenever a consumer i **gets** a data item from its local node Out$i$, the connector empties its corresponding full buffer. The consumers do not necessarily **get** data items in the order in which the connector stored those data items in its buffers. Every round consists of a **put** by the producer and a **get** by a consumer; in every round, two transitions fire.

With EarlyAsyncOutSequencer$_k$ (cf. Figure 1e), whenever the producer **puts** a data item on its local node In, the connector stores this data item in its leftmost buffer. The relieved producer can immediately continue, possibly before a consumer has completed a **get** for its data item (i.e., communication between a producer and the consumers transpires asynchronously). The connector ensures that the consumers can **get** only in the top-to-bottom sequence. Whenever a consumer i **gets** a data item from its local node Out$i$, the connector empties its corresponding full buffer. Every round consists of k **puts** by the producer and a **get** by every consumer; in every round, $2k$ transitions fire.

Finally, Lock$_k$ represents a classical lock (cf. Figure 1j). To acquire the lock, a computation thread i **puts** an arbitrary data item (i.e., a signal) on its local node Acq$i$; to release the lock, this thread **puts** an arbitrary data item on its local node Rel$i$. A **put** on Acq$i$ suspends until every computation thread j that previously performed a **put** on Acq$j$ has performed its complementary **put** on Rel$j$ (i.e., the connector guarantees mutual exclusion). Every round consists of two **puts** by one of the k producers; in every round, two transitions fire.

5   Experimental Results: Compilation

Measurements. We used Compiler$_{\text{hybr}}$ and Compiler$_{\text{centr}}$ to compile the connector families in Figure 1 for the aforementioned values of k with a transition limit of 8096 and a timeout after five minutes. We imposed a transition limit, because the Java compiler cannot conveniently handle Java code generated for CAs with so many transitions; we imposed a compilation timeout, because waiting for longer than five minutes to compile a single connector in practice seems unacceptable to us. Figure 6 shows the measured compilation times; see also [12].

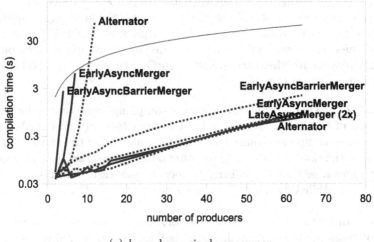

(a) k-producer-single-consumer

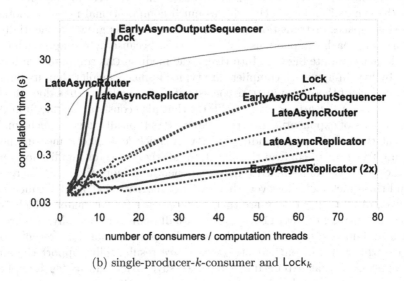

(b) single-producer-k-consumer and Lock$_k$

Fig. 6. Compilation times (continuous lines for Compiler$_{centr}$; dotted lines for Compiler$_{hybr}$; gray lines for proportional growth $x = y$, just as a reference)

For most connector families, $\text{Compiler}_{\text{hybr}}$ required substantially less time than $\text{Compiler}_{\text{centr}}$. In fact, for six of our nine connector families, $\text{Compiler}_{\text{centr}}$ failed to run to completion beyond certain (relatively low) values of k, as witnessed also by their very steep curves in Figure 6:

- For $\text{EarlyAsyncMerger}_{k>7}$, $\text{LateAsyncReplicator}_{k>8}$ and $\text{LateAsyncRouter}_{k>7}$, the transition number of their "big" CAs exceeded the limit (e.g., $\text{EarlyAsync-Merger}_8$ has 23801 transitions, $\text{LateAsyncReplicator}_9$ has 19172 transitions, and LateAsyncRouter_8 has 23801 transitions) or the compiler timed out.
- For $\text{EarlyAsyncBarrierMerger}_{k>4}$, $\text{EarlyAsyncOutSequencer}_{k>14}$, and $\text{Lock}_{k>12}$, the compiler timed out.

In contrast, $\text{Compiler}_{\text{hybr}}$ had no problems compiling these connector families for all values of k under investigation. For LateAsyncMerger_k and $\text{EarlyAsyncRep-licator}_k$, our two compilers required a comparable amount of time for all values of k under investigation. Finally, only for Alternator_k, $\text{Compiler}_{\text{hybr}}$ required substantially more time than $\text{Compiler}_{\text{centr}}$ does. In this case, $\text{Compiler}_{\text{hybr}}$ timed out for $k > 12$, while $\text{Compiler}_{\text{centr}}$ had no problems.

Discussion. In Section 1, we stated that hybrid-approach compilers have the advantage of "reasonably fast compilation at build-time" compared to centralized-approach compilers. The idea behind this statement is that the formation of a big CA in the centralized approach requires much computational resource, notably when state spaces or transition relations of such big CAs grow exponentially in k; hybrid-approach compilers usually avoid this, because hybrid-approach compilers do not compute big CAs. Intuitively, the medium CAs computed for a connector by hybrid-approach compilers are typically much smaller than its big CA. After all, each of those medium CAs consists of fewer small CAs than does this big CA. (The big CA consists of every small CA that also constitutes a medium CA.) Thus, in cases of exponential growth, medium CAs typically have a much smaller exponent than their corresponding big CA. A quick look at our measurements in Figure 6a seems to confirm this intuition: all six connector families for which $\text{Compiler}_{\text{centr}}$ eventually failed require exponentially more time as k increases. Beyond this quick look, however, there are peculiarities that need clarification.

A first, obvious peculiarity are the measurements for Alternator, which $\text{Compiler}_{\text{hybr}}$—instead of $\text{Compiler}_{\text{centr}}$—eventually fails for. Actually, we already made a preliminary *qualitative* analysis of this phenomenon in a recent workshop contribution [11]; our current *quantitative* results fully support the anecdotal analysis in that extended abstract. To save space—an in-depth explanation requires significantly more details of the partitioning algorithm used in hybrid-approach compilation—we only briefly summarize the cause of this phenomenon. Essentially, a hybrid-approach compiler cannot treat every private node of a connector as truly private: $\text{Compiler}_{\text{hybr}}$ cannot use the hide operator to abstract away those private nodes that mark the boundaries between a connector's regions. After all, protocol threads for neighboring regions synchronize their transitions through those nodes, which makes explicitly representing them in compiler-generated code essential. But because those private nodes must remain, also many internal transitions remain, potentially to the extent that they cause the transition relation of "medium" CAs formed for certain problematic regions to explode. This happens with Alternator. $Compiler_{centr}$, in contrast, can incrementally hide *all* private nodes to neutralize this source of explosion.

The second peculiarity concerns centralized-approach compilation. First, by analyzing the big CAs of the k-parametric connector families EarlyAsyncBarrierMerger, EarlyAsyncMerger, EarlyAsyncOutSequencer, LateAsyncReplicator, and LateAsyncRouter, we found that those CAs grow *exponentially* as k increases (due to the many ways in which their k independent transition can concurrently fire). This explains why $Compiler_{centr}$ requires exponentially more time as k increases to compile members of those families, as shown in Figure 6. Now, it seems not unreasonable to assume also the inverse: for k-parametric connector families whose big CAs grow only *linearly* in k, $Compiler_{centr}$ should scale fine. Alternator, EarlyAsyncReplicator, and LateAsyncMerger, which satisfy its premise, seem to validate this assumption. Indeed, Figure 6 shows that $Compiler_{centr}$ has no problems with compiling members of those families. (The big CAs of the EarlyAsyncReplicator family even have a constant number of transitions.) However, this still leaves us with two families whose compilation behavior we have not yet accounted for: EarlyAsyncOutSequencer and Lock. Although the big CAs of both these k-parametric families grow only linearly in k, Figure 6 shows that $Compiler_{centr}$ nevertheless requires exponentially more time as k increases.

It turns out that even if big CAs grow only linearly in k, the "intermediate products" during their formation may "temporarily" grow exponentially. For instance, if we have three CAs α_1, α_2 and α_3, the intermediate product of α_1 and α_2 may grow exponentially in k, while the full product of α_1, α_2, and α_3 grows only linearly. This is easiest to explain for $EarlyAsyncOutSequencer_k$ (cf. Figure 1e), in terms of its number of states. $EarlyAsyncOutSequencer_k$ consists of a subconnector that, in turn, consists of a cycle of k buffered channels (of capacity 1). The first buffered channel initially contains a dummy data item ■ (i.e., its actual value does not matter); the other buffered channels initially contain nothing. As in the literature [1,2], we call this subconnector $Sequencer_k$. Because no new data items can flow into $Sequencer_k$, only ■ cycles through the buffers—ad infinitum—such that only one buffer holds a data item at any time. Consequently, the CA for $Sequencer_k$ has only k states, each of which represents the presence of ■ in a different one of the k buffers. However, when $Compiler_{centr}$ compositionally computes this CA out of a number of smaller CAs by forming their product, it closes the cycle only with the very last application of the product operator: until that moment, the "cycle" still looks to the compiler as an open-ended chain of buffered channels. Because new data items can freely flow into it, such an open-ended chain can have a data item in any buffer at any time. Consequently, the CA for the largest chain (i.e., the chain of $k-1$ buffered channels, just before it becomes closed) has 2^{k-1} states. Only when $Compiler_{centr}$ forms the product of [the CA of the k-th buffered channel] and [the previously formed CA for the chain of $k-1$ buffered channels], the state space of 2^{k-1} states collapses into k states, as the compiler "finds out" that the open-ended chain is actually an input-closed cycle with exactly one data item. Clearly, because Sequencer$_k$ constitutes EarlyAsyncOutSequencer$_k$, also EarlyAsyncOutSequencer$_k$ itself suffers from this problem. A similar argument applies to Lock$_k$.

Thus, even for k-parametric connector families whose big CAs grow only linearly in k, Compiler$_{centr}$ can have scalability issues because of exponential growth in intermediate products. Compiler$_{hybr}$ has no problems with the kind of cycle-based exponential growth discussed above because of how it deals with such cycles in its partitioning algorithm. Generally, however, we can imagine also Compiler$_{hybr}$ to have this problem for other sources of exponential growth.

Conclusion. For the four k-parametric connector families whose big CAs grow exponentially in k (i.e., EarlyAsyncBarrierMerger, EarlyAsyncMerger, LateAsync-Replicator, and LateAsyncRouter), hybrid compilation has clear advantages over centralized compilation, as we already expected. For the two k-parametric connector families whose big CAs and intermediate products grow only linearly in k (i.e., LateAsyncMerger and EarlyAsyncReplicator), centralized-approach compilation and hybrid-approach compilation do not make much of a difference; here, run-time performance—investigated in the next section—becomes the key factor in deciding which approach to apply. For Alternator, centralized compilation has clear advantages over hybrid compilation. Finally, for the two k-parametric connector families whose intermediate products grow exponentially in k (i.e., EarlyAsyncOutSequencer and Lock), hybrid compilation seems to have clear advantages over centralized compilation as suggested by Figure 6b.

We find the latter conclusion slightly rash, though. After all, our previous analysis showed that the big CAs—the only CAs that we actually care about—for both EarlyAsyncOutSequencer and Lock grow only linearly in k. If we can develop technology that enables Compiler$_{centr}$ to avoid temporary exponential growth of intermediate products, Compiler$_{centr}$ should perform similar to Compiler$_{hybr}$.

One option is to equip Compiler$_{centr}$ with a novel static analysis technique to infer, *before* forming the full product, which states will have become unreachable *after* forming the full product. For instance, in the case of EarlyAsyncOutSequencer$_k$ (or its subconnector Sequencer$_k$), every state where two or more buffers contain a data item will have become unreachable in the full product but not so yet in the intermediate products. If Compiler$_{centr}$ can determine such "eventually unreachable states" from the start, it can already remove those states *while* forming the full product to keep the intermediate products as small as possible. This optimization requires significant theoretical work: not only must we formulate the analysis technique itself, but we must also prove that it preserves certain behavioral properties. It seems an interesting form of on-the-fly state space reduction, though, which may have applications also in model checking.

Another option is not really a solution to our problem but a way to avoid it. We observed that the Sequencer$_k$ subconnector of EarlyAsyncOutSequencer$_k$ causes its intermediate products to grow exponentially in k. For simplicity, let us therefore focus on this problematic Sequencer$_k$. The obvious way to construct a connector with the behavior of $Sequencer_k$ is by putting k buffered channels in a cycle, as we did before. An alternative way to construct such a connector, however, is by connecting a $Sequencer_{0.5k}$ to another $Sequencer_{0.5k}$ with a "glue subconnector". The details of this glue subconnector do not matter here: what matters is that in this alternative construction, $Compiler_{centr}$ can first form the products of the $Sequencer_{0.5k}$ subconnectors to get two CAs with $0.5k$ states, and then form the products of those CAs and the two-state CA of the glue subconnector. The largest intermediate CA encountered by the compiler during this process has at most $\max(2^{0.5k}, 0.5k \cdot 0.5k \cdot 2)$ states. In contrast, the largest intermediate CA for the obviously constructed $Sequencer_k$—the one with the cycle—has 2^{k-1} states. This analysis shows that *hierarchically* constructing $Sequencer_k$ out of $Sequencer_{l<k}$ subconnectors reduces its centralized-approach compilation complexity compared to its *flat* design. Generally, we should therefore encourage programmers to design connectors as hierarchically as possible.

6   Experimental Results: Execution

Measurements. We ran every successfully compiled connector with "empty" computation threads: in every iteration of their infinite loop, a producer/consumer had no work and immediately performed a put/get on its own public node. As a result, we measured the performance of only the compiler-generated code. Figure 7 shows our measurements, in completed protocol rounds per four minutes. By dividing this number of rounds by 240, one gets the round-throughput, in rounds per second. By further dividing this number by the number of transitions per round, one gets the (transition-)throughput.

Figures 7a, 7b, 7c, and 7f show the performances in the k-producers-single-consumer category. For LateAsyncMerger, EarlyAsyncMerger, and EarlyAsyncBarrierMerger, their centralized implementations outperform their hybrid implementations in cases involving only few producers (up to/including four in the case of LateAsyncMerger and EarlyAsyncBarrierMerger; up to/including six in the case of EarlyAsyncMerger). In cases involving more producers, either the hybrid implementations outperform the centralized implementations, or $Compiler_{centr}$ failed to compile such that we cannot make a direct comparison. In those latter cases, however, it seems reasonable to assert, by extrapolation, that if compilation had succeeded, these generated centralized implementations would have performed worse than their corresponding hybrid counterparts. For Alternator, in contrast, its centralized implementations always outperform its hybrid implementations.

Figures 7d, 7e, 7g, and 7h show the performances in the single-producer-k-consumers category. The figures for LateAsyncReplicator and LateAsyncRouter are similar to those of LateAsyncMerger, EarlyAsyncMerger, and EarlyAsyncBarrierMerger that we saw before: with only few consumers, their centralized implementations outperform their hybrid implementations, while with more consumers, their hybrid implementations outperform their centralized implementations. For EarlyAsyncReplicator, the performance of its centralized and hybrid implementations is nearly the same. For EarlyAsyncOutSequencer, because $Compiler_{centr}$ failed to generate code for $k > 14$, the comparison remains inconclusive.

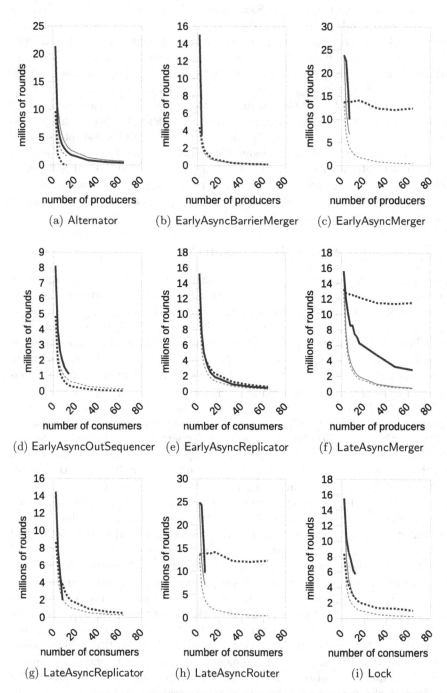

Fig. 7. Performance, in rounds per four minutes (blue continuous/dotted lines for centralized/hybrid implementations; gray lines for inverse-proportional growth)

Discussion. For six of the nine connector families, the obtained results look as expected. For those families, we observe that with low values of k (i.e., little parallelism), their centralized implementations outperform their hybrid implementations. In those cases, the increased throughput of hybrid implementations as compared to their centralized counterparts cannot yet compensate for their increased latency. As k increases and more parallelism becomes available, however, hybrid implementations start to outperform centralized implementations. In those cases, increased throughput does seem to compensate for increased latency. This, however, is not the only reason why hybrid implementations outperform centralized implementations for larger values of k. More importantly, we found that the latency of not only hybrid implementations but also centralized implementations increases with k. In fact, the latency of centralized implementations increases much more dramatically. By analyzing the "big" CAs formed by Compiler$_{centr}$ for the families currently under discussion, we found that their exponential growth (cf. Section 5) causes this steep increase in latency: the more transitions a CA has per state, the more time it takes for a thread to select and check any one of them at run-time. (EarlyAsyncReplicator constitutes a special case, where increased throughput and increased latency roughly balance out.)

Contrasting the families discussed in the previous paragraph, the results obtained for Alternator, EarlyAsyncOutSequencer, and Lock are more peculiar. In Section 5, we already briefly explained why Compiler$_{centr}$ succeeded in generating code for Alternator$_{k>12}$, while Compiler$_{hybr}$ failed. This, however, does not yet explain why centralized implementations of Alternator connectors outperform their hybrid implementations also at run-time. The reason becomes clear when we realize that Alternator$_k$ essentially behaves sequentially: in every round, the producers start by synchronously putting their data items (and the consumer synchronously gets the first data item), after which the consumer asynchronously gets the remaining $k-1$ data items in sequence. The centralized implementation of Alternator$_k$ at run-time sequentially simulates one CA, which consists of k transitions between k states, that represents exactly this sequentiality. Its hybrid implementation, in contrast, at run-time has k parallel protocol threads and, as such, suffers from *overparallelization*: it uses parallelism— and incurs the overhead that parallelism involves—to implement intrinsically sequential behavior. Because also EarlyAsyncOutSequencer and Lock essentially behave sequentially, they suffer from the same problem. For these two families, however, this observation is even more important than for Alternator. After all, hybrid-approach compilation fails for Alternator$_{k>12}$, so for larger k, we must use centralized-approach compilation anyway. For EarlyAsyncOutSequencer$_{k>14}$ and Lock$_{k>12}$, in contrast, centralized-approach compilation fails, even though centralized implementations of those connectors are, by extrapolation, likely to perform better than their hybrid counterparts.

Centralized implementations consist of only one protocol thread, which can do only one thing at a time. If many computation threads each perform an I/O operation roughly simultaneously, depending on the connector, this may result in contention (i.e., every computation thread must wait until the protocol thread has time to process its I/O operation). To further study the effect of contention, we repeated our experiments with z-parametric producers/consumers that wait a random amount of time between 0 and $\lceil z$ times the previously measured round-latency$\rceil$ before they perform their put/get, for $z \in \{1, 10, 100\}$. [12] contains our measurements. The short conclusion is that as z increases, the performance of centralized implementations and hybrid implementations becomes more similar. We doubt whether this can be ascribed to less contention, though. Instead, we consider it more likely that the producers'/consumers' waiting times now dominate our measurements. Although perhaps not too surprising, we nevertheless consider this something that one should be aware of: the more work threads perform, the less important the choice between centralized/hybrid implementation becomes (with respect to run-time performance).

Conclusion. For six of the nine connector families, the obtained results are as we expected: their centralized implementations outperform their hybrid implementations for smaller values of k, while their hybrid implementations outperform their centralized implementations for larger values of k. As k increases and more parallelism becomes available, the higher throughput of hybrid implementations as compared to their centralized counterparts compensates for their higher latency, while the latency of centralized implementations dramatically increases.

Because Alternator, EarlyAsyncOutSequencer, and Lock essentially behave sequentially, their centralized implementations in fact outperform their hybrid implementations for all k. This is a strong incentive to improve our centralized-approach compilation technology (e.g., the optimization at the end of Section 5).

7   Conclusion

Better understanding the differences between centralized-approach compilation and hybrid-approach compilation is crucial to further advance our compilation technology, one of whose promising applications is programming protocols among threads in multicore applications. Initially, we wanted to investigate under which circumstances parallel protocol code generated by a hybrid-approach compiler, with high throughput but also high latency, outperforms sequential protocol code generated by a centralized-approach compiler, with low latency but also low throughput. Based on our comparison, the answer to this question is this:

– Except for cases with overparallelization, hybrid implementations of connectors with more than a few (e.g., at least ten to twelve) parallel computation threads perform at least as good as their centralized counterparts.

Our comparison taught us much more about centralized/hybrid-approach compilation, though. To summarize our other findings:

– Hybrid-approach compilation may suffer from exponentially sized CAs in cases where centralized-approach compilation works fine.
– Centralized-approach compilation may suffer from exponentially sized intermediate products in cases where hybrid-approach compilation works fine.

- Programmers should prefer hierarchically constructed connectors over flat constructed connectors to reduce compilation complexity.
- Hybrid implementations may overparallelize inherently sequential connectors, which leads to poor run-time performance.
- Centralized implementations may in fact have even higher latency than hybrid implementations.
- The more work threads perform, the less important the choice between centralized/hybrid approach becomes (with respect to run-time performance).

In future work, we want to follow up on these findings by developing new optimization techniques (such as the one sketched in Section 5). In particular, we should identify when hybrid-approach compilation should reduce to centralized-approach compilation and improve our partitioning algorithm accordingly.

Although we heavily used Reo/connector terminology in this paper as a narrative mechanism, we really have been talking about and investigating different kinds of implementations of a general kind of communicating automaton (i.e., CAs). Because also other languages can have semantics in terms of such automata (e.g., Rebeca [18] and BIP [5]), our findings have applications beyond Reo.

References

1. Arbab, F.: Reo: a channel-based coordination model for component composition. MSCS 14(3), 329–366 (2004)
2. Arbab, F.: Puff, The Magic Protocol. In: Agha, G., Danvy, O., Meseguer, J. (eds.) Talcott Festschrift. LNCS, vol. 7000, pp. 169–206. Springer, Heidelberg (2011)
3. Arbab, F., Kokash, N., Meng, S.: Towards Using Reo for Compliance-Aware Business Process Modeling. In: ISoLA 2008. CCIS, vol. 17, pp. 108–123. Springer, Heidelberg (2008)
4. Baier, C., Sirjani, M., Arbab, F., Rutten, J.: Modeling component connectors in Reo by constraint automata. SCP 61(2), 75–113 (2006)
5. Basu, A., Bozga, M., Sifakis, J.: Modeling Heterogeneous Real-time Components in BIP. In: SEFM 2006, pp. 3–12. IEEE (2006)
6. Bliudze, S., Sifakis, J.: Causal semantics for the algebra of connectors. Formal Methods in System Design 36(2), 167–194 (2010)
7. Changizi, B., Kokash, N., Arbab, F.: A Unified Toolset for Business Process Model Formalization. In: Preproceedings of FESCA 2010, pp. 147–156 (2010)
8. Groote, J.F., Mousavi, M.R.: Modeling and Analysis of Communicating Systems. MIT Press (2014)
9. Jongmans, S.S., Arbab, F.: Global Consensus through Local Synchronization. In: FOCLASA 2013. CCIS, vol. 393, pp. 174–188. Springer (2013)
10. Jongmans, S.S., Arbab, F.: Modularizing and Specifying Protocols among Threads. In: PLACES 2012. EPTCS, vol. 109, pp. 34–45. CoRR (2013)
11. Jongmans, S.S., Arbab, F.: Toward Sequentializing Overparallelized Protocol Code. In: ICE 2014. EPTCS, vol. 166, pp. 38–44. CoRR (2014)
12. Jongmans, S.S., Arbab, F.: Can High Throughput Atone for High Latency in Compiler-Generated Protocol Code (Technical Report). Tech. Rep. FM-1503, CWI (2015)

13. Jongmans, S.S., Halle, S., Arbab, F.: Automata-based Optimization of Interaction Protocols for Scalable Multicore Platforms. In: Kühn, E., Pugliese, R. (eds.) COORDINATION 2014. LNCS, vol. 8459, pp. 65–82. Springer, Heidelberg (2014)
14. Jongmans, S.S., Santini, F., Arbab, F.: Partially-Distributed Coordination with Reo. In: PDP 2014, pp. 697–706. IEEE (2014)
15. Meng, S., Arbab, F., Baier, C.: Synthesis of Reo circuits from scenario-based interaction specifications. SCP 76(8), 651–680 (2011)
16. Proença, J., Clarke, D., de Vink, E., Arbab, F.: Dreams: a framework for distributed synchronous coordination. In: SAC 2012, pp. 1510–1515. ACM (2012)
17. Proença, J.: Synchronous Coordination of Distributed Components. Ph.D. thesis, Leiden University (2011)
18. Sirjani, M., Jaghoori, M.M., Baier, C., Arbab, F.: Compositional Semantics of an Actor-Based Language Using Constraint Automata. In: Ciancarini, P., Wiklicky, H. (eds.) COORDINATION 2006. LNCS, vol. 4038, pp. 281–297. Springer, Heidelberg (2006)

Painless Support for Static and Runtime Verification of Component-Based Applications

Nuno Gaspar[1,2,3,*], Ludovic Henrio[2], and Eric Madelaine[1,2]

[1] INRIA, Sophia Antipolis, France
{Nuno.Gaspar,Eric.Madelaine}@inria.fr
[2] Univ. Nice Sophia Antipolis, CNRS, I3S, UMR 7271,
06900 Sophia Antipolis, France
Ludovic.Henrio@cnrs.fr
[3] ActiveEon S.A.S
http://www.activeeon.com/

Abstract. Architecture Description Languages (ADL) provide descriptions of a software system in terms of its structure. Such descriptions give a high-level overview and come from the need to cope with arbitrarily complex dependencies arising from software components.

In this paper we present PAINLESS, a novel ADL with a *declarative* trait supporting parametrized specifications and architectural reconfigurations. Moreover, we exhibit its reliable facet on its integration with ProActive — a middleware for distributed programming. This is achieved by building on top of MEFRESA, a Coq framework for the reasoning on software architectures. We inherit its strong guarantees by extracting certified code, and subsequently integrating it in our toolchain.

Keywords: The Coq Proof Assistant, Component-based Engineering, Formal Methods, Architecture Description Language

1 Introduction

Typically, one uses an Architecture Description Language (ADL) as a means to specify the software architecture. This promotes separation of concerns and compels the software architect to accurately define structural requisites. Nevertheless, this task is seldom trivial as arbitrarily complex architectures may need to be defined. It is thus important to provide the means for expressive and intuitive, yet reliable, specifications.

In this paper we present PAINLESS, a novel ADL for describing parametrized software architectures, and its related formal verification support. We discuss its integration with ProActive [1], a middleware for distributed programming, and the reference implementation for the Grid Component Model (GCM) [2].

The GCM ADL lacks support for architectural reconfigurations and parametrization. Further, it is XML-based: while it may be suitable for tools, it is a rather verbose and static description of the architecture. PAINLESS supports

---

* This work is partially supported by ANRT/CIFRE No 2012/0109.

M. Dastani and M.Sirjani (Eds.): FSEN 2015, LNCS 9392, pp. 259–274, 2015.
DOI: 10.1007/978-3-319-24644-4_18

both the definition of parametrized architectures and the specification of reconfigurations in a declarative style. This facilitates deployment tasks and gives a
more comprehensive understanding of the application's topology.

For instance, let us consider the motivating example depicted by Figure 1.

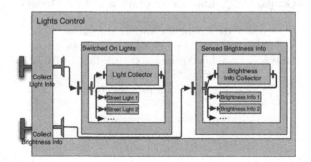

Fig. 1. Architecture of the Lights Control use case

This architecture concerns a previous use case [3] on the saving of power consumption by adequately adding/removing **Street Light** and **Brightness Info** components. For such scenario an ADL solely describing the deployment topology
and unable to handle parametrized specifications becomes cumbersome. In this
paper, our main goal is to provide an ADL specifying at the same time the initial deployment and the possible reconfigurations, while providing support for
describing parametrized topologies. We also want to rely on formal methods to
guarantee a safe deployment and reconfiguration of the considered systems.

In [11], we presented MEFRESA — a Coq [16] framework providing the means
for the formal reasoning on software architectures. Here, we extend MEFRESA
with the ability to interpret PAINLESS specifications, and provably correct functions computing their compliance with the GCM technical specification [10]. We
take advantage of Coq's strong guarantees by extracting certified code, and subsequently integrate it with the ProActive middleware. In our previous work we
focused on the mechanization of the GCM, and facilities for developing arbitrarily complex proofs regarding its intricacies. In this paper, we focus on the
pragmatical aspects of deployment and reconfiguration by providing an ADL,
and all the toolchain that allows us to deploy and reconfigure GCM applications
in ProActive while reusing the guarantees provided by our proven back-end.

We see our contribution as two-fold. Firstly, we propose PAINLESS, a novel
ADL supporting parametrized specifications and architectural reconfigurations.
Its declarative nature promotes concise and modular specifications. Secondly,
we describe the integration of its related tool support with ProActive. This
provides a case study on the use of certified code, fostering the application of
formal methods in a software engineering context.

The remainder of this paper is organised as follows. Section 2 briefly discusses
GCM and MEFRESA. Section 3 overviews our approach for extending the Pro-
Active middleware to cope with PAINLESS specifications. Section 4 introduces

the semantics of PAINLESS. Section 5 shows the specification of the use case depicted by Figure 1 in PAINLESS. Related work is discussed in Section 6. For last, Section 7 concludes this paper.

2 Background

MEFRESA provides a mechanized specification of the GCM, a simple *operation* language for manipulating architectural specifications, and the means to prove arbitrary complex properties about instantiated or parametrized architectures. It is developed with the Coq proof assistant [16].[1]

The GCM is constituted by three core elements: interfaces, components, and bindings.

An interface is defined by an *id* denoting its name, a *signature* corresponding to its *classpath*, and a *path* identifying its location in the component's hierarchy (i.e. the component it belongs to). It is of internal or external *visibility*, has a client or server *role*, is of functional or non-functional *functionality*, has an optional or mandatory *contingency*, and its *cardinality* is singleton, multicast or gathercast.

A component has an *id*, a *path*, a *class*, subcomponents, interfaces, and bindings. This implicitly models GCM's hierarchical nature. Further, components holding subcomponents are called *composite*.

Bindings act as the means to connect components together through their interfaces. They are composed by a *path* indicating the component holding the binding, and *ids* identifying the involved components and interfaces. Moreover, they can be of normal, import or export kind. A normal binding connects two components at the same hierarchical level, that is, they have the same enclosing component. The remaining kind of bindings are connecting together a component with a subcomponent. Whether of import and export kind depends on the client interface being from the subcomponent or from the enclosing one, respectively.

The GCM technical specification [10] dictates the constraints that a GCM application must comply with. They can be summed up into properties regarding the *form* of the architecture and its readiness to start execution. These requirements are encoded by the well-formed and well-typed predicates.

Well-Formed and Well-Typed Architectures. A component is well-formed if its subcomponents are well-formed and uniquely identifiable through their identifiers. Further, its interfaces, and bindings must also be well-formed.

Interfaces are well-formed if they are uniquely identifiable by their identifiers and visibility value: two interfaces may have the same identifier provided that they have a different visibility. bindings are well-formed if they are established between existing components/interfaces, from client to server interfaces, and unique.

A component may be well-formed but still unable to start execution. Further insurances are needed for the overall good functioning of the system in terms of its application dependencies. These are dictated by typing rules (see [10, p. 22]).

---

[1] MEFRESA is available online at http://mefresa.gaspar.link

An interface possesses cardinality and contingency attributes. These determine its supported communication model and the guarantee of its functionality availability, respectively. For instance, for proper system execution we must ensure that client and singleton interfaces are bound at most once. For client interfaces only those of multicast cardinality are allowed to be bound more than once.

Analogously, similar constraints apply to the interfaces' contingency attribute. An interface of mandatory contingency is guaranteed to be available at runtime. This is rather obvious for server interfaces as they implement one or more service methods, i.e., they do have a functionality of their own. Client interfaces however, are used by service methods that require other service methods to perform their task. It therefore follows that a client and mandatory interface must be bound to another mandatory interface of server role. As expected, interfaces of optional contingency are not guaranteed to be available.

MEFRESA captures these requirements by defining a well-typed predicate. Basically, it requires that both the contingency and cardinality concerns are met throughout the component hierarchy. Architectures not meeting these requirements are said to be *ill-typed*.

An Operation Language for Manipulating GCM Architectures. Another important element of MEFRESA is an *operation* language that allows the manipulation of GCM architectures. It possesses seven constructors: Mk_component, Rm_component, Mk_interface, Mk_binding, Rm_binding, Seq, and Done. The meaning of each constructor should be intuitive from its name. The only doubt may arise from the Seq constructor: it stands for operation composition.

Its operational semantics is mechanized by the step predicate, and exhibit the following structure: $op \ / \ \sigma \to op' \ / \ \sigma'$. States are denoted by σ, and in our particular case these have the shape of a component, i.e., an empty state is an empty component, etc. Thus, σ represents the component hierarchy being built.

With Coq, one can use these semantic rules to interactively reduce an operation to its *normal form* done, at which point some final state σ is attained. Naturally, the ability to perform such reduction depends on the demonstration that all required premises for each individual reduction step are met. This lets us wonder about a more general property that one can expect about σ on an overall operation reduction. Let $\longrightarrow^*$ be the reflexive transitive closure of the step predicate. Then, the theorem depicted by Listing 1.1 should be intuitive.

```
1  Theorem validity: forall (s s':state) (op:operation),
2      well_formed s           ->
3      op / s --->* Done / s' ->
4      well_formed s'.
```

Listing 1.1. validity statement

Informally, it expresses that if s is a well-formed state, and if we are able to reduce op to Done, then we know that the resulting state s' is well-formed. Proving this theorem is achieved by induction on the operation language constructors.

3   Overview of Our Approach

Figure 2 gives an overview of our approach. In short, we obtain an extension to ProActive that is able to cope with PAINLESS architectures.

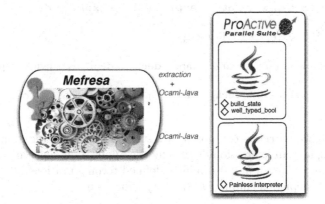

Fig. 2. Integration of Painless with ProActive

We extend MEFRESA with functions — build_state and well_typed_bool — responsible for ensuring the compliance of a deployment/reconfiguration specification with the GCM requirements. We prove these functions correct w.r.t the GCM mechanized specification, and use Coq's extraction mechanism to obtain certified OCaml code. Further, we also define a PAINLESS interpreter that translates PAINLESS expressions to MEFRESA's operation language. This is directly programmed in OCaml. Finally, to ease the integration with ProActive, we use OCaml-Java [5] to produce Java byte code.

3.1   Painless Hello World

PAINLESS provides the software architect with the ability to write parametrized architectures and its possible structural reconfigurations in a declarative style. An excerpt of its grammar is defined by Table 1.

Its elementary — or *normal forms* — expressions include natural numbers, booleans, lists, and strings. Naturally, one can also use variables. Making and removing elements from the component architecture is achieved by the polymorphic mk and rm, respectively. As expected, skip is idempotent. Components, interfaces and bindings are also first-class citizens — where bexp is an expression for the three types of bindings. Facilities for manipulating lists, comparison, and binary operators such as + and - are also built-in features. The standard if-then-else, function application, sequence ; and match constructors conclude the range of allowed expressions. **decl** acts as a declaration layer composed by the usual (potentially recursive) let definitions, indexed by a parameter *P*.

Table 1. PAINLESS syntax (excerpt)

$$\textbf{exp} ::= \text{n} \mid \text{true} \mid \text{false} \mid [] \mid str \mid \text{x} \mid \text{mk } \textbf{exp} \mid \text{rm } \textbf{exp} \mid \text{skip}$$
$$\mid \text{Component } \textbf{exp}_1 \ldots \textbf{exp}_6 \mid \text{Interface } \textbf{exp}_1 \ldots \textbf{exp}_7 \mid \text{Binding } \textbf{bexp}$$
$$\mid \textbf{exp} :: \textbf{exp} \mid \textbf{exp} = \textbf{exp} \mid \textbf{exp} + \textbf{exp} \mid \textbf{exp} - \textbf{exp}$$
$$\mid \text{if } \textbf{exp} \text{ then } \textbf{exp} \text{ else } \textbf{exp} \mid \textbf{exp} \textbf{ exp} \mid \textbf{exp} \text{ ; } \textbf{exp}$$
$$\mid \text{match } \textbf{exp} \text{ with } \textbf{pat}_1 \rightarrow \textbf{exp}_1 \ldots \textbf{pat}_k \rightarrow \textbf{exp}_{k \geq 1} \text{ end}$$

$$\textbf{decl} ::= \text{let } P = \textbf{exp} \mid \text{let rec } P = \textbf{exp}$$

$$\textbf{rcfg} ::= \text{Reconfiguration } str \text{ arg}_0 \ldots \text{arg}_k \text{: } \textbf{decl}_0 \ldots \textbf{decl}_k \text{ reconfigure } \textbf{exp}$$

$$\textbf{arch} ::= \text{Architecture } str \text{ : } \textbf{decl}_0 \ldots \textbf{decl}_{k \geq 0} \text{ deploy } \textbf{exp rcfg}_0 \ldots \textbf{rcfg}_{h \geq 0}$$

An architecture **arch** is composed by a string str representing its name, $k \geq 0$ declarations, and an expression describing the application deployment topology. Further, it may contain $h \geq 0$ similarly defined reconfigurations.

Listing 1.2 depicts a simple PAINLESS specification.

```
1 Architecture "Street Light component":
2 let itf_class = "org.lightscontrol.GetLightInfo"
3 let impl_class = "org.lightscontrol.StreetLight"
4
5 let itf = Interface "GetLightInfo" itf_class ["Street Light"] External
          Server Functional Mandatory Singleton
6 let streetLight = Component "Street Light" [] impl_class [] [itf] []
7 deploy mk streetLight
```

Listing 1.2. A first Painless specification

Its meaning should be intuitive. We give a representative name to the specification (line 1), and define two definitions holding an interface and component class (lines 2-3). Then, we define an interface named *"GetLightInto"*, using the previously defined class, with a path indicating the component it belongs, and followed by its attributes concerning its visibility, role, etc (line 5). Next, we define the component named *"Street Light"*, with an empty path — i.e., at the root of the component hierarchy —, with impl_class as its implementation class, without subcomponents, with itf as its only interface, and without bindings (line 6). Finally, we deploy the application (line 7).

3.2 Computing States from Operations

PAINLESS specifications are translated to MEFRESA's operation language. The details of this process are discussed in Section 4.

As discussed above, one can check the feasibility of reducing an operation by interactively applying its reduction rules and attempting to prove the required premises. This ability is of great value when attempting to prove arbitrary complex properties about parametrized architectures. Yet, if we intend to build a state representing the result of an operation reduction, then we would be better with a function performing such task. This is the purpose of the function depicted by Listing 1.3.

```
1  Function build_state (op:operation) (s:state) : option state :=
2  match op with
3  | Mk_component i p ic cl lc li lb =>
4      if beq_bool (valid_component_path_bool p s && no_id_clash_bool i p
         s
5          && dec_component (Component i p ic cl lc li lb)) false then
6          None
7      else
8          add_component s p i ic cl lc li lb
9      ...
10
11 | Seq         op1 op2              =>
12     match build_state op1 s with
13         | None    => None
14         | Some s' => build_state op2 s'
15     end
16 | Done                            => Some s
17 end.
```

Listing 1.3. Excerpt of the build_state function definition

The above excerpt shows how we can use a function to compute the result of an arbitrary operation reduction. Basically, it pattern matches on the parameter op (line 2), and proceeds depending on the matched constructor. For instance, if it is a Mk_component, it performs the adequate checks w.r.t. to the creation of a component, and invokes the add_component function (lines 3-8). As expected, valid_component_path_bool is a boolean function checking if path p points to an existing component in the state init. no_id_clash checks that the identifier i is not already used by another component at the same hierarchical level. For last, dec_component computes whether the component to be added is well-formed.

Apart from the Seq and Done constructors, the remaining operation constructors are handled analogously. Seq is composed by two operations (line 11), the leftmost operation is fully evaluated, and the resulting state is used for evaluating the rightmost operation (lines 12-15). Done means that the end of the operation was reached, and it simply returns the current state (line 16).

Another important note regards the use of the option type as return type of this function. This is due to the fact that it only returns a state if it was able to fully evaluate the given operation, otherwise, if the operation is *invalid*, it simply returns None. As seen above, the validity theorem (see Listing 1.1) enunciates that reducing an operation to Done from a well-formed state yields a well-formed state. Naturally, the analogous behaviour is expected from the build_state function. Further, we also expect it to always be able to compute a resulting state from an operation op, whenever it is possible to fully evaluate op. Formally, listing 1.4 depicts the relevant theorem.

```
1  Theorem build_state_correctness:
2      forall op s s',
3          well_formed s ->
4          (op / s ---->* Done / s' <-> build_state op s = Some s').
```

Listing 1.4. build_state correctness

Proving build_state_correctness requires a case analysis on the operation constructors, and relating the boolean checks made in build_state with the premises of the step predicate.

Considering the context of a component-based application life-cycle, one deploys its application by performing an operation *op* on an empty state — which is provably well-formed. Then, if *op* can indeed be reduced, we reach a well-formed state s (see Listing 1.1). Performing an architectural reconfiguration boils down to applying an operation *op'* to s, leading to yet another well-formed state s' — provided that *op'* can indeed be reduced —, and this can be repeated indefinitely. Indeed, there is no need to explicitly compute the well-formedness of the attained states, as it is provably guaranteed. There is however such a need regarding their well-typedness. To this end, we define the *well_typed_bool* : *component* → *boolean* function. Basically, it acts as a decision procedure w.r.t. the well-typedness of a component. It is proved as the computational counterpart of the well_typed predicate, that is, it is both *sound* and *complete* w.r.t. the well_typed predicate.

If an issue occurs — invalid operation or ill-typedness of the returned state — an exception is thrown and the deployment aborts. Otherwise, the operation is mapped to the adequate methods composing the ProActive API, and the actual deployment is performed by the middleware. Further, the object holding the state's structure is kept for subsequent reconfiguration tasks.

4   Painless Semantics

Table 2 gives an excerpt of the rules for translating expressions to MEFRESA's operation language. We use $\Gamma \vdash e \Downarrow v$ for denoting the evaluation of e under the environment Γ being reduced to v, and $\vdash_t$ stands for type inference.

Rule nf_{sem} dictates that a *normal form* yields immediately a semantic value. The rule $skip_{sem}$ simply depicts that skip is translated to MEFRESA's done operation. Rules mk^c_{sem} and mk^i_{sem} illustrate the polymorphic constructor **mk** at work. It can be used to build components, interfaces and bindings — making bindings is omitted for the sake of space. These proceed by fully reducing the expression e into a component/interface/binding that can be used into MEFRESA's operations. Rule c_{sem} shows the reduction of a Component: all its elements (identifier, subcomponents, ...) need to be reduced and of adequate type. Analogous rules apply for Interfaces and Bindings. $match_{sem}$ illustrates how pattern matching is performed. First, the expression exp to be matched is reduced to some value val. Then, we reduce the expression exp_k with the corresponding pattern $pat_{k \in \{1,n\}}$ matching with val. As expected, this occurs in an environment Γ enlarged with a mapping between pat_k and val, and patterns are checked by order. var_{sem} shows that a variable is reduced by looking it up in the environment Γ. Finally, the rule seq_{sem} simple attests that a sequence of PAINLESS expressions is translated to MEFRESA's operations.

The complete reduction of an expression should yield a (sequence of) MEFRESA's operations, otherwise it is rejected. For instance, the rule $arch_{sem}$ depicts how an architecture without reconfiguration strategies is evaluated.

Table 2. PAINLESS semantic rules (excerpt)

$$\frac{normal\_form(v)}{\Gamma \vdash v \Downarrow v} \; nf_{sem} \qquad\qquad \frac{}{\Gamma \vdash skip \Downarrow \textbf{Done}} \; skip_{sem}$$

$$\frac{\Gamma \vdash e \Downarrow c \quad c = \textbf{Component } id \; p \; cl \; lc \; li \; lb}{\Gamma \vdash mk \; e \Downarrow \textbf{Mk\_component } c} \; mk^{c}_{sem} \qquad \frac{\Gamma \vdash e \Downarrow i \quad i = \textbf{Interface } id \; p \; sig \; v \; f \; co \; ca}{\Gamma \vdash mk \; e \Downarrow \textbf{Mk\_interface } i} \; mk^{i}_{sem}$$

$$\frac{\begin{array}{c} \Gamma \vdash exp_1 \Downarrow id \quad \Gamma \vdash_t id : string \quad \Gamma \vdash exp_2 \Downarrow p \quad \Gamma \vdash_t p : list \; string \\ \Gamma \vdash exp_3 \Downarrow cl \quad \Gamma \vdash_t cl : string \quad \Gamma \vdash exp_4 \Downarrow lc \quad \Gamma \vdash_t lc : list \; component \\ \Gamma \vdash exp_5 \Downarrow li \quad \Gamma \vdash_t li : list \; interface \quad \Gamma \vdash exp_6 \Downarrow lb \quad \Gamma \vdash_t lb : list \; binding \end{array}}{\Gamma \vdash \textbf{Component } exp_1 \; ... \; exp_6 \Downarrow \textbf{Component } id \; p \; cl \; lc \; li \; lb} \; c_{sem}$$

$$\frac{\Gamma \vdash exp \Downarrow val \quad matches(pat_k, val) \wedge \forall h, h < k \to \neg matches(pat_h, val) \quad \Gamma, (pat_k, val) \vdash exp_k \Downarrow v_k}{\Gamma \vdash match \; exp \; with \; pat_1 \to exp_1 \; ... \; pat_n \to exp_n \; end \Downarrow v_k} \; match_{sem}$$

$$\frac{\Gamma[x] = \alpha}{\Gamma \vdash x \Downarrow \alpha} \; var_{sem} \qquad \frac{\begin{array}{cc} \Gamma \vdash exp_1 \Downarrow \alpha & \Gamma \vdash_t \alpha : operation \\ \Gamma \vdash exp_2 \Downarrow \beta & \Gamma \vdash_t \beta : operation \end{array}}{\Gamma \vdash exp_1 \; ; \; exp_2 \Downarrow \alpha \; ; \; \beta} \; seq_{sem}$$

$$\frac{\forall i, 0 \le i \le k. \; decl_i = (P_i, \; exp_i) \quad \Gamma \vdash exp_i \Downarrow \beta_i \quad \Gamma, (P_0, \beta_0), ..., (P_k, \beta_k) \vdash exp \Downarrow \alpha \quad \Gamma \vdash_t \alpha : operation}{\Gamma \vdash \textbf{Architecture } str\textbf{: } \textbf{decl}_0 \; ... \; \textbf{decl}_{k \ge 0} \; deploy \; \textbf{exp} \Downarrow \alpha} \; arch_{sem}$$

Basically, the deployment expression *exp* is reduced to α, under an environment including all the declarations $decl_i$. Naturally, α must be of type *operation*.

Dealing with reconfigurations is performed analogously. The expression to be evaluated is reduced on a context including the deployment declarations, the ones defined locally, and its instantiated parameters.

4.1 Painless Standard Library

As discussed above, the GCM component model is hierarchical, that is, a component may possess subcomponents. A component communicates with the "outside" world through its *external* interface, whereas it relies on its *internal* interfaces to communicate with its subcomponents. Typically, composite component interfaces are symmetric, that is, for each external interface of server role there is a internal interface of client role, and vice-versa. Listing 1.5 and Listing 1.6 depict a convenient function to ease the specification of such scenarios — with the obvious definition of visibility_symmetry omitted for the sake of space.

```
1 let role_symmetry r =
2   match r with
3     Client -> Server
4   | Server -> Client
5   end
```

Listing 1.5. Role symmetry

```
1 let symmetric i = match i with
2   Interface id si p v r f co ca ->
3     let vs = visibility_symmetry v in
4     let rs = role_symmetry r in
5     Interface id si p vs rs f co ca
  end
```

Listing 1.6. Interface symmetry

Another common scenario regards the need to change the location of a component. For this, we define the function depicted by Listing 1.7.

```
1 let change_component_path p comp =
2   match comp with
3     Component id cp cl lc li lb ->
4
5       let rec change_subcomponents_path p lc =
6         match lc with
7           []       -> []
8         | c :: r -> change_component_path p c ::
                    change_subcomponents_path p r
9         end
10      in
11
12      let lcm = change_subcomponents_path (suffix p id) lc in
13      let lim = change_interfaces_path (suffix p id) li in
14      let lbm = change_bindings_path (suffix p id) lb in
15      Component id p cl lcm lim lbm
16  end
```

Listing 1.7. Changing the path of a component

A component may contain subcomponents, interfaces and bindings. As such, it is also necessary to adjust their paths. We define a inner function (lines 5-9) to deal with nested recursion. The function suffix returns a path with the second parameter suffixed to the first one. Moreover, we use other library functions — change_interfaces_path and change_bindings_path — to adjust the interfaces and bindings paths (lines 13-14).

Another useful function concerns the making of components in a specific path. Listing 1.8 defines such a function.

```
1 let mk_in p c =   mk (change_component_path p c)
```

Listing 1.8. Changing the path of a component

All the discussed functions are part of PAINLESS standard library along with other facilities for dealing with common specification tasks. Further, the user can easily build its own libraries as specifications can be imported.

5   Specifying the Lights Control use case in Painless

In this section we show how the specification of the Lights Control application discussed in Section 1 (see Figure 1) is achieved in PAINLESS. We follow a modular approach by separately specifying the Switched On Lights, Sensed Brightness Info, and Lights Control components.

Listing 1.9 depicts the specification of the Switched On Lights component.

```
1  Architecture "Composite component: Switched On Lights":
2
3  let id = "Switched On Lights"
4  let p = [id]
5
6  let streetLight =
7    Component "Street Light" p "org.lightscontrol.StreetLight"
8    []
9    [Interface "GetLightInfo" "org.lightscontrol.GetLightInfo"
10     [id; "Street Light"] External Server Functional Mandatory Singleton
             ]
11   []
12
13 let collectLightInfo p =
14   Interface "CollectLightInfo" "org.lightscontrol.CollectLightInfo"
15              p External Server Functional Mandatory Singleton
16
17 let getLightInfo =
18   Interface "GetLightInfo" "org.lightscontrol.GetLightInfo"
19       [id; "Light Collector"] External Client Functional Mandatory
             Multicast
20
21 let lightCollector =
22   Component "Light Collector" p "org.lightscontrol.LightCollector"
23   [] [collectLightInfo [id; "Light Collector"] ; getLightInfo] []
24
25 let switchedOnLights nrOfStreetLights =
26   Component id [] "null"
27   (lightCollector :: list_of streetLight nrOfStreetLights)
28   [collectLightInfo p ; symmetric (collectLightInfo p)]
29   (Export p "CollectLightInfo" "Light Collector" "CollectLightInfo" ::
30    normal_bindings p "Light Collector" "GetLightInfo" "Street Light" "
         GetLightInfo" nrOfStreetLights )
```

Listing 1.9. Specification for the Switched On Lights component (from Figure 1)

We start by giving a descriptive name to this ADL (line 1). Then, we define the Street Light component (lines 6-11). It possesses a name, a path indicating where it is in the component hierarchy, a classpath, an empty list of subcomponents, one server interface and no bindings. This definition should be seen as a template, as its instances are the ones dynamically added/removed. Next, we define the Light Collector component (lines 21-23) and its two interfaces (lines 13-19). The first interface is parametrized by its path as we shall use it later when specifying the Lights Control component (see Listing 1.11). Last, we specify the Switched On Lights component parametrized by its number of Street Lights (lines 25-30). As expected, its subcomponents include the Light Collector component and a list of *nrOfStreetLights* Street Light components (line 27). The interfaces are symmetric and their specification is conveniently handled by the interface_symmetry function. Further, the function normal_bindings is responsible for binding Light Collector's multicast interface to the several Street Light instances.

It should be noted that this specification can be used on its own by adding a deployment expression. Listing 1.10 depicts an example of a deployment with one hundred Street Light components.

```
33 deploy mk (switchedOnLights 100)
```

Listing 1.10. Example of a deployment specification for Switched On Lights component

The ADL of the Sensed Brightness Info component follows the same rationale and is omitted for the sake of space. Listing 1.11 depicts the deployment specification of the overall Lights Control application. As an example, the Street Light and Sensed Brightness Info components are instantiated to ten each.

```
1 Require "org.lightscontrol.adl.SwitchedOnLights.painless"
2 Require "org.lightscontrol.adl.SensedBrightnessInfo.painless"
3 Architecture "Lights Control Architecture":
4
5 let p = ["Lights Control"]
6
7 let lightsControl =
8   Component "Lights Control" [] "null" []
9     [collectBrightnessInfo p; symmetric (collectBrightnessInfo p);
10     collectLightInfo p    ; symmetric (collectLightInfo p)    ] []
11
12 let n = 10 //number of sensor components to deploy
13 let m = 10 //number of light components to deploy
14
15 deploy
16   mk (add_subcomponents lightsControl [sensedBrightnessInfo n;
        switchedOnLights m]) ;
17   mk export p "CollectLightInfo" "Switched On Lights" "CollectLightInfo
        ";
18   mk export p "CollectBrightnessInfo" "Sensed Brightness Info" "
        CollectBrightnessInfo"
```

Listing 1.11. Specification for the Lights Control application

We start by importing the ADLs from the Switched On Lights and Sensed Brightness Info components (lines 1-2). This adds all their definitions to the current scope, namely the interfaces collectLightInfo and collectBrightnessInfo. Next, we define the Lights Control without including its subcomponents and bindings (lines 7-10). These are added directly in the deployment expression. The function add_subcomponents belongs to PAINLESS standard library. It places the subcomponents into LightsControl while adequately adjusting their path field (line 16). Finally, the two export bindings are established to the two added subcomponents (lines 17-18).

The last remaining ingredient concerns the structural reconfigurations. Listing 1.12 depicts two reconfiguration strategies regarding the addition and removal of the nth Street Light component.

```
22 Reconfiguration "add light" n:
23   let p = ["Lights Control" ; "Switched On Lights"]
24   reconfigure
25     mk_in p (nth streetLight n);
26     mk normal p "Light Collector" "GetLightInfo" ("Street Light"+n) "
          GetLightInfo"
27
28 Reconfiguration "remove light" n:
29   let p = ["Lights Control" ; "Switched On Lights"]
30   reconfigure
31     rm normal p "Light Collector" "GetLightInfo" ("Street Light"+n) "
          GetLightInfo" ;
32     rm ["Lights Control" ; "Switched On Lights"] ("Street Light"+n)
```

Listing 1.12. Reconfigurations specification for the Lights Control application

Their understanding should pose no doubt. The first adds a Street Light component by making it with the adequate path (line 25) and subsequently binding it to Light Collector's multicast interface (line 26). As expected, the expression nth streetLight n returns a streetLight component with an identifier suffixed by n. The second reconfiguration is handled in a similar manner. We first need to unbind the component to remove (line 31) — where normal is the constructor for normal bindings —, and then we proceed by removing it (line 32).

From a programming perspective, the reconfigurations are available through a simple method call indicating its name and parameters. Further, the evaluation of the deployment specification and subsequent applied reconfigurations is carried out by the machinery originating from MEFRESA. Moreover, it should be noted that checking that a reconfiguration leads to a well-formed and well-typed component architecture is achieved without stopping any component. Indeed, before reconfiguring the application, ProActive needs to stop the involved composite component. The inherent benefit is that only valid reconfigurations w.r.t the mechanized GCM specification are mapped to the ProActive API. For instance, attempting to add a Street Light component with the same identifier as another one already deployed is rejected, i.e., an exception is thrown.

Our ProActive extension is freely available online. The release contains the examples discussed here and several others. The reader is pointed to the following website for more details http://painless.gaspar.link.

6   Related Work

Let us mention the work around the ArchWare ADL [14]. They claim that *"software that cannot change is condemned to atrophy"* and introduce the concept of an *active software architecture*. Based on the higher-order π-calculus, it provides constructs for specifying control flow, communication and dynamic topology. Unlike PAINLESS, its syntax exhibits an imperative style and type inference is not supported, thus not promoting concise specifications. Nevertheless, it is sufficiently rich to provide executable specifications of active software architectures. Moreover, user-defined constraints are supported through the ArchWare Architecture Analysis Language. Yet, their focus is more aimed at the specification and analysis of the ADL, rather than actual application execution and deployment. In our work, the user solely defines the architecture of its application, structural constraints are implicit: they are within the mechanized GCM specification. Further, our tool support is tightly coupled with ProActive.

Also from the realm of process algebras, Archery [15] is a modelling language for software architectural patterns. It is composed by a core language and two extensions: Archery-Core, Archery-Script and Archery-Structural-Constraint. These permit the specification of structural and behavioural dimensions of architectures, the definition of scripts for reconfiguration, and the formulation of structural constraints, respectively. Moreover, a bigraphical semantics is defined for Archery specifications. This grants the reduction of the constraint satisfaction verification to a type-checking problem. However, this process is not guarantee to be automatic, and type-checking decidability remains as future work.

Gerel [9] is a generic reconfiguration language including powerful query constructs based on first-order logic. Further, its reconfiguration procedures may contain preconditions *à la* Hoare Logic [12]. These are evaluated by brute force. It is unclear how they cope with the inherent undecidability of such task.

Di Cosmo et. al. defined the Aeolus component model [6]. Their focus is on the automation of cloud-based applications deployment scenarios. Their proposal is loosely inspired by the Fractal component model [4] whose most peculiar characteristics are its hierarchical composition nature and reconfiguration capabilities. However, while both approaches permit architectural reconfigurations at runtime, its specification is not supported by their ADL, it solely contemplates deployment related aspects. Moreover, support for parametrized specifications is also not covered, forcing the software architect to explicitly define the application's structure.

Regarding Fractal, it is also worth noticing that it tries to overcome the lack of support for reconfiguration specification through Fscript [7]. Fscript embeds FPath — a DSL for navigation and querying of Fractal architectures — and acts as a scripting language for reconfiguration strategies. These are not evaluated for their validity. Nevertheless, system consistency is ensured by the use of *transactions*: a violating reconfiguration is *rolled back*.

Like the Fractal ADL, xMAML [13] is XML-based, yet it permits the specification of reconfigurations. An important difference is that their focus is on processor architectures and aim at producing synthesizable models.

In [8], Di Ruscio et. al. defend the concept of building your own ADL through the BYADL framework. Further, they claim that *"it is not possible to define a general, optimal ADL once and forever"*, and propose the means to incrementally extend and customize existing ADLs by composing their metamodels. This approach offers an interesting perspective regarding the interoperability of PAINLESS with other ADLs.

7   Final Remarks

In this paper we presented PAINLESS and its related novel approach for the specification of software architectures. Its declarative trait allows for intuitive and concise specifications, liberating the software architect from highly verbose specifications such as the ones obtained via machine languages like XML. Moreover, its support for parametrized architectures eases deployment — it becomes a matter of instantiation —, and thus boosts productivity. Further, in ProActive, mapping components to physical resources is achieved through *application/deployment descriptors*. While this information is not an aspect of the architecture *per se*, extending PAINLESS with such feature could be envisaged.

Another key ingredient is the treatment of structural reconfigurations as first-class citizens. Indeed, by supporting the specification of the topological changes that may occur at runtime, it yields a better understanding of the application. Moreover, it is worth noticing that the specified reconfigurations become easily accessible from a programming perspective: through a simple method call with the name of the desired reconfiguration. Furthermore, reconfiguration specifications are evaluated at runtime. The clear benefit is that one can be highly confident that the reconfiguration will not leave the application in a *ill formed* or *ill typed* state as the evaluation process is carried out by provably correct code extracted from MEFRESA. Additionally, a further inherent advantage is that it all happens without stopping the application. Indeed, actually performing the reconfiguration requires it to be stopped at the composite level. By making a prior evaluation, the risk of reconfiguration failure is avoided.

References

1. ActiveEon, S.A.S.: ProActive - A Library for Parallel and Distributed Programming
2. Baude, F., Caromel, D., Dalmasso, C., Danelutto, M., Getov, V., Henrio, L., Pérez, C.: GCM: a grid extension to fractal for autonomous distributed components. Annales des Télécommunications (2009)
3. Baude, F., Henrio, L., Naoumenko, P.: Structural reconfiguration: an autonomic strategy for GCM components. In: Proc. of the Fifth International Conference on Autonomic and Autonomous Systems: ICAS 2009 (2009)
4. Bruneton, E., Coupaye, T., Stefani, J.-B.: The Fractal component model (2004)
5. Clerc, X.: OCaml-Java: OCaml on the JVM. In: Loidl, H.-W., Peña, R. (eds.) TFP 2012. LNCS, vol. 7829, pp. 167–181. Springer, Heidelberg (2013)
6. Cosmo, R.D., Zacchiroli, S., Zavattaro, G.: Towards a formal component model for the cloud. In: Eleftherakis, G., Hinchey, M., Holcombe, M. (eds.) SEFM 2012. LNCS, vol. 7504, pp. 156–171. Springer, Heidelberg (2012)
7. David, P.-C., Ledoux, T., Coupaye, T., Léger, M.: FPath and FScript: Language support for navigation and reliable reconfiguration of Fractal architectures. Annals of Telecommunications 64(1-2), 45–63 (2009)
8. Di Ruscio, D., Malavolta, I., Muccini, H., Pelliccione, P., Pierantonio, A.: ByADL: An MDE framework for building extensible architecture description languages. In: Babar, M.A., Gorton, I. (eds.) ECSA 2010. LNCS, vol. 6285, pp. 527–531. Springer, Heidelberg (2010)
9. Endler, M., Wei, J.: Programming generic dynamic reconfigurations for distributed applications. In: International Workshop on Configurable Distributed Systems, pp. 68–79 (1992)
10. ETSI. ETSI TS 102 829 V1.1.1 - GRID; Grid Component Model (GCM); GCM Fractal Architecture Description Language (ADL). Technical Spec., ETSI (2009)
11. Gaspar, N., Henrio, L., Madelaine, E.: Bringing Coq into the world of GCM distributed applications. International Journal of Parallel Programming, 1–20 (2013)
12. Hoare, C.A.R.: An axiomatic basis for computer programming. Communications of the ACM 12(10), 576–580 (1969)
13. Lallet, J., Pillement, S., Sentieys, O.: xMAML: A modeling language for dynamically reconfigurable architectures. In: Antonio, N., Carballo, P.P. (eds.) DSD, pp. 680–687. IEEE Computer Society (2009)
14. Morrison, R., Kirby, G.N.C., Balasubramaniam, D., Mickan, K., Oquendo, F., Cîmpan, S., Warboys, B., Snowdon, B., Greenwood, R.M.: Constructing Active Architectures in the ArchWare ADL. CoRR (2010)

Linear Evolution of Domain Architecture in Service-Oriented Software Product Lines

Sedigheh Khoshnevis* and Fereidoon Shams

Department of Computer Engineering, Shahid Beheshti University, G.C., Tehran, Iran
{s_khoshnevis,f_shams}@sbu.ac.ir

Abstract. In service-oriented software product lines, when a change occurs in the business process variability model, designing the domain architecture from scratch imposes costs of re-architecture, high costs of change in the domain-level assets; and high costs of change in many products based on the new domain architecture. In this paper, focusing on the linear evolution scenario in service-oriented product lines, which refers to propagating changes in some assets to some other assets, both in the domain level, we deal with the problem of propagating changes in domain requirements (the business process variability model) to the domain architecture level, in a cost-optimal and consistency-preserving way. We present a method to suggest the optimal change propagation options to reach the aforementioned goals. The method showed promising to provide minimal change costs as well as to fully preserve consistency of the target models if no human intervention exists in the change propagation results.

Keywords: variability. service-oriented product line. linear evolution. Pareto optimization. consistency.

1 Introduction

A software product line is a collection of software-intensive systems that share common properties and are developed aiming at meeting specific market needs or special missions based on a set of core assets [1]. Indeed, a software product line contains a family of software systems that share a number of common functionalities and a number of variable ones. To address the common and variable functionalities, reusable core assets (such as requirements, design artifacts, components, test cases, etc.) are developed, which can be reused by different members of the family[2].

There are two main lifecycles in software product line engineering: domain engineering and application engineering[3]. In the domain engineering lifecycle, the main emphasis is on defining the commonalities and the differences, or in other words determining variability among the aimed products, based on which, the reusable artifacts (the core assets) are developed or obtained. Meanwhile,

---

* Corresponding author.

© IFIP International Federation for Information Processing 2015
M. Dastani and M.Sirjani (Eds.): FSEN 2015, LNCS 9392, pp. 275–291, 2015.
DOI: 10.1007/978-3-319-24644-4_19

in application engineering, the core assets are reused in developing particular products of the product line, using the common (mandatory) product elements and selecting optional and variant product elements, both determined in domain engineering lifecycle.

In a service-oriented software product line, the software architecture building blocks are services, which are identified and specified based on the business processes[4]. The business processes are continually changing and hence, a domain engineer may decide to reflect the changes of the business processes to other artifacts in the software product line. Such a change, therefore, can widely affect artifacts both in the domain and application engineering lifecycles [3].

In general, changing or evolution of a software product line can take place in terms of one or a combination of six *evolution scenarios*, namely, linear evolution, synchronization, merge, propagation, cloning and derivation [5] (see Table 1). These evolution scenarios are different in the *change source* and *change target*. For instance, in the linear evolution scenario, the change source and the change target are both in the domain-level.

Table 1. SPL evolution scenarios [5]

Scenario	Change Source	Change Target	Description
Linear Evolution	Domain Variability Models	Domain Variability Models	-
Synchronization	Domain Variability Models	Product Configurations	-
Merge	Product Configurations	Domain Variability Models	-
Propagation	Product Configurations	Other Product Configurations	-
Cloning	-	New Product Configuration	Based on current product configurations
Derivation	-	New Product Configuration	Based on domain variability models

The scope of research in this paper includes the linear evolution scenario, to propagate changes in a service-oriented software product line, from the requirements-level variability model (which is the business process variability model) to the architecture-level variability model (which mainly includes the variability of services). One way to achieve the mentioned propagation is re-architecting the target architecture model back from scratch based on the changed domain requirements. However, using this way will impose costs, not only for the re-architecture itself, but also for providing new single services and service compositions that may be too distant from their previous versions, and thus will result to: (A) wide changes in the core assets in the domain level; and hence, (B) wide changes in the products that are built by reusing them.

On this basis, in this research we aim to: *"propose a semi-automatic method for linear evolution of service-oriented architecture-level variability model due to the changes in the business process variability model in a way that the costs of change are minimized and that the consistency of the changed model is preserved"*.

To reach this goal, we were inspired by the MAPE-K control loop which is widely adopted in software adaptation in response to changes [6] and we made use of multi-objective Pareto optimization mechanisms to minimize change costs.

Decision making for applying the changes may depend on other factors (such as economic conditions, state of the market, etc.) that cannot be comprehensively determined and formulated in terms of computerized processes; therefore, although it is desirable that the change propagation process be fully automated, we emphasize on a semi-automatic method to avoid missing the role of human factors and expertise in the change decisions. We expect that the method minimizes the change costs and preserves the consistency of the target model, keeping it free from logical conflicts.

1.1   Motivating Example

As a simple example, suppose that a service-oriented Office Letter Submission (OLS) product line is established by a company. For such a product line, a business process family model is designed, based on which, a service variability model was carried out. Fig. 1 depicts the business process variability model in terms of a Business Process Family Model (BPFM), which is a notation proposed by Moon and her team [7,8]. It is an extended UML activity diagram augmented with variability-specific elements, such as variation points, optional versus mandatory activities, variant regions (set of variant activities that generally form an optional sub-process), variability relationships (either excludes or requires constraint), etc.

Moreover, we consider the service variability model (which we name SVM for ease) as a set of services and their interfaces (including operations and messages), along with their variability attributes (optional versus mandatory services, operations and messages) and variability relationships ("excludes", "requires", and "or" relationships between services and between operations). An SVM for the sample OLS product line is depicted in Fig. 3.

Suppose that the models represented in Fig. 1 and 3 both belong to the current version (version i) of the sample OLS product line. Note that, for convenience, we have only included the identifiers of activities that are realized by the corresponding service operations in the services; for example in Fig. 3, optional service "Serv1" includes an optional operation "Oper1" that realizes activity "Create Draft for Internal Letters". It has a set of incoming and outgoing messages that are not depicted in Fig. 3, as they are not necessary for the purposes of the current running example.

Let us suppose that the BPFM is requested to change to version $i+1$ as depicted in Fig. 2. As it is obvious, the following items of change have occurred in BPFM version $i+1$ regarding its previous version.

- Mandatory activity (4) is removed.
- Mandatory activity (7) is changed to optional.
- Mandatory activity (9) is added.

Considering specifically the addition of the new activity (9), we have five change options in the SVM: adding the new operation to: "Serv1", "Serv2", "Serv3", "Serv4", or a new empty service "Serv5". If, for example, for the abstract architecture-level service "Serv1" two concrete services CS1 and CS2 are developed, and if there are 20 configurations in which, CS1 or CS2 are invoked,

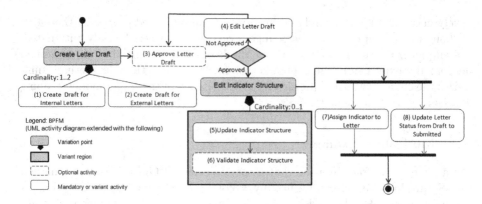

Fig. 1. Current version (i) of the BPFM diagram for the sample Office Letter Submission (OLS) product line

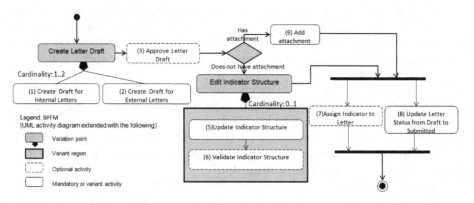

Fig. 2. New version ($i + 1$) of the BPFM diagram for the sample Office Letter Submission (OLS) product line

then a change in "Serv1" propagates not only to those two concrete services, but also to 20 products. Similarly, we would have a number of concrete services for other abstract services in the SVM, each of which could be invoked in a number of product configurations. Therefore, it is crucial to find an optimal set of changes to the SVM so that the change cost, in terms of number of affected artifacts, is minimized.

Moreover, a method to deal with this problem is expected to preserve consistency in the new version of SVM. An inconsistent SVM contains internal logical conflicts between its elements. For example, if there is an "excludes" relationship between two mandatory services, then it is not consistent, since being mandatory implies that in every product configuration, both services are invoked; and the "excludes" relationship implies that only one of them can be invoked in a product configuration, which is contradictory. In another work in progress, we have derived and articulated inconsistency conditions to be checked automatically on SVM models.

In short, the research problem is how to find the set of proper changes in the SVM among a set of change options, so that the cost of change is minimized and the consistency of the target model is preserved. The rest of the paper is organized as follows: In section 2, we take a glance at the previous work on this subject; afterwards, in section 3 we fully describe the proposed method. Section 4 is dedicated to evaluation of the research, while section 5 concludes the paper and proposes a few trends for the future work.

2   State of the Art

The previous work regarding the subject of this research can be divided into two main categories: research works related to software product line evolution, and the research reports on evolution of variability in services and the service-oriented product lines.

Irrespective of service-orientation, there are a number of research works reported for managing and controlling evolution in software product lines (refer to [9] for a wide survey in this regard). The common notion among most of these works is two-fold: emphasis on minimizing the cost of change [10,11,12], and emphasis on consistency preservation in the product line artifacts which are subject to change [10,11,12,13].

Another common point of focus among these works is the steps of encountering with a change request. For instance, Ajila and Kaba in [11] propose evolution management mechanisms that fit in a four-phased process, which includes change identification, change impact analysis, change propagation , and change validation. The same has been proposed in service evolution (irrespective of the product line engineering) [14]; for example for services self-adaptation, the well-known MAPE-K loop has been suggested to Monitor, Analyze, Plan and Execute changes, providing and consuming some change Knowledge [6]. However, all of the research works in this first category are feature-model-based; while in a service-oriented product line, we need to support the business processes; thus these methods cannot fit to our problem.

The research works reported on evolving software with respect to the variability of services within or out of the scopes of a product line, fall into two subcategories: (A) Reports on using the concept of variability to support a set of pre-determined changes in single service-oriented software systems (such as [15] and [16]), none of which are in the scope of a software product line, and thus the works in this subcategory does not fit to our problem.

(B) Reports on supporting some type of evolution in service-oriented product lines (such as [12] and [17]); however, in this subcategory, although the research works are within the scopes of service-oriented product lines, there are no emphasis on the business processes as the main source of continuous change. Gomaa and Hashimoto [17] propose a general service-oriented variability model which uses feature models as the main requirements-level variability model, and do not focus on business process variability model. They concentrate on the basics of self-adaptation in service-oriented product lines. Moreover, Hinchey et al.

[12] discuss general issues in dynamic product lines and do not specifically address evolution scenarios in the service-oriented product lines emerging from the changes in the business processes. Hence, the research works in this subcategory, either, cannot be leveraged to solve the problem mentioned in this paper.

3   The Proposed Method

Considering the linear evolution scenario, the source of changes in the domain architecture of a service-oriented product line is the business process variability model. In this research, we specifically chose the Business Process Family Model (BPFM) notation [7,8] for the purpose of specifying the business process variability. Meanwhile, the change target is the service variability model (SVM). SVM is basically a set of mandatory and/or optional services, each of which contains a nonempty set of mandatory and/or optional operations. Among services and among operations, there can be variability relationships, including, "or", "excludes", and "requires" relationships. Thus, if we consider the proposed method as a black box, then the input to it will be a BPFM' (the changed version of the current BPFM), and the output from it will be an SVM' (the changed version of the current SVM). Inside the black box, we embed four main units and a knowledge repository, which support four main operations by sharing some knowledge among them. These four main operations are: change identification, change impact analysis, change planning and change execution, which can continue over to the change identification operation if the result of change execution is exposed to some new change. Fig. 4 depicts these four main operations besides the knowledge repository in which, all of the changes, their details, and rationales are stored. This paper focuses mostly on the first two operations of the proposed cycle.

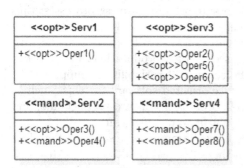

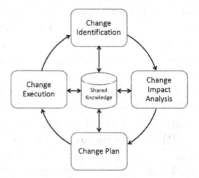

Fig. 3. Current version (*i*) of the SVM diagram for the sample Office Letter Submission (OLS) product line

Fig. 4. The proposed change cycle for linear evolution in service-oriented product line

3.1   Change Identification

"Change identification" operation includes the identification of the elements in the source model (BPFM) that are added, removed, or modified. The result, which we represent by ΔB, is in fact, the set of differences of BPFM′ (the new version) with BPFM (the old version). Each change item in ΔB, can be an element (e) or a variability relationship (r) between the elements in the BPFM, where each element e (such as an activity, a variation point, or a variants region) is a member of all BPFM elements (E); and each relationship r (such as a control flow, a connection or a constraint) is a member of all BPFM relationships (R). Elements can be added, removed or modified, while relationships can only be added or removed. On this basis we will have formula (1), in which *add* means adding an element or a relationship, *rem* means removing an element or a relationship, and *mod* denotes modifying an element.

$$ChangeItem:: = add\ e\ |\ mod\ e\ |\ rem\ e\ |\ add\ r\ |\ rem\ r \qquad (1)$$

Elements and relationships each have their quadruple structures specified in formulas (2) and (3). Formula (2) states that each element has a type (e.g., it is an activity, a variation point, or a variants region), a name, an attribute type, and an attribute value; while formula (3) denotes that a relationship has a category, a type, a source and a target (see [7,8] for details of BPFM).

$$e = (etype, ename, eattrtype, eattrvalue) \qquad (2)$$

$$r = (rcat, rtype, rsource, rdestin) \qquad (3)$$

In the example in subsection 1.1, we depicted a list of change items that occurred to the OLS BPFM.

3.2   Change Impact Analysis

The goal of "change impact analysis" operation is to (1) determine all *change options* for reflecting the change items of BPFM to SVM; (2) calculating the cost of applying each change option; and (3) providing a set of optimal change options for the architects and the domain engineers to help them in decision making about which change options to apply.

Determining SVM Change Options: To designate the changes to SVM (ΔS) as a result of changes in BPFM, we should determine all potential change items that can take place in the SVM (we call them change options) in reflection to each change item existing in ΔB; and then we should analyze costs of each change option. Let CI be the set of all change items residing in ΔB, and CO_i be the set of all possible change options in SVM in response to a change item CI_i. As an example, if currently there exists three services $S1$ to $S3$ in the SVM, and some CI_1 corresponds to adding a mandatory activity "a" to the BPFM, then each of the following four items makes up a change option in the set CO_i:

adding a new operation corresponding to activity "a" to (1) $S1$, (2) $S2$, (3) $S3$, and (4) a new empty service $S4$. Then a set CO is formed from the union of all change options co_j in each CO_i. Fig. 5 depicts the relationship between sets CI and CO. For our running OLS example in subsection 1.1, the set of change items and change options are depicted in Fig. 6.

Change Items in BPFM (CI)	CI_1		CI_2		CI_3			...
Change Options in SVM (CO)	co_1	co_2	co_3	co_4	co_5	co_6	co_7	co_8 ...
Selection Vector	v_1	v_2	v_3	v_4	v_5	v_6	v_7	v_8 ...

Fig. 5. The relationship between change items in BPFM and change options in SVM

Change Items (CI)	Remove activity (4)	Change activity (7) from mandatory to optional	Add new activity (9)				
Change Options (CO)	Apply	Apply	Add to serv1	Add to serv2	Add to serv3	Add to serv4	Add to new serv5
Selection Vector index	v_1	v_2	v_3	v_4	v_5	v_6	v_7
Solution $z1$	1	1	1	0	0	0	0
Solution $z2$	1	1	0	1	0	0	0
Solution $z3$	1	1	0	0	1	0	0
Solution $z4$	1	1	0	0	0	1	0
Solution $z5$	1	1	0	0	0	0	1
$c1$	1	0	1	1	1	1	1
$c2$	1	0	1	1	1	1	1
$c3$	1	0	0	0	0	0	0
Affected Services	$S2$	-	$S1$	$S2$	$S3$	$S4$	New Empty $S5$

Fig. 6. Potential solutions for the OLS sample

Moreover, to build up a single solution (a potential ΔS) we need to select one of the change options for each change item. The selection is done by designating a Boolean selection vector as shown in Fig. 5, with the constraint that for each change item CI_i one and only one of the corresponding change options should be set to 1, and the rest should be set to zero. Fig. 6 depicts the possible selection vectors as well as the affected services by each change option and the values of three Boolean coefficients (which will be discussed later in this subsection).

Analyzing Costs of Change in SVM: We define the total cost of reflecting the changes of BPFM to SVM as a function of (1) the costs due to the changes in service interfaces ($ICost$) and (2) the costs imposed by the changes in relationships between the services ($RCost$).

Since the calculation of economical costs of change is not within the scope of this research, we consider the change cost as the number of affected artifacts.

Here, artifacts are classified into two main classes: first, the domain-level concrete services, and second, the application-level products that use the domain-level services in their configurations.

Therefore, *ICost* imparts two costs: costs due to changes of (domain-level) concrete services developed internally or consumed from external repositories that implement and realize the abstract architecture-level services that are subject to change; and second, costs of change to all (application-level) configured products derived from the product line, which invoke those affected concrete services. The interface cost is calculated in formula (4) in which, z denotes a solution (a potential ΔS), and No_{csi} and No_{appi} represent the number of concrete services and the applications affected by the changes to the interface, respectively.

Similarly, *RCost* can be calculated. However, changes that are imposed by changing the relationships between services do not impose any effects on the domain-level concrete services; however, the products are affected, since it is crucial to keep the products "conforming" to the domain level, i.e., the new constraints (relationships) should hold in each product configuration. Otherwise, products will deviate from the product line, and this imposes extra costs for maintaining the product line. Hence, since product reconfiguration may be required, we will have formula 5, in which, z denotes a potential solution and No_{appr} represents the number of application that need to be reconfigured due to the changes to the relationships between services. Furthermore, changes to relationships in BPFM, require a re-extraction of relationships in SVM. This is achieved by Algorithm 1 , which uses the possible configurations that can be derived from the BPFM and the set of services (from the SVM) to generate the SVM which is modified in its variability relationships (we proposed this algorithm in a previous work [18], which aimed at automating extraction of an SVM from a BPFM).

$$ICost(z) = No_{csi} + No_{appi} \qquad (4)$$

$$RCost(z) = No_{appi} \qquad (5)$$

A change item, regarding its effect on SVM, may result in changes to either the concrete services, the products, both or neither (either impacting their interface or relationships or both). Therefore for each change item, we can define Boolean coefficients $c1$, $c2$ and $c3$, which show whether the change necessitates considering costs for changing interfaces of concrete services ($c1$), costs for changing products because of interface changes in concrete services ($c2$), and costs for reconfiguring the products due to the changes in the relationships ($c3$). Table 2 lists the values of $c1$ to $c3$ per each potential feasible change scenario in SVM. These coefficients for our running OLS example are listed for each change option in Fig. 6.

For a set of potential solutions, Z, we can form a set Obj_z, which is populated with individual objective vectors as ordered pairs of $(ICost, RCost)$ to be minimized. We will use these objective vectors to find a set of the most cost-effective change options in the target SVM in response to the changes in the corresponding BPFM.

Algorithm 1. Service Variability Identification

Input: Service Set (SS), BPFM Configuration Set (CS)
Output: Service variability Model (SVM)

1. $SVM \leftarrow NIL$
2. **for each** *service* in SS **do**
3.   **for each** c in CS **do**
4.   **if** !(IsUsed(*service*,c)) **then**
5.   // service is not used in configuration c
6.   **add** *service* **to** $SVM.OptionalServiceSet$
7. $ServiceIsOptional \leftarrow True$
8.   **break**
9.   **end if**
10.   **if** $!ServiceIsOptional$ **then**
11.   **add** *service* **to** $SVM.MandatoryServiceSet$
12.   **end if**
13.   **end for**
14.   **for each** s_i in *optionalServiceSet* **do**
15.   **for each** $s_j \neq s_i$ in *optionalServiceSet* **do**
16.   **for each** c in CS **do**
17.   **if** !((IsUsed(s_i,c) $\oplus$ (IsUsed(s_j,c))) **then**
18. $AreAlt \leftarrow false$
19.   **end if**
20.   **if** !((IsUsed(s_i,c) $\vee$ (IsUsed(s_j,c))) **then**
21. $AreOR \leftarrow false$
22.   **end if**
23.   **if** !(!(IsUsed(s_i,c) $\vee$ (IsUsed(s_j,c))) **then**
24. $AreIncl \leftarrow false$
25.   **end if**
26.   **end for**
27.   **if** !($AreAlt = false$) $\wedge$ (s_j,s_i) $\notin SVM.AltRelations$ **then**
28.   **add** (s_i,s_j) **to** $SVM.AltRelations$
29.   **end if**
30.   **if** !($AreOr = false$) $\wedge$ (s_j,s_i) $\notin SVM.OrRelations$ **then**
31.   **add** (s_i,s_j) **to** $SVM.OrRelations$
32.   **end if**
33.   **if** !($AreIncl = false$) **then**
34.   **add** (s_i,s_j) **to** $SVM.IncRelations$
35.   **end if**
36.   **end for**
37.   **end for**
38. **end for**
39. **return** SVM

Determining the Most Cost-Effective solution: In this step, for each change item in ΔB we should determine which change options are the least costly. For this purpose, we utilize multi-objective Pareto optimization [19]. If there is a solution z, whose $ICost$ and $Rcost$ are both less than all other change options' $ICost$ and $RCost$ respectively, then z is announced the most cost-effective solution which dominates all other solutions in cost-effectiveness. However, the problem arises when we reach a set of solutions, in which, some solutions have lower $ICost$s but higher $RCost$s, or have higher $ICost$s but lower $RCost$s compared with the other ones. In this case, no single solution can be announced as "dominating"; instead, we only can select a set of solutions, that although not dominating other solutions, are not dominated by other solutions either; that is, the set of "non-dominated" solutions that form the "Pareto-optimal" set of solutions [19]. The results of this step are used in the next step for decision-making on the Pareto-optimal set of solutions. Algorithm 2 represents the triple steps of change impact analysis.

For our OLS example, considering the concrete services and the configured products using them as denoted in Table 3, the objective vectors are those represented in Table 4. Since solution z_2 (see Fig. 6) is selected as the Pareto optimal solution, and assuming that the change is approved by the decision makers, the changes are executed and the new version of SVM (i.e., version $i+1$) is depicted in Fig. 7. In the new version of SVM, operation "$Oper4$" is removed from service "$Serv2$", operation "$Oper7$" in "$Serv4$" has changed from mandatory to optional, and a new operation "$Oper9$" is added to "$Serv2$" (there is no need to remind that each operation "$Oper\ i$" is an operation to realize activity i in the BPFM). No change was made to the variability attributes of the services, and no relationship exists among the services, and thus the new SVM cannot be inconsistent.

Table 2. General change options in SVM due to the change items in BPFM and the corresponding coefficient values

No.	Change Item in BPFM	Change Option in SVM	c1	c2	c3
1	Remove a mandatory activity	Remove mandatory operation from the mandatory service, and the service does not get empty to be removed	1	1	1
2		Remove mandatory operation from the mandatory service, and the service gets empty and is removed	0	1	1
3	Remove a non-mandatory (optional or variant) activity	Remove non-mandatory operation from the mandatory service	1	1	0
4		Remove non-mandatory operation from the optional service, and the service does not get empty to be removed	1	1	1
5		Remove non-mandatory operation from the optional service, and the service gets empty and is removed	0	1	1
6	Add a new mandatory activity	Add a new mandatory operation to a mandatory service	1	1	0
7		Add a new mandatory operation to an optional service	1	1	0
8		Add a new mandatory operation to a new empty service	1	1	0
9	Add a new non-mandatory (optional or variant) activity	Add a new optional operation to a mandatory service	1	0	0
10		Add a new optional operation to an optional service	1	0	1
11		Add a new optional operation to a new empty service	1	0	1
12	Modify data of an existing activity	Modify the operation in the same service that it currently resides	1	1	0
13	Remove a constraint (relationship) b/w activities	(has no impact on service interfaces and their relationships)	0	0	0
14	Add a new constraint (relationship) b/w activities	(has impact on relationships between services)	0	0	1
15	Modify cardinality from (x,y) to (x',y') where $x' \leq x$ and $y' \geq y$	(has no impact on service interfaces and their relationships)	0	0	0
16	Modify cardinality from (x,y) to (x',y') where $x' > x$ or $y' < y$	(has impact on relationships between services)	0	0	1
17	Modify the variability attribute of an activity from mandatory to optional	Modify variability attribute of the operation from mandatory to optional, if the service remains mandatory	0	0	0
18		Modify variability attribute of the operation from mandatory to optional, if the service becomes optional	0	0	0
19	Modify the variability attribute of an activity from optional to mandatory	Modify variability attribute of the operation from optional to mandatory, if the service turns from optional to mandatory	0	0	1
20		Modify variability attribute of the operation from optional to mandatory, if the service was mandatory before change	0	0	0
21	Move activity outside variant regions	(has no impact on service interfaces and their relationships)	0	0	0
22	Move activity from outside to inside variant regions or vice versa	(has impact on relationships between services)	0	0	1

Algorithm 2. Change Impact Analysis

Input: $BPFM, BPFM', SVM$
Output: Pareto optimal set of change solutions($POSC$)
1. $POSC \leftarrow NIL$
2. $\Delta B \leftarrow CalculateDelta(BPFM, BPFM')$
3. $Obj \leftarrow NIL$
4. **for each** CI_i in ΔB **do**
5. $COi \leftarrow$ all potential change options to reflect CI_i in SVM ()
6.   fetch coefficients()
7. **end for**
8. Generate Z //all possible solutions
9. **for each** z_i in Z **do**
10. $ICost \leftarrow$ Calculate_ICost(z_i)
11. $RCost \leftarrow$ Calculate_RCost(z_i)
12. $Obj \leftarrow Obj \cup (Icost, RCost)$
13. **end for**
14. $POSC \leftarrow$ FindPaertoOptimalSet(Z , Obj)
15. **return** $POSC$

Table 3. Concrete services and currently existing products (before change)

abstract service in SVM	concrete services	existing configurations (products)
$S1$	$CS1$	$app1, app2$
$S2$	$CS2$	$app1, app2, app3, app4$
$S3$	$CS3$	$app3$
$S4$	$CS4$	$app1, app2$
	$CS5$	$app3, app4$

Table 4. Values of Objective functions for the potential solutions

Obj	ICost	RCost	Selected in Pareto Optimal Set
$Obj(z1)$	6	4	-
$Obj(z2)$	5	4	✓
$Obj(z3)$	6	4	-
$Obj(z4)$	6	4	-
$Obj(z5)$	6	4	-

3.3   Change Planning and Decision Making

In this step, domain architects and engineers decide between change options among the Pareto-optimal set of change options, and may even disapprove a change item to take place in the product line.

As stated earlier, change cost is not necessarily the main and single factor to consider when deciding on a change; on the contrary, there can be a multitude of other factors such as market state, specific metrics and measures, and other particular features that exists especially for the external services; or other costs

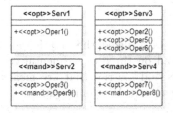

Fig. 7. New version of SVM (version $i + 1$)

and benefits, and miscellaneous priorities that affect the decision, which cannot necessarily be grabbed in a formula to be calculated and included in the optimization process. That is why we emphasize on the human factor and the role the experts play in this regard. Therefore, a fully-automated method is not advisable for propagating the changes from the business process variability model to the abstract and concrete services and to the applications configured based on them; since it is unlikely to identify all effective factors. Details of this step is outside the scope of this research and can be achieved by utilizing different decision making processes such as AHP and its variants.

3.4 Change Execution

A potential way to execute the changes that are determined in the selected change items (ΔS) is using model driven methods, and more specifically, model transformation. The advantage of applying these methods is preserving consistency in the target models by setting consistency constraints on the meta-model (e.g. in OCL) that will prevent inconsistent models to form. Using the change items in ΔS, the modified version of SVM, SVM$'$, is formed.

3.5 Version Control

For supporting traceability between the versions of the product line, we utilize an evolution graph (similar to what is proposed in [20]) as follows: in this graph, the nodes denote different product line versions, and directed edges denote a transition from a version to another. The nodes are attributed with the version number, and other version-related attributes such as creation date, approver, etc., while the edges are attributed with ΔB, ΔS, rationale for transitioning from the previous version to the new one, decisions made, etc. Every approved change in the product line domain must be reflected to and documented in the evolution graph, which acts as a shared knowledge among the four operations. Apache SVN can be utilized as a well-known version (revision) control tool.

4   Evaluation

To evaluate the method, we utilized the GQM approach [21] and controlled experimentation, performed on three experimental cases. In GQM, evaluation goal, evaluation questions and metrics that are measured to answer the evaluation questions are determined. We define the evaluation goal, questions and metric as follows:

Evaluation Goal (G): To analyze the proposed method for the purpose of evaluation from the aspect of specific quality metrics of cost minimization and consistency preservation in linear evolution in service-oriented product lines.

Evaluation Questions (Q): Q1: Does the method minimize change costs?; *Q2:* Does the method preserve consistency of the SVM after applying the change items, in terms of avoiding logical conflicts?

Evaluation Metrics (M): To answer question *Q1*, we calculate change ratio which is the ratio of artifacts changed due to interface change and due to relationship change of the services (Metrics *M1* and *M2*). Moreover, to answer question *Q2*, we introduce consistency degree metric (*M3*) which calculates a ratio of the number of consistent changed SVMs to the total number of changed SVMs that had gone through the change process. Table 5 represents more GQM details of evaluation.

Table 5. GQM details of evaluation

Evaluation Goal	Evaluation Question	Evaluation Metric	Metric Name	Metric Formula	Description
G1	Q1	M1	Change Ratio for Interface Change (CRI)	$CRI = \frac{AAI}{A}$	AAI: number of affected artifacts by interface change A: total number of artifacts
		M2	Change Ratio for Relationship Change (CRR)	$CRR = \frac{AAR}{A}$	AAR: number of affected artifacts by relationship change A: total number of artifacts
	Q2	M3	Consistency Degree (CD)	$CD = \frac{CS}{S}$	CS: number of consistent changed SVMs S: total number of changed SVMs

4.1   Experimentation Materials and Procedure

Ten product lines (A to J) were selected for experimentation, for each of which a distinct BPFM was derived beforehand based on business processes existing in detergent manufacturing, sales and distribution, and food industries, by domain engineers and business experts. Input materials to the experimentation were the current versions of SVMs related to each case, along with their corresponding BPFM models. Other information such as the number of concrete services and the number of applications was also supplied.

Then, to design changes to the BPFM models, a set of random numbers were generated, to designate the number of changes to that BPFM (which we considered between 1 to 8) and the change scenarios for each change (random numbers between 1 and 22). If a change scenario was not applicable on the BPFM, then (rotationally) the next possible scenario was chosen. Moreover, we sometimes re-generated the random numbers for scenarios to make sure we had covered each change scenario at least once. All random numbers were generated in MS Excel.

Then, the changed BPFMs were designed in a way that the change requirements denoted by the numbers and scenarios of changes (random numbers) were met. Some details about the experimental materials are listed in Table 6.

The metrics were measured on the new SVMs generated by the method. Moreover, the consistency of the obtained outputs was then inspected using the SPLOT online consistency checking tool for variability models [22].

Table 6. Details on experimental cases for evaluating the method

Exp.Case	Business process	Business domain	No. of changes in BPFM	Change scenarios	No. of total concrete services	Total No. of Configurations
A	Purchase order processing	Procurement	5	10,18,5,17,14	25	138
B	Order Processing	Sales	3	2,19,13	10	45
C	Adding new asset	Asset management	7	6,1,20,17,10,14,3	9	45
D	Repair order processing	Maintenance, operation and repair	2	19,21	18	107
E	Online sales	Sales	6	11,17,6,21,1,14	7	45
F	Letter submission	Office automation	2	16,20	4	29
G	Issue warehouse note	Warehousing	4	11,9,22,4	4	22
H	Create new bill of materials	Manufacturing	2	7,12	9	49
I	Calculate wages and salaries	Payment	1	11	14	94
J	Issue accounting notes	Accounting	6	5,9,21,8,3,15	6	39

4.2 Experimentation Results

The summary of experimentation results to answer question $Q1$ is shown in Table 7. As it is obvious, average change ratios of 33.6% and 33% are resulted by the method for changes costs caused by interface changes and by relationship changes, respectively. Therefore, in response to question $Q1$, the method has managed to affect an average of only 33.3% (one third) of the artifacts in the product line.

Since the Pareto optimal set, which was obtained by the method is a set of optimal non-dominated solutions, it is obvious that these solutions are the least costly from the aspects of interface and relationships change costs, compared with the other solutions that are not a member of this set. Therefore, if the decision maker selects any of the members of the Pareto optimal set, he or she has chosen one of the least costly choices.

To answer question $Q2$, we measured metric $M3$, namely, the consistency degree, which shows a full (100%) consistency preservation. The reason is that the variability relationships between services must be re-determined by Algorithm 1 when a change occurs to the relationships; and the algorithm guarantees consistency. In other words, the automated process prevents formation of conflicting variability relationships between services, unless a human factor intervenes in the produced results. Hence, the answer to question $Q2$ would be that, in case there is no human intervention in the change results, the method guarantees 100% consistency preservation.

Table 7. A summary of experimentation results for Question Q1

Experimental Case	No. of Total Artifacts	$ICost$	$RCost$	CRI (%)	CRR (%)
A	163	27	26	17	16
B	55	17	24	31	44
C	54	24	42	44	78
D	125	0	28	0	22
E	52	6	32	12	62
F	33	0	4	0	12
G	26	21	22	81	85
H	58	30	0	52	0
I	108	1	0	1	0
J	45	44	5	98	11
Average	71.9	17	18.3	33.6	33

5   Conclusion

In this paper, focusing on linear evolution scenario in service-oriented product lines, we dealt with the problem of propagating changes from domain requirements (the business process variability model) to the domain architecture (the service variability model) so that the costs of change in the concrete domain services and the configured applications are minimal; and simultaneously, the consistency of the target domain architecture model is preserved. This paper provides a method based on Pareto optimization to find an optimal solution, that is, the least costly changes in the target architecture model. The method consists of four main operations, namely, change identification, change impact analysis, change planning and change execution, interrelating with the evolution graph, which is used for version control. These operations along with the evolution graph form the whole evolution cycle to control and manage linear evolution. The evaluation results showed that the method manages to minimize change costs and can fully preserve consistency of the target model.

The future research includes proposing methods to cover other evolution scenarios, implementing model transformation to realize change execution as well as model-driven method to apply the deltas, along with extending the method to support runtime changes and dynamic reconfiguration of service-based applications in the service-oriented product line.

References

1. Clements, P., Northrop, L.: Software product lines: practices and patterns. Addison-Wesley Reading (2002)
2. Gomaa, H.: Designing Software Product Lines with UML: From Use Cases to Pattern-Based Software Architectures. Addison-Wesley, Boston (2004)
3. Van der Linden, F., Pohl, K.: Software Product Line Engineering: Foundations, Principles, and Techniques. Springer, Stuttgart (2005)
4. Erl, T.: Service-oriented architecture (SOA): concepts, technology, and design. Prentice Hall Englewood Cliffs (2005)

5. Wu, Y., Peng, X., Zhao, W.: Architecture Evolution in Software Product Line: An Industrial Case Study. In: Schmid, K. (ed.) ICSR 2011. LNCS, vol. 6727, pp. 135–150. Springer, Heidelberg (2011)
6. Kephart, J., Kephart, J., Chess, D., Boutilier, C., Das, R., Kephart, J.O., Walsh, W.E.: An architectural blueprint for autonomic computing. IEEE Internet Computing 18 (2007)
7. Moon, M., Hong, M., Yeom, K.: Two-level variability analysis for business process with reusability and extensibility. In: 32nd Annual IEEE International Conference on Computer Software and Applications, COMPSAC 2008, pp. 263–270. IEEE (2008)
8. Park, J., Moon, M., Yeom, K.: Variability modeling to develop flexible service-oriented applications. Journal of Systems Science and Systems Engineering 20, 193–216 (2011)
9. Laguna, M.A., Crespo, Y.: A systematic mapping study on software product line evolution: From legacy system reengineering to product line refactoring. Science of Computer Programming 78, 1010–1034 (2013)
10. Peng, X., Yu, Y., Zhao, W.: Analyzing evolution of variability in a software product line: From contexts and requirements to features. Information and Software Technology 53, 707–721 (2011)
11. Ajila, S.A., Kaba, A.B.: Evolution support mechanisms for software product line process. Journal of Systems and Software 81, 1784–1801 (2008)
12. Hinchey, M., Park, S., Schmid, K.: Building dynamic software product lines. Computer, 22–26 (2012)
13. Acher, M., Cleve, A., Collet, P., Merle, P., Duchien, L., Lahire, P.: Extraction and evolution of architectural variability models in plugin-based systems. Software & Systems Modeling, 1–28 (2013)
14. Andrikopoulos, V., Bucchiarone, A., Di Nitto, E., Kazhamiakin, R., Lane, S., Mazza, V., Richardson, I.: Service Engineering. In: Papazoglou, M., Pohl, K., Parkin, M., Metzger, A. (eds.) Service Research Challenges and Solutions for the Future Internet, pp. 271–337. Springer, Heidelberg (2010)
15. Alférez, G.H., Pelechano, V., Mazo, R., Salinesi, C., Diaz, D.: Dynamic adaptation of service compositions with variability models. Journal of Systems and Software 91, 24–47 (2014)
16. Pleuss, A., Botterweck, G., Dhungana, D., Polzer, A., Kowalewski, S.: Model-driven support for product line evolution on feature level. Journal of Systems and Software 85, 2261–2274 (2012)
17. Gomaa, H., Hashimoto, K.: Dynamic software adaptation for service-oriented product lines. In: Proceedings of the 15th International Software Product Line Conference, vol. 2, p. 35. ACM (2011)
18. Khoshnevis, S.: Identifying Variable Services for Multi-Tenant SaaS Applications as a Service-Oriented Product Line Using MOEA/D. International Journal of Software Engineering and Its Applications (2015)
19. Coello, C.C., Lamont, G.B., Van Veldhuizen, D.A.: Evolutionary algorithms for solving multi-objective problems. Springer (2007)
20. Pressman, R.: Software engineering: a practitioner's approach. McGrow-Hill International Edition (2005)
21. Van Solingen, R., Basili, V., Caldiera, G., Rombach, H.D.: Goal question metric (GQM) approach. Encyclopedia of Software Engineering (2002)
22. Mendonca, M., Branco, M., Cowan, D.: SPLOT: software product lines online tools. In: Proceedings of the 24th ACM SIGPLAN Conference Companion on Object Oriented Programming Systems Languages and Applications, pp. 761–762. ACM (2009)

An Interval-Based Approach to Modelling Time in Event-B

Gintautas Sulskus, Michael Poppleton, and Abdolbaghi Rezazadeh

University of Southampton, Southampton, UK
{gs6g10,mrp,ra3}@ecs.soton.ac.uk

Abstract. Our work was inspired by our modelling and verification of a cardiac pacemaker, which includes concurrent aspects and a set of interdependent and cyclic timing constraints. To model timing constraints in such systems, we present an approach based on the concept of *timing interval*. We provide a template-based timing constraint modelling scheme that could potentially be applicable to a wide range of modelling scenarios. We give a notation and Event-B semantics for the interval. The Event-B coding of the interval is decoupled from the application logic of the model, therefore a generative design of the approach is possible. We demonstrate our interval approach and its refinement through a small example. The example is verified, model-checked and animated (manually validated) with the ProB animator.

1 Introduction

Control systems must interact with all possible events that the environment may present. A number of factors contribute to the complexity and challenge of these systems. Concurrent and communicating components tend to exhibit unpredictable interactions that may lead to incorrect behaviours. Moreover, timing constraints add real complexity to real-time control systems.

Formal methods are used for rigorous modelling and verification of safety-critical real-time systems. Mathematical models enable generation of verification conditions which then can be proved using theorem provers. Formalising complex real-time systems is demanding, thus suitable modelling abstractions are desirable.

This work emerges from our work on a cardiac pacemaker case study [1]. The pacemaker is a complex control system that interacts with a non-deterministic environment (the heart) via sensors and actuators, whose functionality depends on its internal model of a normal heart. The pacemaker identifies certain heart dysfunctions and intervenes when necessary in order to maintain a correct heartbeat rate. The normal behaviour of the heart is usually modelled [8] in terms of a set of interconnected time intervals, representing various requirements of the normal pacing cycle. The pacemaker intervenes when the heart is observed to violate these requirements. The pacemaker can be single- or dual-channel, being able to interact with one or both (atrium and ventricle) heart chambers respectively.

© IFIP International Federation for Information Processing 2015
M. Dastani and M.Sirjani (Eds.): FSEN 2015, LNCS 9392, pp. 292–307, 2015.
DOI: 10.1007/978-3-319-24644-4_20

In this paper we present a timing interval approach that builds on the existing notion of delay, deadline and expiry [21]. We introduce the concept of the interval and reusable patterns that are potentially suitable for modelling systems. Their demands range from a single deadline timing constraint to systems with complex timing constraints that are cyclic, concurrent and interdependent.

A timing interval can have lower and upper boundary timing constraints defined in a number of ways. Typically, such timing constraints share many elements, such as trigger and response events. We present a notation for our timing interval approach that helps describe the timing requirements at a high level but hides the underlying implementation complexity from the modeller.

We demonstrate the interval approach through an example model. The example is modelled in the Event-B language [5] with the Rodin [6] tool. Our development process consists of two main stages. In the first stage, we express the system in UML diagrams using the UML-like modelling tool called iUML [3]. In the second stage, we add explicit timing using our interval approach. We leverage the power of abstraction and reuse via templates.

Section 2 introduces Event-B and the related formal approaches to modelling timing. Section 3 gives the Event-B semantics of the timing interval as a pattern-based collection of variables, invariants, event guards and actions. The approach allows the intervals to be specified in a manner that does not interfere with the logic of the model, and in a compositional fashion. This affords the opportunity to a generative description of the approach with a potential for automated support; in section 4 we give Event-B code templates for such potential automation. In section 5 we give an example of the interval refinement. Sections 6, 7 present verification and validation results of the approach and discuss related work on the pacemaker. Section 8 concludes.

2   Preliminaries

The Event-B [5] formalism is an evolution of the Classical B method [4]. Most of the formal concepts it uses were already proposed in Action Systems [7]. Event-B focuses on reactive systems and is aimed at modelling whereas the Classical B is just for software. We prefer Event-B for its simplicity of notations, extensibility and tool support.

An Event-B model is composed of *contexts* and *machines*. Contexts specify the static part of a model such as carrier sets s, constants c and axioms $A(s, c)$. Machines represent the dynamic part of a model and contain variables v, invariants $I(s, c, v)$ and *events*. An event may accept a number of parameters x and consists of at least two blocks: guards $G(x, s, c, v)$ that describe the conditions that need to hold for the occurrence of the event, and actions which determine how specific state variables change as a result of the occurrence of the event. Conceptually, events in Event-B are atomic and instantaneous. Contexts can be extended by other contexts and machines can be refined by other machines. Each machine may refer to one or more contexts.

Event-B employs a strong proof-based verification. The system's safety property requirements are encoded as invariants from which Event-B verification conditions, called *proof obligations* (POs), are then generated. There are various kinds of POs concerned with different proof problems. For instance, an Invariant Preservation PO (INV) indicates that the invariant condition is preserved by an event with before-after predicate R:

$$A(s, c) \wedge I(s, c, v) \wedge G(x, s, c, v) \wedge R(x, s, c, v, v') \vdash i(s, c, v') \qquad (1)$$

where $i(s, c, v')$ is a modified specific invariant.

Systems are usually too complex to model all at once. Refinements help to deal with the complexity in a stepwise manner, by developing a system incrementally. There are two forms of refinement in Event-B. The feature augmentation refinement (*horizontal refinement*) introduces new features of the system. The data refinement (*vertical refinement*) enriches the structure of a model to bring it closer to an implementation structure. Refined variables are linked to the abstract layer state variables by means of *gluing invariants* that ensure the consistency of the system.

One of the key advantages of Event-B is its tooling support. Rodin [6] is an Eclipse based IDE for Event-B that provides effective support for modelling, refinement and proof. Rodin auto-generates POs for project machines. These are then discharged by automated theorem provers, such as AtelierB [2] or SMT [13], or manually via the interactive proving environment. Rodin provides a wide range of plug-ins, such as Camille text editor, statemachine-to-Event-B modelling tool iUML [3] and ProB [17] model checker, which were used in our case study.

2.1   Timing

The Event-B is a general purpose modelling language that lacks explicit support for expressing and verifying timing constraints. However, several concepts were proposed on how to model the time in Event-B. Event-B does not support real numbers natively, hence in this work we discuss only the discrete time related work.

Butler and Falampin [11] describe an approach to model discrete time in Classical B, which is the origin of Event-B. They express current time as a natural number and model the time flow with a tick operation. Deadline conditions are modelled as guards on the tick operation.

Cansell et al. [12] propose a scheme in Event-B. The authors model time as a variable $time \in \mathbb{N}$. An event *post_time* adds a new *active time* to a variable $at \subseteq \mathbb{N}$. Active time elements are the future events' activation times ($min(at) > time$) that must be handled by the system. Event *tick* handles the time flow, where the time progress is limited to the least at element – $min(at)$. Event *process_time* then handles the active time. The paper recommends to introduce timing not too early into the model, to avoid unnecessary complexity, especially in terms of proof obligation discharge.

Rehm [20] extends Cansell's work on the active time approach. The author introduces an event-calendar *atCal* that allows to keep a record of the active times for every process. Let *evts* be the finite set of processes or names for one model. Event-calendar is a function that gives for every element of *evts* a set of activation times in the future: $atCal \in evts \rightarrow \mathbb{P}(\mathbb{N})$. In order to facilitate model-checking, [20] shows an approach to refine an infinite model with absolute timing to a finite model with relative timing and show the equivalence of the two models.

Bryans et al. [10], like Rehm, use the extended version of active times, that maps a set of events to future time and adds the support for *bounded inconsistency*. They remove the guard from the *tick* event to allow time to progress beyond the deadline. Instead, they split event *process_time* into two cases. One event then handles the case when the active time is handled within expected time boundaries. The other handles the case when the timing constraint is not correctly maintained by the system.

Sarshogh [21] categorises timing properties in terms of *delay*, *expiry* and *deadline*. He introduces notation to specify these timing properties and provides Event-B semantics for the notation. The notation hides the complexity of encoding timing properties in an Event-B model, thus making timing requirements easier to perceive for the modeller.

In this approach a typical constraint starts with a trigger event followed by a possible response event. A timing constraint relates a trigger event T and a response event R or a set of response events $R_1...R_n$:

$$Deadline(T;\ R_1...R_n;\ t) \tag{2a}$$

$$Delay(T;\ R;\ t) \tag{2b}$$

$$Expiry(T;\ R;\ t) \tag{2c}$$

$Deadline(T, R_1...R_n, t)$ means that one and only one of the response events $(R_1..R_n)$ must occur within time t of trigger event T occurring. In case of $Delay(T;\ R;\ t)$, the response event R cannot occur before time t of trigger event T occurring. $Expiry(T;\ R;\ t)$ means that the response event cannot occur after time t of trigger event occurring.

In general, Sarshogh's timing properties correspond to timed automata delay, deadline and time-out modelling patterns [25]. However, two significant differences must be pointed out. Firstly, time in Event-B is modelled explicitly whereas in timed automata it is implicit and continuous ($\mathbb{R}$). Secondly, Sarshogh's patterns can be used in a stepwise refinement modelling, whereas timed automata does not natively support such a feature. We build our approach on Sarshogh's timing properties (2a - 2c) and use similarly structured Event-B semantics.

3 Timing Interval Approach

Our aim is to provide a generative, simple to apply approach to enrich an already existing Event-B model with timing interval constraints. The model can be of any size, may include cyclic and concurrent behaviours and have multiple intervals and other timing constraints.

In the following paragraphs we emphasize the limitations that we solve in our contribution. The need for such timing requirements comes from the pacemaker case study [1] that we have performed [24].

In this paper we present a simple Event-B model [23] to illustrate various modelling needs for timing constraints. The model is abstracted from our pacemaker case study model. We choose a visual state representation for ease of discussion. The abstract model is represented in UML-like diagrams that are generated with the iUML tool as a statemachine *SM* with two concurrent regions (Fig. 1). A transition is enabled when all its source states are active. Therefore *e3* is always enabled, *e1* is enabled when the left hand side region is in state *A*. Transition *e2* works as a synchronisation point – it is enabled only when the left hand side region is in state *st_INT*1 and the right hand side region is in state *st_INT*2. *SM* regions act independently unless the shared event *e2* is executed.

At the abstract level, we express the timing interval as time spent in a state. In this example we define two intervals *INT*1 and *INT*2 as the time periods during which states *st_INT*1 and *st_INT*2 respectively are occupied.

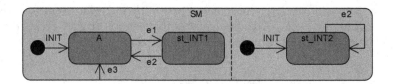

Fig. 1. Example iUML model.

In the left hand side region of the *SM* (Fig. 1), we define an interval *INT*1, triggered by the event *e1* and responded by the event *e2*. We assume that this interval is an aggregate of delay and deadline timing properties, with lower and upper duration limits. We propose the interval as an abstraction over these properties that formally combine these boundaries. An interval is called *active*, when it has been triggered but not yet responded to.

We consider the notion of *interrupt* event, which can interrupt an already active timing interval. For instance, event *e3*, at any point in time, must be able to interrupt the left hand side region's active timing interval *INT*1. Moreover, we require the enabledness of event *e3* to be independent of whether *INT*1 is active or not. In contrast, *e2* is enabled only if there is an active interval to respond to.

The right hand side region contains a timing interval *INT*2. The interval *INT*2 may be triggered by *INIT* or *e2* event, hence it requires a *multiple trigger support*. Timing interval *INT*2 is responded by the event *e2*.

Note that both timing intervals are interdependent – they share the event *e2*, effectively forcing a single event to serve as a response for the *INT*1 and as both trigger and response for $INT2$. We call this phenomenon *event overloading*, when an event serves a number of roles in one or more timing intervals.

3.1 Modelling Notation

In order to model the given example, we introduce the timing interval approach. The interval is characterised by one or two *timing properties TP* and a set of events – optional ones denoted by [ ]. The system may have a number of timing intervals that are identified by a unique name – *Interval_name*. There may be multiple active instances of a given interval that occur independently from each other.

$$Interval\_name(T_1[,...,T_i];\ R_1[,...,R_j];\ [I_1,...,I_k];\ TP_1(t_1)[,TP_2(t_2)]) \quad (3)$$

The interval is defined by three kinds of events. One of a set of trigger events $T \in T_1..T_i$ always creates a new instance of the interval. One of a set of response events $R \in R_1...R_j$ always terminates an interval instance under conditions specified by timing properties. If there is no active interval instance to terminate, the response event is disabled. In order to be well defined, the interval must have at least one trigger and response event. One of a set of optional interrupt events $I \in I_1..I_k$ interrupts the interval. Unlike the response event, the interrupt event is not constrained by timing properties TP and does not block if there is no active interval instance to interrupt. The interrupt event always interrupts an active interval instance (if one exists).

The interval must have at least one timing property $TP(t)$ of duration t, where TP stands for *Deadline*, *Delay* or *Expiry*. Further, the interval can have one of five TP configurations: (i.) Deadline; (ii.) Delay; (iii.) Expiry; (iv.) Delay and Expiry; (v.) Delay and Deadline. If more than one timing property is associated with an interval, then there is a relation between the interval's timing property durations (2a-2c): the delay duration must be less or equal to the deadline duration ($t_{Delay} \leq t_{Deadline}$) and the expiry duration ($t_{Delay} \leq t_{Expiry}$).

Having defined the notation, we can now use it to specify the left hand side region timing constraint $INT1$ ((4), Fig. 1), with trigger $e1$, response $e2$ and interrupt $e3$. Upon event $e1$ execution, a new interval $INT1$ instance is created. The occurrence of the response event $e2$ then becomes constrained by the delay and deadline timing properties whose durations are $INT1\_t\_dly$ and $INT1\_t\_ddl$ respectively. The interrupt event $e3$ can be executed at any given time regardless of the state the model is in. Upon event $e3$ execution the active $INT1$ instance is interrupted (if one exists) and the left hand side region enters state A.

$$INT1(e1;\ e2;\ e3;\ Delay(INT1\_t\_dly), Deadline(INT1\_t\_ddl)) \quad (4)$$

According to the interval $INT2$ specification (5), the right hand side (Fig. 1) interval is triggered by $INIT$ or $e2$ events. Event $INIT$ means that the interval is activated immediately upon the model initialisation. The *overloaded* $e2$ event serves as the trigger and the response for the interval $INT2$. Therefore when executed, event $e2$ responds to an already existing interval instance and initiates a new one. The deadline timing property means that event $e2$ must occur within time $INT2\_t\_ddl$ of trigger event occurring. $INT2$ has no interrupt and therefore can be responded to only by the response event $e2$.

$$INT2(INIT, e2; \; e2; \; ; \; Deadline(INT2\_t\_ddl)) \tag{5}$$

As mentioned before, event $e2$ is an *overloaded* event – it is a response event for $INT1$ and $INT2$ intervals. Therefore $e2$ is constrained by both interval $INT1$ and $INT2$ timing properties.

3.2   Semantics of Example Intervals

We give semantics to our interval construct by translating it to Event-B variables, invariants, guards and actions. The interval timing notation serves as a blueprint, indicating the required Event-B code and its location in the model. In this section we provide semantics of the example interval $INT1$.

Interval. We translate the interval $INT1$ to a set of variables that store the information about interval instances (Fig. 2). Variable $INT1\_trig$ stores the indices of triggered interval $INT1$ instances. When the interval instance is responded to, its index is copied to the $INT1\_resp$ variable. Trigger and response activities are timestamped and the timestamps are stored in $INT1\_trig\_ts$ and $INT1\_resp\_ts$ variables respectively. We model timestamp as a total function $X \rightarrow \mathbb{N}$, where the index set X serves as a unique identification for the interval instance. In case the interval is interrupted, its index is copied to variable $INT1\_intr$. Interval $INT1$-specific variables are prefixed with $INT1\_$.

Invariants $INT1\_consist_1$ and $INT1\_consist_2$ ensure the interval index consistency across the variables (Fig. 2). $INT1\_consist_1$ is the sequencing invariant ensuring that only the triggered indexes can be responded to or interrupted. $INT1\_consist_2$ states that interval instance can be either responded to or interrupted, but not both.

Timing Properties. In Event-B semantics, the timing property is expressed as a set of invariants (Fig. 7). According to $INT1$ specification (4), the interval is constrained by two timing properties: the delay and the deadline. The deadline timing property consists of two invariants. The first invariant $INT1\_inv\_ddl1$ expresses the requirement, that while the active interval instance has not yet been responded to or interrupted, it must not exceed the deadline duration $INT1\_t\_ddl$. The second deadline invariant $INT1\_inv\_ddl2$ requires the active interval $INT1$ instance to be responded to within $INT1\_t\_ddl$ of the trigger event occurring. In order to preserve $INT1$ deadline timing property invariants, a guard $INT1\_grd\_ddl1$ is needed in the *tick* event to ensure that the time will not progress beyond active interval's deadline boundaries (Fig. 6).

The delay timing property of $INT1$ is expressed as one invariant $INT1\_inv\_dly1$ (Fig. 7). The guard $INT1\_grd\_dly1$ in event $e2$ ensures the invariant preservation (Fig. 4). Note that event *tick* (Fig. 6) is not constrained by delay timing properties.

```
INT1_type1 :  INT1_trig ⊆ X
INT1_type2 :  INT1_resp ⊆ X
INT1_type3 :  INT1_intr ⊆ X
INT1_type4 :  INT1_trig_ts ∈ INT1_trig → ℕ
INT1_type5 :  INT1_resp_ts ∈ INT1_resp → ℕ
INT1_consist1 :  ∀ idx · idx ∉ INT1_trig
                   ⇒ idx ∉ INT1_resp ∪ INT1_intr

INT1_consist2 :  INT1_intr ∩ INT1_resp = ∅
```

Fig. 2. Interval *INT*1 variables.

```
Event   e1 ≙
  any  INT1_pTrig
  where
  Grds
  INT1_trg_grd1 :  INT1_pTrig ∈ X
  INT1_trg_grd2 :  INT1_pTrig ∉ INT1_trig
  then
  Acts
  INT1_trg_act1 :
     INT1_trig := INT1_trig ∪ {INT1_pTrig}
  INT1_trg_act2 :
     INT1_trig_ts(INT1_pTrig) := time
  end
```

Fig. 3. Event *e*1.

```
Event   e2 ≙
  any  INT1_pResp INT2_pTrig INT2_pResp
  where
  Grds
  INT1_rsp_grd1 :  INT1_pResp ∈ INT1_trig
  INT1_rsp_grd2 :  INT1_pResp ∉ INT1_resp ∪ INT1_intr
  INT1_grd_dly1 :  time ≥ INT1_trig_ts(INT1_pResp) + INT1_t_dly
  INT2_trg_grd1 :  INT2_pTrig ∈ X
  INT2_trg_grd2 :  INT2_pTrig ∉ INT2_trig
  INT2_rsp_grd1 :  INT2_pResp ∈ INT2_trig
  INT2_rsp_grd2 :  INT2_pResp ∉ INT2_resp ∪ INT2_intr
  then
  Acts
  INT1_rsp_act1 :  INT1_resp := INT1_resp ∪ {INT1_pResp}
  INT1_rsp_act2 :  INT1_resp_ts(INT1_pResp) := time
  INT2_trg_act1 :  INT2_trig := INT2_trig ∪ {INT2_pTrig}
  INT2_trg_act2 :  INT2_trig_ts(INT2_pTrig) := time
  INT2_rsp_act1 :  INT2_resp := INT2_resp ∪ {INT2_pResp}
  INT2_rsp_act2 :  INT2_resp_ts(INT2_pResp) := time
  end
```

Fig. 4. Event *e*2.

```
Event   e3 ≙
  any  INT1_pIntr
  where
  Grds
  INT1_intr_grd1 :  INT1_pIntr ⊆ INT1_trig \ (INT1_resp ∪ INT1_intr)
  INT1_intr_grd2 :  finite(INT1_pIntr)
  INT1_intr_grd3 :  INT1_trig \ (INT1_resp ∪ INT1_intr) ≠ ∅ ⇒ card(INT1_pIntr) = 1
  then
  Acts
  INT1_intr_act1 :  INT1_intr := INT1_intr ∪ INT1_pIntr
  end
```

Fig. 5. Event *e*3.

```
Event   tick ≙
  when
  Grds
  INT1_grd_ddl1 :  ∀ idx·idx ∈ INT1_trig ∧ idx ∉ INT1_resp ∪ INT1_intr
                        ⇒time + 1 ≤ INT1_trig_ts(idx) + INT1_t_ddl
  INT2_grd_ddl1 :  ∀ idx·idx ∈ INT2_trig ∧ idx ∉ INT2_resp ∪ INT2_intr
                        ⇒time + 1 ≤ INT2_trig_ts(idx) + INT2_t_ddl
  then
  Acts
  act1 :  time := time + 1
  end
```

Fig. 6. *tick* event.

```
INT1_inv_ddl1 : ∀ idx·idx ∈ INT1_trig ∧ idx ∉ INT1_resp ∪ INT1_intr
                        ⇒time ≤ INT1_trig_ts(idx) + INT1_t_ddl
INT1_inv_ddl2 : ∀ idx·idx ∈ INT1_trig ∧ idx ∈ INT1_resp
                        ⇒INT1_resp_ts(idx) ≤ INT1_trig_ts(idx) + INT1_t_ddl
INT1_inv_dly1 : ∀ idx·idx ∈ INT1_trig ∧ idx ∈ INT1_resp
                        ⇒INT1_resp_ts(idx) ≥ INT1_trig_ts(idx) + INT1_t_dly
INT1_rel_dly_ddl : INT1_t_dly ≤ INT1_t_ddl
```

Fig. 7. Interval $INT1$ timing property invariants.

Invariant $INT1\_rel\_dly\_ddl$ (Fig. 7) specifies the relation between delay and deadline timing property durations.

Events. According to the $INV1$ specification (4), event $e1$ serves as the trigger for $INT1$ (Fig. 3). To trigger a new instance of the interval, event accepts a parameter $INT1\_pTrig$ that must be an unused index ($INT1\_trg\_grd1$, $INT1\_trg\_grd2$). If the conditions are met, the new index and the timestamp are added to $INT1$ trigger and timestamp sets ($INT1\_trg\_act1$, $INT1\_trg\_act2$). Event $e2$ serves as $INT1$ response (Fig. 4). $e2$ takes a parameter $INT1\_pResp$ that must be an already existing interval $INT1$ index and has not yet been responded to or interrupted ($INT1\_rsp\_grd1$, $INT1\_rsp\_grd2$). Upon response, the selected index is recorded into the responded event set $INT1\_resp$ with its timestamp ($INT1\_rsp\_act1$, $INT1\_rsp\_act2$). *Grds* represents the other guards and *Acts* represents the other actions of the corresponding event.

Event $e2$ is an example of an overloaded event. It serves as the response for $INT1$ and as both, trigger and response for $INT2$ (Fig. 4). $INT2$ trigger parameter $INT2\_pTrig$ and labels $INT2\_trg\_*$ correspond to those of $INT1$; In an analogous manner, $INT2$ response parameter $INT2\_pResp$ and labels $INT2\_rsp\_*$ match the ones of $INT1$. As mentioned in subsection 3.1, the response event must always respond to an active interval instance. Hence $e2$ can be executed only when there are active instances of intervals $INT1$ and $INT2$ to respond to, otherwise the event is disabled. There is no interference between these three roles, as they operate on different variables.

Event $e3$ serves as an interrupt for $INT1$ (Fig. 5). Parameter $INT1\_pIntr$ is modelled as a subset of active but non-responded $INT1$ instance indexes ($INT1\_grd1$). If, upon event execution, there is no active $INT1$ instance, the parameter becomes equal to $\varnothing$ and interval's variable is not affected ($INT1\_act1$). On the other hand, if there is at least one active interval instance available, the parameter is forced to contain one index ($INT1\_grd3$). The guard $INT1\_grd2$ is required for well-definedness, since *cardinality* function can accept only finite parameters. We limit $INT1\_pIntr$ size to 1 to ensure a consistent behaviour with trigger and response parameters that always accept strictly one element.

4   Interval Templates

We provide a generative approach for translating interval specification to Event-B code. Our approach defines a number of generic Event-B code templates that represent elements of the interval notation (3). The templates can potentially be specialised, and thus simplified, to handle, e.g., strictly a single instance interval.

The interval timing approach consists of the *interval base template, event templates* and *timing property templates*. Our process comprises three steps. Firstly, we pick relevant templates according to the interval specification. Then, we instantiate the templates by adding the interval name as a prefix to each template variable (as for *INT1_* and *INT2_* prefixes in the previous sections). Finally, we inject instantiated templates into the model locations, specified by the interval specification.

Interval Base Template. The interval base template is a set of variables and invariants that describe all interval instance states and ensures their consistency (Fig. 8). Prefix **P_** is a place holder for the interval name that gets instantiated in the template code. @ indicates the target Event-B block to be injected with the instantiated template code.

@INVARIANTS
P_type1 : P_trig ⊆ X
P_type2 : P_resp ⊆ X
P_type3 : P_intr ⊆ X
P_type4 : P_trig_ts ∈ P_trig → ℕ
P_type5 : P_resp_ts ∈ P_resp → ℕ

P_consist1 : ∀ idx·idx ∉ P_trig ⇒ idx ∉ P_resp ∪ P_intr
P_consist2 : P_intr ∩ P_resp = ∅

Fig. 8. Interval base template elements.

Timing Property Templates. We define timing property templates for deadline and delay; expiry can be defined similarly. The timing property template is a collection of invariants and guards appropriate for the timing property.

The deadline timing property template consists of two invariants and a guard in *Tick* event (Fig. 9). Invariants **P_***inv_ddl*1 and **P_***inv_ddl*2 expresses the deadline timing property requirement. Guard **P_***grd_ddl*1 is for *Tick* event.[1]

@INVARIANTS
P_inv_ddl1 : ∀ idx·idx ∈ P_trig ∧ idx ∉ P_resp∪ P_intr ⇒ time ≤ P_trig_ts(idx)+P_t_ddl
P_inv_ddl2 : ∀ idx·idx ∈ P_trig ∧ idx ∈ P_resp ⇒ P_resp_ts(idx) ≤ P_trig_ts(idx) + P_t_ddl
@Event   Tick ≙
@where
P_grd_ddl1 : ∀ idx·idx ∈ P_trig ∧ idx ∉ P_resp ∪ P_intr ⇒ time + tick ≤ P_trig_ts(idx) + P_t_ddl
end

Fig. 9. Deadline template.

The delay timing property template consists of a single invariant **P_***inv_dly*1 and a guard **P_***grd_dly*1 on a response event (Fig. 10).

In case interval has delay and deadline (Fig. 11) or delay and expiry (Fig. 12) timing properties, their duration relation is specified as an invariant.

---

[1] We assume, that the time variable *time* and the time flow event *Tick* are present in the model.

```
P_inv_dly1 : ∀ idx·idx ∈ P_trig ∧ idx ∈ P_resp ⇒ P_resp_ts(idx) ≥ P_trig_ts(idx) +
P_t_dly
@Event    R ≙
@where
P_grd_dly1 : time ≥ P_trig_ts(P_pResp) + P_t_dly
end
```

Fig. 10. Delay template.

Interval Event Templates. We define Event-B code templates for trigger T (Fig. 13), response R (Fig. 14) and interrupt I (Fig. 15) interval event types. Templates consist of parameters, guards and actions that are needed for a specific interval role. The templates are analogous to $INT1$ trigger (Fig. 3), response (Fig. 4) and interrupt (Fig. 5).

```
@INVARIANTS
P_rel_dly_ddl : P_t_dly ≤ P_t_ddl
```

Fig. 11. Delay-deadline TP rel. tl.

```
@INVARIANTS
P_rel_dly_xpr : P_t_dly ≤ P_t_xpr
```

Fig. 12. Delay-expiry TP rel. tl.

```
@Event    T ≙
@any  P_pTrig
@where
P_trg_grd1 : P_pTrig ∈ X
P_trg_grd2 : P_pTrig ∉ P_trig
@then
P_trg_act1 : P_trig := P_trig ∪ {P_pTrig}
P_trg_act2 : P_trig_ts(P_pTrig) := time
end
```

Fig. 13. Trigger event template.

```
@Event    R ≙
@any  P_pResp
@where
P_rsp_grd1 : P_pResp ∈ P_trig
P_rsp_grd2 : P_pResp ∉ P_resp ∪ P_intr
@then
P_rsp_act1 : P_resp := P_resp ∪ {P_pResp}
P_rsp_act2 : P_resp_ts(P_pResp) := time
end
```

Fig. 14. Response event template.

```
@Event    I ≙
@any  P_pIntr
@where
P_intr_grd1 : P_pIntr ⊆ P_trig \ (P_resp ∪
    P_intr)
P_intr_grd2 : finite(P_pIntr)
P_intr_grd3 : P_trig \ (P_resp ∪ P_intr) ≠ ∅ ⇒
    card(P_pIntr) = 1
@then
P_intr_act1 : P_intr := P_intr ∪ P_pIntr
end
```

Fig. 15. Interrupt event template.

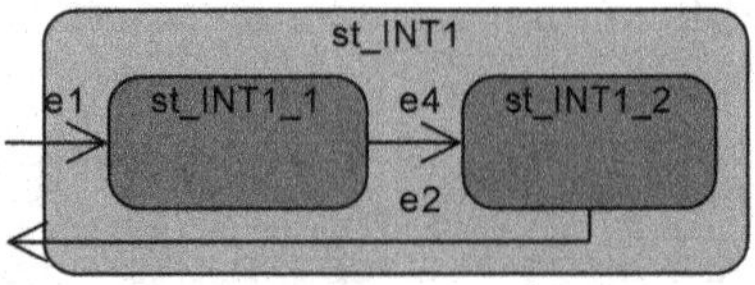

Fig. 16. Ref. of PM example.

5   Example Interval Refinement to Sequential Sub-intervals

We chose one interval refinement pattern out of a number of possible ones [21]. In this section we demonstrate in our example model how the abstract timing interval $INT1$ (4) can be refined into two sub-intervals $INT1\_1$ (6) and $INT1\_2$ (7). We visually express sub-intervals as sub-states st_INT1_1 and st_INT1_2 of the parent state st_INT1 (Fig. 16). Sub-states are connected with a new transition $e4$.

Sub-intervals are modelled in the same way as the abstract interval $INT1$ unless stated otherwise. Concrete sub-intervals $INT1\_1$ and $INT1\_2$ have their own trigger, response and interrupt variables, and at least the same number and type of timing properties. Concrete sub-intervals proceed sequentially, where preceding interval's response serves as succeeding interval's trigger. Thus the $INT1\_1$ response $e4$ serves as the trigger for $INT1\_2$.

$$INT1\_1(e1;\ e4;\ e3;\ Delay(INT1\_1\_t\_dly), Deadline(INT1\_1\_t\_ddl)) \quad (6)$$

$$INT1\_2(e4;\ e2;\ e3;\ Delay(INT1\_2\_t\_dly), Deadline(INT1\_2\_t\_ddl)) \quad (7)$$

This interval refinement is encoded by a set of gluing invariants that map abstract interval variables to concrete sub-interval variables.

Firstly, the concrete sub-interval $INT1\_1$ must data refine all abstract interval $INT1$ trigger variables. Interval $INT1$ trigger index and trigger timestamp variables must map to interval $INT1\_1$ trigger index and timestamp (8). Secondly, abstract interval $INT1$'s response index variables must be refined (9).

$$INT1\_trig = INT1\_1\_trig \wedge INT1\_trig\_ts = INT1\_1\_trig\_ts \quad (8)$$

$$INT1\_resp = INT1\_2\_resp \wedge INT1\_resp\_ts = INT1\_resp\_ts \quad (9)$$

Thirdly, $INT1$'s interrupt indexes must be refined (10).The concrete interrupt indices must be unique to each sub-interval.

$$INT1\_intr = INT1\_1\_intr \cup INT1\_2\_intr \wedge INT1\_1\_intr \cap INT1\_2\_intr = \varnothing \quad (10)$$

Note that in the refined model of subsection 3.2, event $e3$ acts as interrupt for both $INT1\_1$ and $INT1\_2$ intervals (Fig. 17). We reuse the interrupt event pattern. In case there are no active interval instances, both interrupt index parameters become empty sets. Otherwise, guards $INT1\_1\_intr\_grd3$ and $INT1\_2\_intr\_grd3$ force strictly one of the parameters to be a non empty set with the cardinality of 1. The *with* Event-B keyword (*witness*) defines the relation between the abstract parameter that has been refined away and concrete parameters. In event $e3$ witness $INT1\_pIntr$ specifies that the indexes of interrupted abstract and concrete intervals must match.

Finally, interval $INT1\_1$ response indexes and timestamps must map to interval $INT1\_2$ indexes and timestamps (11). This ensures the continuity of concrete intervals.

$$INT1\_1\_resp = INT1\_2\_trig \wedge INT1\_1\_resp\_ts = INT1\_2\_trig\_ts \quad (11)$$

To make sure that concrete sub-intervals do not violate abstract interval durations, the relation between timing property durations is specified as invariants. The sum of sub-interval deadline property durations must be less or equal to the abstract interval's deadline property duration (12). The sum of sub-interval delay property durations must be higher or equal to abstract interval's delay property duration (13).

$$INT1\_1\_t\_ddl + INT1\_2\_t\_ddl \leq INT1\_t\_ddl \quad (12)$$

$$INT1\_1\_t\_dly + INT1\_2\_t\_dly \geq INT1\_t\_dly \quad (13)$$

```
Event   e3 ≙
  refines  e3
  any INT1_1_pIntr INT1_2_pIntr
  where
  seq_grd :  SM = TRUE
  INT1_1_intr_grd1 :  INT1_1_pIntr ⊆ INT1_1_trig \ (INT1_1_resp ∪ INT1_1_intr)
  INT1_2_intr_grd1 :  INT1_2_pIntr ⊆ INT1_2_trig \ (INT1_2_resp ∪ INT1_2_intr)
  INT1_1_intr_grd2 :  finite(INT1_1_pIntr)
  INT1_2_intr_grd2 :  finite(INT1_2_pIntr)
  INT1_1_intr_grd3 :  INT1_1_trig \ (INT1_1_resp ∪ INT1_1_intr) ≠ ∅ ⇒ card(INT1_1_pIntr ∪
  INT1_2_pIntr) = 1
  INT1_2_intr_grd3 :  INT1_2_trig \ (INT1_2_resp ∪ INT1_2_intr) ≠ ∅ ⇒ card(INT1_1_pIntr ∪
  INT1_2_pIntr) = 1
  with
  INT1_pIntr :  INT1_pIntr = INT1_1_pIntr ∪ INT1_2_pIntr
  then
  seq_act :  C := TRUE, A := TRUE, B := FALSE, B2 := FALSE, B1 := FALSE
  INT1_1_intr_act1 :  INT1_1_intr := INT1_1_intr ∪ INT1_1_pIntr
  INT1_2_intr_act2 :  INT1_2_intr := INT1_2_intr ∪ INT1_2_pIntr
  end
```

Fig. 17. m1: refined interrupt event $e3$.

6   Verification and Validation

We have evaluated our timing interval approach in terms of applicability, verification and validation. The refinement model has 3 timing intervals ($INT1\_1$, $INT1\_2$ and $INT2$) and 47 time-related invariants. All 132 generated timing-related POs were automatically discharged. Verification for deadlock freeness is not well integrated into Event-B framework [26], hence we favour model-checking for this task. To further verify our approach, we have model-checked our model with a limited state-space coverage and did not find any deadlocks of invariant violations. Since we model time as an absolute value of $\mathbb{N}$, the infinite state space prevents us from a full state-space coverage. Finally, the model has been manually animated in the ProB and there were no invariant violations or deadlocks found.

A fuller evaluation of our approach is the pacemaker case study [24]. The pacemaker model resulted in three refinements with the final refinement having 10 timing intervals. No customisations were needed to our approach in order to model the timing requirements. Overall, the model has 177 timing related invariants. There are 652 time-related proof obligations, all of which were automatically discharged. A limited coverage model checking has been performed using ProB model-checker. No deadlocks or invariant violations were found, so our approach appears to scale.

We have written a number of test case scenarios for manual validation with the ProB animator in order to test various aspects of the model and the timing interval approach.

Finally, we have developed a heart model in Groovy language for ProB model checker [9]. The heart model has been written as a Java plug-in. It is a simplistic system with two methods *isVentricleContracted*() and *isAtriumContracted*() that return a random boolean value. The simulation engine performs actions in a sequential loop fashion: (i.) invokes the methods to update the heart model state (ii.) if appropriate, executes pacemaker model *sense* events (iii.) arbitrarily executes any non-*sense* pacemaker model event. The simulation did not return any negative results.

7   Related Work

A number of authors have modelled the pacemaker system. Each case study differs in the covered scope of requirements and the modelling challenges that authors have perceived and tackled. For timing, we note some modelling improvement our approach offers over other work.

[19] have developed a single electrode pacemaker system using Event-B. The authors used the *activation times* pattern [12] to model timing constraints. They did not treat timing constraints as a separate element but rather integrated them tightly into the model. Timing constraint implementation is tightly coupled with the model structure, thus does not take advantage of reusability and requires more modelling effort. [16] used timed automata to model a closed loop system of the two-channel pacemaker and the heart. Since UPPAAL lacks a notion of refinement, the complexity of the system is put all at once in a component oriented fashion. The authors modelled pacemaker timing intervals as separate automata that correspond to time counters. The automata communicate via broadcast channels. This is a more complex bottom-up approach than ours. Other works include [18], [14] and [15]. None of the reviewed case studies uses notation specific to timing requirements.

We have chosen to model a dual-channel pacemaker. The support of refinement in Event-B allowed us to use a top-down approach, dealing with the system complexity incrementally. We have expressed the pacemaker system as two interdependent statemachines, representing atrium and ventricle channels. Interdependency and concurrent behaviour are the main factors for the complexity of our the model. To specify the requirements, we used the timing interval notation. We then generated explicit time constraints using our approach, that required no customisations.

8   Conclusions and Future Work

In the simple example model we have highlighted some timing aspects of a complex critical system and demonstrated how to overcome them using our approach. From the case study results we have concluded that the introduced notation gives a sufficient degree of flexibility in terms of timing requirement specification. The example model shows how the interrupt event facilitates event interruption by non-deterministic events and helps to avoid event replication to tackle different cases. As demonstrated in the example model, the event can be overloaded, that is, serve many event roles (trigger, response or interrupt) for multiple intervals. Our approach decouples intervals from other model structure. This affords a template-driven generative approach to modelling timing.

We plan to formalise the interval refinement of section 5 and provide templates for generative modelling. Further, we plan to present more refinement patterns [21].

Two factors prevent the full state-space coverage model-checking. Firstly, we model time as absolute value $\mathbb{N}$. Secondly, the interval instance indexes are not discarded after the use and accumulate. To overcome the infinite state-space problem we consider introducing a relative countdown timer for modelling cyclic intervals [20] and an index reset method for our approach that clears used interval instance indices.

More complex pacemaker systems support variable timing intervals, therefore in future we plan to implement a variable duration t for timing properties. We intend to use a co-simulation plug-in [22] to validate our model against more sophisticated heart models.

Finally, our plan is to develop a plug-in for Event-B code generation, add visualisation support for timing interval representation in iUML diagrams and ProB animations.

References

[1] Pacemaker Challenge (2007). http://sqrl.mcmaster.ca/pacemaker.htm
[2] Interactive Prover Reference Manual 3.7 (2013).
http://www.atelierb.eu/ressources/DOC/
english/prover-reference-manual.pdf
[3] iUML (2013). http://wiki.event-b.org/index.php/IUML-B
[4] Abrial, J.-R.: The B-Book: Assigning Programs to Meanings. Cambridge University Press, New York (1996)
[5] Abrial, J.-R.: Modeling in Event-B: System and Software Engineering, 1st edn. Cambridge University Press, New York (2010)
[6] Abrial, J.-R., Butler, M., Hallerstede, S., Hoang, T.S., Mehta, F., Voisin, L.: Rodin: an Open Toolset for Modelling and Reasoning in Event-B. International Journal on Software Tools for Technology Transfer 12(6), 447–466 (2010)
[7] Back, R.-J., Kurki-Suonio, R.: Decentralization of Process Nets with Centralized Control. In: Symposium on Principles of Distributed Computing, pp. 131–142. ACM, Montreal (1983)
[8] Barold, S.S., Stroobandt, R., Sinnaeve, A.F.: Cardiac Pacemakers and Resynchronization Step-by-Step: an Illustrated Guide. Wiley-Blackwell (2010)
[9] Bendisposto, J.: ProB 2.0 Developer Handbook (2014).
http://nightly.cobra.cs.uni-duesseldorf.de/prob2/
developer-documentation/prob-devel.pdf
[10] Bryans, J., Fitzgerald, J., Romanovsky, A., Roth, A.: Patterns for Modelling Time and Consistency in Business Information Systems, pp. 105–114. IEEE Computer Society, Oxford (2010)
[11] Butler, M., Falampin, J.: An Approach to Modelling and Refining Timing Properties in B. In: Proceedings of Workshop on Refinement of Critical Systems (RCS) (January 2002)
[12] Cansell, D., Méry, D., Rehm, J.: Time Constraint Patterns for Event B Development. In: Julliand, J., Kouchnarenko, O. (eds.) B 2007. LNCS, vol. 4355, pp. 140–154. Springer, Heidelberg (2006)
[13] Déharbe, D., Fontaine, P., Guyot, Y., Voisin, L.: SMT Solvers for Rodin. In: Derrick, J., Fitzgerald, J., Gnesi, S., Khurshid, S., Leuschel, M., Reeves, S., Riccobene, E. (eds.) ABZ 2012. LNCS, vol. 7316, pp. 194–207. Springer, Heidelberg (2012)

[14] Gomes, A.O., Oliveira, M.: Formal Development of a Cardiac Pacemaker: From Specification to Code. In: Davies, J. (ed.) SBMF 2010. LNCS, vol. 6527, pp. 210–225. Springer, Heidelberg (2011)

[15] Jee, E., Wang, S., Kim, J.K., Lee, J., Sokolsky, O., Lee, I.: A Safety-Assured Development Approach for Real-Time Software. In: The Proceedings of the 16th IEEE International Conference on Embedded and Real-Time Computing Systems and Applications, pp. 133–142 (August 2010)

[16] Jiang, Z., Pajic, M., Moarref, S., Alur, R., Mangharam, R.: Modeling and Verification of a Dual Chamber Implantable Pacemaker. In: Flanagan, C., König, B. (eds.) TACAS 2012. LNCS, vol. 7214, pp. 188–203. Springer, Heidelberg (2012)

[17] Leuschel, M., Butler, M.: ProB: A Model Checker for B. In: Araki, K., Gnesi, S., Mandrioli, D. (eds.) FME 2003. LNCS, vol. 2805, pp. 855–874. Springer, Heidelberg (2003)

[18] Macedo, H., Larsen, P., Fitzgerald, J.: Incremental Development of a Distributed Real-Time Model of a Cardiac Pacing System Using VDM. In: Cuellar, J., Sere, K. (eds.) FM 2008. LNCS, vol. 5014, pp. 181–197. Springer, Heidelberg (2008)

[19] Méry, D., Singh, N.K.: Pacemaker's Functional Behaviors in Event-B. Research Report inria-00419973 (2009)

[20] Rehm, J.: From Absolute-Timer to Relative-Countdown: Patterns for Model-Checking (May 2008) (Unpublished)

[21] Sarshogh, M.R.: Extending Event-B with Discrete Timing Properties. PhD thesis, University of Southampton (2013)

[22] Savicks, V., Butler, M., Colley, J.: Co-simulating Event-B and Continuous Models via FMI. In: 2014 Summer Computer Simulation Conference, Society for Modeling & Simulation International (SCS) (July 2014)

[23] Sulskus, G., Poppleton, M., Rezazadeh, A.: Example Event-B project (2014). http://users.ecs.soton.ac.uk/gs6g10/SimplifiedPMExample.zip

[24] Sulskus, G., Poppleton, M., Rezazadeh, A.: An Investigation into Event-B Methodologies and Timing Constraint Modelling. Mini-Thesis, University of Southampton (2014)

[25] Wang, J.: Handbook of Finite State Based Models and Applications. Discrete Mathematics and Its Applications. Chapman and Hall/CRC (2012)

[26] Yang, F., Jacquot, J.-P.: Scaling Up with Event-B: A Case Study. In: Bobaru, M., Havelund, K., Holzmann, G.J., Joshi, R. (eds.) NFM 2011. LNCS, vol. 6617, pp. 438–452. Springer, Heidelberg (2011)

From Event-B Models to Dafny Code Contracts

Mohammadsadegh Dalvandi, Michael Butler, and Abdolbaghi Rezazadeh

Electronic and Computer Science School, University of Southampton
Southampton, United Kingdom
{md5g11,mjb,ra3}@ecs.soton.ac.uk

Abstract. The constructive approach to software correctness aims at formal modelling and verification of the structure and behaviour of a system in different levels of abstraction. In contrast, the analytical approach to software verification focuses on code level correctness and its verification. Therefore it would seem that the constructive and analytical approaches should complement each other well. To demonstrate this idea we present a case for linking two existing verification methods, Event-B (constructive) and Dafny (analytical). This approach combines the power of Event-B abstraction and its stepwise refinement with the verification capabilities of Dafny. We presented a small case study to demonstrate this approach and outline of the rules for transforming Event-B events to Dafny contracts. Finally, a tool for automatic generation of Dafny contracts from Event-B formal models is presented.

Keywords: Event-B, Dafny, Formal Methods, Program Verification, Methodologies.

1 Introduction

The constructive approach to software correctness focuses on early stages of the development and aims at formal modelling of the intended behaviour and structure of a system in different levels of abstraction and verifying the formal specification of it. In contrast, the analytical approach focuses on code level and its target is to verify the properties of the code level. In other words, the constructive approach is concerned with the derivation of an algorithm from the specifications of the desired dynamic behaviour of that, in a way that the algorithm satisfies its specification [5] while the analytical approach is concerned with verifying that a given algorithm satisfies its given specifications. Both approaches are supported through a range of verification tools from groups worldwide. At a high level it would seem that the constructive and analytical approaches should complement each other well. However there is little understanding or experience of how these approaches can be combined at a large scale and very little tool support for transitioning from constructive formal models to annotated code that is amenable to analytical verification. This represents a wasted opportunity, as deployments of the approaches are not benefiting from each other effectively.

This paper presents work in progress on a tool-supported development approach by linking two existing verification tools, Rodin [2] and Dafny [4]. The

© IFIP International Federation for Information Processing 2015
M. Dastani and M.Sirjani (Eds.): FSEN 2015, LNCS 9392, pp. 308–315, 2015.
DOI: 10.1007/978-3-319-24644-4_21

Rodin platform supports the creation and verification of Event-B formal models. The Dafny tool is an extension to Microsoft Visual Studio for writing and verifying programs written in the Dafny programming language. Event-B in its original form does not have any support for the final phase of the development(implementation phase). On the other hand, Dafny has a very little support for abstraction and refinement. Our combined methodology is beneficial for both Event-B and Dafny users. It makes the abstraction and refinement of Event-B available for generating Dafny specifications which are correct with regards to a higher level of abstract specification in Event-B and allows Event-B models to be implemented and verified in a programming language. We discuss our approach for transforming Event-B formal models to annotated Dafny method declarations. Our focus here is only on generating code contracts (pre- and post-conditions) from Event-B models rather than implementations. Generated method contracts with this approach can be seen as an interface that can be implemented and verified later against the high level abstract specification. We also present a tool for automatic generation of Dafny annotations from Event-B models. We have validated our transformation rules by applying our tool to an Event-B model of a map abstract datatype which is presented in this paper.

The organisation of the rest of the paper is as follows: in section 2, background information on Event-B and Dafny is given. Section 3 contains an example of transformation of an Event-B model of a map abstract datatype to Dafny contracts. Transformation rules for transforming an Event-B machine to an annotated Dafny class are described in section 4. In section 5 related and future work are presented and finally section 6 contains conclusions.

2 Background

2.1 Event-B

Event-B is a formal modelling language for system level modelling based on set theory and predicate logic for specifying, modelling and reasoning about systems, introduced by Abrial [1]. Modelling in Event-B is facilitated by a platform called Rodin [2]. Rodin is an extensible open source software which is built on top of the Eclipse IDE. A model in Event-B consists of two main parts: *contexts* and *machines*. The static part (types and constants) of a model is specified in a context and the dynamic part (variables and events) is specified in a machine. To describe the static part of a model there are four elements in the structure of a context: *carrier sets, constants, axioms,* and *theorems.* Carrier sets are represented by their name and they are distinct from each other. Constants are defined using axioms. Axioms are predicates that express properties of sets and constants. Theorems in contexts can be proved from axioms. A machine in Event-B consists of three main elements: (1) a set of *variables*, which defines the states of a model (2) a set of *invariants*, which is a set of conditions on state variables that must hold permanently by all events and (3) a number of *events* which model the state change in the system. Each event may have a number of assignments called actions and also may have a number of guards. Guards are

```
Machine m0 Sees c0
Variables map
Invariants map∈ KEYS↔ VALUES
Initialisation map:= ∅
Event Add                            Event Remove
   any k,v                              any k
   where                                where
      grd1: k∈KEYS                          grd1: k∈dom(map)
      grd2: v∈VALUES                     then
   then                                     act1: map := {k}◁ map
      act1: map(k):= v
```

Fig. 1. Machine m0: the Most Abstract Level of Map ADT Model

predicates that describe the necessary conditions which should be true before an event can occur. An event may have a number of parameters. Event parameters are considered to be local to the event. Figure 1 illustrates machine m0 with two events Add and Remove.

Modelling a complex system in Event-B can benefit from refinement. Refinement is a stepwise process of building a large system starting from an abstract level towards a concrete level [1]. This is done by a series of successive steps in which, new details of functionality are added to the model in each step. The abstract level represents key features and the main purpose of the system. Refining an Event-B machine may involve adding new events or new variables(concrete variables). Concrete variables are connected to abstract variables through *gluing invariants*. A gluing invariant associates the state of the concrete machine with that of its abstraction. All invariants of a concrete model including gluing invariants should preserve by all events. The built-in mathematical language of the Rodin platform is limited to basic types and constructs like integers, boolean, relations and so on. The *Theory Plug-in* [3] has been developed to make the core language extension possible. A theory, which is a new kind of Event-B component, can be defined independently from a particular model and it is the mean by which the mathematical language and mechanical provers may be extended.

2.2 Dafny

Dafny [4] is an imperative sequential programming language which supports generic classes, dynamic allocation and inductive datatypes and has its own specification constructs. A Dafny program may contain both specification and implementation details. Specifications are omitted by the compiler and are used just during the verification process. Programs written and specified in Dafny can be verified using the Dafny verifier which is based on an SMT-solver. Standard pre- and post-conditions, framing construct and termination metrics are included in the specifications. The language offers updatable ghost variables, recursive functions, sets, sequences and some other features to support specification. The verification power of Dafny originates from its annotations (contracts). A program behaviour can be annotated in Dafny using specification constructs such as methods' pre- and post-conditions. The verifier then tries to prove that the code behaviour satisfies its annotations. This approach leads to producing correct programs not only in terms of syntax but also in terms of behaviour. A basic program in Dafny consists of a number of methods. A method in Dafny is a piece of imperative, executable code. Dafny also supports *functions*. A function in Dafny is different from a method and has very similar concept to mathematical functions. A Dafny function cannot write to memory and consists of just one expression. A special form of functions which returns a boolean value is called *predicate*. Dafny uses the **ensures** keyword for post-condition declaration. A post-condition is always a boolean expression. Each method can have more than one post-condition which can either be joined with boolean *and* (&&) operator or be defined separately using the **ensures** keyword. To declare a pre-condition the **requires** keyword is used. Like post-conditions, adding multiple pre-conditions is allowed in the same style. Pre- and post-conditions are placed after method declarations and before method bodies. Dafny does not have any specific construct for specifying class invariants. Class invariants are specified in a predicate named *Valid()* and this predicate is incorporated in all methods pre- and post-conditions so the verifier checks if each method preserve all invariants or not.

3 Case Study: A Map Abstract Data Type

In this section we present a map abstract datatype as a case study and show the Event-B formal model and its transformation to Dafny contracts that is performed by our tool. A map (also called associated array) is an abstract data type which associates a collection of unique keys to a collection of values. This case study is originally taken from [6] where the map ADT is specified, implemented and verified in Dafny. The most abstract model of the map in Event-B (machine *m0*) is illustrated in Figure 1. The map is simply modelled using a partial function from *KEYS* to *VALUES*. *KEYS* and *VALUES* are generic types which are defined in a context (not shown here) as carrier sets. There is only one invariant in this model which says that the variable *map* is a partial function. The model contains two events for add and removing keys and values to the map. By proving that these events preserve the invariant of the model, the uniqueness of the map's keys is verified.

Dafny does not support relations (and functions) as data structures so we cannot directly transform machine *m0* to Dafny annotations. Machine *m0* should be refined in order to reduce the abstraction and syntax gap between the Event-B model and Dafny specification. In the refined machine two new variables *keys* and *values* are introduced to model. Variable *keys* is a sequence of type *KEYS* and variable *values* is a sequence of type *VALUES*. Sequences are built-in data structures in Dafny but they are not part of the built-in mathematical language of Rodin. However sequences are available through the standard library of the Rodin theory plug-in. As the name suggests sequence *keys* stores keys and the other sequence stores values where a value in position i of sequence *values* is

Event *Add1* refines *Add*	Event *Add2* refines *Add*
any k,v	**any** k,v,i
where	**where**
grd1: k∈ *KEYS*	*grd1:* k∈ *KEYS*
grd2: v∈ *VALUES*	*grd2:* v∈ *VALUES*
grd3: k∉ *ran(keys)*	*grd3:* i∈ *1.. seqSize(keys)*
then	*grd4: keys(i)=k*
act1: keys:= seqPrepend(keys,k)	**then**
act2: values:= seqPrepend(values,v)	*act1: values(i):= v*

Fig. 2. Event *Add* is refined to two events *Add1* and *Add2*

associated with the key that is stored in position i of sequence *keys*. An invariant is needed in this refinement to state that both sequences have the same size. A gluing invariants is also needed to prove the consistency between refinements. Figure 2 shows that the event *Add* from machine *m0* is refined to two events *Add1* (for adding new keys to the map) and *Add2* (for updating an associated value to an existing key). Refinement of event *Remove* and other elements of the refined machine are omitted here because of the space limitation. Listing 1.1 shows the transformation of events of the refined machine to an annotated Dafny method called *Add*.

```
method Add(k:KEYS , v:VALUES)
requires Valid();
ensures (k !in old(keys) && keys==[k] + old(keys) &&
values==[v] + old(values))
||
(exists i :: i in (set k0| 0<=k0 && k0<|old(keys)|) &&
old(keys)[i]==k && values==old(values)[i:= v] &&
keys == old(keys));
```

Listing 1.1. Transformation of Machine *m1* to a Dafny Contract

Post-conditions of the *Add* method are directly derived from those events that form the method and they specify the behaviour of the method. Method *Add* is specified by two events in Event-B therefore two **ensures** clauses are generated (beside **ensures** *Valid();*). The reason for specifying a method with two Event-B events is that each event represents a separate case of the method and each case in a Dafny method is represented with a separate post-condition in the method contract. The keyword **old** which is used in the post-conditions of methods represents the value of the variable on entry to the method. Internal variables of each event are defined using existential quantifier with regards to the event's guards. The class declaration, predicate *Valid()* and other details of the generated class are not shown here. The transformation of Event-B events to annotated Dafny methods is discussed in the next section.

4 Transforming Event-B Models to Dafny Contracts

In this section we describe how we generate Dafny contracts from Event-B events. In order to be able to merge different Event-B events together to form a single method from them in Dafny, we have introduced a new element to Event-B machines called *constructor statement*. A constructor statement has the following form:

method *mtd_name(pi_1, pi_2,...)* returns(*po_1, po_2,...*) {*evt_1, evt_2,...*}

In the above statement, *mtd_name* is the name of the target method in Dafny, *(pi_1, pi_2,...)* represents the list of input parameters, *(po_1, po_2,...)* represents the list of output parameters, and *evt_1, evt_2,...* represents the list of Event-B events that must be merged together to form the target method.

A method may or may not have input/output parameters. Input parameters which are stated in the constructor statement must exist in all events which are listed in the the the statement and also the type of the parameters must be explicitly declared in Event-B events as guards of the event. If a method in a constructor statement has a parameter which is not listed as a method's input/output parameter, it should be treated as an *internal parameter*. An internal parameter is a local variable to the method and will be specified using an existential quantifier. A number of post-conditions can be generated from *before-after* predicates of the actions of the events together with their guards. A before-after predicate denotes the relation that exists between the value of a variable just before and just after the execution of an action. In the example shown in the previous section, the method *Add* was generated as a result of the following constructor statement:

method *Add*(k,v) returns() {*Add1, Add2*}

Consider *act1* of event *Add1* from Figure 2. The before-after predicate associated with this action is $keys\prime = seqPrepend(keys, k)$ where the primed variable denotes the value of the variable just after the execution and the unprimed variables denote the value of the variables before the execution. The following expression can be derived from event *Add1* by conjunction of all non-typing guards of the event before-after predicates of all actions of the event. The result would be for event *Add1*:

$$k \notin ran(keys) \wedge keys\prime = seqPrepend(keys, k) \wedge values\prime = seqPrepend(values, v) \tag{1}$$

The same should be done for event *Add2*. As it is obvious from the action of event *Add2*, variable *keys* is not changed by this event therefore the value of this variable after the execution of the event is equal to its value before the execution. The following expression is derived from this event:

$$i \in 1..seqSize(keys) \wedge keys(i) = k \wedge values\prime(i) = v \wedge keys\prime == keys \tag{2}$$

Note that event *Add2* has a third parameter i which is not listed as *Add* method parameter in constructor statement so it is an internal parameter and should be specified using an existential quantifier:

$$\exists i \cdot i \in 1..seqSize(keys) \wedge keys(i) = k \wedge values\prime(i) = v \wedge keys\prime == keys \quad (3)$$

The disjunction of (1) and (3) becomes the post-condition for method *Add* and specifies the desirable behaviour of the method. In addition to the generated contracts from events of the Event-B model, predicate *Valid()*(which contains the conjunction of machines invariants) must be a pre-condition for all method declarations. This is necessary as the verifier needs this information to be able to verify the post-conditions.

4.1 Tool Support for Automatic Transformation

We have developed a Rodin plug-in for automatic transformation of Event-B machines to annotated Dafny classes. The plug-in builds an abstract syntax tree (AST) with regards to the Event-B machine and contexts that it sees and constructor statements that are provided by the user. The AST then is translated to Dafny code by a number of translation rules that are encoded in the plug-in source code. The tool only supports the translation of those Event-B mathematical constructs that have a counterpart in Dafny and ignores the rest. So it is important that the model should be refined to a level that only has those constructs that have a Dafny counterpart.

5   Related and Future Work

To the best of our knowledge, no research has been carried out in order to generate annotated Dafny programs from Event-B models and there is very little research on generating verifiable code from Event-B models. EventB2Dafny [7] is a Rodin plug-in for translating Event-B proof obligations to Dafny code to use Dafny verifier as an external theorem prover for proving Event-B proof obligations. Another research has been carried out in order to translate Even-B models to JML-specified JAVA code. A Rodin plug-in called EventB2JML [8] has been developed to automate the translation from Event-B models to Java specified code. Tasking Event-B [9] is a code generator that generates code from Event-B models to a target language but it does not support verification of the generated code.

Our current transformation rules allow us to generate Dafny contracts for abstract data types. We plan to extend our rules and the tool to be able to generate code contracts from Event-B model of complex algorithms. We have already done another case study for transforming an Event-B model of a model checking algorithm to Dafny contracts.

6   Conclusion

We have presented an approach for generating Dafny code contracts from Event-B models. This approach allows us to start the development with a very high level specification of the program in Event-B and use the Rodin platform facilities to prove the correctness and consistency of specification and refine the specification to a level that is suitable for transformation to Dafny. The implementation can be done later manually and verified against the abstract specification. The abstraction level that can be achieved in a modelling language like Event-B is not achievable at Dafny level therefore using the stepwise manner of Event-B for building specification will help to tackle the complexity that is associated with this task.

Acknowledgments. This work was funded in part by a Microsoft Research 2014 Software Engineering Innovation Foundation Award.

References

1. Abrial, J.R.: Modeling in Event-B: system and software engineering. Cambridge University Press (2010)
2. Abrial, J.R., Butler, M., Hallerstede, S., Hoang, T.S., Mehta, F., Voisin, L.: Rodin: an open toolset for modelling and reasoning in Event-B. International Journal on Software Tools for Technology Transfer 12(6), 447–466 (2010)
3. Butler, M., Maamria, I.: Practical theory extension in Event-B. In: Liu, Z., Woodcock, J., Zhu, H. (eds.) Theories of Programming and Formal Methods. LNCS, vol. 8051, pp. 67–81. Springer, Heidelberg (2013)
4. Leino, K.R.M.: Dafny: An automatic program verifier for functional correctness. In: Clarke, E.M., Voronkov, A. (eds.) LPAR-16 2010. LNCS, vol. 6355, pp. 348–370. Springer, Heidelberg (2010)
5. Dijkstra, E.W.: A constructive approach to the problem of program correctness. BIT Numerical Mathematics 8(3), 174–186 (1968)
6. Leino, K.R.M., Monahan, R.: Dafny meets the verification benchmarks challenge. In: Leavens, G.T., O'Hearn, P., Rajamani, S.K. (eds.) VSTTE 2010. LNCS, vol. 6217, pp. 112–126. Springer, Heidelberg (2010)
7. Catano, N., Leino, K.R.M., Rivera, V.: The eventb2dafny rodin plug-in. In: 2012 2nd Workshop on Developing Tools as Plug-ins (TOPI), pp. 49–54. IEEE (2012)
8. Catano, N., Rueda, C., Wahls, T.: A Machine-Checked Proof for a Translation of Event-B Machines to JML. arXiv preprint arXiv 1309.2339 (2013)
9. Edmunds, A., Butler, M.: Tasking Event-B: An Extension to Event-B for Generating Concurrent Code. Programming Language Approaches to Concurrency and Communication-cEntric Software, 1 (2011)

Author Index

Printed in the United States
By Bookmasters